The Passive Solar
Design and Construction
Handbook

The Passive Solar
Design and Construction
Handbook

STEVEN WINTER ASSOCIATES

EDITED BY MICHAEL J. CROSBIE

John Wiley & Sons, Inc.

New York • Chichester • Weinheim • Brisbane • Singapore • Toronto

An advisory board of building professionals carefully reviewed all technical and construction information. However, due to the variability of all local conditions, construction materials, and personal skills, and so on, neither the authors, the contributors, nor John Wiley & Sons assumes responsibility for any injuries suffered or damages or other losses incurred during or as a result of the construction of any of the details or houses described in the *The Passive Solar Design and Construction Handbook*. It is recommended that, before major construction is undertaken, all plans first be reviewed and approved by a knowledgeable local architect or builder for feasibility and safety, as well as for compliance with all local and other legal and code requirements. All instructions and plans should be carefully studied and clearly under-stood before beginning any construction.

Library of Congress Cataloging in Publication Data:
Passive solar design and construction handbook / Steven Winter
  Associates.
        p.   cm.
    Includes index.
    ISBN 0-471-18308-3 (cloth : alk. paper)
    1. Solar houses—Design and construction.   2. Solar energy—
Passive systems.   I. Steven Winter Associates.
TH7414.P254   1997
690′.8370472—dc21   97-21327

Printed in the United States of America

10 9 8 7 6 5 4 3 2

CONTENTS

ACKNOWLEDGMENTS

The Passive Solar Design and Construction Handbook is based, in part, on a document of the same title written by Steven Winter Associates, Inc. under contract to the U.S. Department of Energy and the National Concrete Masonry Association, and subsequently published in a revised form by Rodale Press in 1983.

The details illustrated in this text are an attempt at developing standard and accepted construction practices for passive solar houses. Many of the details developed were based on a handful of examples selected by the authors from a review of nearly 700 sets of working drawings of existing passive homes. Others are standard industry details, modified, in some cases substantially, to accommodate the requirements of passive design. Much of the information that accompanies these details is of the same nature and was derived from similar sources. Consequently, the text tends to be conservative in scope. Experimental data and construction procedures have been avoided in favor of techniques and information that are "tried and true."

Throughout the development of the original handbook, an advisory board provided direction and assistance on many technical and construction issues. The board was composed of representatives of industry and government groups, including the National Concrete Masonry Association (NCMA); the Portland Cement Association (PCA); the Brick Institute of America (BIA); the National Fenestration Council (NFC); and the Southern Solar Energy Center (SSEC).

Timely and crucial assistance and suggestions were provided by numerous other individuals and organizations. In particular, publications and resources of the Passive Solar Industries Council were critical in developing the content of this book. Equally important have been energy analysis tools, such as *Designing Low-Energy Buildings: Passive Solar Strategies* and Energy-10 software, developed by PSIC and the National Renewable Energy Laboratory on behalf of DOE (PSIC can be contacted at: 1511 K Street, NW, Suite 600, Washington, D.C. 20005 202-628-7400). The authors are indebted to Rodale Press for permission to use portions of *The Passive Solar Energy Book,* © 1979 by Edward Mazria, published by Rodale Press.

Staff members of Steven Winter Associates, Inc. who contributed to this updated book include Michael J. Crosbie (editor), John Amatruda, Adrian Tuluca, Cynthia Gardstein, Peter Stratton, Roque Rey, Paul Romano, Mary Seymour, and Sheila Fabrizio.

Our thanks to Dan Sayre, Janet Feeney, and Jennifer Mazurkie at John Wiley & Sons for their encouragement, support, and care.

1

INTRODUCTION

Over the past two decades, in the wake of the energy crisis of the 1970s and the current growing interest in "green" architecture and building, researchers, builders, economists, architects, and others from a wide variety of disciplines have generated a significant body of information on passive solar technology.

Parallel to the development of the technical foundations of passive solar design is a growing interest among builders and designers in incorporating passive concepts into their standard building practices. They are responding to their market. Homebuyers today are more demanding about the level of comfort in their houses, and passive solar design and construction can deliver a house that is more comfortable and less costly to maintain. Unfortunately, the construction details and information that have developed out of the many successful passive solar projects are dispersed within the enormous volume of literature on passive design and are not readily available to the building community at large. In effect, few publications that focus on the design and construction detailing of passive solar homes have been widely distributed. In most respects, the construction of a passive solar residence utilizes standard construction procedures, although the actual configuration of the materials may not be typical. *The Passive Solar Design and Construction Handbook* represents a comprehensive effort to fill this gap by illustrating methods of adapting standard building practices to passive solar applications.

The information contained in the handbook has been developed primarily for architects, designers, and builders. However, it is hoped that, by providing a variety of construction and technical information, others involved in the building industry and owner-builders will find the contents of value.

The handbook focuses specifically on the construction of passive solar, single-family, detached residential buildings. It will be evident, however, that much of the construction information can be successfully adapted to other building types.

Discussions of construction, of course, cannot stand apart from considerations of design. Where appropriate in the text, basic concepts in the design of passive homes are discussed and general design guidelines are offered. There is also a discussion of the "whole house" approach to passive solar design: how energy efficiency and home comfort are enhanced by design and construction principles that affect the entire building. It should be emphasized that these basic principles are presented only in a general way. More specific design information can be obtained from any of a variety of passive solar design primers (see Bibliography). It is strongly recommended that the handbook be used as a companion volume to one of these design guides.

The illustrations used throughout the text are intended to aid the reader in interpreting the basic concepts of passive solar design. They are general in nature and are not intended to convey a specific or preferred method of design. The construction details, on the other hand, provide suggested use of materials and construction procedures. Details are provided for only those areas of the home that are part of the passive system.

The handbook is intended to be national in scope. As a result, the construction information and details tend to be general in nature, not focusing on specific regional building practices. Many construction-related concerns that would ordinarily be identified and discussed in a regionally oriented text are, therefore, simply identified as areas of regional concern.

This list of regional issues includes the use and location of vapor barriers, the use of termite shields and soil poison, pressure-treating wood, attic ventilation, and various special structural requirements in seismic areas. These and other regional construction considerations will need to be overlaid onto the basic construction information presented in the illustrations and text. The details illustrated in chapters 3 through 6 will then need to be adapted, conforming to local building practices and codes. Thus, the information presented in the handbook is intended to serve as a general construction guide and to convey the basic principles of passive solar design and construction.

The text is organized in a manner intended to acquaint the reader with the basic concepts and provide a source of construction information that can be easily referenced. The discussion that follows briefly outlines this organization, the topics covered in each chapter, and methods for quickly and efficiently using the handbook as a construction reference guide.

Chapter 2: Passive Solar Fundamentals

In Chapter 2, many of the basic elements of passive solar design are reviewed. The discussions are intended to: (1) introduce the reader to the unique design constraints present in passive homes; (2) provide a framework for cataloging passive solar home "types"; (3) discuss the principles of "whole-house" design that are essential for a successful passive solar house; and (4) briefly describe many of the salient issues influencing design decisions, such as economic and energy-saving analysis. The reader familiar with the topics presented may wish to skim the discussions but is advised to read carefully the paragraphs describing the basic passive systems, a section that delineates the organizational framework for the remainder of the text.

Although many significant considerations in designing passive solar homes are outlined in Chapter 2, the section is not intended to substitute for any of the readily available passive solar design guides.

Chapters 3 Through 6: Direct Gain, Thermal Storage Wall, Attached Sunspace, Convective Loop

These four chapters, taken together, contain all of the basic design and construction information. They will serve as a constant guide in the design and construction phases of building passive homes.

Each chapter discusses one of the basic passive system types introduced in Chapter 2. The chapters are all subdivided into three sections: (1) a general discussion, or design overview, of the important design and construction issues that apply to the particular system under review; (2) construction details and notes; and (3) case studies illustrating designed and built examples of the system type.

In reading each chapter, particular attention should be paid to the design overview, which outlines the major advantages and disadvantages of the system type, as well as the more specific rules of thumb for design and construction. These rules will aid in selecting and constructing the passive design.

The actual construction details illustrate both the recommended materials of construction and one suggested design. The precise organization of the details may vary from chapter to chapter. In all chapters, however, a basic set of details is illustrated, typically followed by variations to that detail and/or alternate details, and a set of construction notes. A short introduction summarizes the use of the detail section in each chapter.

The case studies at the end of each chapter describe the design and construction of successful passive solar homes, with particular emphasis on construction detailing. In most instances, each case study demonstrates the use of two or more system types combined in the same home.

Chapter 7: Materials

While quickly thumbing through the details, it may be noted that, although material types are indicated, specific products and material dimensions are not. These designations and selections can be made with the aid of the information contained in this chapter. If used in conjunction with the construction chapters, these discussions provide guidance to available and suitable materials for the various passive solar applications. The information in this chapter is particularly intended to be used with the rules of thumb in the construction chapters.

Glossary

Throughout the text, a variety of terms are used that may be unfamiliar. A glossary has been included to clarify these terms.

Bibliography

For further reading, a bibliography is provided. As noted, it is suggested that one of the design primers be used as a companion volume to the handbook.

2

PASSIVE SOLAR FUNDAMENTALS

Introduction

Over the past two decades, particularly during the "oil crises" of the late 1970s and early 1980s, the implications of our dependence on fossil fuels have created a marked awareness within the building community of the need to conserve energy in the design of residential buildings. Currently, however, prospective homeowners are, with increasing frequency, looking for increased comfort associated with their homes. And whereas it is true that building codes and standards have generally become increasingly stringent with regard to the selection of energy-use-related materials and components, such building codes alone have not significantly increased the public's desire to buy the "energy-efficient" model. Moreover, the incentives and assistance offered by utilities are now being cut back in favor of more competitive approaches.

These trends coincide with a refocusing on energy conservation and renewable energy, which has been called the "whole building" approach. The idea of looking at the entire building—in this case, the house—as an interrelated system, rather than as individual parts, represents the best hope for energy conservation in

the coming years. Such a direction is part of a larger social awareness that grows from a concern about the environment and our stewardship of the planet. The same impetus that propels many of us to recycle bottles and newspapers, to drive more fuel-efficient and less pollution-emitting cars, and to purchase consumer products that are more environmentally benign makes passive solar design and construction the logical choice. Not only do passive solar homes save on heating and cooling bills, but they are also more comfortable. They are also more "sustainable" and "green"—less taxing on our natural resources.

On a more pragmatic level, over the past few years, there has been increased interest in the development of preferential financing products, mortgages, and loans. Such loans are being made available to homeowners and homebuyers who opt to make their homes more energy-efficient. This process typically includes performing a detailed energy analysis or home energy rating. In the case of the passive solar home, this type of preferential financing can be accessed through an energy analysis that will provide projected energy consumption. The energy-efficient mortgage is generally based on a reference point that coincides with a CABO Model Energy Code compliant home. As has been previously mentioned, the success of the passive solar home depends, in large part, on its being energy-conservative in its design and construction. Information on accessing preferential financing can be obtained from federal agencies, such as FHA and EPA; local utilities that may be participating in one of many energy efficiency programs, such as "E Seal" or "Good Cents"; or a Home Energy Rating System provider.

There are numerous techniques and opportunities for conserving energy in residential design. Most remain virtually untapped in the vast majority of new home construction nationwide. Simple and familiar techniques, such as increased insulation levels, multiple glazings instead of single glazing, and high-performance glazing films, are of course, effective and expedient measures to reduce energy use. These and other energy conservation techniques are primarily useful as climatic buffers, protecting against the deleterious effects of, for example, cold outdoor temperatures. They reduce the demand for energy in the home.

There are, however, a variety of additional techniques that effectively utilize the forces of nature to provide energy to the home, reducing—and, in some cases, eliminating—the need for conventional fossil-fuel-fired heating and cooling equipment. In residential design, most of these techniques are based on the use of solar radiation to provide space heating and water heating, and, occasionally, space cooling. These solar techniques can be subdivided into two basic categories: passive and active. Although the distinction between them is not always clear-cut, in general, passive solar techniques or systems heat and/or cool without the need for energy from other nonrenewable sources, such as electric power to run a pump. On the other hand, "active systems," with their roof-mounted solar panels—popular more than a decade ago—are less common today because they require pumps and fans whose consumption of electricity is sometimes significant relative to the amount of energy generated by the overall system.

The "Whole House" Approach

Passive solar techniques are effective in reducing energy use only if they are combined with, not substituted for, energy conservation techniques. Any energy savings that a passive system might generate can be easily offset by the energy use increases that will occur in a poorly designed and constructed building. It is for this reason that the incorporation of energy conservation measures, in both the design and the construction phases of the building, is an absolute prerequisite for the passive solar home to work effectively.

Designers and builders can work with the energy of the sun, natural light, ventilation, and the insulation of the earth to make houses more energy-efficient. This can be accomplished through passive solar strategies, utilizing insulating glass, shading, orientation, thermal mass, and ventilation. As a result, mechanical systems can be smaller to compensate for some or all of the extra cost of a better house. In the long run, money will be saved through lower energy bills, and a more comfortable living environment will result. Such an approach can be thought of as a "whole house" strategy, which combines sensitive environmental design and good construction practices to achieve energy efficiency, comfort, less maintenance, and reduced environmental impact. The following is a concise list of recommendations for improving the energy-conserving capability of a house, according to its location.

1. SITING

It is not always possible to site the house to save energy; however, if the lot allows, the following design principles will help save energy.

a. If the house plan is an elongated shape, position its long axis in the east-west direction. In cold and temperate climates, place most windows toward the south, to gain solar heat. In hot climates, place most windows toward the north, to protect from solar heat. (See more under 3, below.)

b. Make use of natural slopes by berming the house into the ground, when these slopes do not block desirable views or desirable solar access. Berming protects from wind, reduces heat loss during the heating season, and reduces heat gain during the cooling season.

2. LANDSCAPING

a. Plant evergreens to shield the house from cold winds (in cold and temperate climates) or hot winds (usually in hot and dry climates).

b. Consider evergreens or deciduous trees with dense, long-lasting foliage to shade all windows for climates with year-round hot weather.

c. If there are significant heating and cooling requirements, plant deciduous trees to offer seasonal shading. Because the sun is low in the east and west directions, the tree foliage should also be low, and the trees can be distant from the house. On the south side, however, the sun is high during summer; tree foliage needs to be high for shading.

d. To save water, use flowers, grasses, and bushes adapted to the local climate conditions. Many areas of the country do not get abundant rains during summer; xeriscaping is a water-saving and cost-saving method of landscaping.

3. BUILDING DESIGN

Work with the climate, not against it. A solar house accepts sun, heat, and breezes when needed, and blocks them when undesirable. Ideally, a house is like an organism: all of the components work together. It is worthwhile to improve the efficiency of the components one by one. In a retrofit situation, this may be the only feasible solution. However, it is much better to conceive the entire house as an energy-efficient organism. This is achievable in a new design, by using an integrated design concept.

a. In cold and temperate climates:
- Place the most windows on the south side, fewest on the north side, to maximize solar gain and to reduce heat loss. The west elevation should not have many windows. Unless you have high cooling loads, east windows do not have a major effect on energy use.
- Use south-facing clerestories to bring the sun deeper into the house.
- See 2 for shading with trees. South-facing windows can also be shaded with overhangs, and east or west windows with deep porches or with vertical fins.
- Use thermal mass (brick, concrete, tiles, thick gypsum board) in rooms with large, south-facing windows to moderate and store solar heat. Earth berming averages the winter and summer temperatures in the affected rooms. If the earth-bermed rooms can be warmed in winter through south windows, this strategy will be successful.
- Except in regions with high humidity, natural ventilation is usually beneficial for extended periods of time. Enhance it by placing windows on opposite walls of the house. For houses with high spaces, place windows at the top. However, do not encourage air infiltration during winter; specify tight-closing windows.
- In cold climates with brief summers, it may be more important to have fewer openings on the north side than to ventilate by opening opposing windows. Mechanically assisted ventilation (e.g., an exhaust fan placed on the north side) might be a better choice.

b. In locations such as Southern California, where both the summer and winter are mild:
- Place most windows north and south. South-facing windows allow solar gain during heating periods. Opposing north-facing windows allow good cross-ventilation during cooling periods.
- Use south-facing clerestories with operable windows to bring sun and light deeper into the house and to ventilate. Ventilation can also be fan-assisted.
- Use thermal mass (brick, concrete, tiles, thick gypsum board) in rooms with solar exposure (most important south, but also east and west) to moderate and store solar heat. Earth berming can be successful, but is probably not cost-effective unless the ter-

rain easily permits it, since the energy use in such climates is low.

- Shade with trees, as noted in 2, but with emphasis on deciduous trees. South-facing windows are well-shaded with overhangs, while east- and west-facing windows can be shaded by deep porches or by vertical fins.
- Facilitate natural ventilation by placing windows on opposite parts of the house, such as south and north, or low and high. If there are dominant breezes, you might want to place larger operable windows on the leeward side. This arrangement provides greater ventilation than a design where equal openings are placed on both windward and leeward sides.

c. In hot and arid climates, such as Arizona, New Mexico, and Nevada, with year-round high temperatures during the day and cool or cold nights:

- Place most windows on the south side, some on the north side, and few, if any, on the west side. East windows can help heat recovery from cold nights, if the glass area is not excessive, so that it does not create overheating during late morning.
- Use south-facing clerestories to bring sun and light deep into the house.
- See 2 for shading with trees. Evergreens are effective year-round. South-facing windows can also be shaded with overhangs, and east and west windows with deep porches or vertical fins. Interior shading devices (louvers, blinds) are of very little effectiveness because the hot air layer created between blinds and glass cannot release heat to the outside, where it is also hot.
- Use thermal mass throughout the house, including exterior and interior walls, and including floors, to moderate and store solar heat. Earth berming can also provide desirable, year-round cooling.
- Facilitate natural ventilation by placing windows on the north and south sides and high and low parts of the house, such as at the top of a two-story space.

d. In hot and humid climates with year-round high temperatures, small variations between day and night, and extended periods of high humidity, such as southern Texas and Louisiana:

- Place most windows on the north side, fewer on the south, and as few as possible on the east and west.
- See 2 for shading with trees. Evergreens are effective year-round. Shade south-facing windows with overhangs, and east and west windows with deep porches or vertical fins.
- Brick, block, or tile may not be effective unless they are in contact with the ground. Thermal mass is effective if it constitutes a *continuous* heat sink, and it continually cools the house. Earth berming is a good strategy because the ground several feet below the surface remains at a constant temperature of about 50°F.

4. ENERGY-EFFICIENT CONSTRUCTION TECHNIQUES

a. In cold and temperate climates, create a well-insulated, tight shell. Use insulating windows for solar gain and ventilation. Do not count on air infiltration for ventilation. If thermal mass is used, insulate it from contact with the ground. Use efficient lighting and appliances. Use efficient heating, cooling, and domestic hot water (DHW) systems. Use water-saving fixtures.

b. In mild climates, such as Southern California, the construction of opaque walls, roofs, and floors is not very important from an energy perspective, but will make a difference in comfort and indoor air quality. For this reason, it is wise to fill all shell cavities with insulation and to have relatively airtight construction. Use windows for solar gain and ventilation. Do not count on air infiltration for ventilation. Use efficient lighting and appliances, since, in addition to direct energy savings, it may be possible to eliminate significant cooling and heating loads. If you still have cooling and heating, use reasonably efficient equipment. Use efficient

DHW systems and water-saving, economic fixtures.

c. In hot and arid climates, such as Arizona and Nevada, proceed in the same manner as for cold and temperate construction strategies (4a) above.

d. In hot and humid climates, create a well-insulated, tight shell. Use windows for ventilation. Do not count on air infiltration for ventilation. Facilitate contact of any thermal mass with the ground. Use efficient lighting and appliances. Use efficient cooling and DHW systems.

5. INSULATION

For heating climates or hot/arid climates, follow these guidelines:

a. Walls

Masonry

- A thermal mass, good for storing solar heat gains. In sunny climates, this type of construction performs as well as walls with higher R-value.
- Masonry cavity walls in cold climates should have rigid insulation and use thermally broken ties between the wythes.

Wood Frame

- In cold climates, use at least 2 × 6 framing with R-19 insulation.
- In very cold climates, consider additional exterior sheathing, or some of the more innovative concepts, such as truss walls.
- Provide exterior air retarders, such as Tyvek™, which are relatively inexpensive and protect from air intrusion.
- Use a vapor retarder inside, unless engineering calculations show otherwise. (None may be needed for walls with no insulation between studs and with rigid insulation to the outside.)

Structural Insulated Panels (SIPs)

- SIPs consist of rigid insulation between two rigid sheets of plywood or pressed wood. This is a very effective insulation system, since there is no thermal bridging. In cold climates, use at least R-15 insulation, or R-20 if cost-effective.

Log Construction

- This construction provides a good thermal mass for storing solar heat gains. In sunny climates, this construction performs as well as walls with higher R-values.

Steel Frame

- This construction has significant thermal bridging, so, in heating climates, it is important to sheath it with insulation to the exterior. Without sheathing, R-19 insulation behaves more like R-9, or less. With sheathing, the problem is reduced or eliminated, depending on how thick the sheathing is. This is not a concern in cooling climates. In very hot climates, there is a modest increase in cooling load, but sheathing is not necessarily cost-effective.

b. Roofs

- If the attic has wood joists, insulate between and above the joists. This is easily accomplished with blanket, blown, and sprayed insulation.
- If the attic has wood trusses, insulate between them with a blanket. It is worthwhile to insulate above the truss bottom chord not only for the insulation itself, but also because air is prevented from leaking around the insulation between trusses. Above-chord insulation should be blown or sprayed. If a truss roof has blown or sprayed insulation, both between-truss and above-chord areas are easily covered.
- If the attic has steel trusses, insulate above the top chord. All other insulation techniques have severe disadvantages, either because of thermal bridging or because of moisture condensation.

c. Floors

Slab

- Provide perimeter insulation in all climates except mild ones, such as Southern California.

Crawl Space

- A crawl space should have a concrete slab on top of a polyetheylene sheet to prevent moisture from penetrating into the space.

- Insulation in the floor above the crawl space should be tightly fitted between joists.
- Water pipes below an insulated floor should be insulated.
- If the floor above is not insulated, the crawl space must be airtight and its walls must be insulated.

Basement
- If unconditioned, insulate the floor above.
- If conditioned, it is best to insulate outside the walls when waterproofing is applied.

6. AIRTIGHTNESS AND VENTILATION

In frame construction, use air retarders (formerly called air barriers) that are vapor permeable and low-cost. Air retarders prevent air from short-circuiting the insulation and prevent moisture from entering the walls. Use tightly closing windows, such as casements, or awnings.

a. Vapor Retarders
- These are useful where air retarders are not present or where high humidity levels are expected.
- In cold and temperate climates, use on the inside of the wall.
- In hot and humid climates with no heating, use on the outside of the wall.
- Do not use in climates with hot and humid periods, but that also require some heating, since moisture can come from either inside or outside the house. Let the walls breathe.
- Vapor retarders may not be needed, even in climates with significant heating, *if* there is no air movement across the walls, and *if* the temperature profile across the wall does not encourage moisture accumulation.

b. Ventilation
- Use windows, whole-house fans, or heat recovery ventilators.

7. HEATING AND COOLING EQUIPMENT

a. Use heating systems with 80 percent to 95 percent combustion efficiency. Gas, oil, and propane are the conventional fuel sources. Save energy with programmable and multiple thermostats.

b. In mild climates, consider using air-to-air heat pumps, which are cost-effective for heating and cooling where electricity cost is not very high; choose units with seasonal energy efficiency ratings (SEER) of more than 10. This technology is usually not cost-effective in very cold climates.

c. Consider using geothermal heat pumps, which draw cooling and heating from the ground through vertical holes drilled into the ground, or a horizontal pipe loop under the yard. The cost is double or triple that of air-to-air heat pumps, but energy efficiency is also triple in heating and about double in cooling. This technology can be cost-effective even in very cold climates because ground temperature is constant. Choose systems with SEER greater than 16.

d. Use efficient air-conditioners, either through-the-wall or split systems, with SEER of 8 to 12. Save energy with programmable and multiple thermostats.

e. In hot and arid climates, consider using swamp coolers, which humidify the air to make it comfortable without mechanically cooling it.

8. DUCTS AND PIPES

A house with leaky ducts will increase heating costs. If ducts leak outside, heat is lost directly. If they leak inside the house, air and heat are not delivered where they are needed. Some rooms will have excessive air and will be too hot, while rooms with too little air will be too cold. Similar problems arise with leaky ducts in cooling-dominated climates, such as Arizona.

a. Save energy with tight ducts.

b. Insulate pipes, especially if they are located in unconditioned spaces.

9. HVAC CONTROLS

A house without good heating and cooling controls will increase heating and cooling costs.

a. Save energy with programmable thermostats. In winter, the temperature is set back at night, or when the house is unoccupied, and warms to comfort level when residents return. In cooling, programmable thermostats work the same way.

b. Save energy with multiple thermostats. If the house is zoned and each room can be controlled separately, energy can be saved while maintaining comfort conditions in other areas. Overheating or overcooling one area in an attempt to get another area comfortable will also be avoided.

10. LIGHTING

Efficient lighting saves electricity and reduces cooling loads. It also slightly increases heating, but this is of very little consequence. In today's residences, the light level is often too low for many activities (e.g., reading, sewing) for individuals with lower visual acuity. Ceiling lamps are rarely provided, but are often desirable. With increased need for lighting, there is increased opportunity for savings by making this lighting energy-efficient. Energy-efficient lighting makes sense only if the quality of light is adequate. Never save energy at the price of poor light. Today's technologies give good, efficient lighting at an affordable first cost.

a. Replace incandescent lighting with more efficient lighting (typically fluorescent) while maintaining the quality of light.

b. Use T-8 triphosphor fluorescent lamps with electronic ballasts in kitchens and bathrooms. Triphosphor fluorescent lamps have very good color rendition and are energy-frugal (70 percent to 85 percent savings compared to conventional incandescent lamps).

c. Use compact fluorescent lamps in such areas as bedrooms and living rooms to save 60 percent to 75 percent in electricity costs over conventional incandescent lamps. Compact fluorescents have higher first costs but last 10 times longer than incandescents.

d. Use electronic ballasts to save additional energy (25 percent to 40 percent over conventional magnetic ballasts) and reduce noise.

11. APPLIANCES

A house with inefficient appliances can have a greater cooling load in addition to higher energy consumption. Inefficient washing machines, dryers, dishwashers, and refrigerators release heat in the house. An inefficient computer or printer in a home office releases too much heat. Save energy with:

a. Energy-efficient appliances. Look for the Department of Energy-published energy rating and choose those with the lower number.

b. Energy Star computers and printers.

c. Efficient washing machines, dishwashers, refrigerators; efficient dryers vented to the outside.

12. DOMESTIC HOT WATER

a. Hot water heating costs too much if hot water is wasted. Save energy with:
   - Tight faucets.
   - Low-flow shower heads.
   - Dishwashers with programmable "light wash" and "energy saver" cycles.
   - Washing machines with programmable washing cycles that allow low water levels and low water temperatures.

b. Hot water heating costs too much if the water heater is inefficient. Save energy with:
   - Efficient water heaters—80 percent efficiency is common, but up to 95 percent is available.
   - Turn down the tank temperature in the summer.

All of the above recommendations will help create an energy-conserving structure that will reduce the demand for supplemental energy sources. The next step in the design process is to include passive systems that will actually allow the home to provide for its own energy requirements. The result will be a truly "energy conscious" home.

The chapters that follow contain some basic guidelines for the design of such a home, but concentrate primarily on the materials and methods of constructing passive solar features. For more precise information regarding overall design strategies, any of the variety of passive solar design primers listed in the Bibliography can be consulted.

Principles of Passive Solar Design

Passive solar systems rely on the intelligent design and organization of the spaces in a home and on the careful selection of building materials to derive heating and cooling benefits from the free and abundant energy available in the natural environment. Such systems depend on two basic material properties for their effect: (1) the ability of certain materials to store large amounts of heat and to release that heat slowly to the living spaces of the home; and (2) the ability of glass and many other glazing materials to transmit solar radiation (light) but to remain opaque to thermal radiation (heat). When a passive system admits sunlight through its south-facing windows, this light strikes objects and surfaces within the space and is transformed into heat. Much of this heat is prevented from passing back out through the windows because the glazing is opaque to radiant heat. This phenomenon, known as the "greenhouse effect," will be familiar to anyone who has opened the door of a car that has been sitting in the sun with its windows closed on a summer day.

To date, most research and development in the area of passive solar systems has dealt with providing heating, rather than cooling. Thus, the basic passive systems developed and presented in the *Handbook* have been designed primarily for heating, and only secondarily for cooling. In fact, the essential processes of a passive system (collection and storage) are specifically oriented toward gaining heat, rather than rejecting it. This is not to say that aspects of a system cannot be adapted for cooling. Storage elements *can* be used to store "coolth" (coolth is to cooling as warmth is to heating) and to absorb heat from the living space (thereby cooling it) during summer days. Often, this cooling is accomplished in combination with natural ventilation strategies.

Basic Passive Systems

The various strategies for designing and building a passive home can be grouped into four basic system types: direct gain, thermal storage wall, attached sunspace, and convective loop. Each of these systems (discussed in detail later in this chapter) can be visualized as an assembly of *components,* each of which performs a unique function and all of which are required for the effective operation of the overall system.

The basic passive systems are each composed of five mutually dependent basic components:

Collector The solar collector component is composed of transparent or translucent glazing, sealed in a frame and located on the south-facing side of the home. The collector glazing surface can be positioned vertically, as in windows, or sloped, as in a skylight on the roof.

Absorber The absorber is a solid surface, usually dark-colored, that is exposed to the sunlight entering through the collector glazing. The absorber "converts" the solar radiation into heat that is either delivered directly into the space for immediate use or stored in a storage component.

Storage The storage component is composed of material or materials that have the capacity to retain heat for a period of hours or, perhaps, days. The mass of a material is an important measure of its capacity to store heat, and residential construction materials that are high in mass, such as masonry, will be appropriate for storage components. The slow rate of heat discharge from the storage materials helps maintain a steady, comfortable temperature within the spaces to be heated. In some cases, the storage materials can be used to store coolth by absorbing heat from the living spaces and effectively cooling them. The storage material is sized according to the amount of solar heat the collector is intended to provide and is usually located in, or adjacent to, the rooms it is intended to heat and/or cool. The absorber and storage components are often one and the same, as in a masonry floor or wall.

Distribution The distribution component delivers the collected and/or stored heat or coolth into the living spaces to be conditioned. Distribution can be by natural means, such as the radiation of heat from a wall or the movement of air by natural convection, or it can be assisted by small pumps or fans that blow heat away from the absorber to the living spaces or to remote storage.

Control   Control components regulate the heat loss or gain into and out of the passive system. There are three basic types of control components: (1) shading devices, which reduce the amount of radiation allowed to pass through the collector glazing; (2) reflectors, which increase the amount of solar radiation passing through the collector glazing; and (3) movable insulation, which reduces heat flow through the collector and into adjacent spaces.

In summary, all these components interact in the following manner:

- The collector admits solar radiation onto the absorber;

- The absorber "converts" the radiation into heat;

- The storage medium retains the heat not immediately used;

- The distribution component transfers heat between absorber and/or storage and the living spaces; and

- The controls reduce heat loss and increase solar radiation gain in the heating season and/or shade the collector during the cooling season, reducing heat gain.

The precise configuration and appropriate materials for each of the components vary, depending on the system type. Each of the basic passive systems is described below, along with the arrangement of components that characterizes each.

Direct Gain

Of all the passive solar types, a direct gain system is perhaps the easiest to envision and construct. A direct gain design is one in which solar radiation *directly* enters and heats the living spaces. The home itself can be visualized as the collector of solar heat. Direct gain is primarily a heating-type system, used mainly in mild and moderate climates.

In the heating season, during the daylight hours, sunlight enters through south-facing windows, glass doors, clerestories, and skylights, all common *collector* components in direct gain homes. The solar radiation strikes and is *absorbed and stored* by elements within the space. The

most common or primary *absorber/storage* components within a direct gain home are the floors and walls (see Figure 2.1).

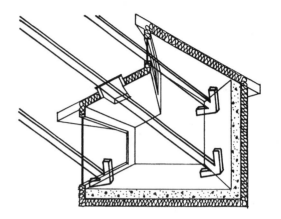

Figure 2.1

Although ceilings and other elements, such as furniture, within the space can be designed to store heat, common direct gain storage component materials are most readily incorporated in the floors and walls. Frequently, the storage component also serves a structural function—as a bearing wall, for example. The *distribution* of heat is generally not crucial to the operation of a direct gain system, since the heat is stored in the same space in which it is used. Heat flow that does occur is by natural convection, usually from one room to another through doorways and stairwells.

In a direct gain design, the amount of solar heat that is collected and retained can be *controlled*. For example, during the daylight hours, light-colored paved surfaces, such as patios and terraces, that are adjacent to the collector components can be used to increase the amount of solar radiation entering the direct gain space. The reflecting component increases the effective collector area without increasing the actual square footage, and the accompanying heat losses, of the collector.

At night, high-performance insulating glazings help to prevent heat flow back out through the collectors. It is also possible to use movable insulation mounted on either the outside or the inside of the collector, although such components require vigilance on the part of the resident. High-performance glazings have reduced the cost-effectiveness of such movable insulation.

During times of the year when heating is not required, the direct gain collector should be shaded to control the amount of solar radiation reaching it. Failure to shade the collector adequately may result in overheating of the direct gain spaces, increasing the cooling load. The most effective shading components are mounted outside, intercepting the sunlight before it passes through the collector. Interior shades (such as venetian blinds) can also be effective, reflecting some or most of the direct and diffuse sunlight, but they will allow some heat buildup to occur. High-performance glazings can be used to cut heat gain without sacrificing natural light.

Thermal Storage Wall

A thermal storage wall system is one in which the storage component is positioned between the collector and the living space. The storage wall typically provides structural support, in addition to serving as the system storage component. Although occasionally used for cooling, thermal storage walls are primarily used to supplement the space-heating requirements. In general, thermal storage walls should be considered for areas that experience mild to severe winters.

In the heating season, solar radiation is allowed to pass through the collector glazing and is absorbed and stored by the wall. The wall heats up, transferring some of its heat to the living space and some to the column of air between the collector and the wall. This column of air can be exhausted directly into the living space, in which case the wall is referred to as a vented, or Trombe, wall (see Figure 2.2), or the heated air can simply remain trapped between the glazing and the wall, in which case it is an unvented, or stagnating, wall (see Figure 2.3). In both cases, the heat in the wall will radiate to the adjacent living space throughout the day and evening hours.

Beyond the action of the vents in the Trombe wall, distribution components are not fundamental to either type of thermal storage wall. In some cases, warmed air is ducted from the airspace

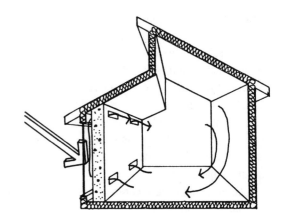

Figure 2.2

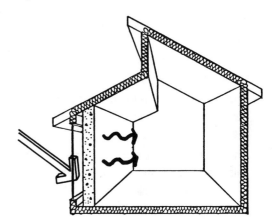

Figure 2.3

between the collector and the storage wall to remote living spaces, but this is not characteristic of the system operation and should be avoided if possible.

In the cooling season, the impact of solar radiation should be controlled by shading the collector and storage components. Shading components are most effective when placed on the exterior, but can also be installed between the collector and the storage wall (see Figure 2.4).

To further promote cooling, the airspace between collector and storage components can be vented to the outside. This is particularly effective in areas where the nighttime temperatures drop below the indoor temperatures. Venting the airspace will cool the storage wall in the evening, allowing it to absorb heat from the space during the day and reducing the space-cooling requirements.

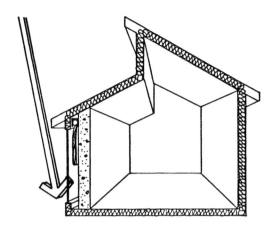

Figure 2.4

Attached Sunspace

Attached sunspaces are typically built as glass-enclosed spaces, frequently constructed as extensions to homes. They are generally considered secondary-use spaces, in which heat is collected and either stored for later use or exhausted directly into the living space. The solar energy collected and absorbed by an attached sunspace is used to heat both the sunspace itself and the adjacent living areas. The ways in which this energy is stored and distributed form the basis for distinguishing five separate attached sunspace subsystems, which differ significantly from each other in terms of their operation, construction, and configuration of basic components. These are:

- Open wall subsystem
- Direct gain subsystem
- Air exchange subsystem
- Thermal storage wall subsystem
- Remote storage subsystem

During the heating season, sunlight enters the attached sunspace through the south-facing collector (an expanse of glass or plastic), is absorbed by elements within the sunspace, and is converted to heat. This basic process is the same for all the attached sunspace subsystems. It is only in the operation and location of the storage, distribution, and control components that these subsystems differ significantly from each other. (For

further information, see Chapter 5: Attached Sunspace.)

All attached sunspaces will be designed for one of two basic modes of operation. In the first, the sunspace is thermally isolated from the living area (see Figure 2.5). As a result of this isolation, the sunspace cannot be used year-round, since

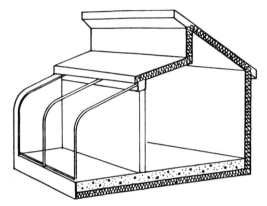

Figure 2.5

the temperature within the space is allowed to fluctuate outside the comfort range.

In the second mode, the sunspace is not thermally isolated, but is treated as an additional living space (see Figure 2.6). In this case, temper-

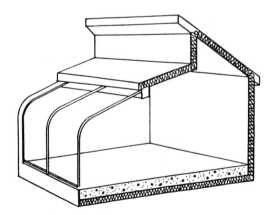

Figure 2.6

atures are not allowed to fluctuate but are maintained—by a conventional heating system, when necessary—within the comfort range.

Similarly, the design and selection of the control components will vary with the selection of subsystem and operational characteristics. To prevent heat loss, high-performance glazings can be used, or a movable insulating component can be placed along the collector glazing or between the sunspace and adjacent living spaces, depending on the type of operation (see Figure 2.7).

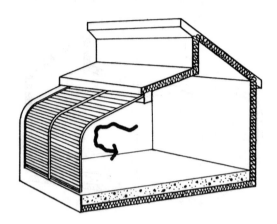

Figure 2.7

In the cooling season, the attached sunspace is particularly susceptible to overheating. Control of solar heat gain by shades and ventilation is critical to proper system functioning. In climates where the nighttime temperatures drop below comfort levels, it is often possible to use the attached sunspace mass for storing coolth, thus reducing daytime cooling loads.

Convective Loop

The convective loop is primarily a heating-type system, most appropriate in areas experiencing moderate to severe winters. It is based on the principle that a fluid, such as air, will rise when heated.

During the heating season, the convective loop collector admits sunlight, which, in turn, strikes an absorber surface and is converted to heat. This heat is transmitted to the air in the space between the absorber surface and the collector. As the heat is collected at the lowest point in the system, the heated air rises up, passing out through a duct located at the top of the absorber, to be replaced by cooler return air drawn in from below. This warm air can be dumped directly into the living spaces, or it can be diverted into a

storage area, such as a radiant slab, and used to provide heat as required (see Figure 2.8).

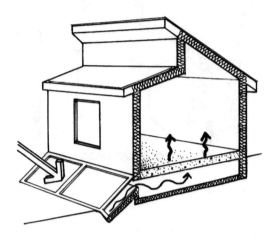

Figure 2.8

The major control component required by this system is a method for preventing the loop from reversing itself at night or during prolonged cloudy periods, drawing heated air out of storage. Simple backdraft or automatic, thermostatically controlled dampers can be used to prevent this backflow. If such controls are provided, it will not be necessary to insulate the collector during the heating season.

It may be desirable to provide some form of reflector to enhance the amount of solar radiation striking the collector. Such reflectors are particularly appropriate for a convective loop because the system is thermally isolated, and often physically separated, from the living spaces. This isolation prevents the glare problems that occur in direct gain systems or attached sunspaces equipped with reflectors.

During the cooling season, the collector should be well shaded (see Figure 2.9) or covered to prevent possible damage to the absorber surface as a result of excessive heat buildup in the system.

Typically, a convective loop system is constructed directly on the south wall of a home or is a separate structure placed slightly in front of and below the first floor. In both designs, a small fan is usually employed to assist the natural flow of heat throughout the system.

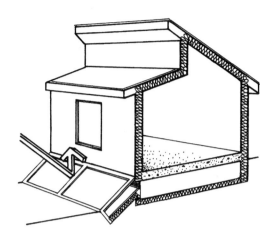

Figure 2.9

Passive Solar Design

A well-designed passive home should not be considered as simply an extension of conventional design principles with the addition of "mass and glass." On the contrary, the desire to create a home that is attractive while also saving energy passively will require serious consideration of some basic principles of passive solar design and energy planning.

While the handbook is a useful guide to building passive homes, the discussions assume that the reader has some prior knowledge of passive design principles, such as room layouts that take full advantage of opportunities for passive heating and cooling.

For example, in a well-designed passive home, the living spaces should be placed on the south. Although this planning principle is implied throughout the text, there is no comprehensive discussion of passive solar space planning, a topic that only indirectly influences the construction of the home. On the other hand, the sizing of the storage component in a thermal storage wall, for instance, *is* a design issue that will affect construction and is, therefore, discussed later in a design rule of thumb.

There are, in fact, four design-related topic areas that influence both the design and the construction of a passive home: selecting the appropriate system, specifying the components, estimating the energy savings, and assessing the economics.

Selecting a System

Much of the experience of builders and researchers to date indicates that each of the individual systems described earlier in this chapter will perform best and tend to be most cost-effective in a particular climate region. In defining the four passive system types earlier, four climate types are mentioned: mild, moderate, moderate to severe, and severe. One or more of these regions is identified as being most appropriate for each of the systems.

The recommendations used throughout the text can be summarized as follows:

System	Appropriate climate(s)
Direct gain	Mild to moderate
Thermal storage wall	Mild to severe
Attached sunspace	Moderate to severe
Convective loop	Moderate to severe

The map in Figure 2.10 indicates the boundaries for each of these climate regions (excluding the desert areas). These recommendations are intended to serve only as a general guide to system selection, and should not supersede specific economic and energy analysis, prior experience, or particular preference. However, these recommendations do indicate, to some extent, the climates to which the inherent operating characteristics of the systems are best suited.

Specifying the Components

Once a system is selected, the components that comprise the system need to be specified. As discussed briefly in the handbook's introduction, once a construction detail is chosen, the exact selection and sizing of the materials comprising that detail will require the information and data contained in chapters 3 through 7.

In most cases, the specification procedure is a simple and straightforward one. For example, if, in selecting the thermal storage wall system, the storage component is to be specified, the first step is to consult the "Storage Rules of Thumb" in Chapter 4 (see page 118). These rules of thumb are basic guidelines that will assist in the design of the system. They also indicate criteria for material selection and sizing. Once such criteria are estab-

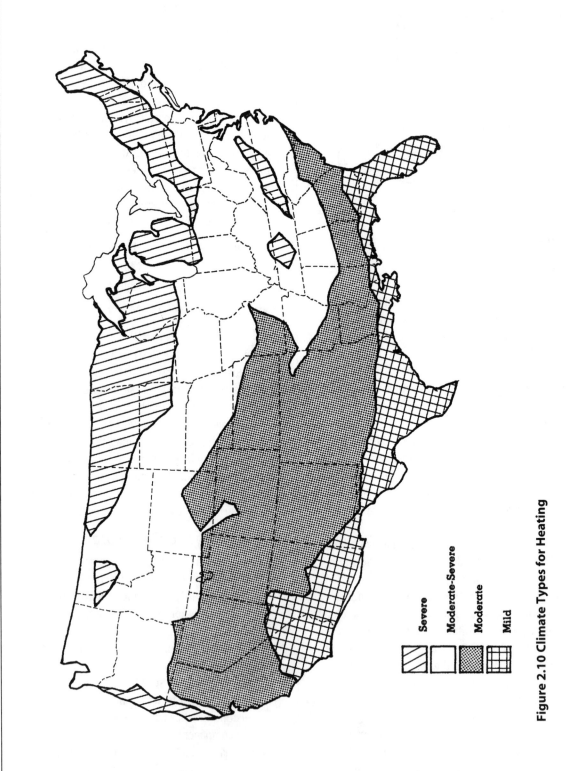

Figure 2.10 Climate Types for Heating

Severe

Moderate-Severe

Moderate

Mild

lished, Chapter 7: Materials is consulted and particular materials are selected for use.

Continuing with the example above, the detail illustrates a thermal storage wall with masonry selected as the storage component, with sizing criteria obtained from the "Storage Rules of Thumb," and particular masonry materials specified.

In some cases, such as specification of the collector component, options for materials selection are too numerous to be covered in one book. In these instances, the information in Chapter 7 is of a general nature. For instance, glazing types (such as double-pane, low-e glazing) are discussed, but particular manufacturers' products are not presented. In these cases, a check of the products locally available that conform to the rules of thumb will need to be made before a particular material is selected.

Energy Use Analysis

At many points in the design process, it is useful to have access to design and energy use analysis methods for the purpose of sizing the passive solar components and estimating the energy use of the home. Depending on the complexity of the design and required accuracy of results, a variety of methods are available for design and energy use analysis. These methods can be grouped into two categories reflecting the tools required to use the method and, to a limited extent, the degree of difficulty in using the method, the flexibility of the method to evaluate a range of design and material types, and the accuracy of the results. The two categories are manual procedures and computer programs, which are discussed below.

MANUAL METHODS

The first category, manual procedures, includes methods in which the projected energy use can be calculated using paper and pencil and, frequently, preprinted charts, tables, and graphs.

The manual methods are often simplified codifications of computer programs. In the process of simplification, however, some of the flexibility to change building characteristics, allowed in the computer program, is lost. For example, in esti-

mating the performance of a thermal storage wall, most manual methods assume that the wall is 18″ thick. Later, it will become evident that such a wall can have a range of thicknesses. Unfortunately, the user of these manual methods may not have the flexibility to vary the material dimension and must, therefore, expect that the projected energy use will be in slight error if a thickness other than 18″ is used. The computer program from which the manual method was derived may have allowed the user to vary the thickness, but the manual method may be applicable only if characteristics such as the wall thickness of the home to be analyzed are similar to the assumptions.

This loss of flexibility may also prohibit the evaluation of innovative designs. The manual methods are, therefore, applicable only for a limited number of design cases (usually the most typical types of designs), yielding only gross estimates of estimated building energy use. Most require a one- to two-day familiarization period. A single analysis can take from a few minutes to a few hours, depending on the method.

One of the most user-friendly manual methods available is a series of worksheets from the Passive Solar Industries Council (PSIC). *Passive Solar Design Strategies: Guidelines for Home Building,* which was developed by PSIC and the National Renewable Energy Laboratory (NREL) with support from the U.S. Department of Energy, contains simple-to-use worksheets and reference tables (see Table 2.1). The guidelines offer information about passive solar techniques and how they work. Specific examples of systems that save various amounts of energy are provided. The worksheets provide a simple, fill-in-the-blank method to evaluate the performance of a specific design. There is also a worked example that demonstrates how to complete the worksheets for a typical residence.

COMPUTER PROGRAMS

By far the most flexible, complex, and detailed analysis methods are computer programs. These programs compute, in a few moments, a very accurate profile of the energy usage patterns of the designed home. A similar analysis, performed

(Text continues on page 26.)

Table 2.1

General Project Information

Project Name	PASSIVE SOLAR EXAMPLE	Floor Area	1504 SF
Location	SEATTLE, WASHINGTON	Date	02/21/96
Designer	BC		

Worksheet I: Conservation Performance Level

A. Envelope Heat Loss

Construction Description	Area		R-value [Table A]		Heat Loss
Ceilings/roofs R-49 IN ATTIC	1084	÷	46.9	=	23
R-38 IN CATHED. CEILING	420	÷	25.7	=	16
Walls R-19 + R-5 SHEATHING	992	÷	24.7	=	40
R-19 AT GARAGE	140	÷	17.7	=	8
Insulated Floors		÷		=	
		÷		=	
Non-solar Glazing WOOD FRAME W/VINYL CLAD.	52	÷	2.4	=	22
- 1/2" AIR GAP, LOW-E $.40		÷		=	
Doors METAL W/FOAM CORE	40	÷	5.9	=	7
		÷		=	
					116 Total	Btu/°F-h

B. Foundation Perimeter Heat Loss

Description	Perimeter		Heat Loss Factor [Table B]		Heat Loss
Slabs-on-Grade R-11	82	×	0.30	=	25
Heated Basements R-11	82	×	0.60	=	49
Unheated Basements		×		=	
Perimeter Insulated Crawlspaces		×		=	
					74 Total	Btu/°F-h

C. Infiltration Heat Loss

$$\underset{\text{Building Volume}}{12483} \times \underset{\substack{\text{Air Changes} \\ \text{per Hour}}}{0.50} \times .018 = \underline{112} \quad \text{Btu/°F-h}$$

D. Total Heat Loss per Square Foot

$$24 \times \underset{\substack{\text{Total Heat Loss} \\ \text{(A+B+C)}}}{302} \div \underset{\text{Floor Area}}{1504} = \underline{4.81} \quad \text{Btu/DD-sf}$$

E. Conservation Performance Level

$$\underset{\substack{\text{Total Heat} \\ \text{Loss per} \\ \text{Square Foot}}}{4.81} \times \underset{\substack{\text{Heating Degree} \\ \text{Days [Table C]}}}{5121} \times \underset{\substack{\text{Heating Degree} \\ \text{Day Multiplier} \\ \text{[Table C]}}}{0.92} = \underline{22661} \quad \text{Btu/yr-sf}$$

F. Comparison Conservation Performance (From Previous Calculation or from Table D)

$$\underline{38747} \quad \text{Btu/yr-sf}$$

Compare Line E to Line F

Table 2.1 *(Continued)*

Worksheet II: Auxiliary Heat Performance Level

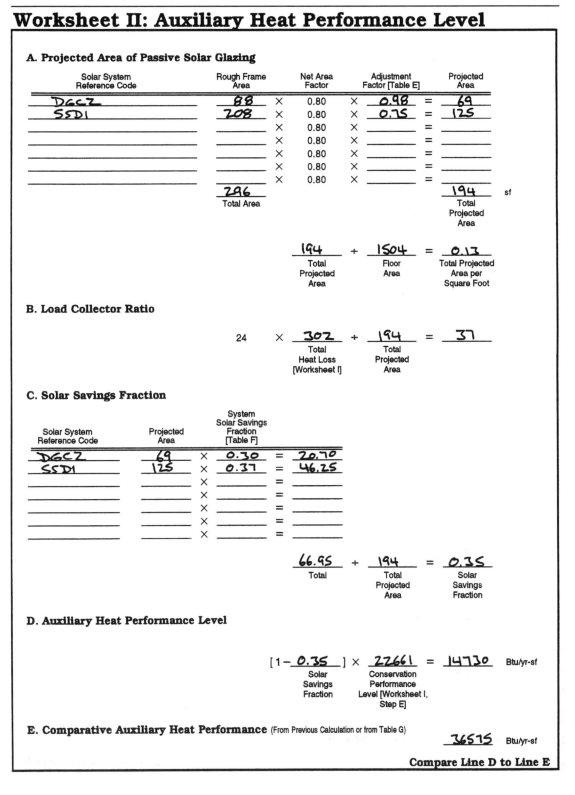

A. Projected Area of Passive Solar Glazing

Solar System Reference Code	Rough Frame Area		Net Area Factor		Adjustment Factor [Table E]		Projected Area
DGC2	88	×	0.80	×	0.98	=	69
SSD1	208	×	0.80	×	0.75	=	125
		×	0.80	×		=	
		×	0.80	×		=	
		×	0.80	×		=	
		×	0.80	×		=	
		×	0.80	×		=	
	296 Total Area						194 sf Total Projected Area

$$\frac{194}{\text{Total Projected Area}} + \frac{1504}{\text{Floor Area}} = \frac{0.13}{\text{Total Projected Area per Square Foot}}$$

B. Load Collector Ratio

$$24 \times \frac{302}{\substack{\text{Total Heat Loss}\\\text{[Worksheet I]}}} + \frac{194}{\substack{\text{Total Projected Area}}} = \frac{37}{}$$

C. Solar Savings Fraction

Solar System Reference Code	Projected Area		System Solar Savings Fraction [Table F]		
DGC2	69	×	0.30	=	20.70
SSD1	125	×	0.37	=	46.25
		×		=	
		×		=	
		×		=	
		×		=	
		×		=	

$$\frac{66.95}{\text{Total}} + \frac{194}{\substack{\text{Total Projected Area}}} = \frac{0.35}{\substack{\text{Solar Savings Fraction}}}$$

D. Auxiliary Heat Performance Level

$$[1 - \underset{\substack{\text{Solar Savings Fraction}}}{0.35}] \times \underset{\substack{\text{Conservation Performance Level [Worksheet I, Step E]}}}{22661} = \underset{}{14730} \text{ Btu/yr-sf}$$

E. Comparative Auxiliary Heat Performance (From Previous Calculation or from Table G)

36575 Btu/yr-sf

Compare Line D to Line E

Table 2.1 *(Continued)*

Worksheet III: Thermal Mass/Comfort

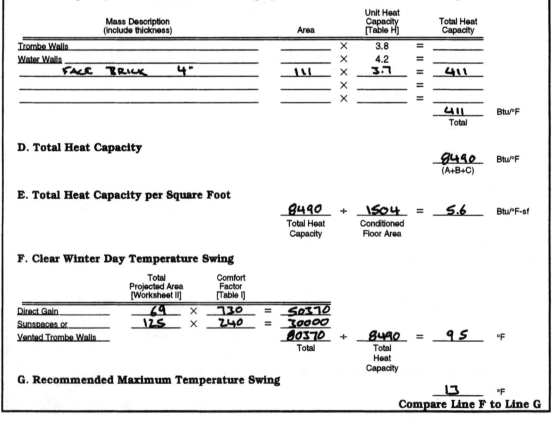

A. Heat Capacity of Sheetrock and Interior Furnishings

	Floor Area		Unit Heat Capacity		Total Heat Capacity	
Rooms with Direct Gain	464	×	4.7	=	2181	
Spaces Connected to Direct Gain Spaces	949	×	4.5	=	4271	
					6452	Btu/°F
					Total	

B. Heat Capacity of Mass Surfaces Enclosing Direct Gain Spaces

Mass Description (include thickness)	Area		Unit Heat Capacity [Table H]		Total Heat Capacity	
Trombe Walls		×	8.8	=		
Water Walls		×	10.4	=		
Exposed Slab in Sun	103	×	13.4	=	1380	
Exposed Slab Not in Sun	137	×	1.8	=	247	
		×		=		
		×		=		
		×		=		
					1627	Btu/°F
					Total	

C. Heat Capacity of Mass Surfaces Enclosing Spaces Connected to Direct Gain Spaces

Mass Description (include thickness)	Area		Unit Heat Capacity [Table H]		Total Heat Capacity	
Trombe Walls		×	3.8	=		
Water Walls		×	4.2	=		
FACE BRICK 4"	111	×	3.7	=	411	
		×		=		
		×		=		
					411	Btu/°F
					Total	

D. Total Heat Capacity

8490	Btu/°F
(A+B+C)	

E. Total Heat Capacity per Square Foot

8490	+	1504	=	5.6	Btu/°F-sf
Total Heat Capacity		Conditioned Floor Area			

F. Clear Winter Day Temperature Swing

	Total Projected Area [Worksheet II]		Comfort Factor [Table I]			
Direct Gain	69	×	730	=	50370	
Sunspaces or	125	×	240	=	30000	
Vented Trombe Walls					80370	+ 8490 = 9.5 °F
					Total	Total Heat Capacity

G. Recommended Maximum Temperature Swing

13	°F

Compare Line F to Line G

Table 2.1 *(Continued)*

Worksheet IV: Summer Cooling Performance Level

A. Opaque Surfaces

Description	Heat Loss [Worksheet I]		Radiant Barrier Factor [Table J]		Absorptance [Table K]		Heat Gain Factor [Table L]		Load
Ceilings/roofs	23	×	1.00	×	0.47	×	23.7	=	256
	16	×	1.00	×	0.47	×	23.7	=	178
		×		×		×		=	
Walls	40	×	n/a		0.70	×	12.9	=	361
		×	n/a			×		=	
Doors	3	×	n/a		0.30	×	12.9	=	12
									807 kBtu/yr Total

B. Non-solar Glazing

Description	Rough Frame Area		Net Area Factor		Shade Factor [Table M]		Heat Gain Factor [Table L]		Load
North Glass	40	×	0.80	×	0.68	×	13.0	=	283
		×	0.80	×		×		=	
East Glass	6	×	0.80	×	0.80	×	36.2	=	139
		×	0.80	×		×		=	
West Glass	6	×	0.80	×	0.90	×	35.9	=	138
		×	0.80	×		×		=	
Skylights		×	0.80	×		×		=	
		×	0.80	×		×		=	
									560 kBtu/yr Total

C. Solar Glazing

Solar System Description	Rough Frame Area		Net Area Factor		Shade Factor [Table M]		Heat Gain Factor [Table L]		Load
Direct Gain	88	×	0.80	×	0.70	×	29.1	=	1434
		×	0.80	×		×		=	
Storage Walls		×	0.80	×		×		=	
		×	0.80	×		×		=	
Sunspace	208	×	0.80	×	1.00	×	6.8	=	1132
		×	0.80	×		×		=	
									2566 kBtu/yr Total

D. Internal Gain

<u>880</u> + (<u>370</u> × <u>3</u>) = <u>1990</u> kBtu/yr

Constant Component [Table N]   Variable Component [Table N]   Number of Bedrooms

E. Cooling Load per Square Foot

1,000 × <u>5923</u> + <u>1504</u> = <u>3938</u> Btu/yr-sf

(A+B+C+D)   Floor Area

F. Adjustment for Thermal Mass and Ventilation

– No Night Vent. w/ Ceiling Fan   <u>4572</u> Btu/yr-sf [Table O]

G. Cooling Performance Level

<u>-634</u> Btu/yr-sf (E -F)

H. Comparison Cooling Performance (From Previous Calculation or from Table P)

<u>2250</u> Btu/yr-sf

Compare Line G to Line H

Table 2.1 *(Continued)*

Table A—Equivalent Thermal Performance of Assemblies R-values (hr-F-sf/Btu)

A1–Ceilings/Roofs

Attic Construction	Insulation R-value			
	R-30	R-38	R-49	R-60
	27.9	35.9	46.9	57.9

Framed Construction	Insulation R-value			
	R-19	R-22	R-30	R-38
2x6 at 16"oc	14.7	15.8	16.3	–
2x6 at 24"oc	15.3	16.5	17.1	–
2x8 at 16"oc	17.0	18.9	20.6	21.1
2x8 at 24"oc	17.6	19.6	21.6	21.9
2x10 at 16"oc	18.1	20.1	24.5	25.7
2x10 at 24"oc	18.4	20.7	25.5	26.8
2x12 at 16"oc	18.8	21.0	25.5	30.1
2x12 at 24"oc	19.0	21.4	27.3	31.4

A2–Framed Walls

Single Wall Framing	Insulation R-value			
	R-11	R-13	R-19	R-25
2x4 at 16"oc	12.0	13.6	–	–
2x4 at 24"oc	12.7	13.9	–	–
2x6 at 16"oc	14.1	15.4	17.7	19.2
2x6 at 24"oc	14.3	15.6	18.2	19.8

Double Wall Framing	Total Thickness (inches)			
	8	10	12	14
	25.0	31.3	37.5	43.8

The R-value of insulating sheathing should be added to the values in this table.

A3–Insulated Floors

Framing	Insulation R-value			
	R-11	R-19	R-30	R-38
2x6s at 16"oc	18.2	23.8	29.9	–
2x6s at 24"oc	18.4	24.5	31.5	–
2x8s at 16"oc	18.8	24.9	31.7	36.0
2x8s at 24"oc	18.9	25.4	33.1	37.9
2x10 at 16"oc	19.3	25.8	33.4	38.1
2x10 at 24"oc	19.3	26.1	34.4	39.8
2x12 at 16"oc	19.7	26.5	34.7	39.8
2x12 at 24"oc	19.6	26.7	35.5	41.2

These R-values include the buffering effect of a ventilated crawlspace or unconditioned basement.

A4–Windows

	Air Gap		
	1/4 in.	1/2 in.	1/2 in. argon
Standard Metal Frame			
Single	.9		
Double	1.1	1.2	1.2
Low-e (e<=0.40)	1.2	1.3	1.3
Metal frame with thermal break			
Double	1.5	1.6	1.7
Low-e (e<=0.40)	1.6	1.8	1.8
Low-e (e<=0.20)	1.7	1.9	2.0
Wood frame with vinyl cladding			
Double	2.0	2.1	2.2
Low-e (e<=0.40)	2.1	2.4	2.5
Low-e (e<=0.20)	2.2	2.6	2.7
Low-e (e<=0.10)	2.3	2.6	2.9

These R-values are based on a 3 mph wind speed and are typical for the entire rough framed opening. Manufacture's data, based on National Fenestration Rating Council procedures, should be used when available. One half the R-value of movable insulation should be added, when appropriate.

Table A–continued ..

A5–Doors

Solid wood with Weatherstripping	2.2
Metal with rigid foam core	5.9

Table B–Perimeter Heat Loss Factors for Slabs-on-Grade and Unheated Basements (Btu/h-F-ft)

Perimeter Insulation	Slabs-on-Grade	Heated Basements	Unheated Basements	Insulated Crawlspaces
None	0.8	1.3	1.1	1.1
R-5	0.4	0.8	0.7	0.6
R-7	0.3	0.7	0.6	0.5
R-11	0.3	0.6	0.5	0.4
R-19	0.2	0.4	0.5	0.3
R-30	0.1	0.3	0.4	0.2

Table C–Heating Degree Days (F-day)

C1–Heating Degree Days (Base 65°F)

Seattle	5,121
Aberdeen	5,298
Bremerton	5,193
Buckley	5,510
Centralia	5,081
Clearwater	5,691
Everett	5,352
Kent	5,073
McMillin	5,649
Olympia	5,709
Puyallup	5,144
Quilcene	5,615
Shelton	5,229
Snoqualmie	5,505
Startup	5,505

C2–Heating Degree Day Multiplier

	Passive Solar Glazing Area per per Square Foot				
Heat Loss per Square Foot	.00	.05	.10	.15	.20
12.00	1.13	1.14	1.14	1.15	1.15
11.50	1.12	1.13	1.13	1.14	1.14
11.00	1.11	1.12	1.13	1.13	1.14
10.50	1.10	1.11	1.12	1.12	1.13
10.00	1.09	1.10	1.11	1.11	1.12
9.50	1.08	1.09	1.10	1.11	1.11
9.00	1.06	1.07	1.08	1.09	1.10
8.50	1.05	1.06	1.07	1.08	1.09
8.00	1.03	1.04	1.06	1.07	1.08
7.50	1.01	1.03	1.04	1.05	1.06
7.00	0.99	1.01	1.02	1.03	1.05
6.50	0.97	0.98	1.00	1.02	1.03
6.00	0.94	0.96	0.98	0.99	1.01
5.50	0.91	0.93	0.95	0.97	0.99
5.00	0.87	0.90	0.92	0.94	0.96
4.50	0.82	0.85	0.89	0.91	0.94
4.00	0.77	0.81	0.84	0.87	0.90
3.50	0.70	0.75	0.79	0.83	0.86
3.00	0.61	0.68	0.73	0.78	0.82
2.50	0.49	0.58	0.65	0.71	0.76
2.00	0.34	0.45	0.55	0.62	0.69

Table D–Base Case Conservation Performance (Btu/yr-sf)

Base Case	38,747

Table E–Projected Area Adjustment Factors

Degrees off True South	Solar System Type			
	DG, TW, WW, SSC	SSA, SSD	SSB, SSE	
0	1.00	0.77	0.75	
5	1.00	0.76	0.75	
10	0.98	0.75	0.74	
15	0.97	0.74	0.73	
20	0.94	0.72	0.70	
25	0.91	0.69	0.68	
30	0.87	0.66	0.65	

Table F–Solar System Saving Fractions

F1–Direct Gain

Load Collector Ratio	DGC1 Double Glazing	DGC2 Low-e Glazing	DGC3 R-9 Night Insulation
400	0.03	0.04	0.05
300	0.05	0.05	0.07
200	0.07	0.08	0.10
150	0.09	0.11	0.13
100	0.12	0.15	0.19
80	0.14	0.18	0.22
60	0.17	0.22	0.28
50	0.20	0.25	0.32
45	0.21	0.27	0.35
40	0.22	0.29	0.38
35	0.24	0.32	0.41
30	0.26	0.35	0.46
25	0.28	0.39	0.51
20	0.31	0.44	0.57
15	0.33	0.49	0.64

F2–Trombe Walls

Load Collector Ratio	TWF3 Unvented Non-selective	TWA3 Vented Non-selective	TWJ2 Unvented Selective	TWI4 Unvented Night Insulation
400	0.02	0.05	0.02	0.00
300	0.03	0.06	0.04	0.01
200	0.05	0.08	0.09	0.05
150	0.07	0.10	0.12	0.08
100	0.11	0.14	0.19	0.14
80	0.13	0.16	0.24	0.18
60	0.17	0.20	0.30	0.24
50	0.19	0.22	0.34	0.28
45	0.21	0.24	0.37	0.30
40	0.22	0.25	0.40	0.33
35	0.24	0.28	0.43	0.37
30	0.27	0.30	0.47	0.41
25	0.30	0.33	0.52	0.45
20	0.33	0.37	0.58	0.51
15	0.38	0.42	0.65	0.59

Table 2.1 *(Continued)*

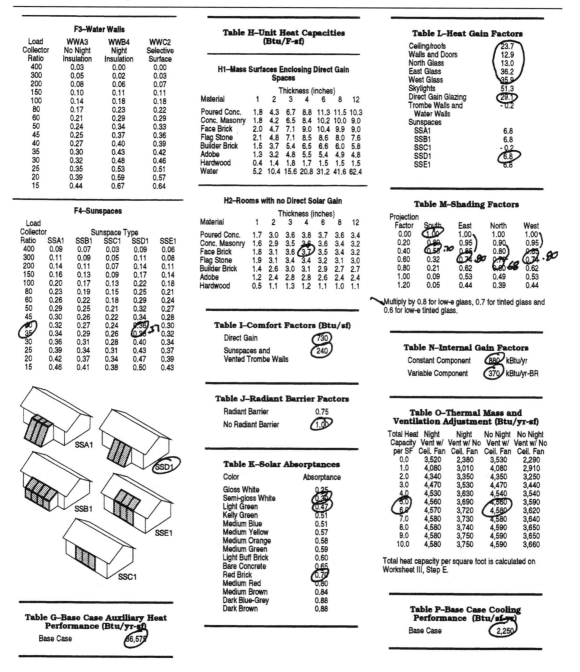

F3—Water Walls

Load Collector Ratio	WWA3 No Night Insulation	WWB4 Night Insulation	WWC2 Selective Surface
400	0.03	0.00	0.00
300	0.05	0.02	0.03
200	0.08	0.06	0.07
150	0.10	0.11	0.11
100	0.14	0.18	0.18
80	0.17	0.23	0.22
60	0.21	0.29	0.29
50	0.24	0.34	0.33
45	0.25	0.37	0.36
40	0.27	0.40	0.39
35	0.30	0.43	0.42
30	0.32	0.48	0.46
25	0.35	0.53	0.51
20	0.39	0.59	0.57
15	0.44	0.67	0.64

F4—Sunspaces

Load Collector Ratio	SSA1	SSB1	SSC1	SSD1	SSE1
400	0.09	0.07	0.03	0.09	0.06
300	0.11	0.09	0.05	0.11	0.08
200	0.14	0.11	0.07	0.14	0.11
150	0.16	0.13	0.09	0.17	0.14
100	0.20	0.17	0.13	0.22	0.18
80	0.23	0.19	0.15	0.25	0.21
60	0.26	0.22	0.18	0.29	0.24
50	0.29	0.25	0.21	0.32	0.27
45	0.30	0.26	0.22	0.34	0.28
40	0.32	0.27	0.24	0.36	0.30
35	0.34	0.29	0.26	0.38	0.32
30	0.36	0.31	0.28	0.40	0.34
25	0.39	0.34	0.31	0.43	0.37
20	0.42	0.37	0.34	0.47	0.39
15	0.46	0.41	0.38	0.50	0.43

Table H—Unit Heat Capacities (Btu/F-sf)

H1—Mass Surfaces Enclosing Direct Gain Spaces

Material	\- Thickness (inches)						
	1	2	3	4	6	8	12
Poured Conc.	1.8	4.3	6.7	8.8	11.3	11.5	10.3
Conc. Masonry	1.8	4.2	6.5	8.4	10.2	10.0	9.0
Face Brick	2.0	4.7	7.1	9.0	10.4	9.9	9.0
Flag Stone	2.1	4.8	7.1	8.5	8.6	8.0	7.6
Builder Brick	1.5	3.7	5.4	6.5	6.6	6.0	5.8
Adobe	1.3	3.2	4.8	5.5	5.4	4.9	4.8
Hardwood	0.4	1.4	1.8	1.7	1.5	1.5	1.5
Water	5.2	10.4	15.6	20.8	31.2	41.6	62.4

H2—Rooms with no Direct Solar Gain

Material	\- Thickness (inches)						
	1	2	3	4	6	8	12
Poured Conc.	1.7	3.0	3.6	3.8	3.7	3.6	3.4
Conc. Masonry	1.6	2.9	3.5	3.6	3.6	3.4	3.2
Face Brick	1.8	3.1	3.6	3.7	3.5	3.4	3.2
Flag Stone	1.9	3.1	3.4	3.4	3.2	3.1	3.0
Builder Brick	1.4	2.6	3.0	3.1	2.9	2.7	2.7
Adobe	1.2	2.4	2.8	2.8	2.6	2.4	2.4
Hardwood	0.5	1.1	1.3	1.2	1.1	1.0	1.1

Table I—Comfort Factors (Btu/sf)

Direct Gain	730
Sunspaces and Vented Trombe Walls	240

Table J—Radiant Barrier Factors

Radiant Barrier	0.75
No Radiant Barrier	1.00

Table K—Solar Absorptances

Color	Absorptance
Gloss White	0.25
Semi-gloss White	0.30
Light Green	0.47
Kelly Green	0.51
Medium Blue	0.51
Medium Yellow	0.57
Medium Orange	0.58
Medium Green	0.59
Light Buff Brick	0.60
Bare Concrete	0.65
Red Brick	0.70
Medium Red	0.80
Medium Brown	0.84
Dark Blue-Grey	0.88
Dark Brown	0.88

Table G—Base Case Auxiliary Heat Performance (Btu/yr-sf)

Base Case	36,575

Table L—Heat Gain Factors

Ceiling/roofs	23.7
Walls and Doors	12.9
North Glass	13.0
East Glass	36.2
West Glass	35.9
Skylights	51.3
Direct Gain Glazing	29.1
Trombe Walls and Water Walls	-0.2
Sunspaces	
SSA1	6.8
SSB1	6.8
SSC1	-0.2
SSD1	6.8
SSE1	6.8

Table M—Shading Factors

Projection Factor	South	East	North	West
0.00	1.00	1.00	1.00	1.00
0.20	0.80	0.95	0.90	0.95
0.40	0.58	0.85	0.80	0.85
0.60	0.32	0.74	0.80	0.74
0.80	0.21	0.62	0.68	0.62
1.00	0.09	0.53	0.49	0.53
1.20	0.05	0.44	0.39	0.44

Multiply by 0.8 for low-e glass, 0.7 for tinted glass and 0.6 for low-e tinted glass.

Table N—Internal Gain Factors

Constant Component	880	kBtu/yr
Variable Component	370	kBtu/yr-BR

Table O—Thermal Mass and Ventilation Adjustment (Btu/yr-sf)

Total Heat Capacity per SF	Night Vent w/ Ceil. Fan	Night Vent w/ No Ceil. Fan	No Night Vent w/ Ceil. Fan	No Night Vent w/ No Ceil. Fan
0.0	3,520	2,380	3,530	2,290
1.0	4,080	3,010	4,080	2,910
2.0	4,340	3,350	4,350	3,250
3.0	4,470	3,530	4,470	3,440
4.0	4,530	3,630	4,540	3,540
5.0	4,560	3,690	4,560	3,590
6.0	4,570	3,720	4,580	3,620
7.0	4,580	3,730	4,580	3,640
8.0	4,580	3,740	4,590	3,650
9.0	4,580	3,750	4,590	3,650
10.0	4,580	3,750	4,590	3,660

Total heat capacity per square foot is calculated on Worksheet III, Step E.

Table P—Base Case Cooling Performance (Btu/sf-yr)

Base Case	2,250

manually, would require months of calculation by a knowledgeable mathematician. This high degree of accuracy in computing energy may, in fact, be well out of proportion to the design being evaluated. To program a single home may require several days.

Choosing Software for Energy Analysis

The biggest problem in developing schematic design software is the lack of specificity inherent to the schematic design phase, which conflicts with the need for precise building dimensions and detailed operating schedules required for computer analysis. Describing a building at that level of specificity would be too time-consuming and also irrelevant, since many original assumptions will change. Conversely, a too-sketchy description can give misleading results.

ENERGY-10 software (described below) addresses this difficulty by providing libraries and a database with building defaults for almost any entry required. The libraries include thermal properties of materials and construction systems, as is typically done for most programs. However, ENERGY-10 goes a step further. For any construction type in its repertory, it assigns default walls, roofs, and windows based on typical construction practice. Defaults are also assigned for levels of lighting, equipment, building use, and even a simplified building geometry. A simulation of a house can be performed quickly, with very few changes required. As more is known about the building, more specific information can be input to replace the defaults.

The following sections describe available energy analysis programs, starting with the most basic and easy to use, and proceeding to the more complex. The more complex a program is, generally, the more accurate its analysis is. However, the less complex and easier-to-use programs are often better geared to residential buildings, and will yield results that are usable for house design and construction.

PEAR Software PEAR is a software package developed by Lawrence Berkeley Laboratory under U.S. Department of Energy sponsorship. It contains a series of look-up table algorithms, which access results from detailed hour-by-hour simulations created using the DOE-2.1 program (see description below). These simulations were performed in 45 U.S. locations, representative of all major weather areas. The results of these simulations are extended to about 900 locations using extrapolations based on weather characteristics. For the building types described (seven configurations of detached houses and townhouses), PEAR is accurate, fast, and user-friendly.

BuilderGuide's Construction Emphasis A builder-friendly software package, BuilderGuide was developed by the Passive Solar Industries Council to automate the calculations for the energy use worksheets of PSIC's workbook, *Passive Solar Design Strategies: Guidelines for Home Building,* described above. The program operates like a spreadsheet—the user fills in values for the building, such as passive solar design and construction features, conservation performance, auxiliary heat performance, thermal mass and comfort, and summer cooling performance. The computer completes the calculations, including searching files containing data on climate and component performance for 228 locations within the United States. The user can adjust for local conditions so that the performance of a building located virtually anywhere can be calculated. BuilderGuide then prints out the answers. This automated method allows the user to vary the input values and to quickly evaluate a wide range of design strategies.

ENERGY-10 ENERGY-10 design software represents the most important advance in energy-efficient predesign tools, and, for that reason, it is probably the tool best suited for the readers of this book—architects and builders. ENERGY-10 was produced through a partnership of the U.S. Department of Energy's Office of Building Technology, the National Renewable Energy Laboratory, the Lawrence Berkeley National Laboratory, and PSIC. Steven Winter Associates personnel served on the PSIC technical committee charged with the project. Through this committee, ENERGY-10 received input from architects, engineers, builders, and utility representatives. ENERGY-10 requires, for good performance, an IBM-compatible 486 DX2, Windows 3.1, and a minimum of 7 MB of hard disk space.

ENERGY-10 facilitates decision making early in the design process. It relies on a whole building approach and integrates daylighting, passive solar heating, and low-energy cooling strategies with energy-efficient shell design and mechanical equipment.

ENERGY-10 shows the consequences of various design decisions. The evaluations are based on hour-by-hour calculations through all 8,760 hours of the year. Weather data used are representative of typical (long-term) average conditions for a large selection of U.S. locations. Version 1 of the program, released in 1996, evaluates a range of building types—including low-rise residential—with one or two thermal zones.

With ENERGY-10, a building can be defined and evaluated before it is designed, using a process called *Autobuild.* To start, a *Reference Case* is described by entering only a few inputs which are known during the predesign phase of a project. Three of these choices are location (to determine the weather file), building size in square feet, and building use. Also needed are the number of stories (one or two), type of HVAC system, and the utility rates. Starting with these inputs, ENERGY-10 can define and evaluate a simple "shoebox" building.

After performing an energy analysis on the *Reference Case* building, ENERGY-10 provides graphic results that indicate how energy is used (e.g., heating versus cooling versus lighting) and where the major opportunities for savings are. With this information, one is able to focus on the design areas with the maximum savings potential.

Autobuild goes one step further. It generates, from the beginning, not just one building description, but two. The second building is derived from the *Reference Case.* It is the same simple shoebox, but with a variety of energy-efficient strategies that the designer applies. The purpose of this second building is to show the range of energy savings that can be expected for that specific building type in that specific climate. Energy-efficient strategies include additional insulation, efficient lights, daylighting, shading, improved glazing, passive solar heating with extra mass for heat storage, and high-efficiency

HVAC equipment. (The user selects the strategies from a menu.) This building is also evaluated, and the results for both buildings are illustrated in many graphic formats, such as annual energy use in thousands of Btus per square foot. An additional feature of ENERGY-10 is called RANK, which sequentially applies several energy-efficient strategies, evaluates their consequences, and rank-orders the results by various indicators, such as annual energy savings and annual dollar savings.

The first set of results from ENERGY-10 illustrates the opportunity for energy savings, but the figures are based on a shoebox, while the building conceived by the designer is different. After the advantageous energy-efficient strategies have been identified, the shoebox can be easily modified to conform to the actual form and to the characteristics of the actual building design, including actual window openings. The modifications are easy, since throughout ENERGY-10, everything is defaulted and everything can be edited. This saves time in setup, yet gives the flexibility in defining the building. For example, the designer can edit the libraries (e.g., material properties, glazing properties, wall constructions) and save them for later use.

High-Powered Analysis with DOE-2 and BLAST The federal government has developed the most comprehensive and accurate energy simulation packages of all. The DOE-2.1A version came into use in the early 1980s. Subsequent versions refined the algorithms for solar gain, daylighting, and control strategies, and increased the number of HVAC systems that can be simulated.

For analysis of large buildings, DOE-2 is the premier tool. The traditional DOE-2 input is very detailed and technical, using its own codified language. The output can be brief or exhaustive, according to need. In either case, the output is hard to interpret by persons without specific training. A new version of DOE-2, Power-DOE, employs screen-oriented input backed up by defaults. This version is much easier to use by practitioners. Graphics software serving to document the plans and volume of the simulated building is already available and continues to be improved. BLAST, developed at the National Institute of Standards and Technology, has also been widely validated. It is more accurate than DOE-2 in its simulation of thermal mass, but is less detailed in modeling HVAC equipment. Like DOE-2, its input and output procedures are very complex and its use for HVAC design is limited. Graphic output is restricted to presentation of energy use patterns.

Assessing the Economics

Whether or not a home sells has traditionally been a function of a number of factors, not the least of which is cost—specifically, first cost. In the past, other costs associated with home ownership—specifically, operating costs—rarely entered into home purchase discussions. Consequently, most economic decisions relating to design, material selection, and site planning tended to be based on first-cost criteria. By far, the major costs of home ownership were monthly mortgage payments, a reflection of the first cost and current interest rates. Due to low fuel cost, energy efficiency was seldom a factor in home design.

At present, although still important, the first-cost approach to decision making is being replaced by an economic indicator capable of reflecting the impact of energy costs. Such an indicator combines both first cost and energy cost into a single value familiar to all homeowners: total monthly cost. The total monthly cost includes both mortgage payments (interest and principal) and energy costs.

As a simple example, suppose a home built in New York state costs $180,000. The buyer makes an initial payment of 20 percent, or $36,000, and takes a $144,000 mortgage. Assuming an 8 percent, 30-year term rate, the monthly mortgage payments are $1,057. An analysis of the energy use indicates an average monthly expenditure of $124, or $1,488 per year on fuel. The total monthly cost to the home-owner is, therefore, $1,057 + $124 = $1,181.

Another buyer purchases an equivalent home, except that the design has been modified to incorporate passive solar and energy-conservation features. The passive home uses an attached sun-

space and additional insulation to reduce the home heating requirements.

The following example summarizes the significant criteria for comparing the homes:

Description
4-bedroom home in New York state

Heated Area
2,124 sq ft

Solar Features
Attached sunspace with low-e high-performance glazing

Manufactured sunspace	$3,000
Additional masonry	$700
Exterior shades	$300
Added insulation	$400
Total	$4,400

Monthly Expenses
Base case

Mortgage	$1,057
Fuel	$ 124
Total	$1,181

Passive Home

Mortgage	$1,082
Fuel	$74
Total	$1,156

It is evident from this example that the solar features add $4,400 to the first cost of the base-case home. Again, assuming that 80 percent of the total cost of $184,400 is financed, the initial cash outlay is $36,880, or $880 higher than the base case, and the mortgage amount is $147,520. With the 8 percent, 30-year term mortgage, the monthly payments are increased to $1,082, or $25 above the base-case home. However, due to the energy-saving features, the estimated costs for fuel are now $881 per year, or about $74 per month on average. The total monthly home-owner expenditures equal $1,156, or $25 less than the base home. With this $300-per-year savings, the initial additional outlay of $880 is recovered in less than three years. In addition to continually accruing these savings (relative to the less energy-efficient home), the owner of the passive solar home has the additional amenity of the sunspace.

ENERGY EFFICIENCY FINANCING PRODUCTS

Another major change over the past few years is the advent of energy efficiency financing products—mortgages and loans—which benefit homebuyers and homeowners who are increasing the energy efficiency of their new or existing home (see Table 2.2 on the next page). Homes that incorporate passive solar features may qualify for such financial products. Essentially, lenders are recognizing the total monthly cost of home ownership expressed above. Therefore, lenders will increase the amount of the mortgage without requiring additional down payment. The ap-

praised value of the home is then automatically increased to include cost-effective energy measures. A Home Energy Rating System (HERS) energy analysis may be required, and can be performed by qualified raters. For details on specific programs available in your area, contact your state energy office, local utility, local FHA office, or the HERS Council at 1511 K Street, NW, Suite 600, Washington, DC 20005; 202-638-3700.

Ultimately, the decision whether or not to invest in a passive solar technique should be an economic one. Throughout the text, numerous design recommendations and rules of thumb are presented to aid in the design process. Design guides should be checked and, if required, superseded by design decisions based on specific economic analysis using actual local costs.

Table 2.2 Guidelines for Energy-Efficiency Financing Products

	Home Types	Loan Types	Construct. Req't	Debt-to-Income Ratio	Cost Limits	Loan Limits	Qualifying
FHA	1- and 2-Unit	Purchase and Refinance	Must Meet MEC 4★ Home	2% Stretch for 4★ Home	$4000 or 5% of Property Value up to $8000	Statutory Limits May Be Exceeded by E-E Escrow Amt.	No Additional Req't
203K-EEM	1- to 4-Unit	Purchase and Refinance	Existing Construct.	N/A	Same as FHA Regular	Statutory Limits May Be Exceeded by E-E Escrow Amt.	No Additional Req't
CONVEN-TIONAL	1- to 4-Unit	Purchase and Refinance	Benefits for % over MEC 4★ Home	2% Stretch for 4★ Home	10% Base Loan Amount	May Not Be Exceeded	Buyer must Qualify
VA	1- and 2-Unit	Purchase and Refinance	Must Meet MEC 4★ Home	Higher Residual Income Calc	Up to $3000 w/o Rating; up to $6000 w/Rating	May Not Be Exceeded	No Additional Req't
EPA ENERGY STAR	Single Family Detach	Purchase Only	5★ Home 30% over MEC	2%–5% Income Stretch[1]	New Construct.	Determined on Individual Basis[1]	Buyer must Qualify
E-SEAL	1- and 2-Unit	Purchase Only	10%–30% over MEC	2%–5% Income Stretch[1]	New Construct.	Determined on Individual Basis[1]	Buyer must Qualify
HELP 2000	1- to 4-Unit	Equity or Consumer	Existing Construct.	N/A	Up to $25,000 for 15 years	Determined on Individual Basis	Borrower must Qualify

[1]Consult mortgage company for specific interest rates, loan limits, and other incentives.
October, 1996 National HERO.

Down Payment	LTV	Appraisal	Time Limit	Post Test and Release	Rating Fee Financing	Other Incentive
No Additional Req't	May Exceed 100%	No Additional Req't	90 Days	By Rater and HERS Provider	Up to $200	None
No Additional Req't	May Exceed 100% (Energy Only)	Appraisal for Non-Energy Improvement	150 Days	By Rater and HERS Provider	Up to $200	None
In Accordance with LTV	Not to Exceed 95%	Increased by Cost of Energy Upgrade	120 Days	By Rater and HERS Provider	Up to $200 if w/in LTV	None
None, for Cost-Effective Improvement	May Exceed 100% w/Positive 1st Yr. Cash Flow	No Additional Req't	180 Days	By Rater and HERS Provider	Up to $200	None
In Accordance with LTV	Determined on Individual Basis[1]	No Additional Req't	N/A	N/A	Builder/ Utility Financed	Low er Int. Rate/ $350 for Closing[1]
No Additional Req't	Determined on Individual Basis[1]	No Additional Req't	N/A	N/A	Builder/ Utility Financed	Lower Int. Rate/ Cash Back[1]
None	100%	No Req't	120 Days	By Rater and HERS Provider	Up to $200	None

Design Overview

Direct gain systems are designed to be used primarily for heating, and are most effective in areas with mild or moderate winter climates. In a direct gain system, the collection, absorption, and storage of solar energy occur directly within the living space. The conceptual simplicity of this arrangement is compelling. As a result of intelligent planning and minor modifications in standard building practice, the home itself becomes the passive solar system. Living within the system can pose certain problems, however, and attention must be paid, during the design of the building, to questions of space planning, privacy, natural lighting, glare, overheating, and fading and deterioration of fabrics exposed to direct sunlight.

Seasonal Operation—Heating

During the heating season, sunlight enters the living space through an expanse of south-facing collector (usually glass). This solar radiation is, in turn, absorbed by elements in the space (e.g., floor, walls, ceiling, and furnishings) and converted to heat, which either warms the air in the space or is stored in interior storage elements for later use (see Figure 3.1). These storage elements are generally made of high-mass materials—typically masonry, which may serve as basic structural components (e.g., walls and floors), or water in suitable containers.

Interior storage mass should be as evenly distributed as possible throughout the spaces to be heated, rather than concentrated in one area. For example, 400 sq. ft. of 4″-thick exposed mass is more effective than 200 sq. ft. of 8″-thick material. It is also recommended that as much mass as possible be located so that sunlight strikes it directly.

It is often difficult, however, when distributing mass throughout a direct gain space, to provide direct sunlight over the entire surface area. Mass not located in direct sun will absorb heat from warmed air, but will not absorb and store as much heat as mass in direct sun. Therefore, in cases where storage mass is evenly distributed throughout the direct gain space, some method for distributing the sunlight to this mass should be investigated.

Reflecting sunlight from light-colored nonstorage surfaces to the dark surface of the storage material is one technique. Another effective, although less common, technique is to use a glazing that diffuses and scatters the sunlight. Standard glazing materials and construction pro-

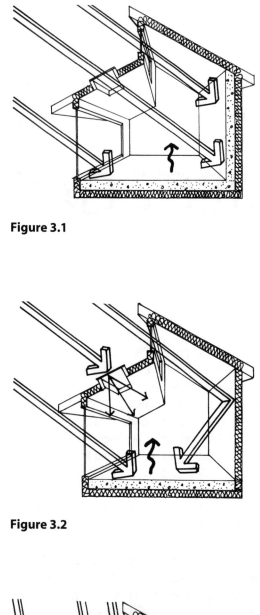

Figure 3.1

Figure 3.2

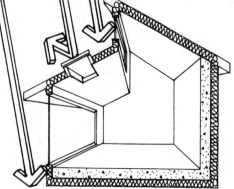

Figure 3.3

cedures can be used in either approach (see Figure 3.2).

Seasonal Operation—Cooling

During the cooling season, the large areas of south-facing collector should be well-shaded to prevent excessive solar heat gain (see Figure 3.3).

Shading elements, such as overhangs, should be sized so as to maximize *overall* system performance. If they are too large, overhangs may completely prevent unwanted solar gain during the cooling season, but they will also block a significant amount of radiation during the later part of the heating season. Conversely, if they are too small, solar gain will be maximized when heat is needed, but overheating will occur during the late part of the cooling season, adding to the overall load on the cooling equipment.

Advantages

- Conceptually the most straightforward, direct gain can also be the easiest to build using standard construction materials and methods.

- The system does not radically alter the appearance of the home.

- The system provides natural light and view in addition to energy savings and can, therefore, reduce lighting energy consumption.

- The system can have a very low additional cost relative to identical buildings without solar features. The use of direct gain systems, whether through the "solar-tempered" approach, or through the use of more substantial thermal storage components, can decrease energy use and allow reductions in the size of the heating and/or air conditioning equipment in a residence. The reduction in cost from smaller mechanical equipment can often equal the additional costs incurred from the passive solar design features.

- The combination of increased insulation levels, high-performance windows, and "tight" building construction can improve the comfort of a home. Common comfort complaints, such as air drafts and cold exterior walls or windows, are substantially reduced using passive solar methods.

Disadvantages

- Large expanse of south-facing glazing can cause glare and privacy problems.

- Ultraviolet radiation in sunlight can fade and degrade fabrics. However, some glazings now used in windows and skylights can substantially reduce the amount of ultraviolet light that passes through.

- Manual operation of movable insulation, which can increase the performance of a direct gain system, requires regular, conscientious attention to be effective. Homeowners may wish to choose high-performance window and skylight units instead, which require no additional maintenance.

Collectors

The principal function of a direct gain collector is to admit and trap solar energy so that it can be absorbed and stored by elements within the direct gain space. Although generally perceived as energy losers, the large expanses of south-facing collector used in direct gain applications can, if properly designed, gain significantly more energy than they lose. There are three basic types of direct gain collectors: solar windows, clerestories, and skylights (see Figure 3.4).

SOLAR WINDOWS

A solar window is simply a standard, off-the-shelf window or patio door installed in a south-facing direct gain wall using conventional construction

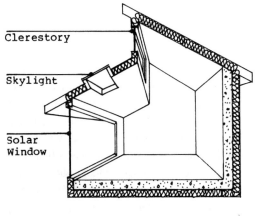

Figure 3.4

methods. The collector frame can be wood or metal and should be well caulked and weatherstripped. If metal is used, the frame should contain thermal breaks.

The solar window can be vertical, or it can be slightly tilted to maximize the amount of incoming solar radiation. A tilted collector is often difficult to install, however, and may require tempered glass. It can also be hard to shade and may pose significant overheating problems during the cooling season.

Glazing materials other than glass can be used in solar windows, although they are not generally available in preframed, off-the-shelf configurations. Such materials include various forms of fiberglass, acrylics, and polycarbonate (possible local building code restrictions on the use of these alternate materials should be investigated before they are specified). Some of these materials can diffuse and scatter the incoming light, which can improve the overall performance of a direct gain system by increasing the amount of radiation reaching the distributed mass. Note that light-scattering materials are typically translucent or patterned, which can result in the loss of view through these areas.

CLERESTORIES

Clerestories serve the same function as solar windows but can prevent problems with privacy, glare, and fading of fabrics. They also allow light to penetrate deeper into a space than may be possible with windows alone, often enabling direct sunlight to strike the north wall of the home. In situations where site obstructions, such as trees, prevent light from reaching standard solar windows, clerestories can be used to admit solar radiation to a direct gain space.

As in solar windows, clerestories can be vertical or tilted, and the problems associated with the latter configuration are the same for both collector types. The full range of collector materials available for solar windows can also be used in clerestories. Special attention should be paid to properly sealing and caulking the clerestory, especially in tilted installations.

In mild climates, several clerestories can be used together in a sawtooth pattern in order to increase the total amount of solar radiation entering a building (see Figure 3.5). If applying the sawtooth design in colder climates, careful consideration must be made for the issues of snow buildup and water leakage at the roof/clerestory connections.

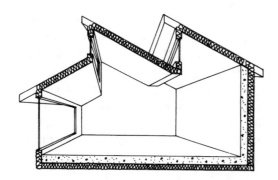

Figure 3.5

SKYLIGHTS

Skylights serve the same function as the other direct gain collectors and can be placed flat on a flat roof or tilted in a south-facing sloped roof. Skylights are often the least effective collector type. Their horizontal position receives the least sunlight during the heating season, when the sun is low in the sky and the heating requirements are highest, and maximum sunshine in the cooling season, when solar heat should be avoided. Because of their relatively low insulative properties, skylights can also become significant areas for heat to escape in an otherwise well-insulated roof.

For these reasons, skylights using high-performance glazings are typically recommended. In addition, the use of reflectors to enhance the amount of solar energy hitting the collector in the heating season, and shades to reduce solar heat gain in the cooling season, are options to improve skylight performance in a direct gain system (see Figure 3.6). Movable insulation to prevent heat losses at night are also effective in extreme climates, or when high-performance glazings are not specified.

In some cases, lighter, translucent materials may be preferable to glass because of their optical and handling characteristics; a variety of plastic "bubble" skylights are available off-the-shelf.

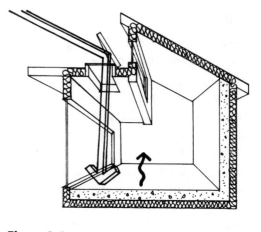

Figure 3.6

Note, however, that most plastic skylights will not perform as well thermally as those with high-performance glazings, and thus the need for shades and movable insulation increases.

As in clerestory installations, special attention should be paid to properly sealing and caulking a skylight because of the increased potential for water leakage in a flat or tilted configuration.

COLLECTOR RULES OF THUMB

All Collectors

- *Orientation:* Collector wall must face south. Variations up to 20° east or west of true south, however, will not significantly affect thermal performance. A slight east-of-south orientation may be desired to allow the sun to "wake up" the living space in the morning.

- *Collector Area:* A preliminary collector area size per square foot of floor area to be heated can be determined from Table 3.1. For example, for Madison, Wisconsin, at 43° NL with an average January temperature of 21.8°F (data available from local and/or national weather bureau), the intersection of the closest latitude (44° NL) and the closest "Average Winter Outdoor Temperature" (20°F) indicates that 0.29 sq. ft. of glazing per square foot of floor area is required. For a living space with a floor area of 200 sq. ft. to be heated, 58 sq. ft. (200 × 0.29) of south-facing glazing will be required.

Table 3.1

Average Winter Outdoor Temperature (Clear Day)*	Glazing/Floor Area**			
	36° NL	40° NL	44° NL	48° NL
COLD CLIMATES				
20°F	.24	.25	.29	.31 (w/NI)
25°F	.22	.23	.25	.28 (w/NI)
30°F	.19	.20	.22	.24
TEMPERATE CLIMATES				
35°F	.16	.17	.19	.21
40°F	.13	.14	.16	.17
45°F	.10	.11	.12	.13

Note: NI indicates night insulation.

* Temperatures listed are for December and January, usually the coldest months.

** These ratios apply to a well insulated space with a heat loss of 8 Btu/degree day/square foot of floor area/°F. If space heat loss is more or less than this figure, adjust the ratios accordingly.

- *Glazing Type:* Double glazing is recommended as the standard for most climates. The use of high-performance glazings, with low-e coatings, gas fills, and even suspended plastic films (which effectively create "triple-pane" glazings or better), can often be justified, economically and otherwise, in moderate to extreme climates. The additional use of movable insulation can also be effective in severe climates, or, conversely, in mild climates where single glazing is employed. (For more information on windows and movable insulation, refer to Chapter 7, on Materials.)

- *Operation:* Collectors should be operable to provide natural ventilation during the cooling season.

Clerestories

- *Color:* The ceiling adjacent to the clerestory should be light in color to reflect sunlight into the direct gain space and onto interior storage elements.

- *Location:* Clerestories should be placed in front of a direct gain storage wall at a distance of roughly 1.0 to 1.5 times the height of the wall (see Figure 3.7).

- *Sawtooth clerestories:* The angle of a sawtooth clerestory (as measured from the horizontal) should be equal to, or less than, the altitude of the sun at noon on December 21, the winter solstice. Angle A can be determined from the following formula: A = 66.5° − latitude. For example, at latitude 36°, angle A will equal 66.5° − 36°, or 30.5° (see Figure 3.8).

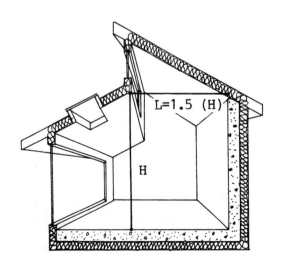

Figure 3.7

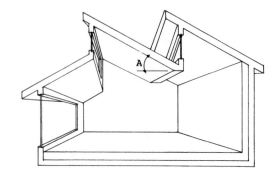

Figure 3.8

Skylights

- *Reflector:* Where horizontal skylights represent a significant portion of the solar collectors, consider the use of a reflector to increase winter solar gain (see "Control" later in this chapter).

Storage

In direct gain systems, solar energy can be stored in the floor, walls, ceiling, and/or furnishings of the living space if these components have sufficient capacity to absorb and store heat and to reradiate this heat to the living space slowly (see Figure 3.9). Most common high-mass materials (concrete, brick, and water) have this capability and can be used effectively in direct gain applications.

The amount of distributed mass required for effective performance will vary, depending on the requirements of each specific installation. In

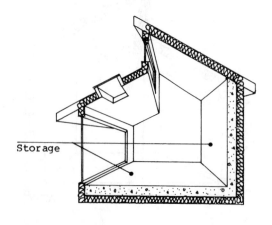

Storage

Figure 3.9

general, within the thickness ranges covered in the Storage Rules of Thumb, thin material spread over a large area will perform better than thick material concentrated in one part of the space. Care should be taken to ensure a balanced distribution of mass throughout the direct gain space.

Storage materials should be located so that they are struck by direct or diffuse sunlight for as much of the day as possible. Storage mass that is heated only indirectly by warm air from the living space requires roughly four times as much area as the same mass in direct sun to provide the same thermal effect. Storage mass that is located in direct sunlight will perform slightly better in a vertical (wall) rather than in a horizontal (floor, ceiling) configuration.

If masonry pavers are used in a storage floor, they should be laid so that no voids exist between adjacent units. Good thermal contact should be maintained (by grouting or actual physical contact) between all units to ensure efficient transfer and even distribution of heat.

Storage floors, walls, and ceilings in direct sunlight should be dark in color to increase the absorption of solar energy. All adjacent nonmass surfaces should be light-colored in order to reflect as much solar radiation as possible onto the storage surfaces.

If walls and floors are both used for storage, walls can be light if the floor is dark. Interior finishes over the storage materials (other than dark paint) will reduce the ability of the mass to absorb and reradiate heat. Plaster and wallpaper will reduce performance only slightly, and gypsum board can be acceptable (although it is not recommended) if care is taken during installation to apply a very thick coat of construction adhesive in order to increase the thermal connection between the wall and the gypsum board. Wall-to-wall carpet over a storage floor is emphatically *not* recommended.

STORAGE RULES OF THUMB*

- *Area:* It is recommended that, for every square foot of south-facing glazing area, 3 sq.

---

* Dimensions cited are *actual,* not nominal. If restrictions on local availability of materials require using thicknesses out-

ft. of storage mass, designed to receive direct sun, be provided.

- *Thickness (floor):* Recommended thickness of the storage floor material is 2 to 6″ (generally, 4″). Dimensions for water containers can vary but are typically 6 to 18″ thick. If prefabricated units are used, consult the manufacturers' literature regarding these products.

- *Thickness (wall):* Recommended thickness of storage wall materials is 2 to 4″. Dimensions for water containers can vary significantly. Consult the manufacturers' literature regarding these products.

- *Color:* Storage mass exposed to direct sunlight should be a dark color.

- *Masonry grouting:* Masonry units should be solid or have grout-filled cores. A full mortar bedding is recommended.

Control

SHADING

To avoid excessive heat gain in the cooling season and to increase overall system performance, it is recommended that some method be provided for shading the direct gain collector. The most thermally effective shading devices are those placed on the exterior of the home, such as simple overhangs (fixed or adjustable), trellises, vegetation (deciduous trees and the like), awnings, louvers (horizontal or vertical, fixed or adjustable), and wing walls (see Figure 3.10).

Interior shading devices, while often not as thermally effective as exterior units, are generally easier to operate and maintain. Common interior shading devices include roller shades, blinds, drapes, and movable panels. For optimum overall performance of the system, these interior shading elements should also be designed to provide insulation during the day in the cooling season and at night in the heating season (see "Insulating—Movable Insulation" later in this chapter).

---

side the ranges listed, it is generally more thermally efficient to employ thicker, rather than thinner, units. (At floor thicknesses greater than 4″, performance will increase, but not significantly. At thicknesses greater than 8″, performance can decrease.)

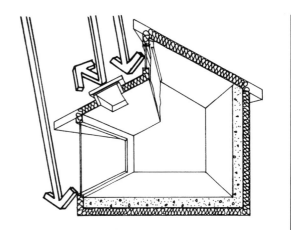

Figure 3.10

REFLECTING

Reflectors placed horizontally above or below a collector can help increase overall system performance by increasing the amount of sunlight reaching the collector (see Figure 3.11).

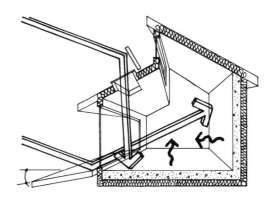

Figure 3.11

In certain cases, where physical obstructions (e.g., trees or other buildings) on or around the building site shade the collector, the provision of reflectors can increase solar collection by 30 percent to 40 percent. Reflectors can also improve the performance of skylights placed in a flat roof that may not receive sufficient winter sunlight in the horizontal position.

From the standpoint of practicality and economy, it is recommended to use existing architectural elements in the building design as reflectors, where possible. Light-colored exterior landscape elements, such as patios or terraces, are examples of such elements (see Figure 3.12). While not as effective as reflector panels, these architectural elements require no additional maintenance, and do not present the glare and overheating problems sometimes associated with reflector panels.

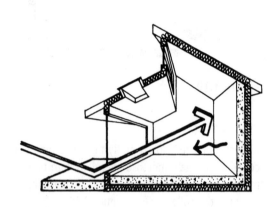

Figure 3.12

For cases in extreme environments, or for those committed to making daily or seasonal adjustments, the more efficient reflector panels may be appropriate. Reflector panels are usually coated on one side with a material of high reflectance, and are placed directly in front of a vertical, south-facing collector, or behind a horizontal collector (skylight). When the collector extends all the way to the ground (e.g., a patio door), the reflector is simply laid on the ground in front of it. In the case of collector openings higher up in the wall, or in cases where the reflector is placed above the collector, some form of support will be needed. Reflectors for horizontal skylights can be placed vertically on the roof on the north side of the skylight.

All horizontal panels should be placed so that they slope slightly away from a vertical collector to increase the amount of reflected sunlight and to facilitate drainage (5° is recommended). To be more economically and/or aesthetically justifiable, they should also be insulated so that they can serve as movable insulation when not in the reflecting mode. It should be noted that reflect-

ing panels may cause glare and/or overheating problems within the direct gain living spaces.

INSULATING—FIXED EXTERIOR INSULATION

Direct gain storage walls and floors that are exposed to the outside should be insulated on their exterior surfaces. Insulating the interior surface of a direct gain storage wall effectively nullifies any thermal storage capability of the wall, since it prevents solar energy from being absorbed by the wall and then reradiated back into the direct gain space. Therefore, insulation should be placed on the outside of any exterior wall, above and below grade, that is used for direct gain storage (see Figure 3.13).

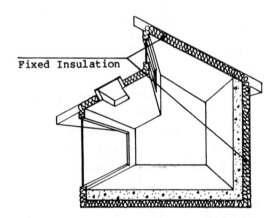

Fixed Insulation

Figure 3.13

The case of direct gain storage floors is a bit more complicated. Storage floors supported by wood frame construction over vented crawl spaces *should* be insulated, and standard batt insulation will work well. The effectiveness of insulating under a slab-on-grade will depend on factors such as the moisture content and minimum winter temperatures of the ground under the slab. If the moisture content is high or the minimum temperature low (less than 50°F), the tendency for heat to be lost through the floor to the ground will increase. In these instances, insulating under the slab, for a minimum of 2′ along the entire perimeter and, preferably, under the entire slab, is recommended. Two inches of rigid insulation (R-10) is appropriate for direct gain slabs-on-grade.

INSULATING—MOVABLE INSULATION

Although direct gain collectors can admit and trap a great deal of solar energy during clear, sunny days, they can also lose a great deal of heat during prolonged overcast periods and at night. While the introduction of high-performance glazings has significantly improved the ability of collectors to retain heat during cold weather (or reject it in warm weather), conditions still exist in extreme climates where additional provisions can be useful. Providing some form of movable insulation during periods of heat loss can result in very significant increases in overall thermal performance. Movable insulation can also be used to prevent excessive heat gain during the cooling season.

As in the case of shading devices, there are two basic types of movable insulation: those applied to the outer face of the collector, and those applied on the inside. Both can be effective at reducing heat loss during the heating season and, when used like shades, at preventing excessive heat gain during the cooling season.

Insulation on the inside is generally easier to operate and maintain and is not subject to degradation due to weathering. Exterior insulation, on the other hand, is a more efficient shading device, reducing heat gain during the cooling season by intercepting the solar radiation before it can penetrate the collector and be converted to heat (see Figure 3.14).

There are a variety of possible insulating devices, including rigid panels (if placed on the exterior, these can also be used as reflectors—see "Reflecting" earlier in this chapter), insulating shutters, and insulating drapes and shades. These devices can be hand-operated or motor-driven. In choosing the appropriate technique, the willingness of the homeowner to become involved in the day-to-day management of these elements must be carefully weighed. When using movable insulation, care must be taken to ensure a tight seal between the insulation and the collector to avoid heat loss around the edges of the insulation. This is particularly crucial when the insulation's total R-value exceeds R-4.

CONTROL RULES OF THUMB

Shading

- *Overhang:* The projection of the overhang that will be adequate (that will provide 100 percent shading at noon on June 21) at particular latitudes can be quickly calculated by using the following formula:

Projection (L)

$$= \frac{\text{window opening, i.e., collector (H)}}{\text{F (see Table 3.2)}}$$

A slightly longer overhang may be desirable at latitudes where this formula does not provide enough shade during the later part of the cooling

Table 3.2

North Latitude	F Factor*
28°	5.6–11.1
32°	4.0–6.3
36°	3.0–4.5
40°	2.5–3.4
44°	2.0–2.7
48°	1.7–2.2
52°	1.5–1.8
56°	1.3–1.5

* Select a factor according to your latitude. The higher values will provide 100% shading at noon on June 21, the lower values on August 1.

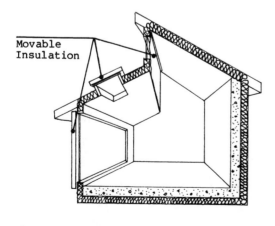

Movable
Insulation

Figure 3.14

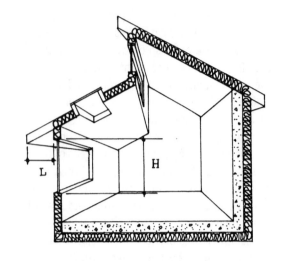

Figure 3.15

season (see Figure 3.15). For example, for Madison, Wisconsin, at 43° NL, select an F factor between 2.0 and 2.7 (values for 44° NL). Assuming shade is desired on August 1, choose the lower value of 2.0. If the window opening (H) is 8′, the projection (L) of the overhang placed at the top of the collector will be: ⁸⁄₂ = 4′.

Reflecting

- *Sizing:* If reflector panels are used, they should be sized according to the following:
    1. Solar windows and clerestories: same width as the collector and roughly 1 to 2 times the height.
    2. Skylights: roughly equal in size to the collector.

- *Slope:* A downward slope (away from the collector) of roughly 5° is recommended for drainage (see Figure 3.16).

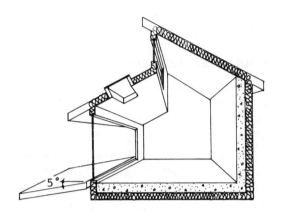

Figure 3.16

Insulating

- *R-values (fixed insulation):* Fixed exterior insulation R-values should meet or exceed the levels that would be maintained by the same element in a nonsolar building, which should in turn meet or exceed local building code requirements.

- *R-values (movable insulation):* Rigid movable insulation will typically have an R-value between R-4 and R-9. Insulating drapes and shades, for interior use, will typically have lower R-values.

- *Seals:* Insulation should provide a tight seal to prevent problems with heat loss at its edges.

DIRECT GAIN DETAILS

The drawings that follow illustrate sample construction detailing for direct gain systems using thermal mass.

The details are divided into three sections. The first two sections illustrate construction options where an interior wall of the home is designed as the storage component. Section one reviews masonry storage, while section two reviews water storage. The third section illustrates the construction of the storage component on an exterior wall. Details in this section illustrate the use of masonry storage.

In general, the details in all three sections employ standard, platform-framed wood construction as the main structural system. Due to the emerging use of light-gauge steel and structural insulated panels in residential building, however, examples of these systems are represented in the first section, directly following the standard wood details. The issues noted in these alternate details can be used to adapt and modify the other wood frame details included throughout the book.

In each section, there are four individual details that, together, suggest one possible configuration for all the system components. Variations follow, highlighting additional details, alternate construction methods, and the use of materials other than those suggested on previous pages. The following pages contain the construction notes referenced from the details. These notes provide guidelines, troubleshooting tips, and other information useful in building a direct gain home.

At the end of the first section, skylight and clerestory details are also included. These collector variations, with the associated construction notes, are applicable in all three direct gain sections.

Further, at the end of both the first and third sections, additional component material options are illustrated. These constructions can be substituted for the original sample details shown at the beginning of these sections.

Interior Wall
(Wood Framing with Masonry)

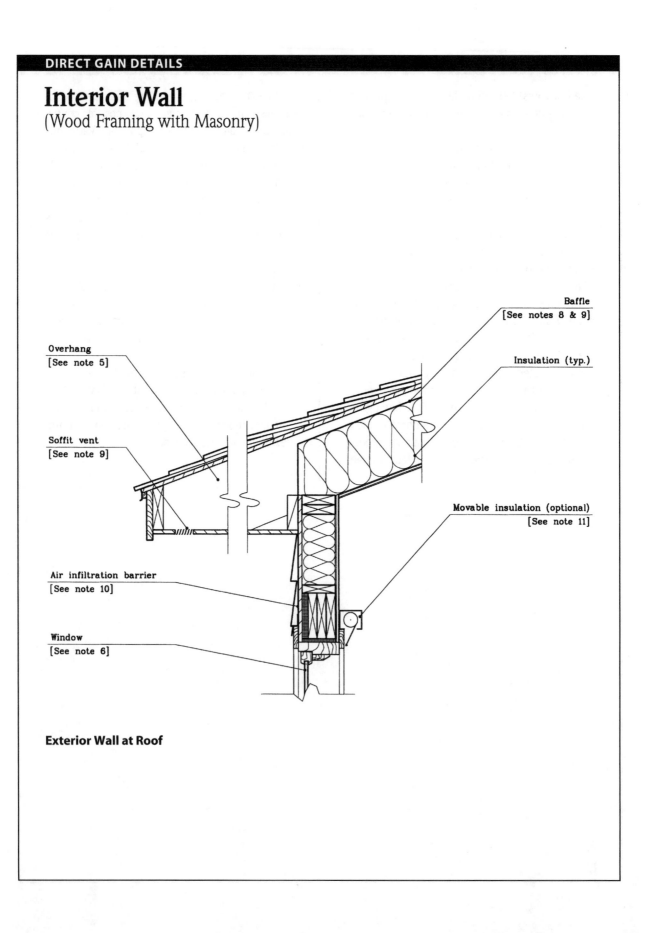

Baffle
[See notes 8 & 9]

Overhang
[See note 5]

Insulation (typ.)

Soffit vent
[See note 9]

Movable insulation (optional)
[See note 11]

Air infiltration barrier
[See note 10]

Window
[See note 6]

Exterior Wall at Roof

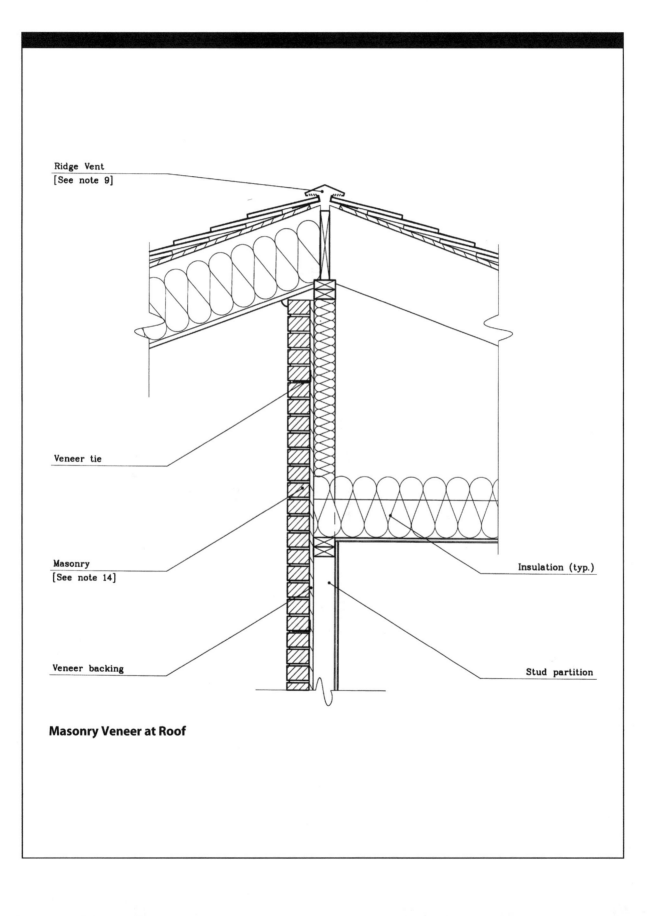

Ridge Vent
[See note 9]

Veneer tie

Masonry
[See note 14]

Veneer backing

Insulation (typ.)

Stud partition

Masonry Veneer at Roof

DIRECT GAIN DETAILS

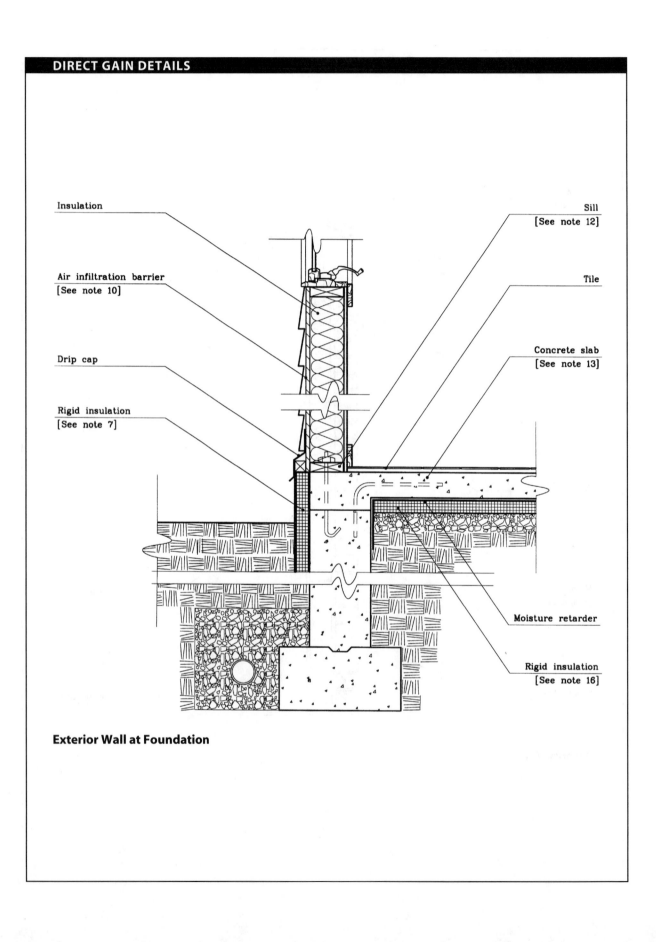

Insulation

Air infiltration barrier
[See note 10]

Drip cap

Rigid insulation
[See note 7]

Sill
[See note 12]

Tile

Concrete slab
[See note 13]

Moisture retarder

Rigid insulation
[See note 16]

Exterior Wall at Foundation

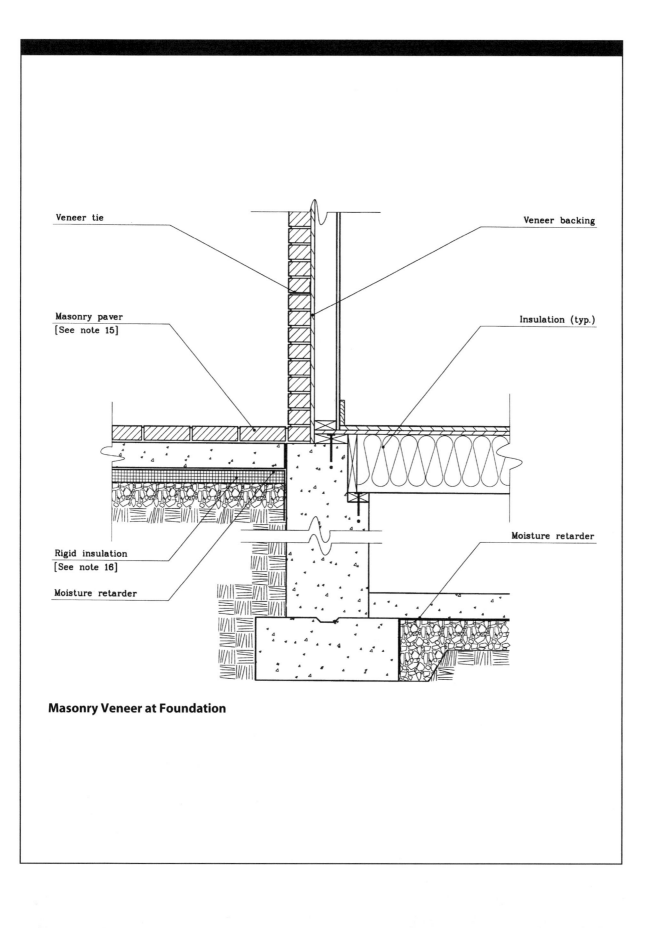

Veneer tie

Veneer backing

Masonry paver
[See note 15]

Insulation (typ.)

Rigid insulation
[See note 16]

Moisture retarder

Moisture retarder

Masonry Veneer at Foundation

DIRECT GAIN DETAILS

Interior Wall Variations
(Wood Framing with Masonry)

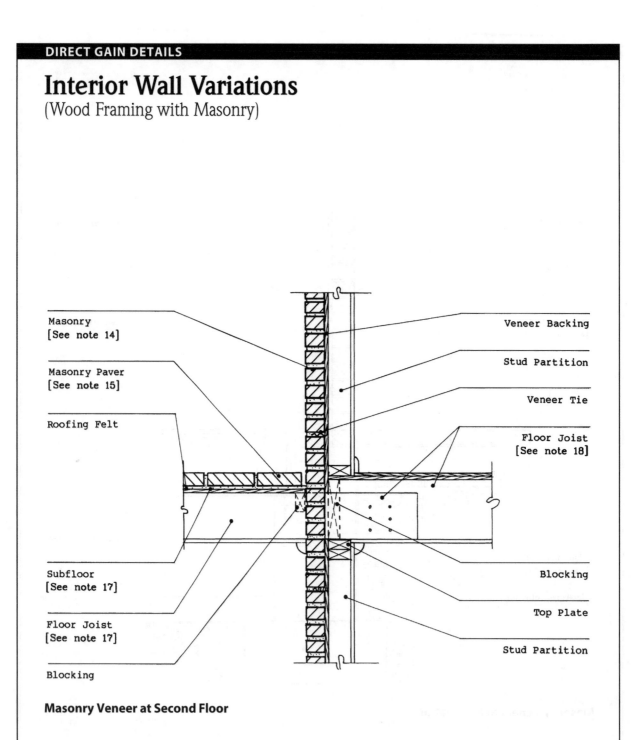

Masonry
[See note 14]

Masonry Paver
[See note 15]

Roofing Felt

Subfloor
[See note 17]

Floor Joist
[See note 17]

Blocking

Veneer Backing

Stud Partition

Veneer Tie

Floor Joist
[See note 18]

Blocking

Top Plate

Stud Partition

Masonry Veneer at Second Floor

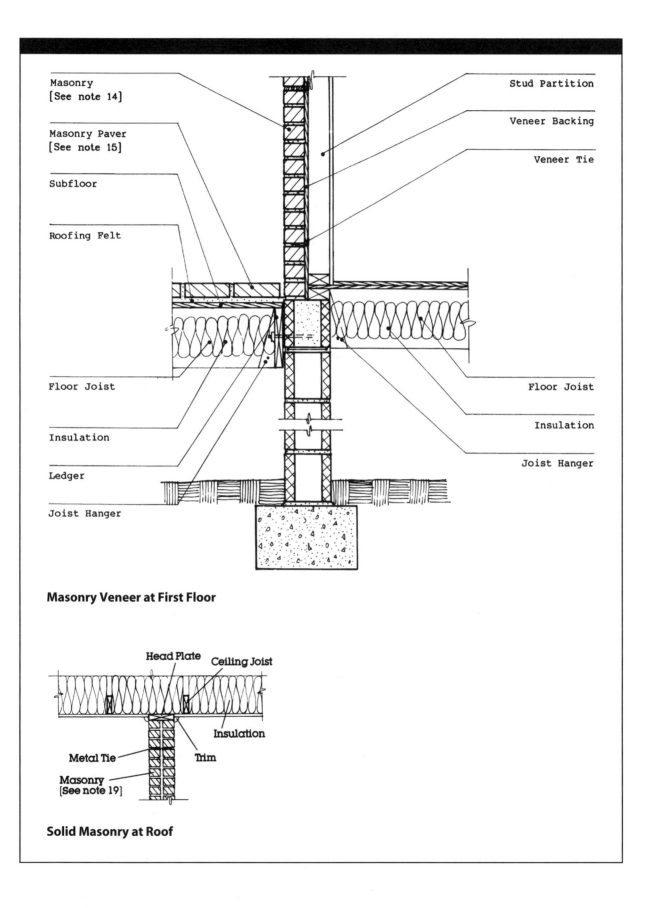

Masonry
[See note 14]

Masonry Paver
[See note 15]

Subfloor

Roofing Felt

Floor Joist

Insulation

Ledger

Joist Hanger

Stud Partition

Veneer Backing

Veneer Tie

Floor Joist

Insulation

Joist Hanger

Masonry Veneer at First Floor

Head Plate   Ceiling Joist

Insulation

Metal Tie   Trim

Masonry
[See note 19]

Solid Masonry at Roof

DIRECT GAIN DETAILS

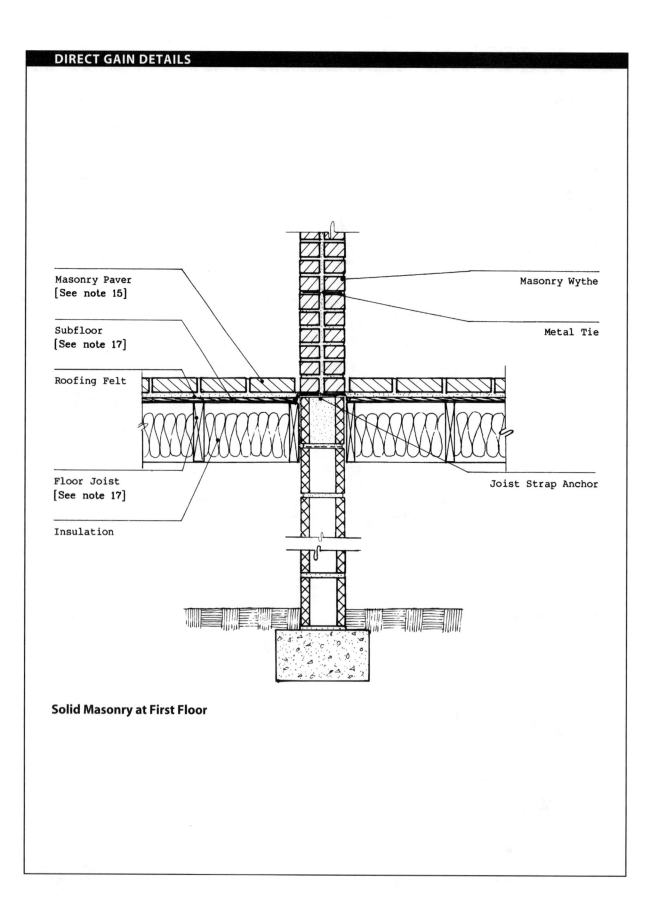

Masonry Paver
[See note 15]

Subfloor
[See note 17]

Roofing Felt

Floor Joist
[See note 17]

Insulation

Masonry Wythe

Metal Tie

Joist Strap Anchor

Solid Masonry at First Floor

Collector Variations

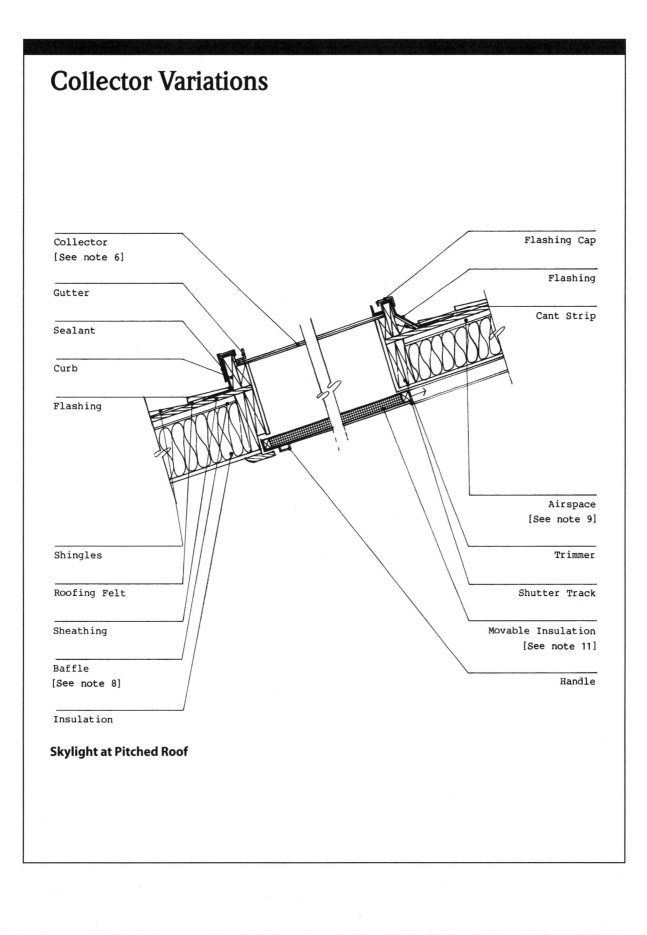

Collector
[See note 6]

Gutter

Sealant

Curb

Flashing

Shingles

Roofing Felt

Sheathing

Baffle
[See note 8]

Insulation

Flashing Cap

Flashing

Cant Strip

Airspace
[See note 9]

Trimmer

Shutter Track

Movable Insulation
[See note 11]

Handle

Skylight at Pitched Roof

DIRECT GAIN DETAILS

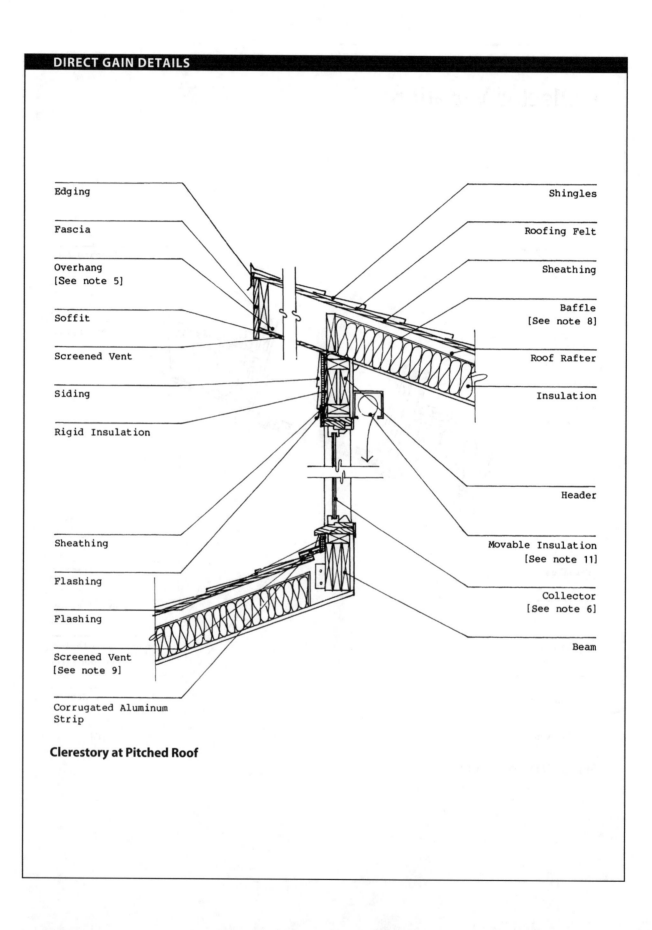

Edging

Fascia

Overhang
[See note 5]

Soffit

Screened Vent

Siding

Rigid Insulation

Sheathing

Flashing

Flashing

Screened Vent
[See note 9]

Corrugated Aluminum
Strip

Shingles

Roofing Felt

Sheathing

Baffle
[See note 8]

Roof Rafter

Insulation

Header

Movable Insulation
[See note 11]

Collector
[See note 6]

Beam

Clerestory at Pitched Roof

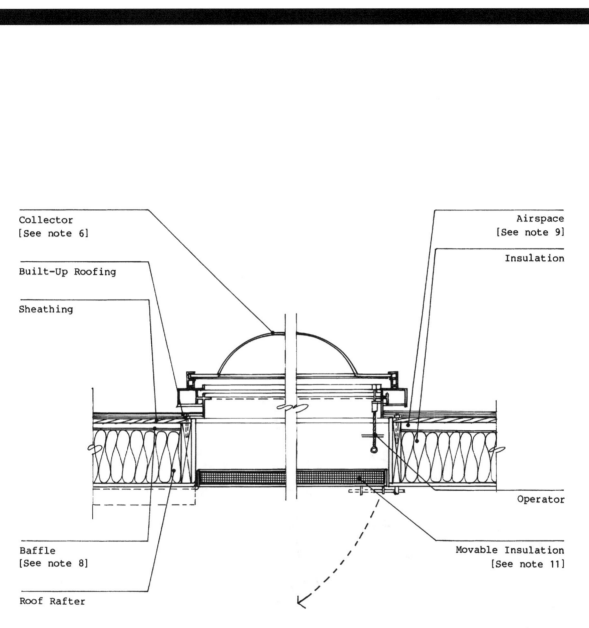

Collector
[See note 6]

Built-Up Roofing

Sheathing

Airspace
[See note 9]

Insulation

Operator

Baffle
[See note 8]

Roof Rafter

Movable Insulation
[See note 11]

Skylight at Flat Roof

DIRECT GAIN DETAILS

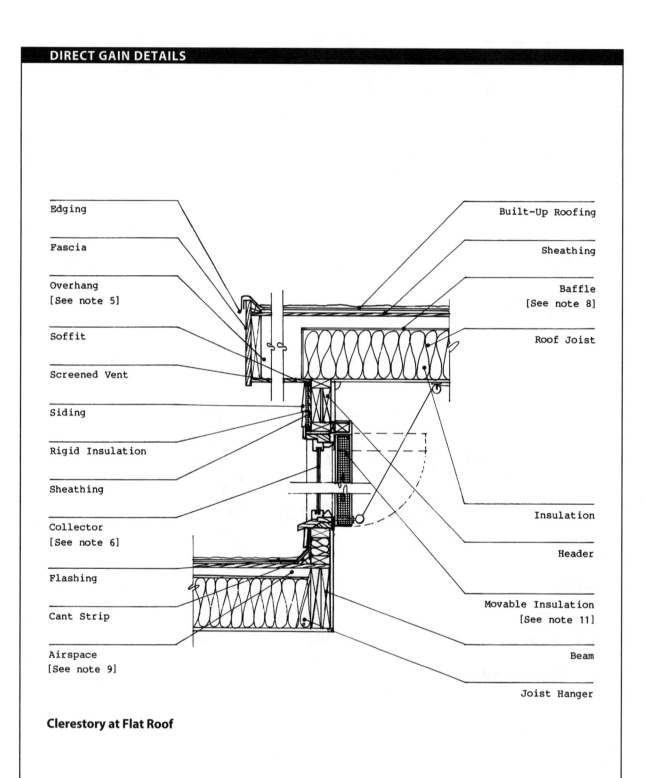

Edging

Fascia

Overhang
[See note 5]

Soffit

Screened Vent

Siding

Rigid Insulation

Sheathing

Collector
[See note 6]

Flashing

Cant Strip

Airspace
[See note 9]

Built-Up Roofing

Sheathing

Baffle
[See note 8]

Roof Joist

Insulation

Header

Movable Insulation
[See note 11]

Beam

Joist Hanger

Clerestory at Flat Roof

Interior Wall Notes
(Wood Framing with Masonry)

GENERAL NOTES

1. All footings must bear on undisturbed soil. Adjust footing size, reinforcing, and depth below grade as required by site conditions and/or local building code restrictions. Placement of all reinforcing, metal ties, and anchor bolts is to be determined by local codes and/or accepted practice. Reinforcing in concrete slab-on-grade construction is not recommended, except where required by local conditions and/or code. Expansion joints should be provided, as required, at the connection between concrete or masonry floors and stud, concrete, or masonry walls to prevent cracking.

2. Insulation levels in foundation/floor, walls, and ceiling must meet or exceed requirements of local building and energy codes. Floor/foundation insulation may be provided between floor joists over crawl space or unheated basement, or on foundation/basement walls and/or under slab. The installation of a continuous vapor retarder on the warm side of the building insulation is strongly recommended (if not required by local code) in this type of construction.

3. Other roof configurations may be used at builder's option. Consult local building codes for restrictions and special requirements concerning roof/wall connections, especially in seismic and/or high-wind areas.

4. Provide gutters and downspouts as required.

DETAIL NOTES

5. Overhang at collector should be sized to optimize solar gains during heating season and prevent overheating during cooling season. (For further information, see "Control Rules of Thumb" in this chapter.)

6. For optimum thermal performance, it is generally recommended that double glazing be provided, preferably a high performance glazing using one or more of the following: low-e coating(s), gas fill, or suspended plastic film(s). (See the "Collector Components" section in Chapter 7 for more information on glass or plastic collector materials.) Collectors can be standard preframed wood or metal frame windows, patio doors, prefabricated "bubble" skylights, any of a wide variety of off-the-shelf glazing units currently available, or site-built custom units. Where metal frames are used, it is generally recommended that thermal breaks be specified. All installations of prefabricated configurations must conform with manufacturers' specifications to ensure proper performance.

7. Insulation must be protected where exposed above grade. Cement or synthetic stucco over lath, or other methods, may be employed. Where dampproofing is used, allow for complete curing before applying insulation. Consult insulation manufacturer for recommended installation methods.

8. Provide baffles where necessary to maintain 1″ minimum airspace for venting an attic.

9. An opaque roof must be vented to ensure proper performance of the insulation. Vents are typically located at the overhang soffits and at the ridge, depending on the roof construction. An airspace is provided to allow for circulation.

10. The use of an air infiltration barrier is generally recommended to reduce air infiltration and exfiltration through construction joints in exterior walls. Air infiltration barriers should allow the transpiration of moisture vapor. All air barrier products must be

DIRECT GAIN DETAILS

installed according to the manufacturer's specifications to ensure proper performance.

11. Movable insulation can be provided to improve the system's thermal performance. Insulating shades or drapes may be specified for interior applications. Insulated shutters or weather-resistant panels may be specified for exterior use. Care must be taken to ensure a tight fit between the insulation and the collector to reduce heat loss at the edges, particularly if the insulation has an R-value greater than R-4. (For further information, see "Control Components" in Chapter 7.)

12. Continuous sill sealer is recommended to provide protection against infiltration.

13. Concrete slab-on-grade may be used as a storage component. Alternate storage floor materials may be specified at the builder's option. (For further information, see "Interior Floor Types" in this chapter.)

14. Interior masonry veneer may be used for direct gain storage. (For information on finishes, material variations, and thermal performance characteristics, see "Interior Wall Types" in this chapter and "Storage Components" in Chapter 7.)

15. For information on masonry pavers used for direct gain storage, including recommended installation procedures, see "Storage Components" in Chapter 7.

16. In cooler climates, install continuous insulation under the slab used for direct gain storage. (For further information, see "Control" in this chapter.)

17. Consideration must be given to the additional weight of pavers and concrete used as direct gain storage. Consult structural design loading tables and local codes to determine suitable grade and spacing of joists, and grade and thickness of the subfloor.

18. Joists are framed through continuous masonry veneer wall into structural framing. Joists are lapped and nailed together and bear on the double plate of the stud partition below. The joists are unequal in depth to maintain the floor level.

19. Solid masonry interior partition used for direct gain storage wall is perpendicular to south glazing (collector). For information on finishes, material variations, and thermal performance characteristics, see "Storage Components" in Chapter 7.

Interior Wall
(Steel Framing with Masonry)

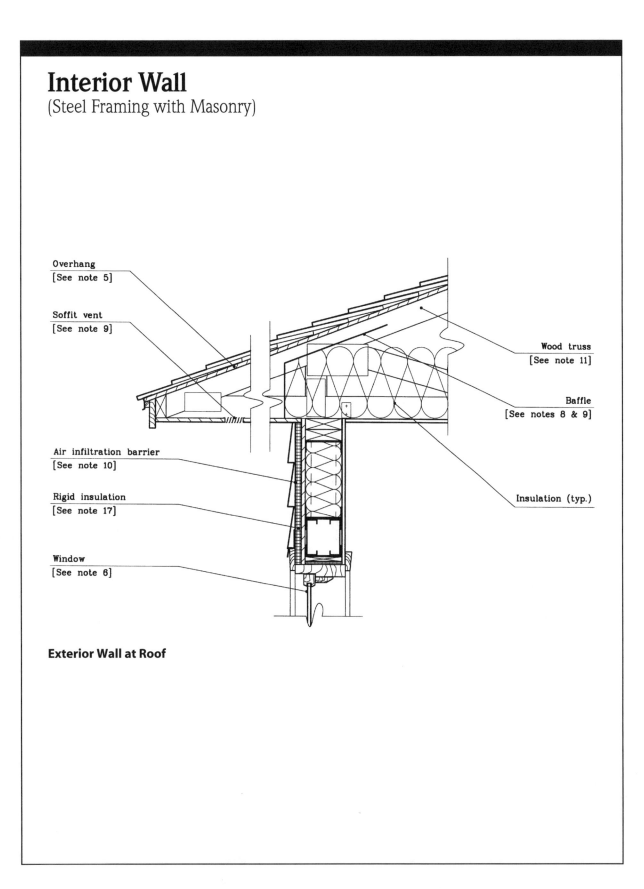

Overhang
[See note 5]

Soffit vent
[See note 9]

Air infiltration barrier
[See note 10]

Rigid insulation
[See note 17]

Window
[See note 6]

Wood truss
[See note 11]

Baffle
[See notes 8 & 9]

Insulation (typ.)

Exterior Wall at Roof

DIRECT GAIN DETAILS

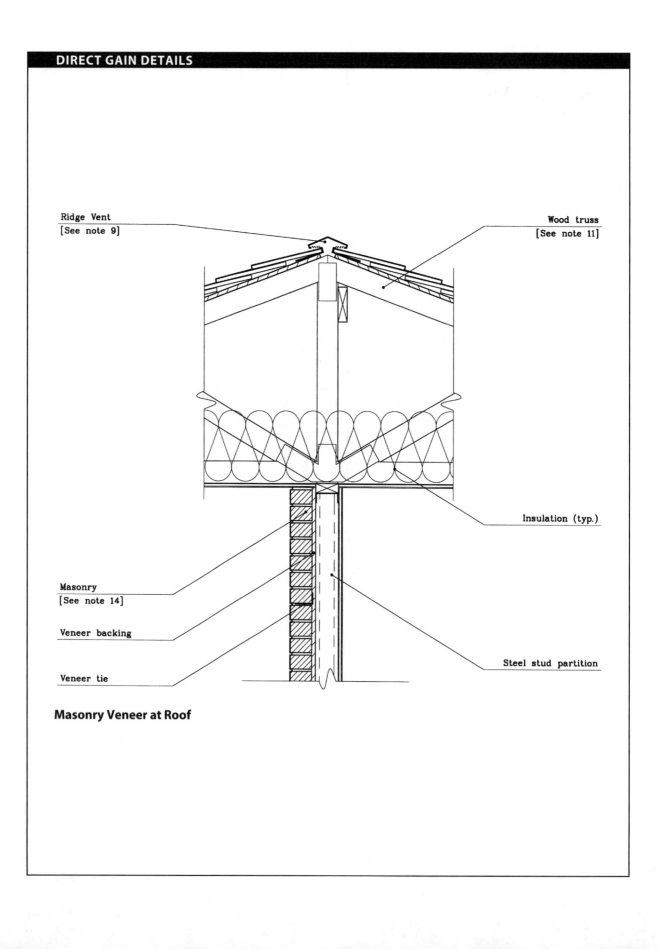

Ridge Vent
[See note 9]

Wood truss
[See note 11]

Insulation (typ.)

Masonry
[See note 14]

Veneer backing

Steel stud partition

Veneer tie

Masonry Veneer at Roof

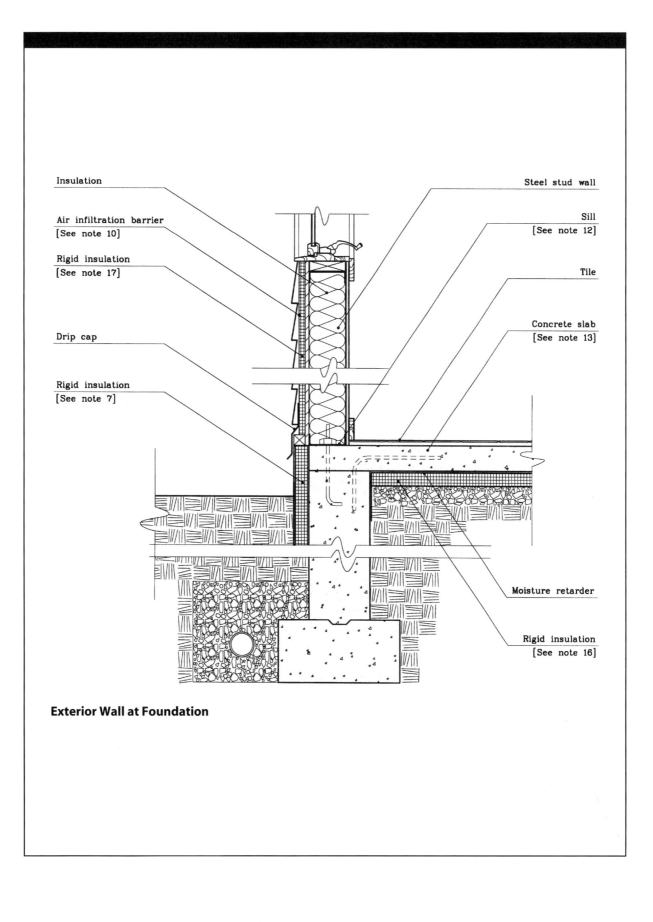

Insulation

Air infiltration barrier
[See note 10]

Rigid insulation
[See note 17]

Drip cap

Rigid insulation
[See note 7]

Steel stud wall

Sill
[See note 12]

Tile

Concrete slab
[See note 13]

Moisture retarder

Rigid insulation
[See note 16]

Exterior Wall at Foundation

DIRECT GAIN DETAILS

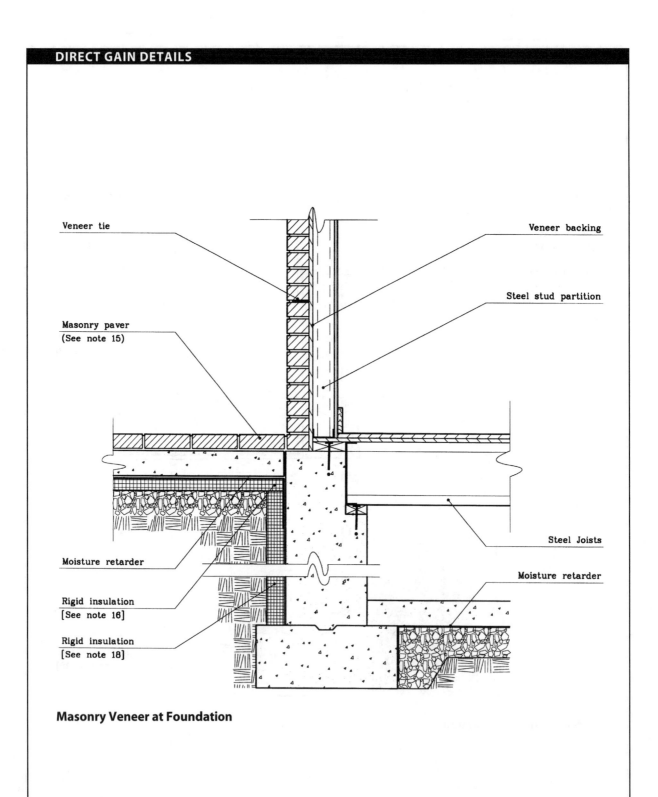

Veneer tie

Masonry paver
(See note 15)

Moisture retarder

Rigid insulation
[See note 16]

Rigid insulation
[See note 18]

Veneer backing

Steel stud partition

Steel Joists

Moisture retarder

Masonry Veneer at Foundation

Interior Wall Notes
(Steel Framing with Masonry)

Introduction

The use of light-gauge steel framing for residential building has been steadily increasing since the early 1980s. Besides the economic reasons for this growth, steel offers a number of distinct qualities as a building system. Light-gauge steel framing is strong, noncombustible, lightweight, insect- and rot-resistant, and dimensionally stable. Steel is also a readily recyclable material, which lessens its long-term environmental impact.

There are three basic residential framing assembly methods in steel: stick-built construction, which is similar to wood framing; panelized systems, where walls, floors, and roofs are prefabricated off-site and delivered as full panels; and pre-engineered systems, which combine widely spaced structural members with secondary framing (often horizontal furring channels) to take advantage of steel's exceptional strength.

When using steel as the structural system in a direct gain passive solar building, attention must be paid to the placement and detailing of the building insulation. Steel is a highly conductive material (approximately 380 times more conductive than wood), and this property leads to a condition known as thermal bridging. In an exterior wall, thermal bridging refers to the ability of the steel studs to conduct heat so efficiently that, in effect, they short-circuit the surrounding insulation. Because of this, the overall insulation values of the wall can be significantly downgraded. For example, the ASHRAE standard 90.1 downgrades the value of R-19 fiberglass in a 6″ steel stud wall (studs at 24″ on-center) to R-8.6 due to thermal bridging properties. In addition, thermal bridging can cause condensation to form on steel studs during cold weather, when humidity levels in the house are high (particularly in kitchens and bathrooms). Prolonged exposure to conden-

sation can result in deterioration of the wall finish, the batt insulation, and even the studs themselves.

It is thus critical to account for thermal bridging when determining the type and placement of insulation to be used with a steel-framed building. One solution, illustrated in the accompanying details, is to provide a layer of rigid foam insulation on the exterior of the steel framing. While this method is effective for the wall studs (see notes below for more details), a similar solution at the roof tends to be less practical. Additionally, thermal bridging problems can occur at roof overhangs, where the steel framing extends from the interior of the building to the exterior. Because of these difficulties, it is often desirable to combine the steel framed walls with a wood framed roof, such as the truss shown in the accompanying details.

GENERAL NOTES

1. All footings must bear on undisturbed soil. Adjust footing size, reinforcing, and depth below grade as required by site conditions and/or local building code restrictions. Placement of all reinforcing, metal ties, and anchor bolts is to be determined by local codes and/or accepted practice. Reinforcing in concrete slab-on-grade construction is not recommended except where required by local conditions and/or code. Expansion joints should be provided, as required, at the connection between concrete or masonry floors and stud, concrete, or masonry walls to prevent cracking.

2. Insulation levels in foundation/floor, walls, and ceiling must meet or exceed requirements of local building and energy codes. Floor/foundation insulation may be pro-

DIRECT GAIN DETAILS

vided between floor joists over crawl space or unheated basement, or on foundation/basement walls and/or under slab. The installation of a continuous vapor retarder on the warm side of the building insulation is strongly recommended (if not required by local code) in this type of construction.

3. Other roof configurations may be used at builder's option. Consult local building codes for restrictions and special requirements concerning roof/wall connections, especially in seismic and/or high-wind areas.

4. Provide gutters and downspouts as required.

DETAIL NOTES

5. Overhang at collector should be sized to optimize solar gains during heating season and prevent overheating during cooling season. For further information, see "Control Rules of Thumb" in this chapter.

6. For optimum thermal performance, it is generally recommended that double glazing be provided, preferably a high-performance glazing using one or more of the following: low-e coating(s), gas fill, or suspended plastic film(s). (See the "Collector Components" section in Chapter 7 for more information on glass or plastic collector materials.) Collectors can be standard preframed wood or metal frame windows, patio doors, prefabricated "bubble" skylights, any of a wide variety of off-the-shelf glazing units currently available, or site-built custom units. Where metal frames are used, it is generally recommended that thermal breaks be specified. All installations of prefabricated configurations must conform to manufacturers' specifications to ensure proper performance.

7. Insulation must be protected where exposed above grade. Cement or synthetic stucco over lath, or other methods, may be employed. Where dampproofing is used, allow for complete curing before applying insulation. Con-

sult insulation manufacturer for recommended installation methods.

8. Provide baffles where necessary to maintain 1″ minimum airspace for venting the attic.

9. The opaque roof must be vented to ensure proper performance of the insulation. Vents are typically located at the overhang soffits and at the ridge, depending on the roof construction. An airspace is provided to allow for circulation.

10. The use of an air infiltration barrier is generally recommended to reduce air infiltration and exfiltration through construction joints in exterior walls. Air infiltration barriers should allow the transpiration of moisture vapor. All air barrier products must be installed according to the manufacturers' specifications to ensure proper performance.

11. Consult structural engineer, local code, and/or truss manufacturer for sizes, spans, and spacing of pre-engineered wood trusses.

12. Continuous sill sealer is recommended to provide protection against infiltration.

13. Concrete slab-on-grade may be used as a storage component. Alternate storage floor materials may be specified at the builder's option. (For further information, see "Interior Floor Types" in this chapter.)

14. Interior masonry veneer may be used for direct gain storage. (For information on finishes, material variations, and thermal performance characteristics, see "Interior Wall Types" in this chapter and "Storage Components" in Chapter 7.)

15. For information on masonry pavers used for direct gain storage, including recommended installation procedures, see "Storage Components" in Chapter 7.

16. In cooler climates, install continuous insulation under the slab used for direct gain storage. (For further information, see "Control" in this chapter.)

17. Rigid foam insulation is recommended to decrease the thermal bridging properties of the steel framing (see introduction notes above). In moderate to extreme climates, and where interior humidity levels are high, 1″-thick rigid insulation (minimum R-4) is recommended. Where interior humidity is not a concern, a minimum of ½″ to ⅝″ rigid insulation is recommended. The batt insulation can be eliminated entirely if the exterior rigid foam is increased in thickness to meet local energy codes. In this case, a stucco-type finish or masonry veneer wall is usually required, due to the increased thickness of the rigid insulation.

18. To avoid the thermal bridging properties of the steel floor framing, two approaches are suggested. In the detail shown, the crawl space below the floor is insulated using exterior rigid foam boards, which eliminates the need for batt insulation at the floor. A second approach, more appropriate when a full basement exists, is to hang the batt insulation below the level of the steel floor framing. This can be accomplished through the use of a suspended ceiling system, or by suspending a wire mesh below the joists. Note that other insulation solutions may be more practical or economical based on the particulars of the actual construction project and/or the requirements of the local building and energy codes.

Interior Wall
(Structural Insulated Panels with Masonry)

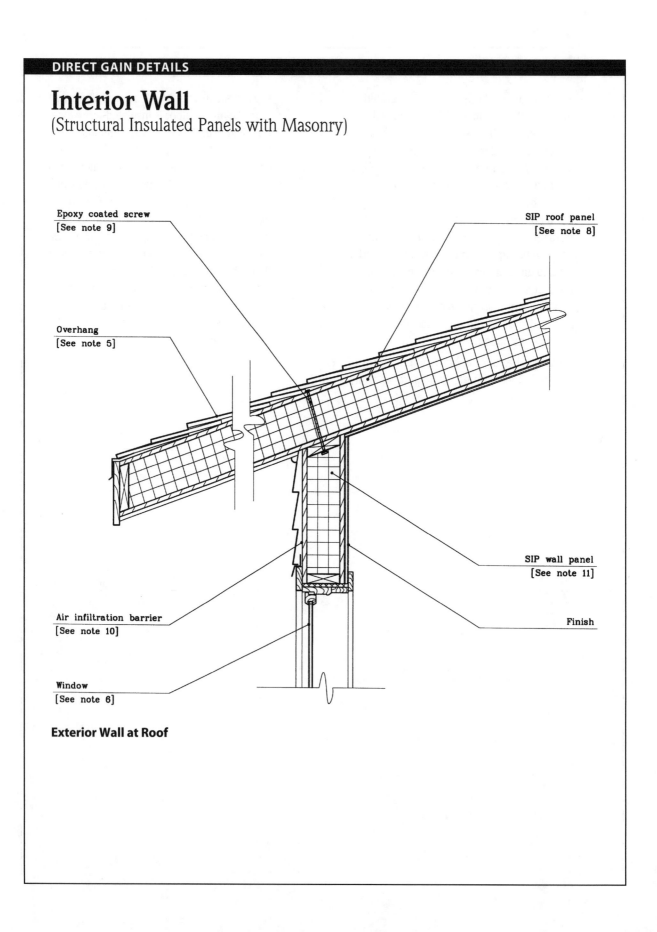

Epoxy coated screw
[See note 9]

SIP roof panel
[See note 8]

Overhang
[See note 5]

SIP wall panel
[See note 11]

Air infiltration barrier
[See note 10]

Finish

Window
[See note 6]

Exterior Wall at Roof

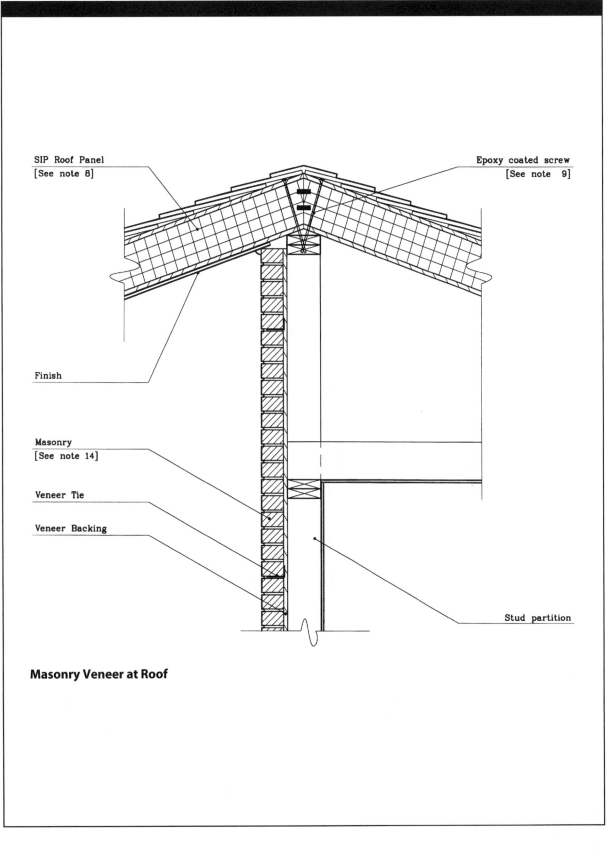

Masonry Veneer at Roof

DIRECT GAIN DETAILS

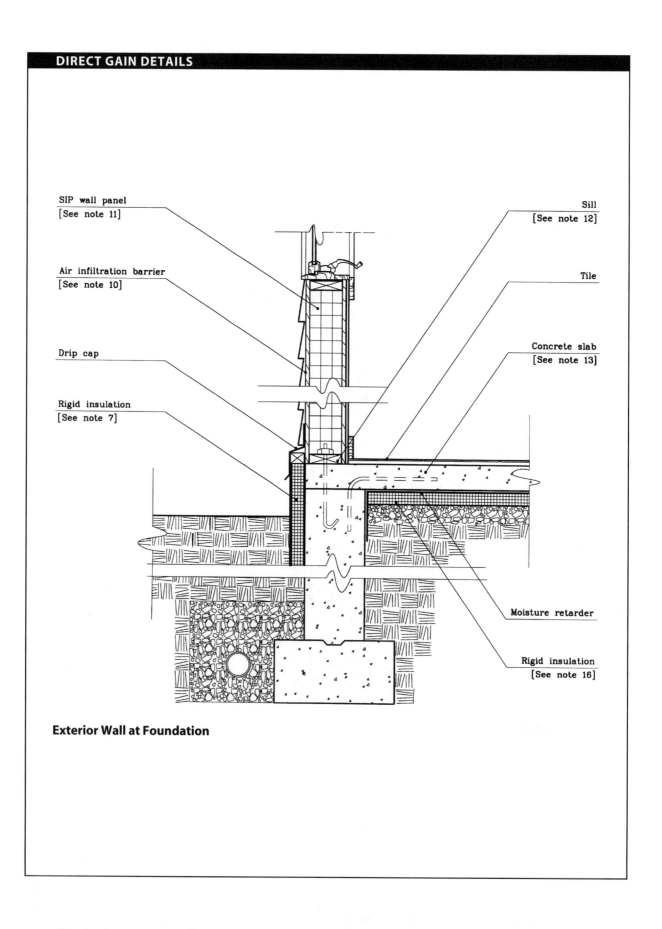

SIP wall panel
[See note 11]

Air infiltration barrier
[See note 10]

Drip cap

Rigid insulation
[See note 7]

Sill
[See note 12]

Tile

Concrete slab
[See note 13]

Moisture retarder

Rigid insulation
[See note 16]

Exterior Wall at Foundation

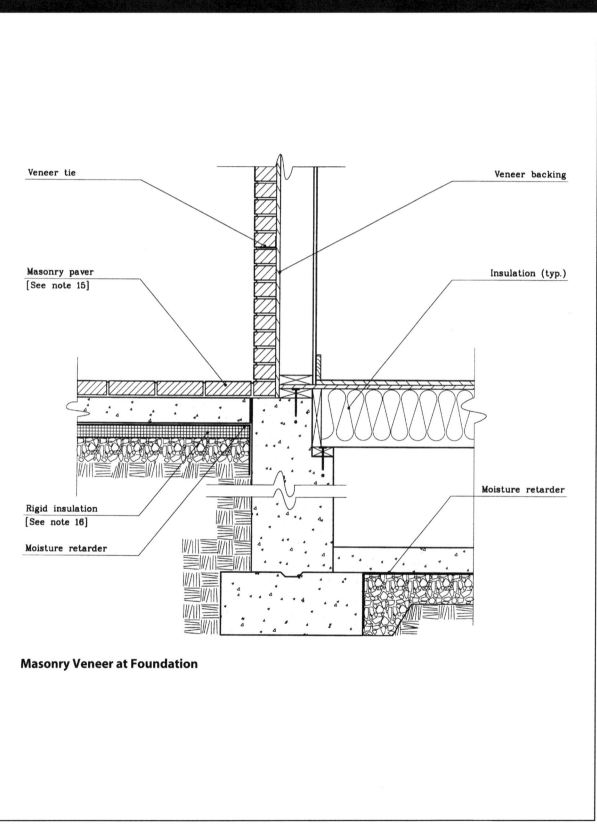

Veneer tie

Masonry paver
[See note 15]

Veneer backing

Insulation (typ.)

Rigid insulation
[See note 16]

Moisture retarder

Moisture retarder

Masonry Veneer at Foundation

DIRECT GAIN DETAILS

Interior Wall Notes
(Structural Insulated Panels with Masonry)

Introduction

Structural insulated panels (SIPs), sometimes known as stress skin panels, represent another building system that has recently gained popularity in residential building. SIPs combine the attributes of energy efficiency and resource efficiency in a high-strength, lightweight building system.

SIPs consist of two exterior skins, usually oriented strand board or plywood, adhered to a rigid core of plastic foam insulation. These panels, which are typically factory fabricated, come in standard sizes ranging from $4' \times 8'$ to $8' \times 24'$, with thickness ranging from 11 to 12". Panels are also custom-engineered for specific building projects. The panels can be used as stand-alone structural elements for walls and roofs, or can be used as infill panels in post-and-beam-type construction.

SIPs can provide an exceptionally energy-efficient envelope for a direct gain passive solar building. The rigid foam insulation cores (usually of expanded polystyrene) have higher per-inch R-values than batt insulations. In addition, SIP walls and roofs contain very few joints compared to standard frame construction, and avoid the thermal bridging effects inherent in exterior stud walls. This combination typically gives SIP buildings higher overall R-values, and significantly reduced air infiltration—both energy-saving advantages.

Consult local building codes for the requirements for SIP construction. SIPs are accepted by most building codes for residential and light commercial buildings. Typically, code compliance is, in part, based on the panel manufacturer meeting quality control requirements for SIP production.

GENERAL NOTES

1. All footings must bear on undisturbed soil. Adjust footing size, reinforcing, and depth below grade as required by site conditions and/or local building code restrictions. Placement of all reinforcing, metal ties, and anchor bolts is to be determined by local codes and/or accepted practice. Reinforcing in concrete slab-on-grade construction is not recommended except where required by local conditions and/or code. Expansion joints should be provided, as required, at the connection between concrete or masonry floors and stud, concrete, or masonry walls to prevent cracking.

2. Insulation levels in foundation/floor, walls, and ceiling must meet or exceed requirements of local building and energy codes. Floor/foundation insulation may be provided between floor joists over the crawl space or unheated basement, or on foundation/basement walls and/or under slab.

3. Other roof configurations may be used at builder's option. Consult local building codes for restrictions and special requirements concerning roof/wall connections, especially in seismic and/or high-wind areas.

4. Provide gutters and downspouts as required.

DETAIL NOTES

5. Overhang at the collector should be sized to optimize solar gains during heating season and prevent overheating during cooling season. For further information, see "Control Rules of Thumb" in this chapter.

6. For optimum thermal performance, it is generally recommended that double glazing be

provided, preferably a high-performance glazing using one or more of the following: low-e coating(s), gas fill, or suspended plastic film(s). (See the "Collector Components" section in Chapter 7 for more information on glass or plastic collector materials.) Collectors can be standard preframed wood or metal frame windows, patio doors, prefabricated "bubble" skylights, any of a wide variety of off-the-shelf glazing units currently available, or site-built custom units. Where metal frames are used, it is generally recommended that thermal breaks be specified. All installations of prefabricated configurations must conform with manufacturers' specifications to ensure proper performance.

7. Insulation must be protected where exposed above grade. Cement or synthetic stucco over lath, or other methods, may be employed. Where dampproofing is used, allow for complete curing before applying insulation. Consult insulation manufacturer for recommended installation methods.

8. Consult structural engineer, local code, and/or SIP manufacturer for roof panel sizes and allowable spans. Insulation types include expanded polystyrene, extruded polystyrene, polyurethane, and polyisocyanurate (R-4 to R-7 per inch). A vapor retarder is not required at the roof or ceiling in SIP construction.

9. Screw size and spacing are to be determined by the structural engineer, local building code, and/or structural insulated panel manufacturer.

10. The use of an air infiltration barrier is generally recommended to reduce air infiltration and exfiltration through construction joints in exterior walls. Air infiltration barriers should allow the transpiration of moisture vapor. All air barrier products must be installed according to the manufacturer's specifications to ensure proper performance.

11. Consult the structural engineer, local code, and/or SIP manufacturer for wall panel sizes and allowable loads. Insulation types include expanded polystyrene, extruded polystyrene, polyurethane, and polyisocyanurate (R-4 to R-7 per inch). A vapor retarder is not required at the exterior walls in SIP construction.

12. Continuous sill sealer is recommended to provide protection against infiltration.

13. Concrete slab-on-grade may be used as a storage component. Alternate storage floor materials may be specified at the builder's option. (For further information, see "Interior Floor Types" in this chapter.)

14. Interior masonry veneer may be used for direct gain storage. (For information on finishes, material variations, and thermal performance characteristics, see "Interior Wall Types" in this chapter and "Storage Components" in Chapter 7.)

15. For information on masonry pavers used for direct gain storage, including recommended installation procedures, see "Storage Components" in Chapter 7.

16. In cooler climates, install continuous insulation under the slab used for direct gain storage. (For further information, see "Control" in this chapter.)

Interior Wall Types
(Masonry)

Masonry Veneer

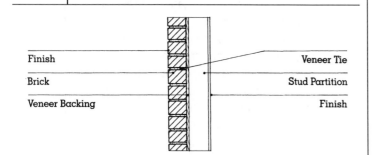

Finish

Brick

Veneer Backing

Veneer Tie

Stud Partition

Finish

GENERAL NOTES

- Veneer may be attached to the frame wall using either anchored or adhered construction methods. In anchored construction (as shown), metal ties are used to attach the masonry to a veneer backing (e.g., plywood or building paper) or directly to the frame wall studs. In adhered construction, the masonry is secured to a veneer backing material, using a binding material such as mortar. Units specified for adhered construction are generally limited to a maximum weight of 15 lb/ft^2 of surface area.

FINISH

- For optimum thermal performance, masonry should be a dark color and should be left exposed wherever feasible. Certain finishes (e.g., plaster and gypsum board) can be acceptable if properly applied. Particular colors can also be specified from the manufacturer, or the masonry can be stained or painted. (For further information on finishes and their effect on thermal performance, see "Storage" in this chapter and "Storage Components" in Chapter 7.)
- Wall finish on the nonveneer side of wall construction has no effect on thermal performance and may be specified per builder's option.

MASONRY

- Any of the wide variety of standard brick, concrete block, concrete brick, or split, slump, fluted, scored, or recessed block are suitable for thermal storage. To ensure proper thermal performance, masonry must be solid, or hollow with grout-filled cores. (For further material information, see "Storage Components" in Chapter 7. For recommended thicknesses, see Storage Rules of Thumb in this chapter.)
- Veneer is assumed to support no load other than its own weight.

VENEER BACKING

- In anchored veneer construction (as shown), veneer backing is not required, although some form of backing (e.g., plywood, gypsum board, or building paper) can make wall construction easier and may be desirable.
- In adhered veneer construction (not shown), some form of veneer backing is required. Plywood, gypsum board, metal lath over building paper, or other similar materials are suitable.

VENEER TIE

- Corrosion-resistant, corrugated metal ties, of a minimum 22-gauge thickness and 7/8" width, are typically specified. Corrosion-resistant 8d nails, located at the bend in the tie and having a minimum penetration of 1½" into the stud, are recommended. The tie should be embedded a minimum of 2" into the mortar joint at the veneer. Spacing of the ties is to be determined by local building code requirements and/or standard practice.

STUD PARTITION

- The interior stud partition walls can be of standard wood or metal frame construction.

Concrete Masonry Unit

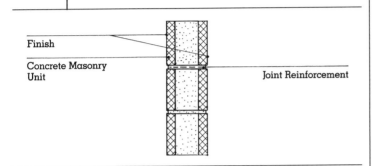

Finish

Concrete Masonry Unit

Joint Reinforcement

GENERAL NOTES

- Single-wythe masonry units may be built with conventional mortar joints.

- Openings in masonry walls may be spanned by arches, steel angle lintels, or reinforced masonry lintels constructed of standard and/or specially shaped masonry units, mortar, grout, and reinforcing steel. Specifications for all three types should conform to local building code requirements with regard to load, span, and type of wall construction.

FINISH

- For optimum thermal performance, masonry should be a dark color and should be left exposed wherever feasible. Certain finishes (e.g., plaster and gypsum board) can be acceptable if properly applied. Particular colors can also be specified from the manufacturer, or the masonry can be stained or painted. (For further information on finishes and their effect on thermal performance, see "Storage" in this chapter and "Storage Components" in Chapter 7.)

- Wall finish on the nonveneer side of wall construction has no effect on thermal performance and may be specified per builder's option.

- For further information on finishes and their effect on thermal performance, see "Storage" in this chapter and "Storage Components" in Chapter 7.

CONCRETE MASONRY UNIT

- Concrete block, concrete brick, or architectural facing units, such as split, slump, fluted, scored, or recessed block, may be used for thermal storage. To ensure optimum thermal performance, units must be solid, or hollow with grout-filled cores. (For further material information, see "Storage Components" in Chapter 7. For recommended thicknesses, see "Storage Rules of Thumb" in this chapter.)

JOINT REINFORCEMENT

- Joint reinforcement should be provided to control cracking caused by thermal movement and shrinkage. Truss, ladder, or x-tie configurations are suitable and can be embedded in the wall at vertical intervals per local code requirements or industry recommendations. Splices in reinforcing should be lapped a minimum of 6", and the width of the reinforcement should be 2" less than the nominal width of the storage wall.

Brick

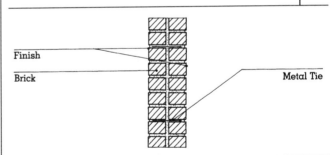

Finish

Brick

Metal Tie

GENERAL NOTES

- Openings in brick walls may be spanned by arches, steel angle lintels, or reinforced brick lintels constructed of standard and/or specially shaped brick units, mortar, grout, and reinforcing steel. Specifications for all three should conform to the Brick Institute of America recommendations and local building code requirements with regard to load, span, and all types of wall construction.

DIRECT GAIN DETAILS

FINISH

- For optimum thermal performance, brick should be a dark color and should be left exposed wherever feasible. Certain finishes (e.g., plaster and gypsum board) can be acceptable if properly applied. (For further information on finishes and their effect on thermal performance, see "Storage" in this chapter and "Storage Components" in Chapter 7.)

BRICK

- Any of the wide variety of standard bricks are suitable for thermal storage. To ensure proper performance, bricks must be solid, or hollow with grout-filled cores. (For further information, see "Storage Components" in Chapter 7.) For recommended thicknesses, see "Storage Rules of Thumb" in this chapter.

Interior Floor Types
(Masonry)

Concrete Slab-on-Grade

Finish
Concrete
Reinforcing
Vapor Barrier
Rigid Insulation

FINISH

- For optimum thermal performance, the concrete slab should be a dark color and should be left exposed wherever feasible. Certain finishes (e.g., exposed aggregate, embossed surface, and thin vinyl tile, ceramic tile, and quarry tile) will not significantly affect thermal performance and can be specified. Covering the concrete with carpet is emphatically *not* recommended. (For further information on finishes and their effects on thermal performance, see "Storage" in this chapter and "Storage Components" in Chapter 7.)

CONCRETE SLAB

- Concrete slab-on-grade construction can be used for direct gain storage. (For material information, see "Storage Components" in Chapter 7. For recommended thicknesses, see "Storage Rules of Thumb" in this chapter.)

REINFORCING

- Reinforcing is generally not recommended except where required by soil conditions and/or local building codes.

VAPOR BARRIER

- A vapor barrier should be placed directly under the slab.

RIGID INSULATION

- In the cooler climates, it is generally recommended that rigid insulation be placed under

slabs-on-grade that are acting as direct gain storage components. (For further information, see "Control" in this chapter.)

Masonry Paver on Slab

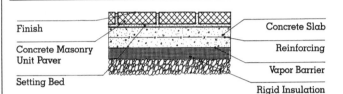

Finish
Concrete Masonry Unit Paver
Setting Bed
Concrete Slab
Reinforcing
Vapor Barrier
Rigid Insulation

FINISH

- For optimum thermal performance, pavers should be a dark color and should be left exposed wherever feasible. Covering the pavers with carpet is emphatically *not* recommended. Sealers can be used to provide an impervious finish for the pavers, making them easier to clean, without affecting thermal performance. (For further information on finishes and their effect on thermal performance, see "Storage" in this chapter and "Storage Components" in Chapter 7.)

PAVER

- Any of the wide variety of standard brick and concrete masonry pavers are suitable for thermal storage. (For material information, see "Storage Components" in Chapter 7. For recommended thicknesses, see "Storage Rules of Thumb" in this chapter.)

SETTING BED

- Pavers are generally laid in a mortar setting bed. Type N mortar is suitable for interior applications.

- Pavers can also be set in a dry mixture of sand and cement. After the pavers are laid, the sur-

DIRECT GAIN DETAILS

face is wetted down with water to set the mixture. In this application, pavers are typically laid without mortar joints.

- Pavers can be laid without mortar. Care must be taken to maintain continuous contact between units to ensure optimum thermal performance.

CONCRETE SLAB

- Concrete slab-on-grade construction can be used for direct gain storage. (For material information, see "Storage Components" in Chapter 7. For recommended thicknesses, see "Storage Rules of Thumb" in this chapter.)

REINFORCING

- Reinforcing is generally not recommended except where required by soil conditions and/or local building codes.

VAPOR BARRIER

- A vapor barrier should be placed directly under the slab.

RIGID INSULATION

- In the cooler climates, it is generally recommended that rigid insulation be placed under slabs-on-grade that are acting as direct gain storage components. (For further information, see "Control" in this chapter.)

Lightweight Concrete on Wood Floor

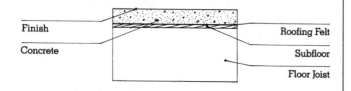

FINISH

- For optimum thermal performance, the concrete slab should be a dark color and should be left exposed wherever feasible. Certain finishes (e.g., exposed aggregate, embossed surface, and thin vinyl tiles) will not significantly affect thermal performance and can be specified. Covering the concrete with carpet is emphatically *not* recommended. (For further information on finishes and their effect on thermal performance, see "Storage" in this chapter and "Storage Components" in Chapter 7.)

CONCRETE

- A structural lightweight concrete slab over floor joists can be used for direct gain storage. (For further material information, see "Storage Components" in Chapter 7. For recommended thicknesses, see "Storage Rules of Thumb" in this chapter.)

ROOFING FELT

- The installation of two layers of 15-lb roofing felt between the setting bed and the subfloor is recommended. The felt serves as a cushion for the masonry, as well as a moisture barrier for the floor assembly. In mortarless applications, it aids in reducing the effects of minor surface irregularities in the base material.
- The felt also serves as a bond break between the setting bed and subfloor.
- Individual sections of roofing felt should be lapped 6".

SUBFLOOR

- Consideration must be given to the additional weight of the masonry when selecting the subfloor.

FLOOR JOIST

- Consideration must be given to the additional weight of the masonry when selecting and sizing the floor joists.

Masonry Paver on Wood Floor

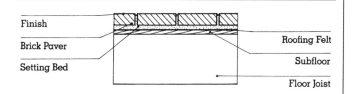

Finish
Brick Paver
Setting Bed
Roofing Felt
Subfloor
Floor Joist

GENERAL NOTES

- The pavers and the setting bed act together as the thermal storage mass. The recommended overall thickness of the storage floor can be attained by increasing or decreasing the depth of the setting bed, depending on the thickness of the pavers specified. (For recommended floor thickness, see "Storage Rules of Thumb" in this chapter.)

FINISH

- For optimum thermal performance, pavers should be a dark color and should be left exposed wherever feasible. Covering the pavers with carpet is emphatically *not* recommended. Sealers can be used to provide an impervious finish for the pavers, making them easier to clean, without affecting thermal performance. (For further information on finishes and their effect on thermal performance, see "Storage" in this chapter and "Storage Components" in Chapter 7.)

PAVER

- Any of the wide variety of standard brick and concrete masonry pavers are suitable for thermal storage. (For material information, see "Storage Components" in Chapter 7. For recommended thicknesses, see "Storage Rules of Thumb" in this chapter.)

SETTING BED

- Pavers are generally laid in a mortar setting bed. Type N mortar is suitable for interior applications.

- Pavers can also be set in a dry mixture of sand and cement. After the pavers are laid, the surface is wetted down with water to set the mixture. In this application, pavers are typically laid without mortar joints.

- Pavers can be laid without mortar. Care must be taken to maintain continuous contact between units to ensure optimum thermal performance.

ROOFING FELT

- The installation of two layers of 15-lb roofing felt between the setting bed and the subfloor is recommended. The felt serves as a cushion for the assembly. In mortarless applications, it aids in reducing the effects of minor surface irregularities in the base material.

- The felt also serves as a bond break between the setting bed and subfloor.

- Individual sections of roofing felt should be lapped 6″.

SUBFLOOR

- Consideration must be given to the additional weight of the masonry when selecting the subfloor.

FLOOR JOIST

- Consideration must be given to the additional weight of the masonry when selecting and sizing the floor joists.

Interior Wall
(Water)

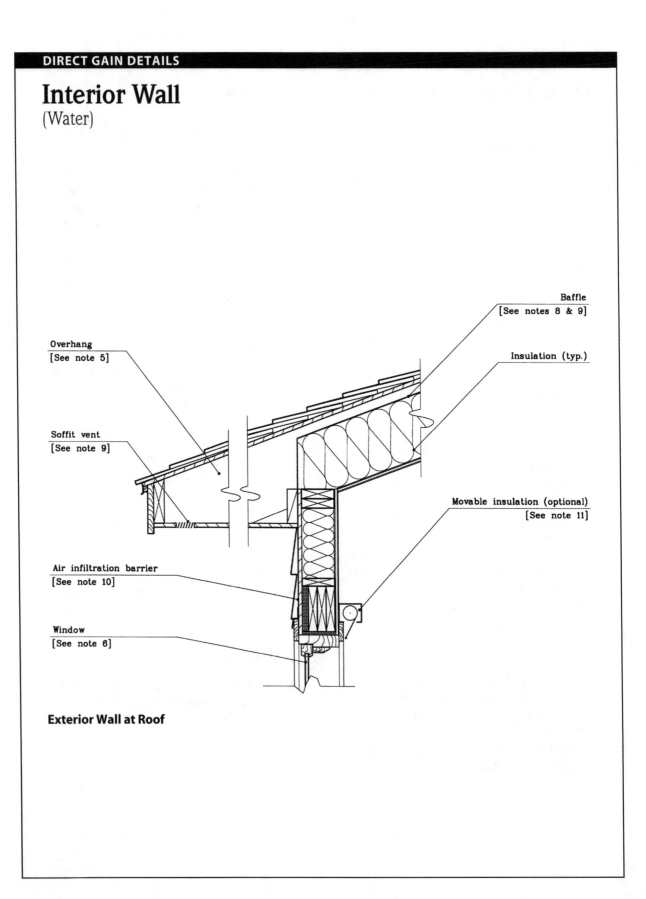

Baffle
[See notes 8 & 9]

Insulation (typ.)

Overhang
[See note 5]

Soffit vent
[See note 9]

Movable insulation (optional)
[See note 11]

Air infiltration barrier
[See note 10]

Window
[See note 6]

Exterior Wall at Roof

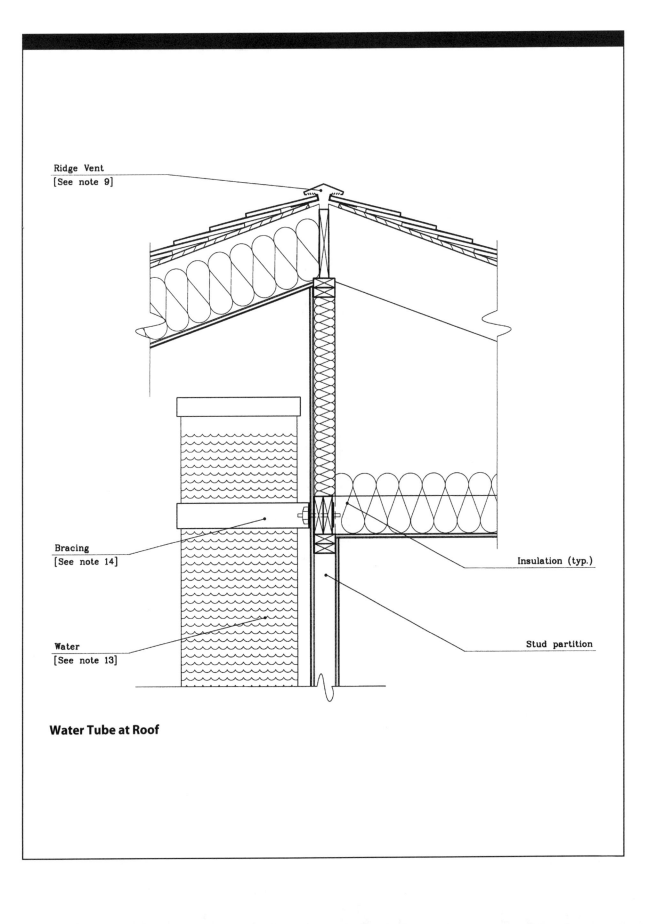

Ridge Vent
[See note 9]

Bracing
[See note 14]

Water
[See note 13]

Insulation (typ.)

Stud partition

Water Tube at Roof

DIRECT GAIN DETAILS

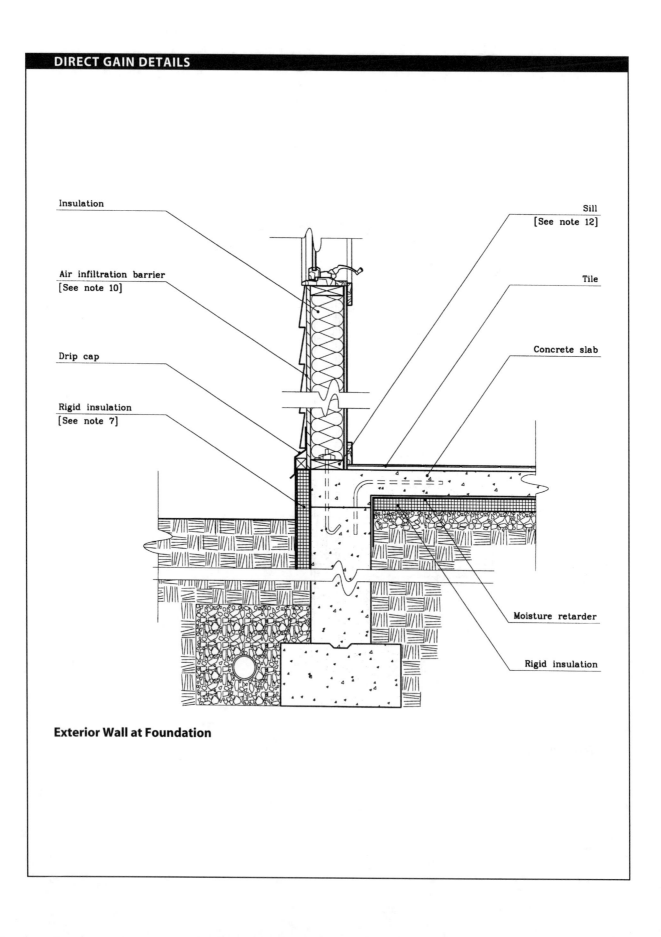

Insulation

Air infiltration barrier
[See note 10]

Drip cap

Rigid insulation
[See note 7]

Sill
[See note 12]

Tile

Concrete slab

Moisture retarder

Rigid insulation

Exterior Wall at Foundation

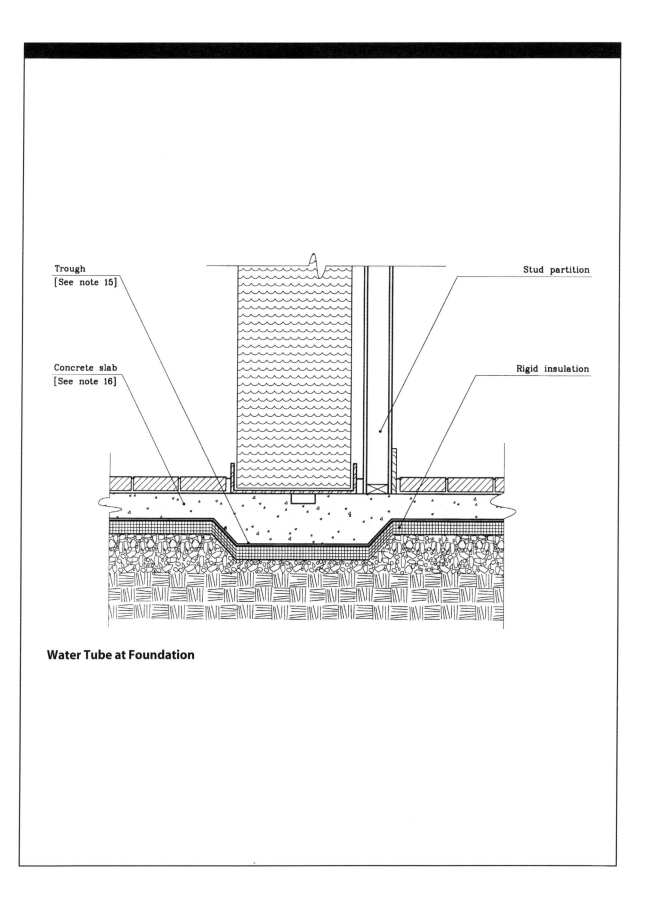

Trough
[See note 15]

Concrete slab
[See note 16]

Stud partition

Rigid insulation

Water Tube at Foundation

DIRECT GAIN DETAILS

Interior Wall Notes
(Water)

GENERAL NOTES

1. All footings must bear on undisturbed soil. Adjust footing size, reinforcing, and depth below grade as required by site conditions and/or local building code restrictions. Placement of all reinforcing, metal ties, and anchor bolts is to be determined by local codes and/or accepted practice. Reinforcing in concrete slab-on-grade construction is not recommended except where required by local conditions and/or code. Expansion joints should be provided, as required, at the connection between concrete or masonry floors and stud, concrete, or masonry walls to prevent cracking.

2. Insulation levels in foundation/floor, walls, and ceiling must meet or exceed requirements of local building and energy codes. Floor/foundation insulation may be provided between floor joists over the crawl space or unheated basement, or on foundation/basement walls and/or under slab.

3. Other roof configurations may be used at the builder's option. Consult local building codes for restrictions and special requirements concerning roof/wall connections, especially in seismic and/or high-wind areas.

4. Provide gutters and downspouts as required.

DETAIL NOTES

5. Overhang at the collector should be sized to optimize solar gains during heating season and prevent overheating during cooling season. (For further information, see "Control Rules of Thumb" in this chapter.)

6. For optimum thermal performance, it is generally recommended that double glazing be provided, preferably a high-performance glazing using one or more of the following: low-e coating(s), gas fill, or suspended plastic film(s). (See the "Collector Components" section in Chapter 7 for more information on glass or plastic collector materials.) Collectors can be standard preframed wood or metal frame windows, patio doors, prefabricated "bubble" skylights, any of a wide variety of off-the-shelf glazing units currently available, or site-built custom units. Where metal frames are used, it is generally recommended that thermal breaks be specified. All installations of prefabricated configurations must conform with manufacturers' specifications to ensure proper performance.

7. Insulation must be protected where exposed above grade. Cement or synthetic stucco over lath, or other methods, may be employed. Where dampproofing is used, allow for complete curing before applying insulation. Consult insulation manufacturer for recommended installation methods.

8. Provide baffles where necessary to maintain 1″ minimum airspace for venting the attic.

9. The opaque roof must be vented to ensure proper performance of the insulation. Vents are typically located at the overhang soffits and at the ridge, depending on the roof construction. An airspace is provided to allow for circulation.

10. The use of an air infiltration barrier is generally recommended to reduce air infiltration and exfiltration through construction joints in exterior walls. Air infiltration barriers should allow the transpiration of moisture vapor. All air barrier products must be installed according to the manufacturer's specifications to ensure proper performance.

11. Movable insulation can be provided to improve the system's thermal performance. Insulating shades or drapes may be specified for interior applications. Insulated shutters or weather-resistant panels may be specified for exterior use. Care must be taken to ensure a tight fit between the insulation and the collector to reduce heat loss at the edges, particularly if the insulation has an R-value greater than R-4. (For further information, see "Control Components" in Chapter 7.)

12. Continuous sill sealer is recommended to provide protection against infiltration.

13. Water, stored in appropriate containers, is an effective material for thermal storage. Suitable containers include fiberglass tubes, polyethylene or steel drums, and metal culverts. Care should be taken to ensure that steel and metal containers are lined with corrosion-resistant materials. In all cases, water should be treated with algae-retardant chemicals. (For further information on the use of water as thermal storage, including descriptions of appropriate containers, see "Storage Components" in Chapter 7.)

14. It is recommended that all cylindrical containers that are located within or near a traffic or living area be braced at top and bottom against lateral movement. Taller containers should also be braced at midpoint. Bracing may be in the form of a framed valance, a broad steel band tied into a wall, or any other bracketing device.

15. Troughs should be provided as a precaution against leakage of water from containers or from condensation. Troughs may be formed of corrosion-resistant materials and attached or set into the supporting floor system to provide added lateral bracing at the base of the container. Troughs may be designed for a single container or a row of containers. It is generally recommended that each trough be provided with a slight slope of the base to a central drain that is tied to the main plumbing system of the building.

16. Concrete slab should be thickened to take the additional weight of water containers. Consult local codes for requirements.

17. Interior stud partition walls can be of standard construction. Wall finish may be specified per builder's option, but it is generally recommended that lighter colors be incorporated behind water storage, since they provide good reflective capabilities.

18. Rigid insulation should be provided to prevent heat losses from the water storage to the ground.

DIRECT GAIN DETAILS

Exterior Walls
(Masonry)

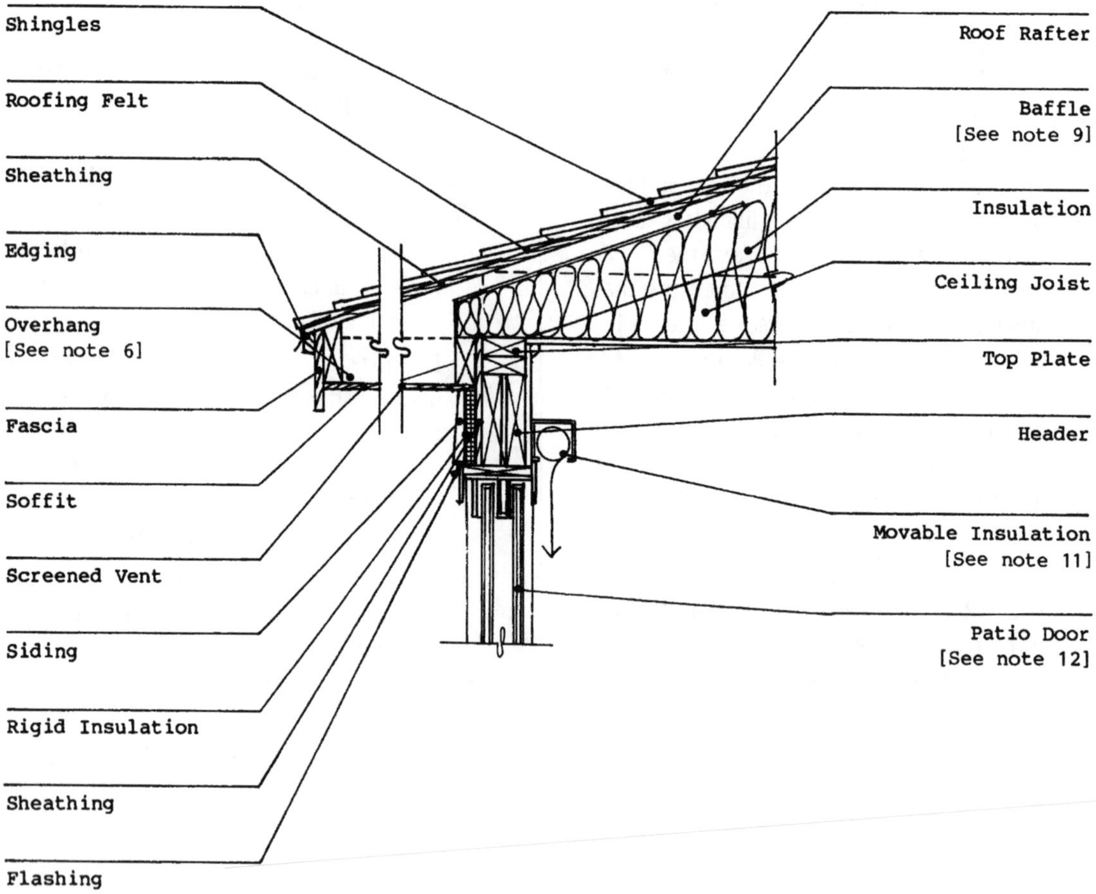

Shingles

Roofing Felt

Sheathing

Edging

Overhang
[See note 6]

Fascia

Soffit

Screened Vent

Siding

Rigid Insulation

Sheathing

Flashing

Roof Rafter

Baffle
[See note 9]

Insulation

Ceiling Joist

Top Plate

Header

Movable Insulation
[See note 11]

Patio Door
[See note 12]

Patio Door at Roof

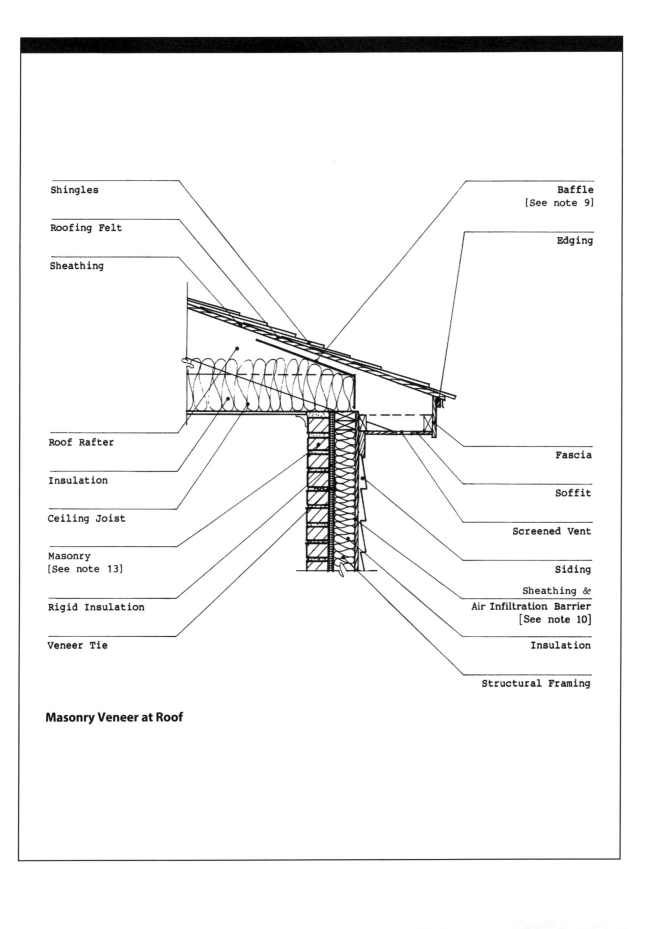

Shingles

Roofing Felt

Sheathing

Roof Rafter

Insulation

Ceiling Joist

Masonry
[See note 13]

Rigid Insulation

Veneer Tie

Baffle
[See note 9]

Edging

Fascia

Soffit

Screened Vent

Siding

Sheathing &
Air Infiltration Barrier
[See note 10]

Insulation

Structural Framing

Masonry Veneer at Roof

DIRECT GAIN DETAILS

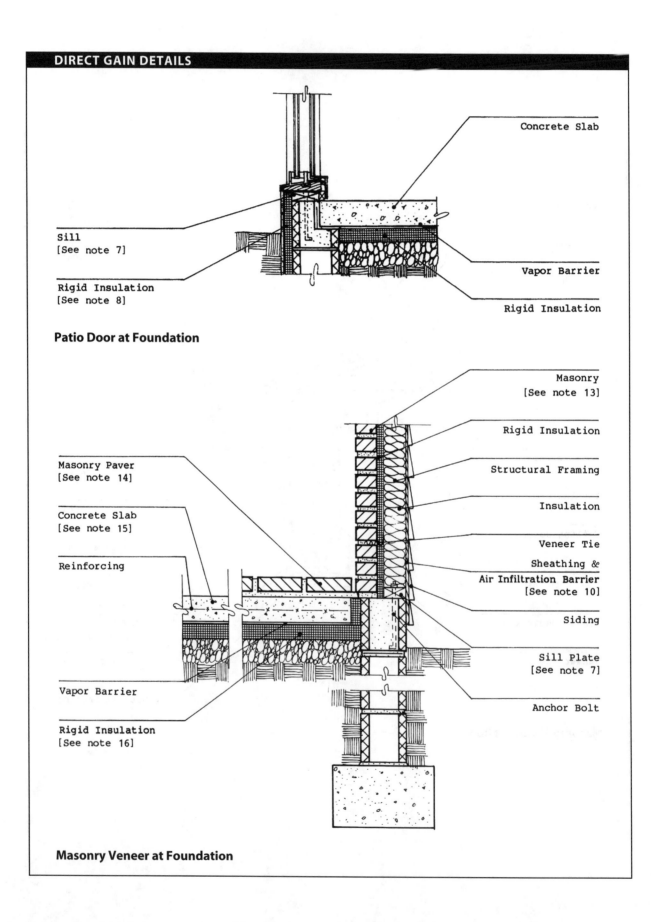

Concrete Slab

Sill
[See note 7]

Vapor Barrier

Rigid Insulation
[See note 8]

Rigid Insulation

Patio Door at Foundation

Masonry
[See note 13]

Rigid Insulation

Masonry Paver
[See note 14]

Structural Framing

Concrete Slab
[See note 15]

Insulation

Reinforcing

Veneer Tie

Sheathing &
Air Infiltration Barrier
[See note 10]

Siding

Sill Plate
[See note 7]

Vapor Barrier

Anchor Bolt

Rigid Insulation
[See note 16]

Masonry Veneer at Foundation

Exterior Wall Variations
(Masonry)

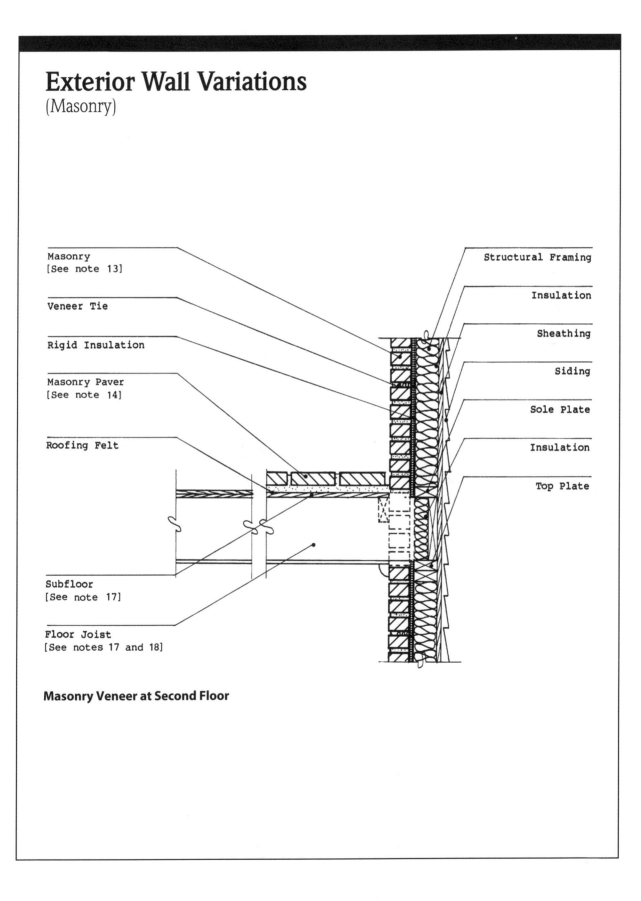

Masonry
[See note 13]

Veneer Tie

Rigid Insulation

Masonry Paver
[See note 14]

Roofing Felt

Subfloor
[See note 17]

Floor Joist
[See notes 17 and 18]

Structural Framing

Insulation

Sheathing

Siding

Sole Plate

Insulation

Top Plate

Masonry Veneer at Second Floor

DIRECT GAIN DETAILS

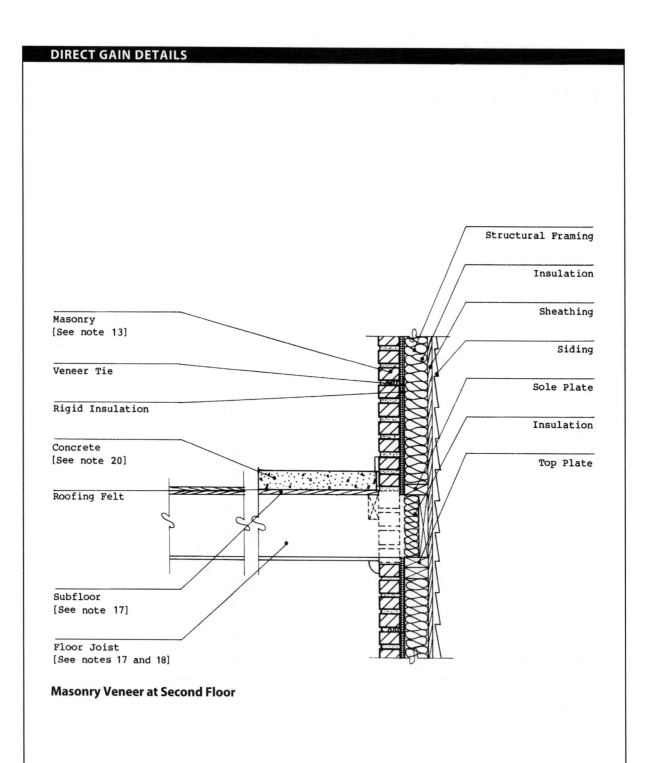

Masonry
[See note 13]

Veneer Tie

Rigid Insulation

Concrete
[See note 20]

Roofing Felt

Subfloor
[See note 17]

Floor Joist
[See notes 17 and 18]

Structural Framing

Insulation

Sheathing

Siding

Sole Plate

Insulation

Top Plate

Masonry Veneer at Second Floor

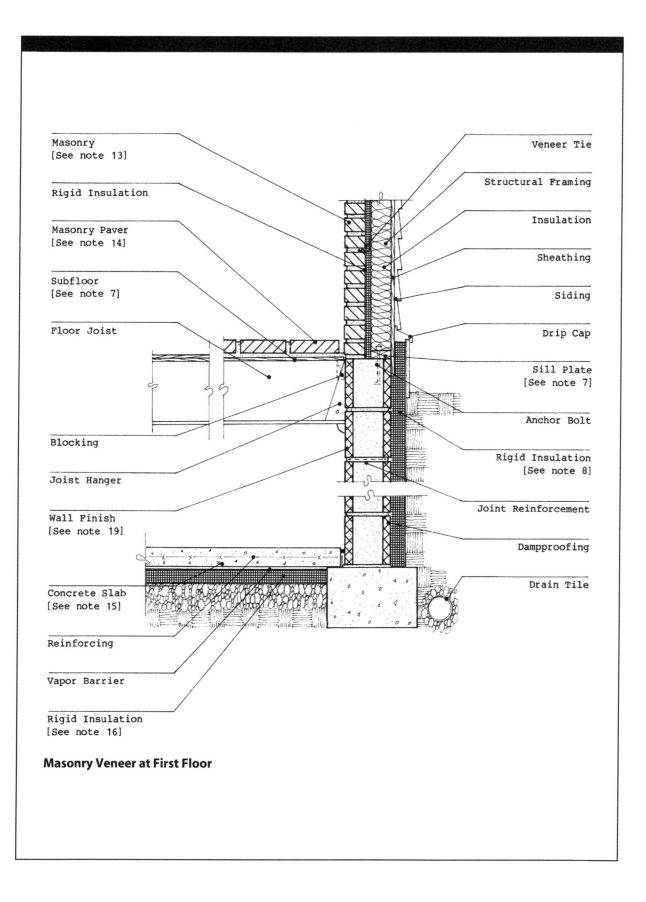

Masonry
[See note 13]

Rigid Insulation

Masonry Paver
[See note 14]

Subfloor
[See note 7]

Floor Joist

Blocking

Joist Hanger

Wall Finish
[See note 19]

Concrete Slab
[See note 15]

Reinforcing

Vapor Barrier

Rigid Insulation
[See note 16]

Veneer Tie

Structural Framing

Insulation

Sheathing

Siding

Drip Cap

Sill Plate
[See note 7]

Anchor Bolt

Rigid Insulation
[See note 8]

Joint Reinforcement

Dampproofing

Drain Tile

Masonry Veneer at First Floor

DIRECT GAIN DETAILS

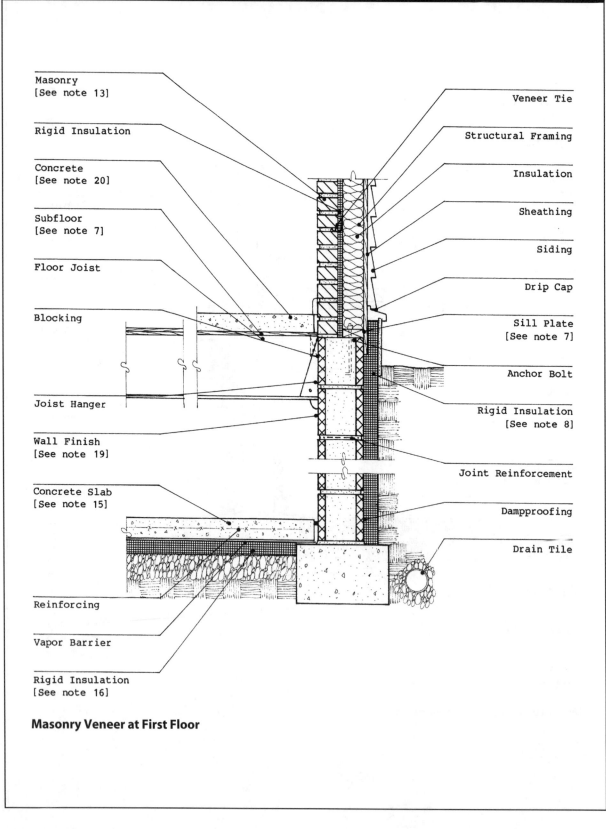

Masonry
[See note 13]

Rigid Insulation

Concrete
[See note 20]

Subfloor
[See note 7]

Floor Joist

Blocking

Joist Hanger

Wall Finish
[See note 19]

Concrete Slab
[See note 15]

Reinforcing

Vapor Barrier

Rigid Insulation
[See note 16]

Veneer Tie

Structural Framing

Insulation

Sheathing

Siding

Drip Cap

Sill Plate
[See note 7]

Anchor Bolt

Rigid Insulation
[See note 8]

Joint Reinforcement

Dampproofing

Drain Tile

Masonry Veneer at First Floor

Exterior Wall Variations
(Masonry)

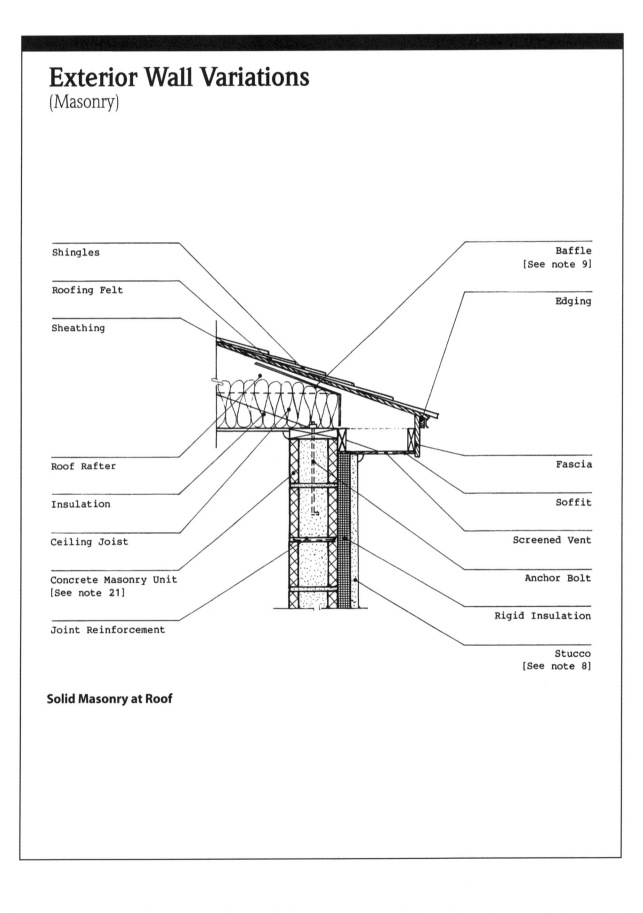

Shingles

Roofing Felt

Sheathing

Roof Rafter

Insulation

Ceiling Joist

Concrete Masonry Unit
[See note 21]

Joint Reinforcement

Baffle
[See note 9]

Edging

Fascia

Soffit

Screened Vent

Anchor Bolt

Rigid Insulation

Stucco
[See note 8]

Solid Masonry at Roof

DIRECT GAIN DETAILS

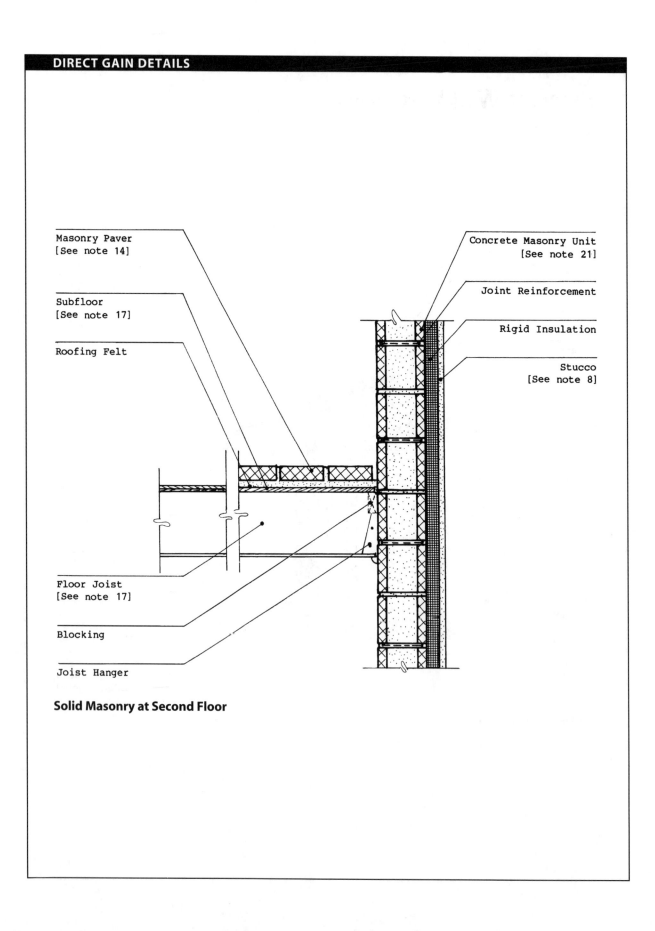

Masonry Paver
[See note 14]

Subfloor
[See note 17]

Roofing Felt

Concrete Masonry Unit
[See note 21]

Joint Reinforcement

Rigid Insulation

Stucco
[See note 8]

Floor Joist
[See note 17]

Blocking

Joist Hanger

Solid Masonry at Second Floor

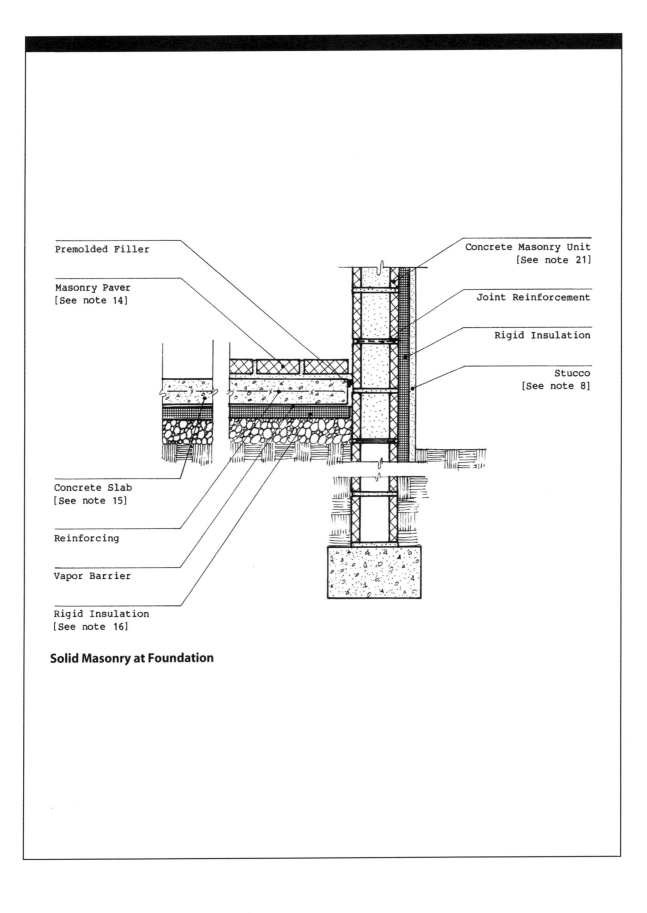

Premolded Filler

Masonry Paver
[See note 14]

Concrete Masonry Unit
[See note 21]

Joint Reinforcement

Rigid Insulation

Stucco
[See note 8]

Concrete Slab
[See note 15]

Reinforcing

Vapor Barrier

Rigid Insulation
[See note 16]

Solid Masonry at Foundation

DIRECT GAIN DETAILS

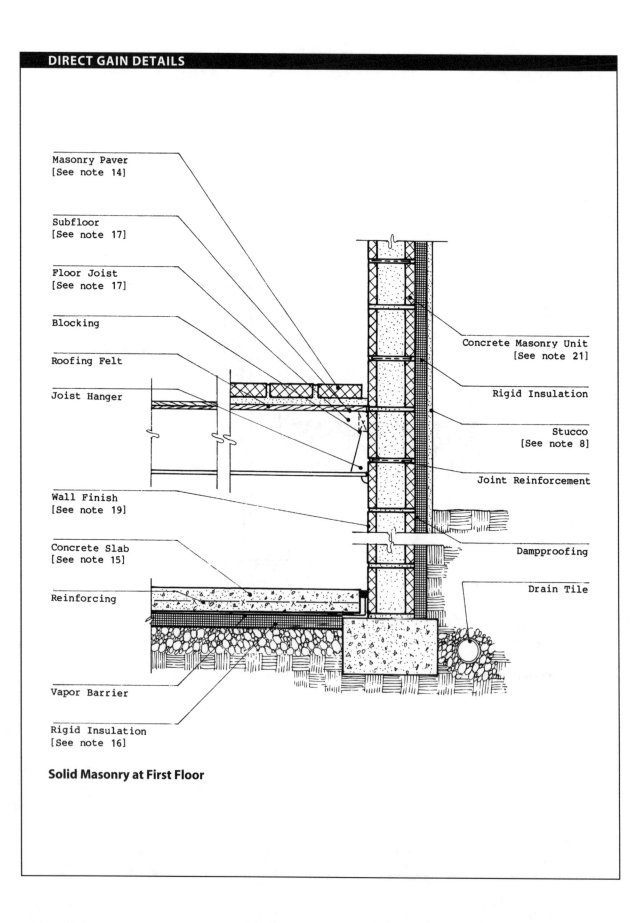

Masonry Paver
[See note 14]

Subfloor
[See note 17]

Floor Joist
[See note 17]

Blocking

Roofing Felt

Joist Hanger

Wall Finish
[See note 19]

Concrete Slab
[See note 15]

Reinforcing

Vapor Barrier

Rigid Insulation
[See note 16]

Concrete Masonry Unit
[See note 21]

Rigid Insulation

Stucco
[See note 8]

Joint Reinforcement

Dampproofing

Drain Tile

Solid Masonry at First Floor

Exterior Wall Notes
(Masonry)

GENERAL NOTES

1. All footings must bear on undisturbed soil. Adjust footing size, reinforcing, and depth below grade as required by site conditions and/or local code. Where groundwater problems exist, provide sufficient granular fill to prevent water penetration at slab-on-grade. Reinforcing in concrete slab-on-grade construction is not recommended, except where required by local conditions and/or code. Expansion joints should be provided, as required, at the connection between concrete or masonry floors and stud or masonry walls to prevent cracking.

2. Sizing of headers is to be determined by local building codes and/or accepted practice.

3. Insulation levels at foundation, floors, walls, and ceiling must meet or exceed requirements of local building and energy codes.

4. Other roof configurations may be used at the builder's option. Consult local building codes for restrictions and special requirements concerning roof/wall connections, especially in seismic and/or high-wind areas. The opaque roof must be vented to ensure proper performance of the insulation. Vents may be located at the sides of the roof or at the ridge, depending on the roof construction. An airspace is provided to allow for circulation.

5. Provide gutters and downspouts as required.

DETAIL NOTES

6. Overhang at the collector should be sized to optimize solar gains during heating season and prevent overheating during cooling season. (For further information, see "Control Rules of Thumb" in this chapter.)

7. Continuous sill sealer is recommended to provide protection against infiltration.

8. A cement or synthetic stucco finish (applied on lath over exterior insulation) is recommended. Other finishes may be specified at the builder's option, but rigid insulation must be protected where exposed above grade.

9. Provide baffles where necessary to maintain 1″ minimum airspace for venting the attic.

10. The use of an air infiltration barrier is generally recommended to reduce air infiltration and exfiltration through construction joints in exterior walls. Air infiltration barriers should allow the transpiration of moisture vapor. All air barrier products must be installed according to the manufacturer's specifications to ensure proper performance. Note that the application of an air infiltration barrier may not be required at the solid masonry/exterior insulation and stucco wall assemblies.

11. Movable insulation can be provided to improve the system's thermal performance. Insulating shades or drapes may be specified for interior applications. Insulated shutters or weather-resistant panels may be specified for exterior use. Care must be taken to ensure a tight fit between the insulation and the collector to reduce heat loss at the edges, particularly if the insulation has an R-value greater than R-4. (For further information, see "Control Components" in Chapter 7.)

12. For optimum thermal performance, it is generally recommended that double glazing be provided, preferably a high-performance glazing using one or more of the following: low-e coating(s), gas fill, or suspended plastic film(s). (See the "Collector Components"

DIRECT GAIN DESIGN DETAILS

section in Chapter 7 for more information on glass or plastic collector materials.) Collectors can be standard preframed wood or metal frame windows, patio doors, prefabricated "bubble" skylights, any of a wide variety of off-the-shelf glazing units currently available, or site-built custom units. Where metal frames are used, it is generally recommended that thermal breaks be specified. All installations of prefabricated configurations must conform with manufacturers' specifications to ensure proper performance.

13. Interior masonry veneer is shown for the direct gain storage component. (For information on finishes, material variations, and thermal performance characteristics, see "Interior Wall Types" in this chapter and "Storage Components" in Chapter 7.)

14. For information on masonry pavers used for direct gain storage, including recommended installation procedures, see "Interior Floor Types" in this chapter and "Storage Components" in Chapter 7.

15. Concrete slab-on-grade is shown as a storage component. (For further information, see "Interior Floor Types" in this chapter and "Storage Components" in Chapter 7.)

16. In cooler climates, install continuous insulation under the slab used for direct gain storage. (For further information, see "Control" in this chapter.)

17. Consideration must be given to the additional weight of pavers and concrete. Consult structural design loading tables and local codes to determine suitable grade and spacing of joists, and grade and thickness of the subfloor.

18. Masonry veneer must be continuous. Floor joists are framed through veneer.

19. Below-grade wall may be used for direct gain storage if it is designed to be in direct sunlight. (For information on interior finishes, see "Interior Wall Types" in this chapter and "Storage Components" in Chapter 7.)

20. For information on concrete used as direct gain storage, including recommended installation procedures, see "Storage Components" in Chapter 7.

21. Single-wythe concrete masonry unit is shown for the direct gain storage component. (For information on finishes, material variations, and thermal performance characteristics, see "Storage Components" in Chapter 7.)

Exterior Walls
(Masonry)

Masonry Veneer

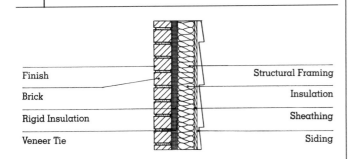

Finish | Structural Framing
Brick | Insulation
Rigid Insulation | Sheathing
Veneer Tie | Siding

FINISH

- For optimum thermal performance, masonry should be a dark color and should be left exposed wherever feasible. Certain finishes (e.g., plaster and gypsum board) can be acceptable if properly applied. Particular colors can also be specified from the manufacturer, or the masonry can be painted. (For further information on finishes and their effect on thermal performance, see "Storage" in this chapter and "Storage Components" in Chapter 7.)

MASONRY

- Any of the wide variety of standard brick, concrete block, concrete brick, and architectural facing units, such as split, slump, fluted, scored, or recessed block, are suitable for thermal storage. To ensure proper thermal performance, bricks must be solid, or hollow with grout-filled cores. (For further material information, see "Storage Components" in Chapter 7. For recommended thicknesses, see "Storage Rules of Thumb" in this chapter.)
- Veneer is assumed to support no load other than its own weight.

RIGID INSULATION

- Use of rigid insulation between masonry veneer and frame wall may be necessary to develop an acceptable R-value for the exterior wall.

VENEER TIE

- Corrosion-resistant, corrugated metal ties, of a minimum 22-gauge thickness and ⅞" width, are typically specified. Corrosion-resistant 8d nails, located at the bend in the tie and having a minimum penetration of 1½" into the stud, are recommended. The tie should be embedded a minimum of 2" into the mortar joint at the veneer. Spacing of the ties is to be determined by local building code requirements and/or standard practice.

STRUCTURAL FRAMING

- The structural frame walls can be of standard wood or metal frame construction.

INSULATION

- Selection of insulation materials for frame walls is to conform with local code requirements and/or standard practice.

SHEATHING

- Plywood, building board, or other similar materials can be specified as sheathing. The use of structural insulative sheathing as a substitute will reduce air infiltration and improve overall thermal performance if properly installed.

SIDING

- Material selection and color of siding is to be subject to builder's preference.

DIRECT GAIN DETAILS

Solid Concrete Masonry

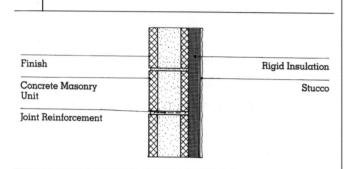

Finish

Concrete Masonry Unit

Joint Reinforcement

Rigid Insulation

Stucco

FINISH

- For optimum thermal performance, masonry should be a dark color and should be left exposed wherever feasible. Certain finishes (e.g., plaster and gypsum board) can be acceptable if properly applied. Particular colors can also be specified from the manufacturer, or the masonry can be stained or painted. (For further information on finishes and their effect on thermal performance, see "Storage" in this chapter and "Storage Components" in Chapter 7.)

CONCRETE MASONRY UNIT

- Concrete block, concrete brick, or architectural facing units, such as split, slump, fluted, scored, or recessed block may be used for thermal storage. To ensure optimum thermal performance, units must be solid, or hollow with grout-filled cores. (For further material information, see "Storage Components" in Chapter 7. For recommended thicknesses, see "Storage Rules of Thumb" in this chapter.)

JOINT REINFORCEMENT

- Joint reinforcement should be provided to control cracking by thermal movement and shrinkage. Truss, ladder, or x-tie configurations are suitable and can be embedded in the wall at vertical intervals according to local code requirements or industry recommendations. Splices in reinforcing should be lapped a

minimum of 6", and the width of the reinforcement should be 2" less than the nominal width of the storage wall.

RIGID INSULATION

- Rigid insulation may be applied directly to the masonry with mechanical fasteners and/or with adhesive (type and application per insulation manufacturers' recommendations and/or standard practice).

STUCCO

- Wire mesh or expanded metal lath for stucco finishes is laid over the rigid insulation and mechanically fastened to the concrete masonry. In general, the insulation surface must be free of mud and dust before stucco finish is applied. Alternately, a synthetic stucco exterior insulation and finish system (EIFS) may be applied as per the manufacturer's specifications.

Solid Concrete

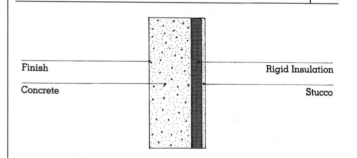

Finish

Concrete

Rigid Insulation

Stucco

FINISH

- For optimum thermal performance, concrete should be a dark color and should be left exposed wherever feasible. Textured finishes can be obtained, using standard construction practice, without significant impact on thermal performance.

- Certain finishes (e.g., plaster and gypsum board) can be acceptable if properly applied. Particular colors can also be specified from the supplier, or the concrete can be stained or painted. (For further information on finishes and their effect on thermal performance, see "Storage" in this chapter and "Storage Components" in Chapter 7.)

CONCRETE

- The use of normal-weight concrete (140 to 150 lb) is generally recommended. Placement of formwork and pouring of concrete should follow standard practice and/or local building codes. (For further information, see "Storage Components" in Chapter 7. For recommended material thicknesses, see "Storage Rules of Thumb" in this chapter.)

RIGID INSULATION

- Rigid insulation may be applied directly to the masonry with mechanical fasteners and/or with adhesive (type and application per insulation manufacturers' recommendations and/or standard practice).

STUCCO

- Wire mesh or expanded metal lath for stucco finishes is laid over the rigid insulation and mechanically fastened to the concrete masonry. In general, the insulation surface must be free of mud and dust before stucco finish is applied. Alternately, a synthetic stucco exterior insulation and finish system (EIFS) may be applied per the manufacturer's specifications.

TVA Solar House #10

Integrated into a south-facing slope, this 1,660-sq.-ft. two-level house incorporates direct gain and thermal storage wall systems for passive solar heating. The site is well suited to conserving energy because it requires minimal exposure of the home on the north, which reduces heat loss, and because a substantial building area is available for solar gain on the south.

Fixed double-glazed skylights illuminate an interior wall composed of grout-filled 12″ masonry units. Ceiling-mounted rigid panels insulate the skylights. The panels sit in a track and operate on a counterweight system operated from the first floor.

Thermal storage wall panels of fully grouted 8″ hollow-core concrete masonry units alternate with double direct gain glazing, combining the advantages of both system types. Exterior insulated vents located at the upper and lower edges of the collector frames ventilate the thermal storage wall airspace, reducing heat gain during the cooling season.

A sunscreen spanning the south face of the house affords summer sun protection, while its plywood fins are angled to optimize winter solar heat gain. Designed as a trellis, the sunscreen frames the front porch located on both sides of the air lock entry.

The hollow-core concrete block foundation is filled with loose-fill insulation, reducing ground heat losses. Additionally, 2″ of rigid insulation for the foundation wall, R-30 batt in the ceiling, R-19 batt in the wall, and R-7 duct insulation wrap complete a thermally tight home.

Supplementary heating is provided by a wood-burning stove. Solar collectors can be added to reduce the conventional fuel needed to meet domestic hot water heating requirements.

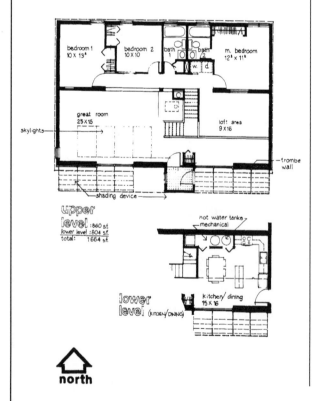

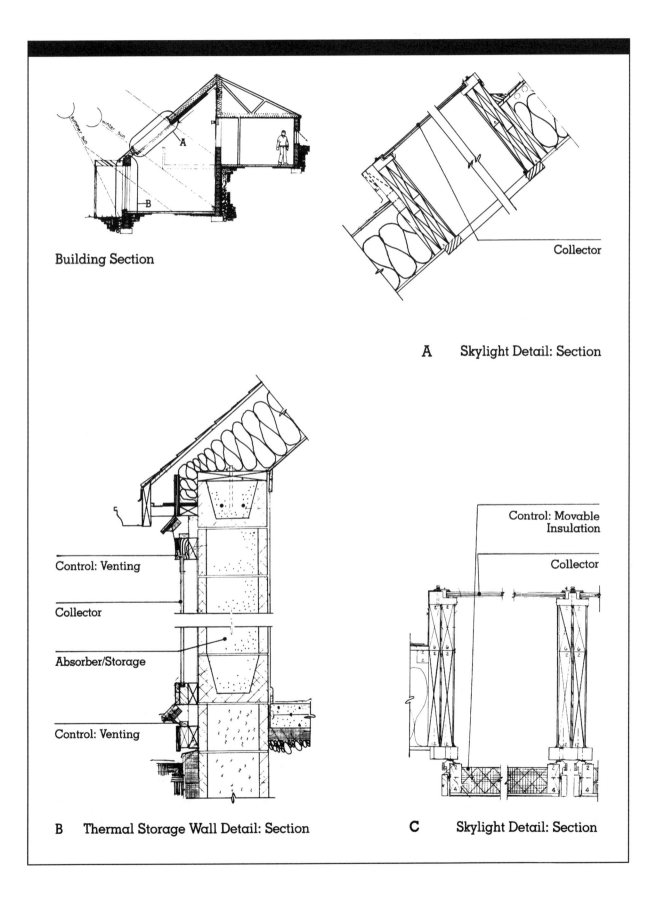

Building Section

A   Skylight Detail: Section

Collector

Control: Venting

Collector

Absorber/Storage

Control: Venting

Control: Movable
Insulation

Collector

B   Thermal Storage Wall Detail: Section

C   Skylight Detail: Section

DIRECT GAIN CASE STUDY

TVA Solar House #11

This 1,200-sq.-ft. single-story gabled house provides passive solar heating through both direct gain and thermal storage wall systems. Designed for flat or slightly sloping sites, its flexible square floor plan can be rotated and, with only minor changes, can be redesigned to place its passive features on any one of its four façades.

A continuous row of tempered glass skylights lines the upper edge of the south slope of the roof. At their interior, insulated shutters, which have a reflective interior skin and which roll in a track and are operated by a counterweight system, function in several modes to offer climate control. At night and on cloudy days in the heating season, they are closed to reduce heat losses; in the cooling season, they are closed during the day to control heat gain. The insulating panels consist of 3″ of rigid insulation sandwiched between ¼″ masonry boards. The panels are painted to match the interior walls.

A louvered roof overhang with angled slats positioned to allow the winter sun to strike the collector intercepts the summer sun, protecting the south-facing thermal storage wall from overheating during summer. Its mortar-filled 12″ heavyweight concrete masonry units have a cement plaster interior finish. Upper and lower exterior vents in the collector frames may be opened to cool the shaded wall and airspace during the summer.

In addition to warming the interior, the skylights allow sunlight to penetrate to the direct gain storage wall on the north side of the home. Its interior veneer of 4″ solid concrete masonry units is coated with a dark cement plaster finish for greater heat absorption.

Operable exterior vents high in the east and west gables provide natural ventilation for summer cooling. Adjacent to the entry, a wood-burning stove whose chimney runs through an interior masonry wall offers auxiliary heat.

In addition to loose-fill insulation filling the 8″ concrete masonry unit foundation wall, a 2″ layer of rigid waterproof R-16 insulation improves the thermal resistance of the vertical foundation. Beneath the slab, another 2″ of rigid waterproof R-16 insulation extends 4′ in from the perimeter. Roof insulation is specified to a level of R-30.

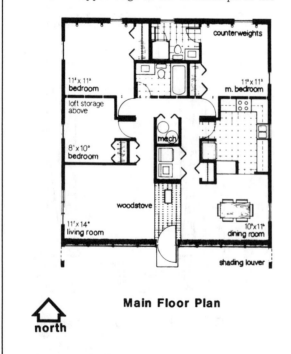

Main Floor Plan

north

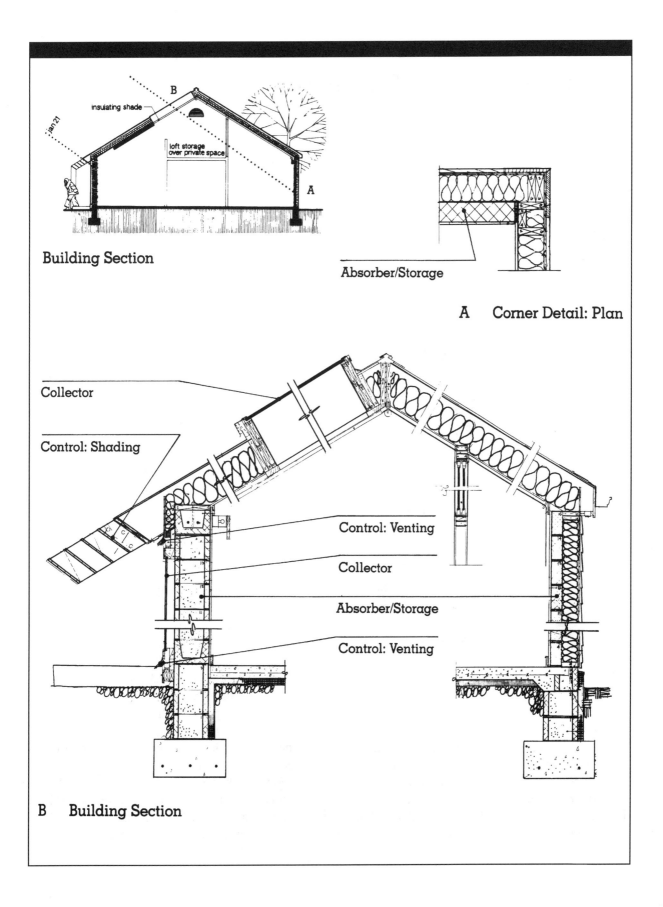

Building Section

Absorber/Storage

A   Corner Detail: Plan

Collector

Control: Shading

Control: Venting

Collector

Absorber/Storage

Control: Venting

B   Building Section

insulating shade

jan 21

loft storage
over private space

Burnside House—Seagroup

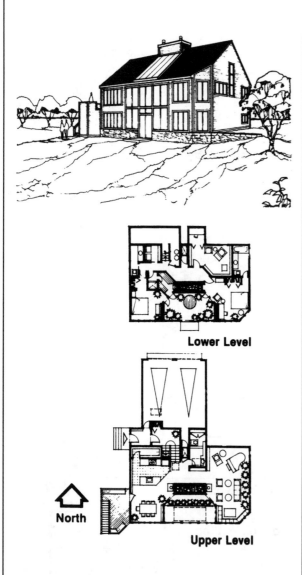

Lower Level

North

Upper Level

A double-height attached sunspace with vertical and horizontal rock bed and masonry thermal storage supplies passive solar heating to the Burnside house in Pawlet, Vermont. The home is vertically zoned, with the bedrooms on the lower level and the living areas above. Both share the aesthetic and heating advantages of a double-height sunspace centrally located on the south side of the home.

Partial earth berming and a north-facing garage shelter the north façade of the house from cold winter winds. Limited fenestration to the east is strategically located to provide morning light into the kitchen and dining room while minimizing heat losses. To the south, large expanses of glazing provide direct gain to all the major living spaces.

A skylight with movable insulation increases solar gain into the sunspace. Thermal mass is provided by brick pavers over concrete slab-on-grade floor in the sunspace. In adjacent direct gain spaces, the slab floors are finished with stone. Both spaces share a brick-veneered concrete masonry wall.

Operable doors and windows into the sunspace allow heated air to circulate throughout the home. Insulating shades reduce heat losses from all south- and southwest-facing fenestration at night.

On the north side of the sunspace, a 1½-story vertical rock bed provides central heat for the home. Additionally, a horizontal rock bed has been constructed beneath the floor under the living spaces to the north. During the day, warmed air rises in the sunspace and is circulated down and across the rock beds with the aid of induction fans. The air releases its heat to the rocks, which, in turn, warm the adjacent masonry surfaces. This heat slowly dissipates throughout the day and evening hours. When needed for supplemental heat, two wood-burning stoves at either end of the vertical rock bed contribute heat to the space and thermal mass.

At the peak of the cathedral ceiling, above the sunspace and rock beds, pole-operated latched vents exhaust excess heat through the louvered thermal chimney for summer cooling.

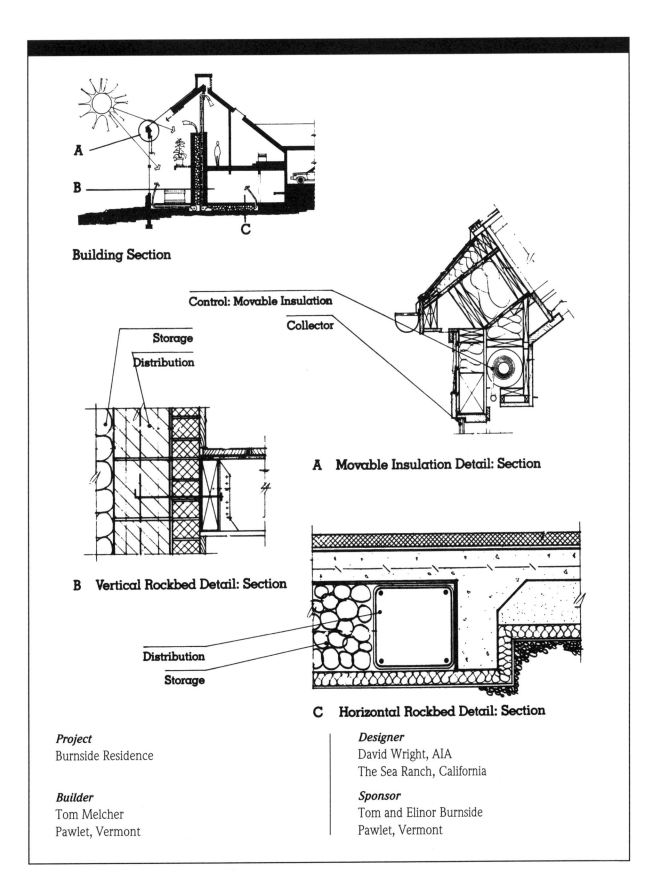

Building Section

Control: Movable Insulation

Collector

A Movable Insulation Detail: Section

Storage

Distribution

B Vertical Rockbed Detail: Section

Distribution

Storage

C Horizontal Rockbed Detail: Section

Project
Burnside Residence

Builder
Tom Melcher
Pawlet, Vermont

Designer
David Wright, AIA
The Sea Ranch, California

Sponsor
Tom and Elinor Burnside
Pawlet, Vermont

DIRECT GAIN CASE STUDY

McCaffrey House

Upper Floor Plan

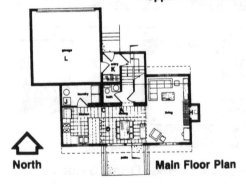

North   **Main Floor Plan**

A south-facing, two-story direct gain dining room with a masonry interior wall beyond combine to provide passive solar heating for the 1,360-sq.-ft. McCaffrey house in Lafayette, Colorado. Partial earth berming on all sides reduces the home's overall heat loss. A protected entry into an air-lock vestibule adjacent to the garage, and service areas on the north, buffer the north, further reducing the home's heating needs. In addition, the absence of glazing along the east and west façades eliminates a major source of summer heat gain.

At the center of the south wall, two sets of double-glazed sliding glass doors on each level illuminate the direct gain spaces. On the exterior, a light-colored concrete patio slab acts as a reflector, increasing solar gain into this space. The dining room is open to the kitchen and living room on the first floor, allowing for an even distribution of heat throughout these spaces.

Thermal storage is provided by a two-story-high wall in the center of two layers of 4″ brick units. The wall receives direct gain sunlight through a large second collector. A vent at the wall allows heated air to flow into the rooms on the north side of the home. The quarry tile over 5″ concrete slab dining room and kitchen floor provides additional thermal storage. R-4 quilted rolling shades insulate the glazing against night-time and cloudy-day heat losses.

A sunscreen trellis at the first floor and a roof overhang above are designed to shade the south façade in the summer. Additionally, the second floor is cantilevered on the south side to shade the first floor. Above the direct gain dining area, two thermostatically controlled paddle fans circulate air through the house

A heat-circulating fireplace and a gas forced-air furnace meet the auxiliary heating needs. The building envelope is constructed with R-38 ceiling and R-19 wall insulation.

Project
SERI #3

Builder
Tradition Homes
Lafayette, Colorado

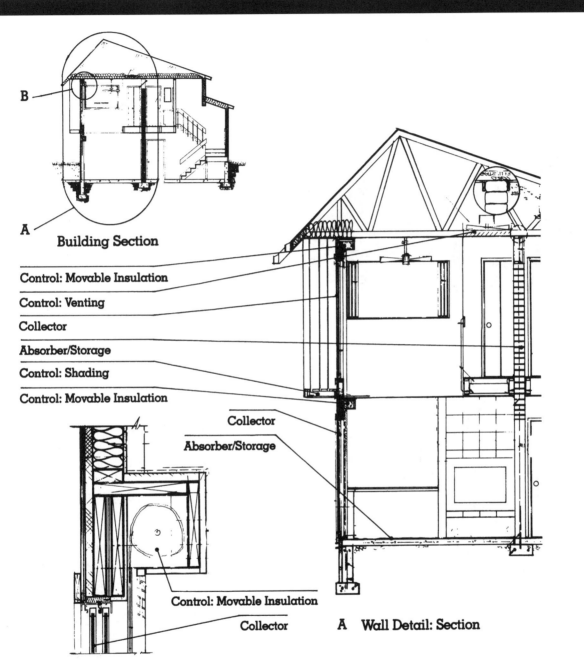

Building Section

Control: Movable Insulation

Control: Venting

Collector

Absorber/Storage

Control: Shading

Control: Movable Insulation

Collector

Absorber/Storage

Control: Movable Insulation

Collector

A Wall Detail: Section

B Movable Insulation Detail: Section

Designer
William J. McCaffrey
WJM Associates
Ft. Collins, Colorado

Sponsor
Solar Energy Research Institute,
Denver Metro Home Builders Association
Denver, Colorado

DIRECT GAIN CASE STUDY

TVA Solar House #7

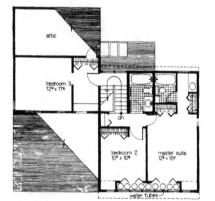

Upper Level

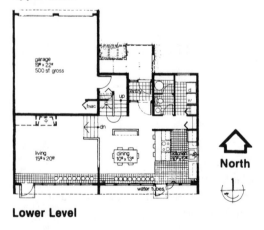

Lower Level

North

An air-lock entry and garage protect the northern exposure of the TVA Solar House #7 against heat loss. Water-filled tubes lining portions of the fenestrated south wall, along with a masonry floor slab, provide thermal storage for this two-story 2,300-sq.-ft. direct gain passive house.

Floor-to-ceiling fiberglass water storage tubes alternate with open areas of operable glazing on both floors along the south wall. The water contained in the 12″- and 18″-diameter tubes is treated with dark-colored dyes in order to increase the solar heat absorbptivity. Quarry tile over the concrete slab beneath the first floor tubes and in other selected areas provides additional thermal storage mass. Insulated drapes in the space between these storage tubes and the glazing are essential for the effective operation of the system.

On the upper level, the tubes, which are cantilevered beyond the line of the first floor, are placed between the exterior glazing and pairs of bifold interior doors. In the closed position, these doors enable heat to build up in the water storage tubes. The doors are opened when heat is required in the living spaces.

The house has been designed to accommodate either a flat site or an east- or west-sloping site. Deciduous trees to the southeast and southwest, overhangs, and wing walls provide summer shading. Evergreens have been used as a windbreak on the north. The cantilevered second floor and roof overhang above protect the large expanse of water wall from direct summer sun without interfering with winter solar gain.

The envelope is constructed with R-30 ceiling insulation, R-19 wall insulation, and R-4 insulated window coverings over the predominantly double- and triple-glazed casement windows.

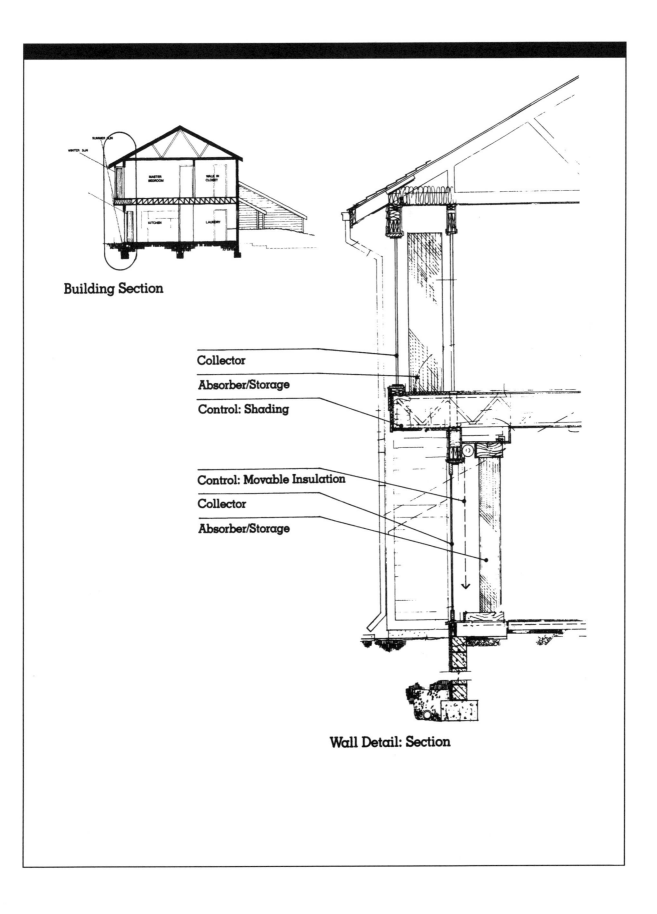

Building Section

Collector

Absorber/Storage

Control: Shading

Control: Movable Insulation

Collector

Absorber/Storage

Wall Detail: Section

DIRECT GAIN CASE STUDY

Perez House

This four-bedroom Colonial-style house in Albany, New York, incorporates a number of passive solar design strategies. The house encompasses 2,750 sq. ft. on two floors, with an unfinished basement and third story. The houses faces south, with large collector areas equal to approximately 17 percent of the finished square footage.

The collectors are 1″-thick double-pane, with welded vinyl frames. On the first floor, the living room, family room, and foyer are flooded with daylight, while two bedrooms on the second floor are given ample fenestration. A double-height space near the south wall, opening up the foyer, allows natural light to penetrate deep into the floor plan. There are also large collector areas in the foundation wall to admit sunlight into the basement.

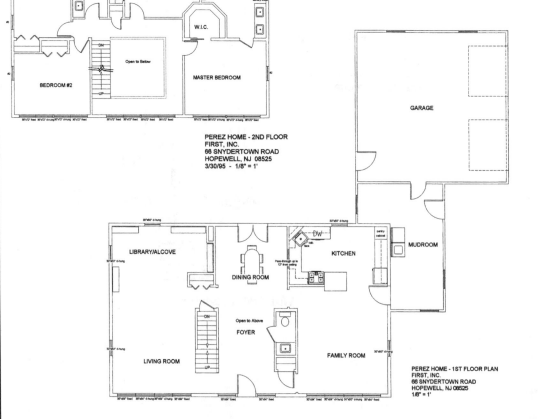

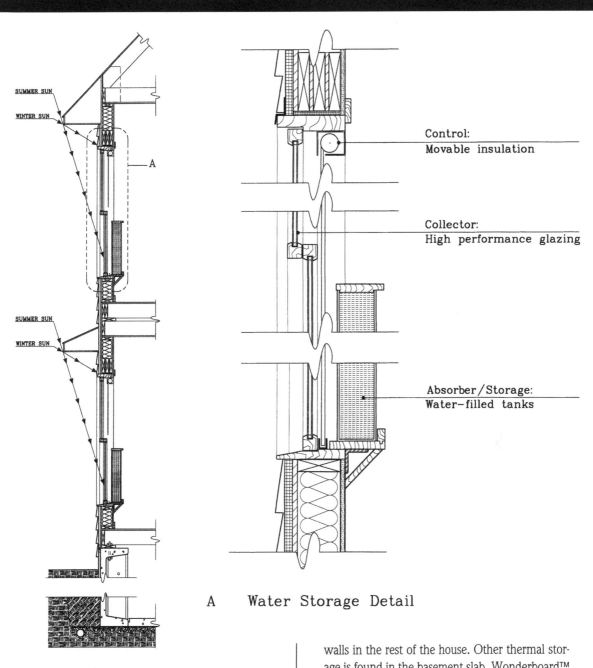

Control:
Movable insulation

Collector:
High performance glazing

Absorber/Storage:
Water—filled tanks

A   Water Storage Detail

Building section

For thermal storage, the south-facing windows incorporate galvanized steel water containers, approximately 30″ high and 5″ thick. Painted the same color as the walls and trimmed with pine, these "water walls" essentially blend in with the walls in the rest of the house. Other thermal storage is found in the basement slab, Wonderboard™ concrete underlayment, and ceramic tile flooring throughout.

Other passive solar features include double-cell pull-down shades for night insulation, with an estimated R-value of R-4, and overhangs for blocking solar gain in the summer. Boosted insulation in the shell delivers R-28 walls and R-38

DIRECT GAIN CASE STUDY

ceilings. The insulated basement wall has an R-value of R-30.

A unique element of the house's heating and cooling profile is the earth tube air system that extends out from the house beneath the ground and draws in cool air in for summer cooling and tempered fresh air in the winter. The Perez House also incorporates an active photovoltaic system on the roof to supply electric power from charged batteries.

Project
Perez House

Designer
Lyle Rawlings
Fully Independent Residential Solar
    Technology, Inc.
Hopewell, New Jersey

Sponsor
Richard Perez
Albany, New York

Exemplary House

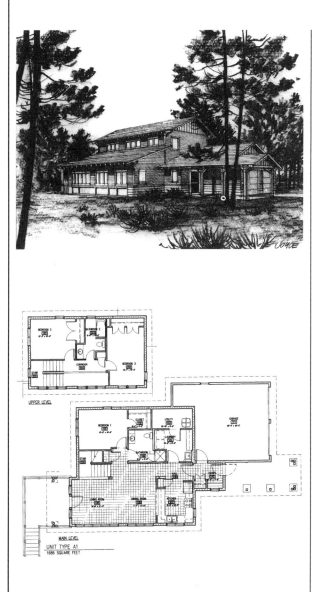

This prototype house is one of 59 single-family units built for employee housing in Grand Canyon National Park in Arizona. The 1,350-sq.-ft., two-story, three-bedroom house was designed to get the most from direct solar gain, along with other passive solar features.

The plan is relatively compact, providing maximum living space within a small footprint. The living room, dining room, and kitchen are found on the south side of the first floor, with few, if any, walls separating these spaces. On both the first and second floors, there are large collectors on the south elevation, with a total collector area of nearly 100 sq. ft. The collectors are double-glazed with low-e coating to reduce radiation heat transfer. The air space between the panes is filled with krypton gas to reduce convection, and the spacers are fiberglass.

Directly below the collectors on the south side is an 8"-thick masonry Trombe wall. The wall is covered on the exterior with a black selective-surface foil and double-pane glazing. The foil greatly reduces thermal radiation heat flow from the wall to the glazing. The Trombe wall glazing, which is clear glass without coatings, makes the house's windows appear to extend to the ground. Inside, the Trombe wall is concealed with gypsum board. The Trombe walls provide a balance to the daytime heating of the direct gain, and heat the space primarily at night by radiation and convection.

The house's walls and roof are constructed of structural insulated panels (SIPs) made of CFC-free polystyrene foam sandwiched between strandboard. Because the construction site is in a nature conservation area, the SIPs permitted quick erection (four days for one house) with minimal site disturbance. The SIP wall panels deliver an R-value of R-34, while the 10" roof panels perform at R-45. Rigid insulation of 2" was added to the exterior of the foundation wall and under the 4" slab-on-grade.

DIRECT GAIN CASE STUDY

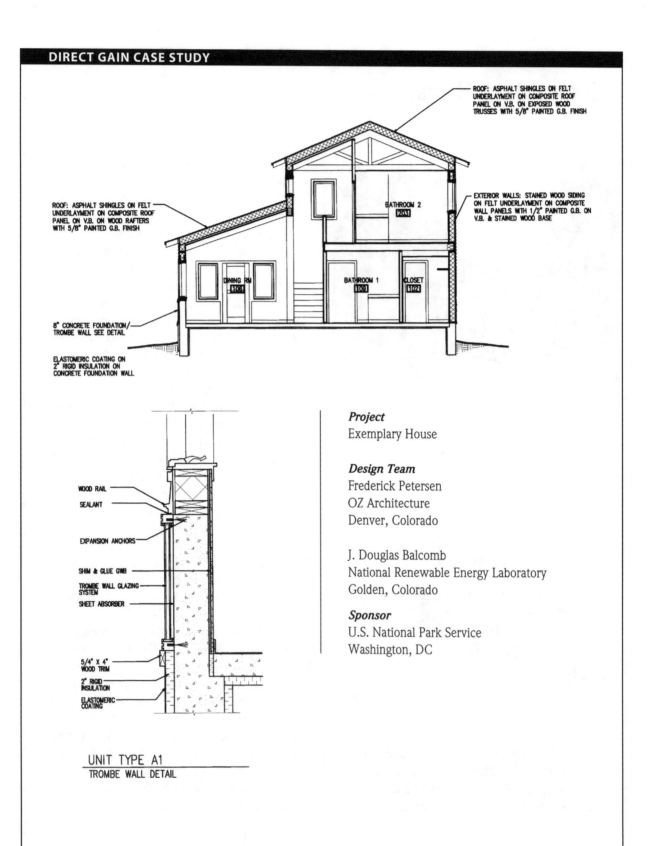

ROOF: ASPHALT SHINGLES ON FELT UNDERLAYMENT ON COMPOSITE ROOF PANEL ON V.B. ON EXPOSED WOOD TRUSSES WITH 5/8" PAINTED G.B. FINISH

EXTERIOR WALLS: STAINED WOOD SIDING ON FELT UNDERLAYMENT ON COMPOSITE WALL PANELS WITH 1/2" PAINTED G.B. ON V.B. & STAINED WOOD BASE

ROOF: ASPHALT SHINGLES ON FELT UNDERLAYMENT ON COMPOSITE ROOF PANEL ON V.B. ON WOOD RAFTERS WITH 5/8" PAINTED G.B. FINISH

8" CONCRETE FOUNDATION/ TROMBE WALL SEE DETAIL

ELASTOMERIC COATING ON 2" RIGID INSULATION ON CONCRETE FOUNDATION WALL

BATHROOM 2
201

DINING RM
104

BATHROOM 1
103

CLOSET
102

WOOD RAIL
SEALANT
EXPANSION ANCHORS
SHIM & GLUE GWB
TROMBE WALL GLAZING SYSTEM
SHEET ABSORBER
5/4" X 4" WOOD TRIM
2" RIGID INSULATION
ELASTOMERIC COATING

UNIT TYPE A1
TROMBE WALL DETAIL

Project
Exemplary House

Design Team
Frederick Petersen
OZ Architecture
Denver, Colorado

J. Douglas Balcomb
National Renewable Energy Laboratory
Golden, Colorado

Sponsor
U.S. National Park Service
Washington, DC

THERMAL STORAGE WALL

Design Overview

Thermal storage wall systems are designed primarily for space heating but can be used in certain climate conditions to provide cooling. For heating, they are effective in areas with mild to severe winters. For cooling, they are best suited to areas with high daily temperature swings (see "Seasonal Operation," below).

The collector component in a thermal storage wall system is generally a wall of south-facing glass or plastic placed directly in front of a wall that serves as the storage component. Movable insulation control components can be applied outside the collector or in the airspace between the collector and the storage wall. Shading and reflecting devices can be placed on the exterior.

In a thermal storage wall system, collection, absorption, storage, and control of solar energy occur outside the living space. Heat is transferred to the living space by the storage wall itself, which generally forms one side of the space. The wall can be unvented, or vents can be provided at the top and bottom. Windows can also be integrated into the wall to provide light, view, and some direct gain heating.

Seasonal Operation—Heating

During the heating season, sunlight passes through the collector (usually some form of glass or plastic), strikes the storage wall, and heats it. In an unvented thermal storage wall (see Figure 4.1), this heat is stored and slowly migrates to the interior, where it heats the adjacent living space.

If properly designed, the wall can provide adequate heat to the living space throughout the night.

Some of the heat generated in the airspace between the collector and the storage wall is lost through the glass or plastic back to the outside. The hotter the air in the airspace, the greater this heat loss. These potential heat losses can be reduced by venting the storage wall (see Figure 4.2).

Because of the tendency of hot air to rise and cool air to fall, a natural system for providing warm air to the living space can be set up in a vented wall system. Vents placed at the top of the wall allow air, which has been heated in the airspace, to flow naturally into the adjacent living area. Vents low in the wall then pull cooler replacement air into the airspace from the living

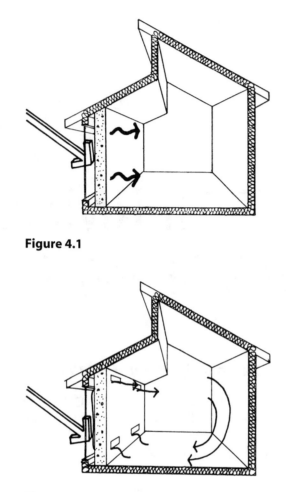

Figure 4.1

Figure 4.2

area, thus setting up a loop for circulating the heated air (thermocirculation). No mechanical means for moving the air is required, although the addition of a small fan can increase the system efficiency. Care should be taken to ensure that the circulation pattern does not reverse itself at night, when temperatures in the airspace drop, allowing heated air from the living space to flow into the airspace, pushing cooler airspace air into the living area. The provision of simple backdraft dampers or operable louvers on the upper vents will prevent this reverse flow from occurring.

In a vented system, heated air enters the living space at roughly 90°F. The loss of this heat from the airspace consequently reduces the amount of heat available to be stored by the wall. An unvented system does not lose heat in this way,

and thus has the advantage of storing a greater percentage of the solar energy available to it than does a vented wall. This stored heat is not, however, readily available for immediate use, but radiates slowly into the living area.

The delay between the time when sunlight first strikes the unvented storage wall and the time when the heat has finally traveled through the wall and reached the living space is called time lag. It is characteristic of certain materials, such as masonry, that are commonly used to construct thermal storage walls. Depending on the thickness and thermal properties of the selected wall materials, this lag period can last from several hours to an entire day. In a vented system, this time lag still occurs, but some of the heat is short-circuited by the vents that provide heat to the living space throughout the day. Such a tradeoff makes sense in colder climates, where daytime as well as nighttime heating requirements are high, and it is desirable to provide a certain amount of heat directly to the living space. In such situations, a vented wall should be specified. In most moderate climates, on the other hand, where daytime heating is not as important as nighttime heating, an unvented system will be preferable. If properly designed, such a system will be able to store heat throughout the day and release it to the living space throughout the night.

Note that windows integrated into thermal storage walls to provide light, view, and/or some direct gain daytime heating will also reduce the effective area of the storage wall.

Seasonal Operation—Cooling

The south-facing collector should be well shaded to prevent excessive heat gain during the cooling season, when heat is not required from the system (see Figure 4.3).

Shading elements, such as overhangs, should be sized to maximize overall system performance. If they are too large, they may completely shade the wall, preventing unwanted gain during the cooling season, but they will also block a significant amount of radiation during the later part of the heating season. Conversely, if they are too small, solar gain will be maximized when heat is

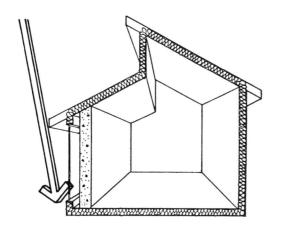

Figure 4.3

needed, but overheating will occur during the later part of the cooling season, adding to the load on the auxiliary energy system.

A thermal storage wall system can contain two sets of vents. In addition to the wall vents discussed earlier, vents can and should be placed on the exterior in the collector component. In the former case, the vents are placed in the storage wall itself to provide heated air to the living space. Vents placed in the collector are used to prevent overheating during the cooling season by admitting and expelling outside air to the airspace (see Figure 4.4).

These external vents can be opaque panels in the collector system, or they can simply be opera-

ble glazing elements. In situations where the collector is shaded by a fixed device, such as an overhang, an opaque vent may be preferable to glazing for use at the top of the collector. This area will generally receive little or no sun, especially if the overhang is large, but will conduct considerable amounts of heat if it is glazed. Opaque vents, if properly designed, can allow for the inclusion of adequate insulation to reduce such heat flow. Lower vents can be opaque or glazed, depending on builder preference. Glazed units have the advantage of transmitting sunlight onto an unshaded part of the wall, improving system performance.

A combination of high and low exterior vents in the collector wall will remove much of the solar heat generated in the airspace. By opening both the high exterior vents in the collector wall and the low interior vents in the storage wall, air will be drawn across the living space and through the low vents to replace the warm air in the airspace, rising naturally out the upper vents. This method not only prevents heat buildup in the airspace, but also provides some natural ventilation to the living space (see Figure 4.5).

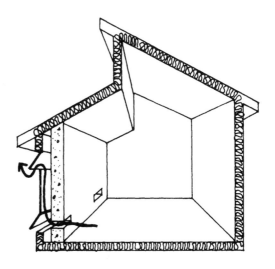

Figure 4.5

In areas of the country with high daily temperature swings, the thermal storage wall can be used to further reduce the cooling energy requirements by releasing heat to the cool night air. In the evening, the exterior vents are opened

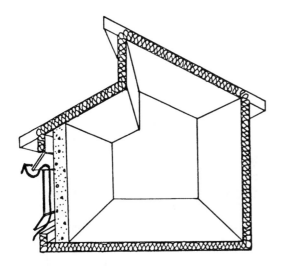

Figure 4.4

to the storage wall by natural convection or fans. By morning, the wall temperature will be low enough to allow the wall to absorb heat from the living space during the day.

Movable insulation should be used during this daytime period to cover the collector from the outside and to preserve the cool temperature of the wall for as long as possible. At the end of the day, the insulation is removed and the cycle is repeated (see Figure 4.6).

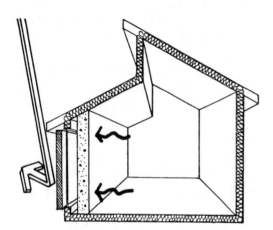

Figure 4.6

Advantages

- Glare and ultraviolet degradation of fabrics are not problems, as they are in direct gain systems.

- The time lag between the absorption of solar energy by the exterior surface of the wall and the delivery of the resulting heat to the interior living space provides this heat in the evening, when it is most needed.

- Sufficient storage mass to achieve a desired level of thermal performance can be provided in a relatively small, concentrated area within the living space.

- The high mean radiant temperature of the thermal storage wall can improve the comfort of the adjacent living space.

Disadvantages

- Two south-facing walls, one glazed and one constructed of the storage material, are required.

- Mass storage walls can be expensive and may require specially sized foundations and footings. They may also be subject to special building code restrictions, especially in earthquake-prone areas.

- The mass storage wall can take up valuable square footage in a residence.

- Without movable insulation, the high temperature differential between outside night air and inside airspace air will cause considerable heat to be lost through the collector glazing at night during the heating season. Therefore, some form of movable insulation is highly recommended, but it can be expensive and awkward to operate.

- The storage wall can block view and daylight.

Collectors

Thermal storage wall collectors can be constructed using off-the-shelf window units, simple patio-door replacement glass, various glazing materials, or some combination of these elements incorporated into a framing system specially designed for the specific installation.

If the collector framing system is metal, it should be separated from the storage wall, either by a space or by wood blocking, to avoid conductive heat losses from the wall through the metal to the outside. If the frame is wood, rough-sawn and green wood should be avoided in favor of kiln-dried lumber. Wood framing, although generally less expensive than metal, is subject to greater degradation over time, especially considering that temperatures in the wall cavity can reach 150° to 180°F. Any paint used on the frame should be resistant to high temperatures.

Collector framing systems can be attached to, and supported by, the storage wall itself, or they can be framed conventionally and be supported on a foundation (see Figures 4.7 and 4.8). Both approaches work well, and a choice may be based on specific design considerations and local material costs. Whatever system is chosen, the dimensions of the framing members should be kept to a minimum to maximize the glazing area and, consequently, the amount of sunlight striking the wall.

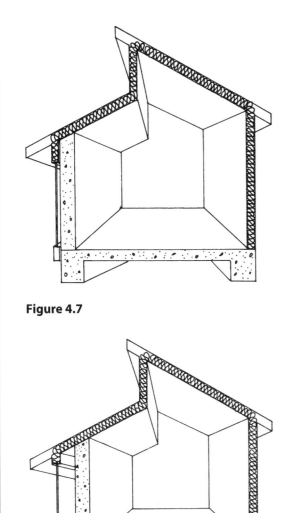

Figure 4.7

Figure 4.8

The collector material can be glass or any one of a variety of glazing materials, including fiberglass, acrylics, and polycarbonates. When reviewing the physical properties of these materials, attention should be paid to the maximum operating temperature of the material, since temperatures within an unvented storage wall airspace can get quite high (150° to 180°F) and may cause some materials to degrade rapidly.

Double glazing, preferably high-performance glazings using low-e coatings, gas fills, and/or suspended plastic films, are recommended for most installations to reduce heat losses back out

through the collector. Single glazing may be cost-effective in mild climates, although movable insulation may need to be provided.

Whatever material is chosen, attention should be paid to expansion, contraction, and sealing. Collector frame joints should allow for significant expansion (½" inch minimum) due to the high temperatures possible in the airspace, particularly in unvented walls. Caulking and sealants used in these applications must be able to accommodate such movement, and it is recommended that only high-quality products be used.

The collector should be periodically checked for possible sealant repair, as some separation may occur during the first few months of operation. It is also recommended that the collector elements be operable or removable to allow for periodic maintenance and cleaning. This is particularly important for reasons of indoor air quality in the vented Trombe wall applications. In systems where the collector material is used to vent summer heat to the exterior, such operability is already partially built in.

COLLECTOR RULES OF THUMB

- *Orientation:* Orient the thermal storage wall system to face south. Orientations up to 20° east or west of due south will not significantly affect performance.

- *Design:* The thermal storage wall should be one wall of the living space(s) to be heated.

- *Area:* The surface area of the collector should be equal to the surface area of the storage component (see "Storage Rules of Thumb" in this chapter).

- *Airspace:* The airspace between the wall and the collector can vary from 2" to 6", depending on the space needed for movable insulation if it is to be included between the wall and collector.

- *Number of glazings:* For optimum thermal performance, it is generally recommended that double glazing be provided, preferably a high-performance glazing using one or more of the following: low-e coatings, gas fill, or suspended plastic films. (See the "Collector Components" section in Chapter 7 for more information on glass or plastic collector materials.) Collectors can be standard preframed wood or metal frame windows, patio doors, prefabricated "bubble" skylights, any of a wide variety of off-the-shelf glazing units currently available, or site-built custom units. Where metal frames are used, it is generally recommended that thermal breaks be specified. All installations of prefabricated configurations must conform with manufacturers' specifications to ensure proper performance.

Storage

The storage wall component of a thermal storage wall system can be made of any one of a variety of materials exhibiting a high capacity to store heat (e.g., concrete, brick, or water). These materials will transfer heat to the living space slowly and evenly, delivering this heat, if the system is properly designed and sized, when it is most needed.

In general, materials used for a storage wall will require larger foundations and footings to accommodate the extra weight of the wall. Special reinforcing requirements must also be considered for a masonry wall if, as is typically the case, it is taken to the roof and used as a bearing wall.

The exterior face of the wall should be a dark color to increase absorption of incoming solar energy. The exposed surface can be painted, or specific colors can be specified from the material manufacturer (see Table 7.4 in Chapter 7 for the absorbtivities of various materials and colors).

A new type of exterior finish material is gaining popularity in thermal storage wall applications: the selective surface. The selective surface materials, usually manufactured in thin sheets that are adhered directly to the storage wall surface, absorb almost all incoming solar radiation but emit only a very small portion as heat. They thus reduce heat loss back out through the collector glazing and can increase efficiency to the point where movable night insulation may no longer be necessary.

The interior surface of the wall can be painted or left untreated. However, finishes other than paint will decrease the efficiency of the wall by restricting its ability to absorb and reradiate heat. Plaster and wallpaper will have only a minor effect in this regard. Gypsum board can be acceptable if it is attached directly to the wall and if care is taken during installation to apply a very thick coat of construction adhesive in order to increase the thermal connection between the wall and the gypsum board. Interior finishes attached on furring strips will not perform as well and should be avoided.

Water containers used as thermal storage walls pose a slightly different finishing condition. Such containers are generally designed and manufactured to be freestanding and unfinished. In cases where the water containers are to be concealed for aesthetic reasons, it is not advisable to attach the finish material directly to the containers. A puncture from decorative material (e.g., wall hangings) can result in leaks from the containers. One option is to build out a stud wall with a conventional gypsum board finish. Vents placed in the top and bottom of the wall will allow heat to be drawn off the water wall. This isolated water container configuration will not perform as well as the exposed-mass thermal storage wall described earlier.

STORAGE RULES OF THUMB

- *Area:* In general, the farther north the building is, the larger the thermal storage wall system should be. The rough area of storage material per square foot of adjacent living space to be heated can be determined from Table 4.1 (collector area will be equal to the storage area). For example, for Madison, Wisconsin, at 43° NL with an average January temperature of 21.8°F (data available from local and/or national weather bureau), go to the intersection of the closest latitude (44° NL) and the closest "Average Winter Outdoor Temperature" (20°F) to find that 0.85 sq. ft. of storage wall—and, therefore, glazing—is required per square foot of floor area. For a living space of 200 sq. ft. to be heated, 170 sq. ft. of thermal storage wall will be required, assuming all other rules of thumb for system sizing have been followed.

Table 4.1

Average Winter Outdoor Temperature (Clear Day)*	Masonry Wall/Space Floor Area**			
	36° NL	40° NL	44° NL	48° NL
COLD CLIMATES				
20°F	.71	.75	.85	.98 (w/NI)
25°F	.59	.63	.75	.84 (w/NI)
30°F	.50	.53	.60	.70
TEMPERATE CLIMATES				
35°F	.40	.43	.50	.55
40°F	.32	.35	.40	.44
45°F	.25	.26	.30	.33

Note: NI indicates Night Insulation.

* Temperatures listed are for December and January, usually the coldest months.

** These ratios apply to a well insulated space with a heat loss of 8 Btu/degree day/square foot of floor area/°F. If space heat loss is more or less than this figure, adjust the ratios accordingly. The surface area of the wall is assumed to be the same as the glazing.

- *Thickness:* The recommended storage component thickness ranges from 8″ to 18″.

- *Vent area:* The area of the thermocirculation vents in the storage wall should be roughly 2 sq. ft. per 100 sq. ft. of wall, divided evenly between upper and lower vents.

- *Vent dampers:* Vents should be provided with backdraft dampers to prevent reverse thermocirculation.

Control

SHADING

To prevent excessive overheating during the cooling periods, it is recommended that some method of shading the thermal storage wall system be provided. The range of possible methods is roughly the same as that for direct gain shading. Exterior devices include overhangs (see Figure 4.9), trellises, awnings, louvers (horizontal or vertical, fixed or operable), and wing walls.

These exterior devices can form part of the building frame, or they may be attached to it. They can be stationary, or they may require daily operation. If interior devices are used, they should be placed in the airspace between the storage wall and the collector (see Figure 4.10).

Interior shades are typically curtains, blinds, or roller shades. They must be opened and closed daily if the storage wall is used for passive cooling (see "Seasonal Operation—Cooling" earlier in this chapter). Thermostatically controlled, motor-driven interior shades are generally most acceptable to the homeowner, but manually operated interior shades are generally less expensive, with fewer maintenance problems. In both cases, special attention must be paid to the method of operation of a specific shade to ensure

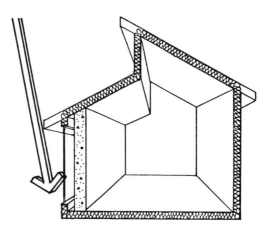

Figure 4.9

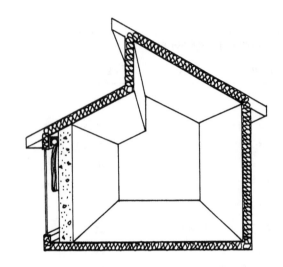

Figure 4.10

safe and maintenance-free operation from the living space. For optimum performance, these interior shading elements should also be designed to provide insulation during the day in the cooling season and at night in the heating season (see "Insulation—Movable Insulation" later in this chapter).

REFLECTING

Reflectors placed horizontally above or below the thermal storage wall collector can increase overall system performance by increasing the amount of sunlight reaching the collector (see Figure 4.11).

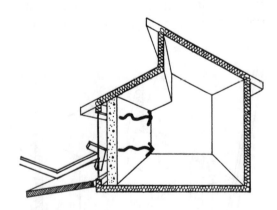

Figure 4.11

In certain cases where physical obstructions (e.g., trees or other buildings) on or around the building site shade the collector, the provision of

reflectors can increase solar collection by 30 percent to 40 percent. Reflectors can also improve the performance of skylights placed in a flat roof that may not receive sufficient winter sunlight in the horizontal position.

From the standpoint of practicality and economy, it is recommended to use existing architectural elements in the building design as reflectors, where possible. Light-colored exterior landscape elements, such as patios or terraces, are examples of such elements. While not as effective as reflector panels, these architectural elements require no additional maintenance, and do not present the glare and overheating problems sometimes associated with reflector panels.

For cases in extreme environments, or for those committed to making daily or seasonal adjustments, the more efficient reflector panels may be appropriate. Reflector panels are usually coated on one side with a material of high reflectance, and are placed directly in front of a vertical south-facing collector, or behind a horizontal collector (e.g., a skylight). When the collector extends all the way to the ground (e.g., a patio door), the reflector is simply laid on the ground in front of it. In the case of collector openings higher up in the wall, or in cases where the reflector is placed above the collector, some form of support will be needed. Reflectors for horizontal skylights can be placed vertically on the roof on the north side of the skylight.

All horizontal panels should be placed so that they slope slightly away from a vertical collector to increase the amount of reflected sunlight and to facilitate drainage (5° is recommended). To be more economically and/or aesthetically justifiable, they should also be insulated so that they can serve as movable insulation when not in the reflecting mode. It should be noted that reflecting panels may cause glare and/or overheating problems within the living spaces.

INSULATING—MOVABLE INSULATION

Although thermal storage walls can trap a great deal of solar energy during clear, sunny days, they can also lose a great deal of heat during prolonged overcast periods and at night. While the introduction of high-performance glazings has

Thermal Storage Wall   121

significantly improved the ability of collectors to retain heat during cold weather (or reject it in warm weather), conditions still exist in extreme climates where additional provisions can be useful. Providing some form of movable insulation during periods of heat loss can result in significant increases in overall thermal performance. Movable insulation can also be used to prevent excessive heat gain during the cooling season.

There are two basic applications of movable insulation: (1) insulation that is applied to the exterior of the collector; and (2) insulation that is placed in the airspace between the collector and the storage wall. The former are usually rigid panels and can be difficult to store, maintain, and operate. If designed properly, however, they can be used as both reflecting panels during the day and insulation at night (see "Reflecting" above). They will also be more effective at reducing unwanted heat gain during the cooling season because they serve as shades intercepting the sunlight before it can enter the collector and be converted to heat. Care must be taken to ensure that there is a tight, well-sealed fit between the exterior insulation and the collector to prevent heat losses at the edges of the insulation (see Figure 4.12). Placing the

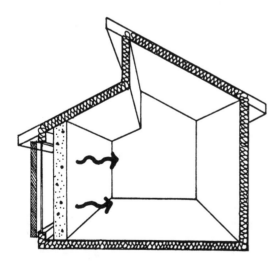

Figure 4.12

insulation in the airspace generally solves the problems of storage and reduces those of maintenance (see Figure 4.13).

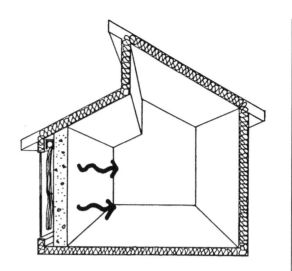

Figure 4.13

Providing for easy operation of airspace insulation, however, can pose significant problems. It is recommended that an adequate operating mechanism, whether manual or automatic, be developed very early in the design process to avoid potential future problems. Care should also be taken that this airspace insulation not interfere with the proper operation of the interior vents (if provided) or the exterior summer cooling vents.

CONTROL RULES OF THUMB

Shading

• *Overhang:* The projection of the overhang that will be adequate (provide 100 percent shading at noon on June 21) at particular latitudes can be quickly calculated by using the following formula:

Projection (L)

$$= \frac{\text{window opening, i.e., collector (H)}}{\text{F (see Table 4.2)}}$$

A slightly longer overhang may be desirable at latitudes where this formula does not provide enough shade during the later part of the cooling season (see Figure 4.14). For example, for Madison, Wisconsin, at 43° NL, select an F factor between 2.0 and 2.7 (values for 44° NL). Assum-

Table 4.2

North Latitude	F Factor*
28°	5.6–11.1
32°	4.0–6.3
36°	3.0–4.5
40°	2.5–3.4
44°	2.0–2.7
48°	1.7–2.2
52°	1.5–1.8
56°	1.3–1.5

* Select a factor according to your latitude. The higher values will provide 100% shading at noon on June 21, the lower values on August 1.

ing shade is desired on August 1, choose the lower value of 2.0. If the window opening (H) is 8′, the projection (L) of the overhang placed at the top of the collector will be 4′.

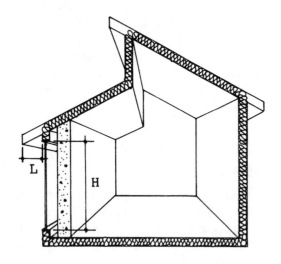

Figure 4.14

Reflecting

If reflector panels are used, the following should be applied:

- *Slope:*   A downward slope (away from collector) of roughly 5° is recommended for reflector (see Figure 4.15).

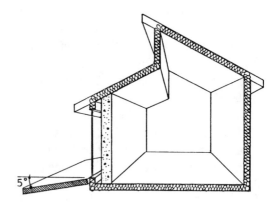

Figure 4.15

- *Sizing:*   The reflector should be the same length as the collector and roughly as wide as the collector is high.

Insulating

- *Movable insulation:*   Movable insulation will typically have an R-value between R-4 and R-9.

THERMAL STORAGE WALL DETAILS

The drawings on the following pages illustrate common construction detailing for thermal storage wall systems. The details are divided into two sections, denoting the major material and construction options available in the design of a thermal storage wall system.

Each section focuses on one of the primary storage materials: masonry or water. In each section there are two sets of details illustrating the major construction type options. Variations that highlight alternate construction methods and the use of materials other than those shown in the basic details are found on the subsequent pages. Following the variations are the construction notes referenced from the details. The notes provide guidelines, troubleshooting tips, and other information useful in building a thermal storage wall.

In the first section, masonry thermal storage wall details, several pages are added after the notes suggesting masonry material substitutions. These material alternates can be substituted for the storage material shown on the first page of the section.

Masonry

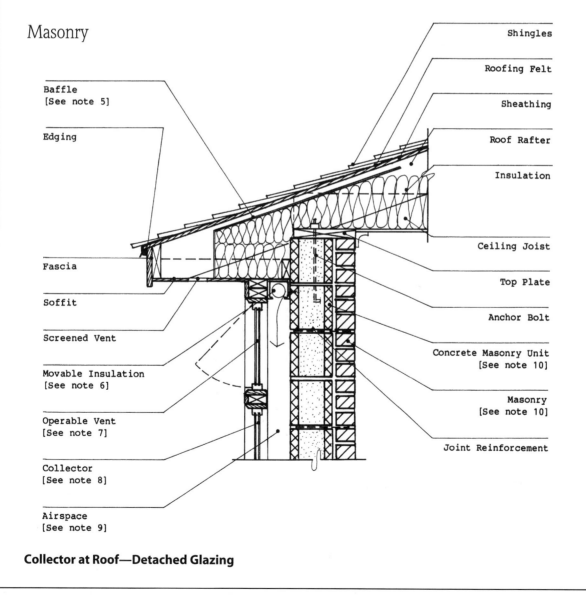

Collector at Roof—Detached Glazing

THERMAL STORAGE WALL DETAILS

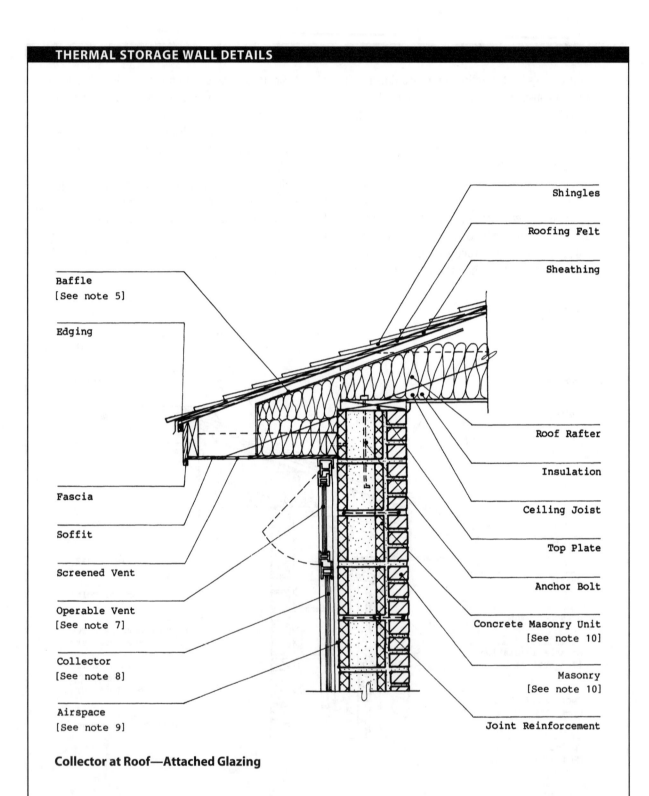

Baffle
[See note 5]

Edging

Fascia

Soffit

Screened Vent

Operable Vent
[See note 7]

Collector
[See note 8]

Airspace
[See note 9]

Shingles

Roofing Felt

Sheathing

Roof Rafter

Insulation

Ceiling Joist

Top Plate

Anchor Bolt

Concrete Masonry Unit
[See note 10]

Masonry
[See note 10]

Joint Reinforcement

Collector at Roof—Attached Glazing

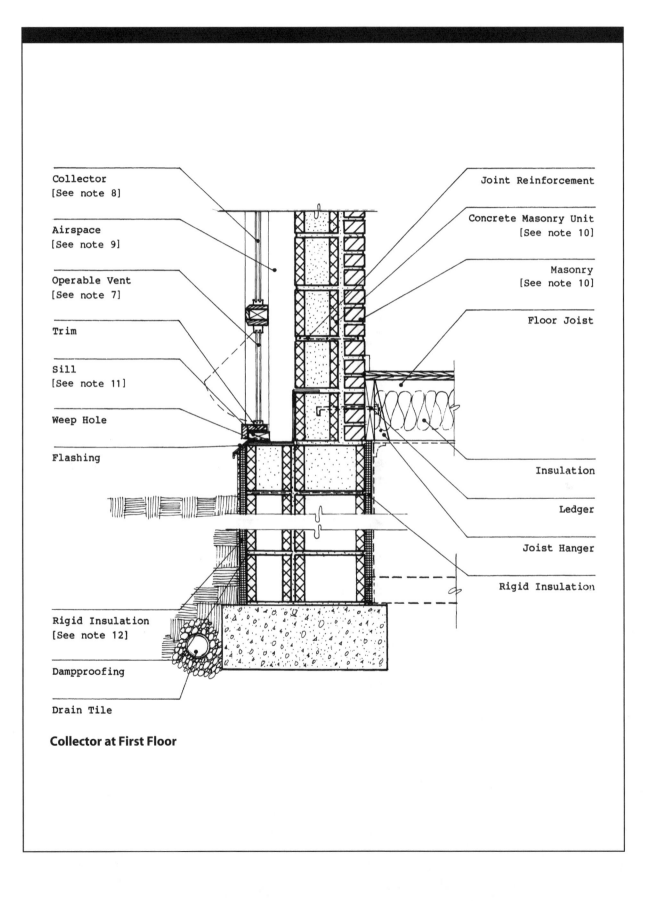

Collector
[See note 8]

Airspace
[See note 9]

Operable Vent
[See note 7]

Trim

Sill
[See note 11]

Weep Hole

Flashing

Rigid Insulation
[See note 12]

Dampproofing

Drain Tile

Joint Reinforcement

Concrete Masonry Unit
[See note 10]

Masonry
[See note 10]

Floor Joist

Insulation

Ledger

Joist Hanger

Rigid Insulation

Collector at First Floor

THERMAL STORAGE WALL DETAILS

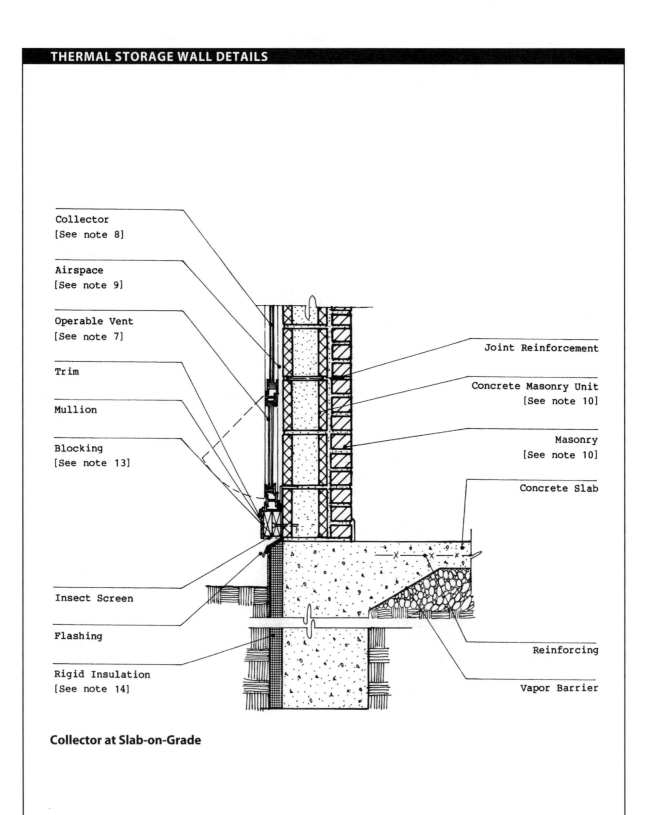

Collector
[See note 8]

Airspace
[See note 9]

Operable Vent
[See note 7]

Trim

Mullion

Blocking
[See note 13]

Insect Screen

Flashing

Rigid Insulation
[See note 14]

Joint Reinforcement

Concrete Masonry Unit
[See note 10]

Masonry
[See note 10]

Concrete Slab

Reinforcing

Vapor Barrier

Collector at Slab-on-Grade

Variations: Detached Glazing
(Masonry)

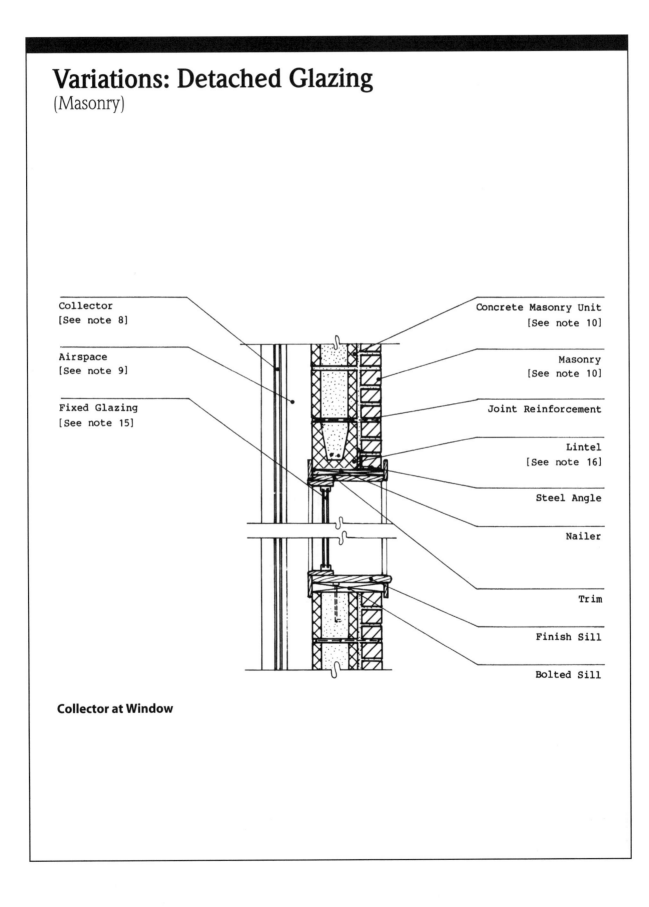

Collector
[See note 8]

Airspace
[See note 9]

Fixed Glazing
[See note 15]

Concrete Masonry Unit
[See note 10]

Masonry
[See note 10]

Joint Reinforcement

Lintel
[See note 16]

Steel Angle

Nailer

Trim

Finish Sill

Bolted Sill

Collector at Window

THERMAL STORAGE WALL DETAILS

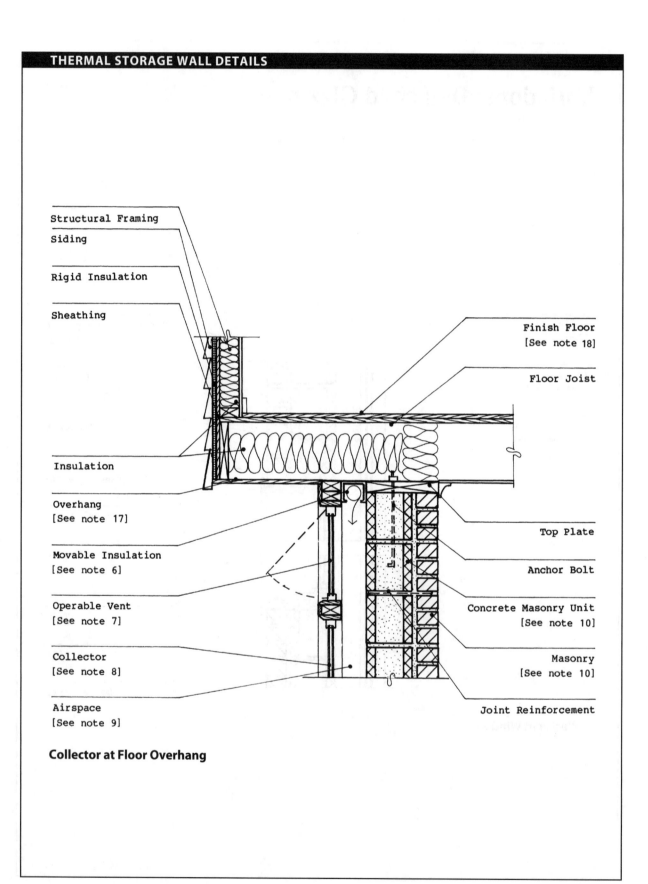

Structural Framing

Siding

Rigid Insulation

Sheathing

Finish Floor
[See note 18]

Floor Joist

Insulation

Overhang
[See note 17]

Movable Insulation
[See note 6]

Top Plate

Operable Vent
[See note 7]

Anchor Bolt

Concrete Masonry Unit
[See note 10]

Collector
[See note 8]

Masonry
[See note 10]

Airspace
[See note 9]

Joint Reinforcement

Collector at Floor Overhang

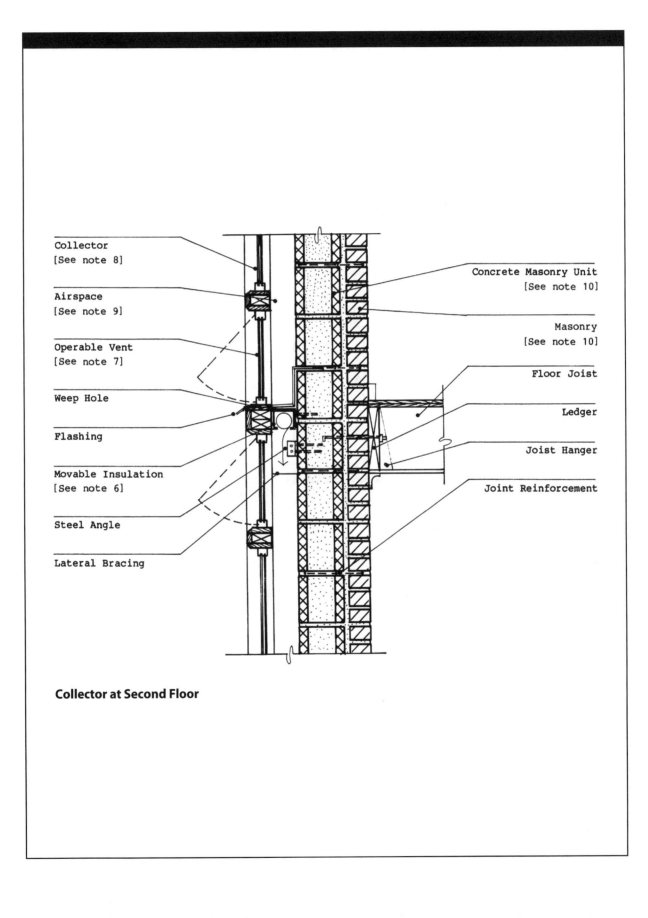

Collector
[See note 8]

Airspace
[See note 9]

Operable Vent
[See note 7]

Weep Hole

Flashing

Movable Insulation
[See note 6]

Steel Angle

Lateral Bracing

Concrete Masonry Unit
[See note 10]

Masonry
[See note 10]

Floor Joist

Ledger

Joist Hanger

Joint Reinforcement

Collector at Second Floor

THERMAL STORAGE WALL DETAILS

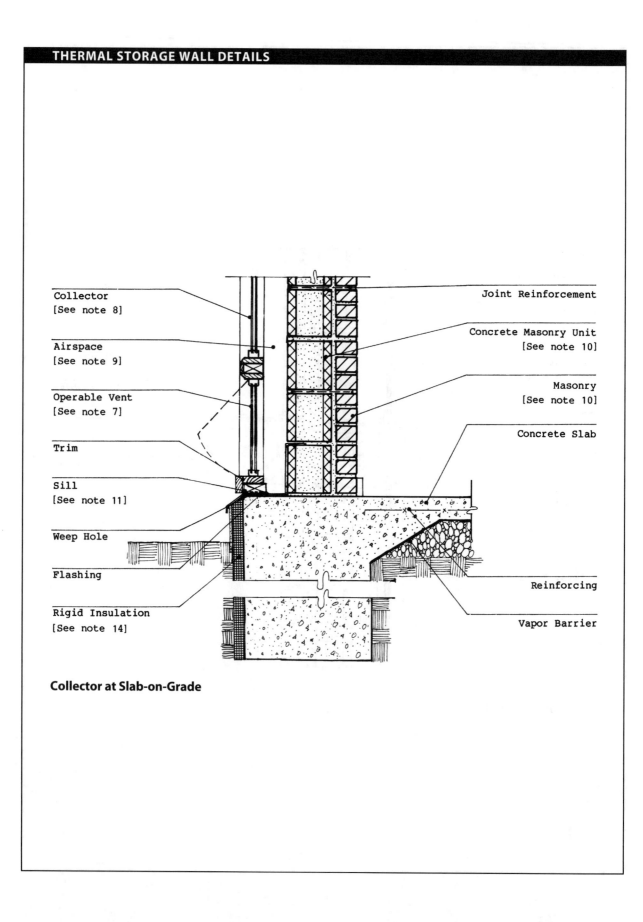

Collector
[See note 8]

Airspace
[See note 9]

Operable Vent
[See note 7]

Trim

Sill
[See note 11]

Weep Hole

Flashing

Rigid Insulation
[See note 14]

Joint Reinforcement

Concrete Masonry Unit
[See note 10]

Masonry
[See note 10]

Concrete Slab

Reinforcing

Vapor Barrier

Collector at Slab-on-Grade

Variations: Attached Glazing
(Masonry)

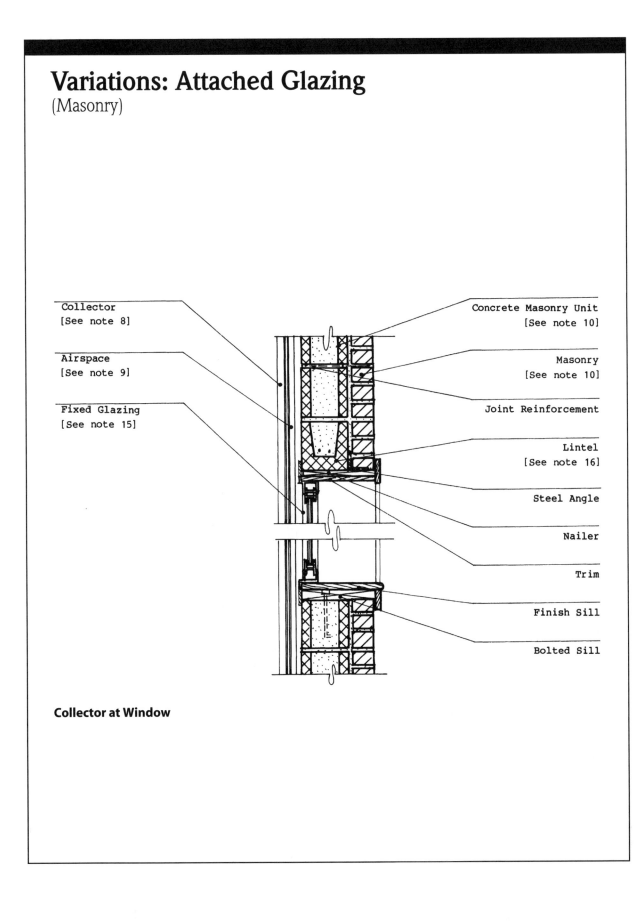

Collector
[See note 8]

Airspace
[See note 9]

Fixed Glazing
[See note 15]

Concrete Masonry Unit
[See note 10]

Masonry
[See note 10]

Joint Reinforcement

Lintel
[See note 16]

Steel Angle

Nailer

Trim

Finish Sill

Bolted Sill

Collector at Window

THERMAL STORAGE WALL DETAILS

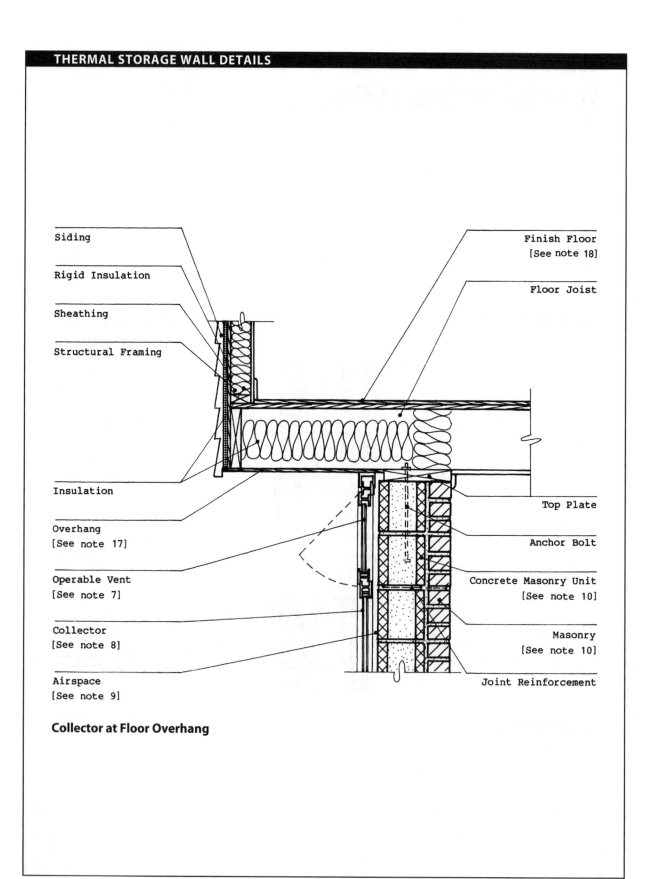

Siding

Rigid Insulation

Sheathing

Structural Framing

Insulation

Overhang
[See note 17]

Operable Vent
[See note 7]

Collector
[See note 8]

Airspace
[See note 9]

Finish Floor
[See note 18]

Floor Joist

Top Plate

Anchor Bolt

Concrete Masonry Unit
[See note 10]

Masonry
[See note 10]

Joint Reinforcement

Collector at Floor Overhang

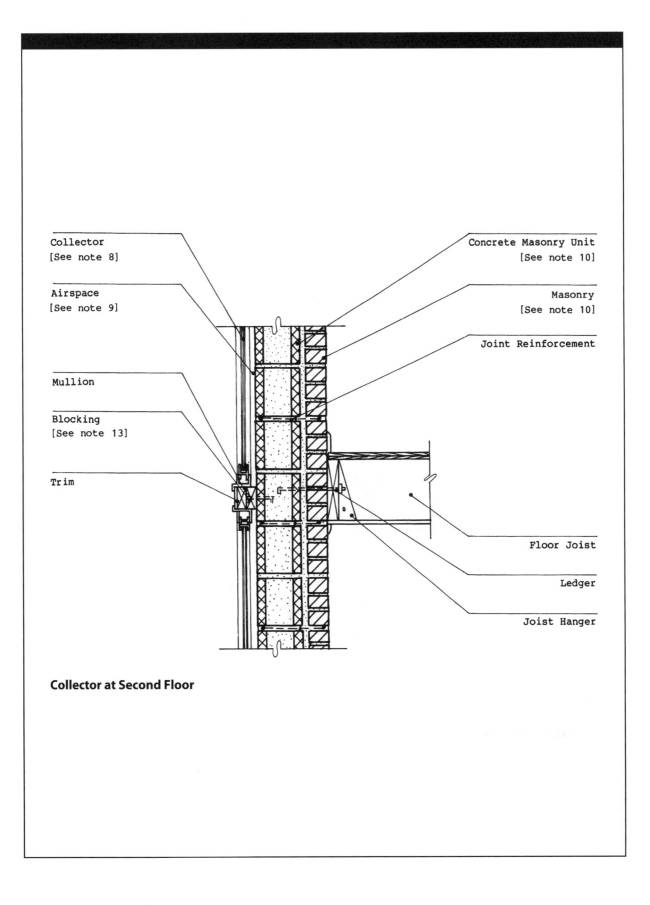

Collector
[See note 8]

Airspace
[See note 9]

Mullion

Blocking
[See note 13]

Trim

Concrete Masonry Unit
[See note 10]

Masonry
[See note 10]

Joint Reinforcement

Floor Joist

Ledger

Joist Hanger

Collector at Second Floor

THERMAL STORAGE WALL DETAILS

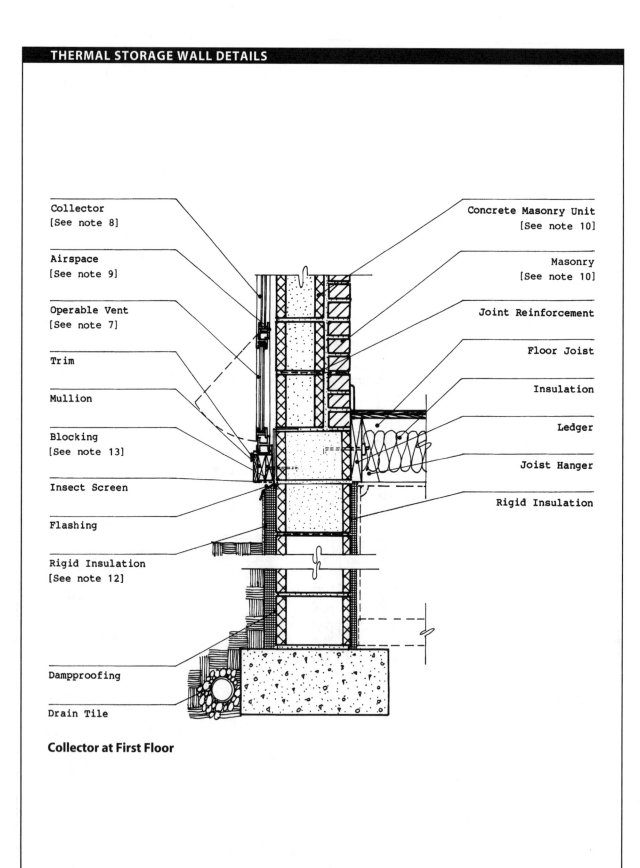

Collector
[See note 8]

Airspace
[See note 9]

Operable Vent
[See note 7]

Trim

Mullion

Blocking
[See note 13]

Insect Screen

Flashing

Rigid Insulation
[See note 12]

Dampproofing

Drain Tile

Concrete Masonry Unit
[See note 10]

Masonry
[See note 10]

Joint Reinforcement

Floor Joist

Insulation

Ledger

Joist Hanger

Rigid Insulation

Collector at First Floor

Notes
(Wood Framing with Masonry)

GENERAL NOTES

1. All footings must bear on undisturbed soil. Adjust footing size, reinforcing, and depth below grade as required by site conditions and/or local code. Where groundwater problems exist, provide sufficient granular fill to prevent water penetration at slab-on-grade.

2. Placement of reinforcing, metal ties, anchor bolts, flashing, and weep holes is to be determined by local building codes and/or accepted practice. Reinforcing in concrete slab is not recommended except where required by local conditions and/or code.

3. Insulation levels at foundation/slab and/or floor, and roof/ceiling, must meet or exceed requirements of local building and energy codes. The storage mass should not be insulated. In crawl space or basement construction, it is recommended that the thermal storage wall foundation be insulated on both sides to prevent losses to the outside and to the ground except where the basement or crawl space is heated. In these cases, insulation is not required on the inside.

4. Other roof configurations may be used at the builder's option. Consult local building codes for restrictions and special requirements concerning roof/wall connections, especially in seismic and/or high-wind areas. The roof/attic section should be vented to ensure proper performance of insulation. Vents may be located at sides of roof construction or at soffit and/or ridge vents. Provide gutters and downspouts as required. Overhang at collector should be sized to optimize solar gains during heating season and prevent overheating during cooling season (see "Control Rules of Thumb" in this chapter and "Control Components" in Chapter 7).

DETAIL NOTES

5. Provide baffles where necessary to maintain 1″ minimum airspace for venting attic.

6. Movable insulation can be provided to control nighttime and cloudy-day heat loss and to prevent overheating during the cooling season. Insulation may be installed within the airspace or placed on the exterior of the collector. In the latter case, insulating shutters or panels can be used. Care must be taken to ensure a tight fit between the insulation and the collector to reduce heat loss at the shutter or panel edges. When provided within the airspace, care must be taken to ensure adequate space for proper installation and operation. Where upper and lower portions of the thermal storage wall are separated, movable insulation must be installed in each section. Note that the use of movable insulation can generally be avoided by specifying high-performance glazings and frames for the collector. (For further information, see "Control Components" in Chapter 7.)

7. Portions of the collector should be operable to allow venting of the thermal storage wall during periods of excessive heat gain. Awning-type or other operable windows may be specified and should be equipped with demountable insect screens that can be removed during the heating season.

8. For optimum thermal performance, it is generally recommended that double glazing be provided, preferably a high-performance glazing using one or more of the following: low-e coatings, gas fill, or suspended plastic films. (See the "Collector Components" section in Chapter 7 for more information on glass or plastic collector materials.) The collector unit should be demountable or exter-

THERMAL STORAGE WALL DETAILS

nally operable to aid in maintenance and cleaning. The collector frame may be detached from the masonry wall and designed to support the glazing, glazing frame (if preframed), roof, and other related loads, or it may be attached to and supported by the masonry wall. Framing should be kept to a minimum, since it reduces the effective collector area and may cast shadows, both of which will affect the thermal performance of the wall. All structural framing and connections should be designed to conform with local building code restrictions and/or accepted practice. Frames should be continuous at edges. 2x framing members bolted to the masonry wall can serve as spacers, ensuring adequate airspace. They should be discontinuous, allowing for free circulation of air behind the collector.

9. It is generally recommended that the airspace between the glazing and the storage mass be a minimum of ¾″ and a maximum of 6″ to avoid excessive heat loss.

10. Brick or concrete brick, or architectural concrete masonry units, such as split, slump, fluted, scored, or recessed blocks, may be used for facing. The concrete masonry backup unit must be solid, or hollow with grout-filled cores. (For information on finishes, material variations, and thermal performance characteristics, see "Storage" in this chapter and "Storage Components" in Chapter 7.)

11. Sill can be wood or masonry at the builder's option, although wood is generally recommended for the collector frame. Where applicable, lumber should be pressure-treated.

12. It is recommended that the thermal storage wall foundation be insulated on both sides to prevent heat losses to the outside. In heated basements and heated crawl spaces, insulation is not required on the inside. Insulation levels on both sides should be equal and should meet code requirements for foundation insulation. Insulation must be protected where exposed outside above grade. Cement plaster over wire lath or other methods may be employed. Where dampproofing is used, allow for complete curing before applying insulation. Consult the insulation manufacturer for recommended installation methods.

13. Blocking can be discontinuous to provide weep holes where required. It is recommended that insect screens be provided at weep holes.

14. Insulation must be protected where exposed outside above grade. Cement plaster or synthetic stucco over lath, or other methods, may be employed. Where dampproofing is used, allow for complete curing before applying insulation. Consult the insulation manufacturer for recommended installation methods.

15. Conventional windows for light, view, and/or direct gain may be incorporated into the thermal storage wall design (see "Collector Rules of Thumb" in Chapter 3).

16. Lintel may be bond beam, lintel, or standard concrete masonry units with depressed, cutout, or grooved webs, or precast concrete. Provide 6″ minimum bearing at each end. Reinforcing is to be designed for loading and clear span to conform with local building codes and/or accepted practice. Facing unit is supported by steel angle.

17. Overhang at collector should be sized to optimize solar gains during heating season and prevent overheating during cooling season. (For further information, see "Control Rules of Thumb" in this chapter and "Control Components" in Chapter 7.)

18. A direct gain system may be incorporated into upper-level design. (For further information on direct gain systems, see Chapter 3.)

Alternates
(Masonry)

Detached Glazing at Roof

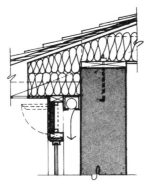

Opaque Insulated Exterior Vent

- The exterior vent of a thermal storage wall is frequently constructed of an opaque, rigid insulating material. This is justified by the fact that the collector directly underneath the roof overlay receives little sunlight.

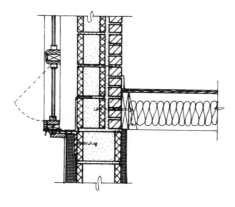

Steel Angle Glazing Support

Detached Glazing Support

- For detached glazing applications, the collector can be supported by a metal angle fastened directly into the masonry wall.

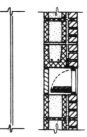

Interior Opaque Wall Vent

Trombe Wall Vent

- When the thermal storage wall is vented into the living space, it is referred to as a vented or Trombe wall. This detail illustrates one possible vent construction. The damper shown here prevents reverse thermocirculation. A hinged insulating panel isolates the airspace from the living space during the cooling season. Note that in this type of design, regular cleaning and maintenance of the collector and storage elements are crucial to maintaining proper indoor air quality.

THERMAL STORAGE WALL DETAILS

Wall Types
(Masonry)

Composite Wall

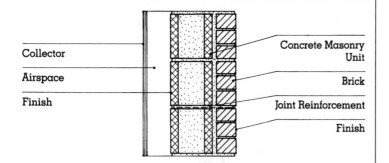

Collector
Airspace
Finish

Concrete Masonry Unit
Brick
Joint Reinforcement
Finish

GENERAL NOTES

- Thicknesses of individual wythes can vary. (For information on recommended composite wall thickness, see "Storage Rules of Thumb" in this chapter.)

- It is recommended that wythes be laid simultaneously. The first wythe laid is parged (back-plastered) with mortar not less than ⅜″ thick before the adjacent wythe is laid.

- Openings in masonry walls may be spanned by arches, steel angle lintels, or reinforced masonry lintels (constructed using standard and/or specially shaped masonry units, mortar, grout, and reinforcing steel). Specifications for all three should conform to local building code requirements, depending on the load, span, and type of wall construction.

AIRSPACE

- It is generally recommended that the airspace between the storage and collector components be a minimum of ¾″ and a maximum of 6″ to ensure optimum performance of the thermal storage wall system.

- If movable insulation is installed within the airspace, sufficient space should be provided to allow for proper installation, operation, and maintenance.

FINISH

- For optimum thermal performance, masonry exposed to solar radiation should be a dark color and should be left exposed wherever feasible. A slurry mix of Portland cement and sand can be used as a finish and will not affect the thermal performance of the wall. Particular colors can be specified from the masonry manufacturer, or the masonry/slurry can be stained or painted. (For further information on finishes and their effects on thermal performance, see "Storage" in this chapter and "Storage Components" in Chapter 7.)

- For optimum thermal performance, interior masonry finish should be left exposed wherever feasible. Certain finishes (e.g., plaster and gypsum board) can be acceptable if properly applied. Particular colors can also be specified from the manufacturer, or the masonry can be stained or painted. (For further information on finishes and their effect on thermal performance, see "Storage" in this chapter and "Storage Components" in Chapter 7.)

MASONRY

- Concrete block, concrete brick, or architectural facing units, such as split, slump, fluted, scored, or recessed block, may be used for thermal storage. To ensure optimum thermal performance, units must be solid, or hollow with grout-filled cores. (For further material information, see "Storage Components" in Chapter 7. For recommended thicknesses, see "Storage Rules of Thumb" in this chapter.)

- Any of the wide variety of standard bricks are suitable for thermal storage. To ensure proper thermal performance, bricks must be solid, or hollow with grout-filled cores. (For further material information, see "Storage Components" in Chapter 7. For recommended thicknesses, see "Storage Rules of Thumb" in this chapter.)

JOINT REINFORCEMENT

- Joint reinforcement should be provided to control cracking caused by thermal movement and shrinkage. Truss, ladder, or x-tie configurations are suitable and can be embedded in the wall at vertical intervals in conformance with local code requirements or industry recommendations. Splices in the reinforcing should be lapped a minimum of 6", and the width of the reinforcement should be 2" less than the nominal width of the storage wall.

Cavity Wall

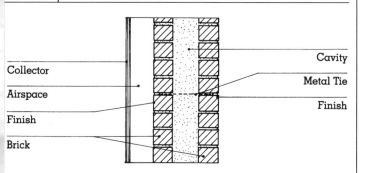

Collector
Airspace
Finish
Brick

Cavity
Metal Tie
Finish

AIRSPACE

- It is generally recommended that the airspace between the storage and collector components be a minimum of ¾" and a maximum of 6" to ensure optimum performance of the thermal storage wall system.
- If movable insulation is installed within the airspace, sufficient space should be provided to allow for proper installation, operation, and maintenance.

FINISH

- For optimum thermal performance, masonry exposed to solar radiation should be a dark color and should be left exposed wherever feasible. Particular colors can be specified from the manufacturer, or the masonry can be stained or painted. (For further information on finishes and their effect on thermal performance, see "Storage" in this chapter and "Storage Components" in Chapter 7.)
- For optimum thermal performance, interior masonry should be left exposed wherever feasible. Certain finishes (e.g., plaster and gypsum board) can be acceptable if properly applied. Particular colors can also be specified from the manufacturer, or the masonry can be painted. (For further information on finishes and their effect on thermal performance, see "Storage" in this chapter and "Storage Components" in Chapter 7.)

MASONRY

- Any of the wide variety of standard bricks, concrete bricks, or architectural facing units, such as split, slump, fluted, scored, or recessed blocks, are suitable for thermal storage. To ensure proper thermal performance, masonry must be solid, or hollow with grout-filled cores. (For further material information, see "Storage Components" in Chapter 7. For recommended thicknesses, see Storage Rules of Thumb in this chapter.)

CAVITY

- It is generally recommended that the cavity be 2" to 4½" in width. The cavity must be filled solid in order to ensure proper thermal performance. The cavity may be filled with grout or other suitable materials. A curing period of not less than three days is recommended before filling the cavity with grout. This is necessary to prevent "blowouts" caused by fluid pressure from the grout.

THERMAL STORAGE WALL DETAILS

METAL TIE

- Adjacent wythes must be tied together. Use of ³⁄₁₆″ corrosion-resistant steel ties or metal tie wire of equivalent stiffness, embedded in the horizontal mortar joints, is generally recommended. Use one tie for each 4½ sq. ft. of wall area. The maximum vertical distance between ties should not exceed 36″. Individual ties in alternate courses should be staggered.

- Continuous horizontal wall ties (joint reinforcement) of either truss or ladder type may be used instead of individual metal ties. Individual lengths of reinforcement should be lapped at least 6″ to provide continuity. Vertical spacing of joint reinforcement at 8″, 16″, or 24″ is recommended, depending on the length and height of wall and the number of openings.

- Metal ties or joint reinforcement should be of sufficient strength to resist "blowout" due to fluid pressure of grout when filling cavity.

Solid Concrete Masonry Unit

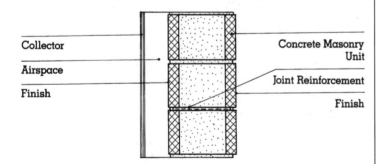

Collector

Airspace

Finish

Concrete Masonry Unit

Joint Reinforcement

Finish

GENERAL NOTES

- Single-wythe concrete masonry units may be built with conventional mortar joints or may be surface bonded. (For further information on surface bonding, see "Storage Components" in Chapter 7.)

AIRSPACE

- It is generally recommended that the airspace between the storage and collector components be a minimum of ¾″ and a maximum of 6″ to ensure optimum performance of the thermal storage wall system.

- If movable insulation is installed within the airspace, sufficient space should be provided to allow for proper installation, operation, and maintenance.

FINISH

- For optimum thermal performance, masonry exposed to solar radiation should be a dark color and should be left exposed wherever feasible. A slurry mix of Portland cement and sand can be used as a finish and will not affect the thermal performance of the wall. Particular colors can be specified from the masonry manufacturer, or the masonry/slurry can be stained or painted. (For further information on finishes and their effects on thermal performance, see "Storage" in this chapter and "Storage Components" in Chapter 7.)

CONCRETE MASONRY UNIT

- Concrete block, concrete brick, or architectural facing units, such as split, slump, fluted, scored, or recessed block, may be used for thermal storage. To ensure optimum thermal performance, units must be solid, or hollow with grout-filled cores. (For further material information, see "Storage Components" in Chapter 7. For recommended thicknesses, see "Storage Rules of Thumb" in this chapter.)

JOINT REINFORCEMENT

- Joint reinforcement should be provided to control cracking caused by thermal movement and shrinkage. Truss, ladder, or x-tie configurations are suitable and can be embedded in the wall at vertical intervals per local code requirements or industry recommendations. Splices in the reinforcing should be lapped a minimum of 6", and the width of the reinforcement should be 2" less than the nominal width of the storage wall.

Concrete

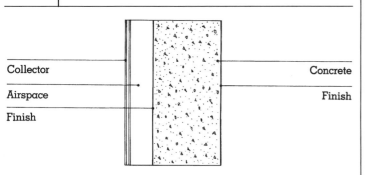

Collector
Airspace
Finish

Concrete
Finish

- The use of normal-weight concrete (140 to 150 lb) is generally recommended. Placement of formwork and pouring of concrete should follow standard practice and/or local building codes. (For further information, see "Storage Components" in Chapter 7. For recommended material thicknesses, see "Storage Rules of Thumb" in this chapter.)

FINISH

- For optimum performance, concrete exposed to solar radiation should be a dark color wherever feasible. Particular colors can be specified from the supplier, or the concrete can be stained or painted. (For further information on finishes and their effect on thermal performance, see "Storage" in this chapter and "Storage Components" in Chapter 7.)
- For optimum thermal performance, masonry exposed to solar radiation should be a dark color and left exposed wherever feasible. A slurry mix of Portland cement and sand can be used as a finish and will not affect the thermal performance of the wall. Particular colors can

be specified from the masonry manufacturer, or the masonry/slurry can be stained or painted. (For further information on finishes and their effects on thermal performance, see "Storage" in this chapter and "Storage Components" in Chapter 7.)

AIRSPACE

- It is generally recommended that the airspace between the storage and collector components be a minimum of ½" and a maximum of 6" to ensure optimum performance of the thermal storage wall system.
- If movable insulation is installed within the airspace, sufficient space should be provided to allow for proper installation, operation, and maintenance.

Brick

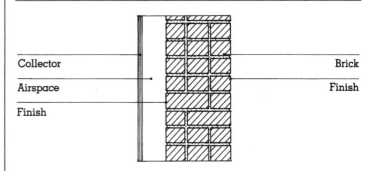

Collector
Airspace
Finish

Brick
Finish

GENERAL NOTES

- Structural bonding of the wall may be accomplished by overlapping (interlocking) masonry units. The maximum vertical and horizontal distance between headers is generally recommended to be 24", subject to local code restrictions.
- Openings in brick walls may be spanned by arches, steel angle lintels, or reinforced brick lintels (constructed using standard and/or specially shaped brick units, mortar, grout, and

THERMAL STORAGE WALL DETAILS

reinforcing steel). Specifications for all three should conform to the Brick Institute of America recommendations and local building code requirements, depending on load, span, and type of wall construction.

AIRSPACE

- It is generally recommended that the airspace between the storage and collector components be a minimum of ¾" and a maximum of 6" to ensure optimum performance of the thermal storage wall system.

- If movable insulation is installed within the airspace, sufficient space should be provided to allow for proper installation, operation, and maintenance.

FINISH

- For optimum thermal performance, masonry exposed to solar radiation should be a dark color and should be left exposed wherever feasible. A slurry mix of Portland cement and sand can be used as a finish and will not affect the thermal performance of the wall. Particular colors can be specified from the masonry manufacturer, or the masonry/slurry can be stained or painted. (For further information on finishes and their effects on thermal performance, see "Storage" in this chapter and "Storage Components" in Chapter 7.)

BRICK

- Any of the wide variety of standard bricks are suitable for thermal storage. To ensure proper thermal performance, bricks must be solid, or hollow with grout-filled cores. (For further material information, see "Storage Components" in Chapter 7. For recommended thicknesses, see "Storage Rules of Thumb" in this chapter.)

- Through-the-wall units may also be specified for thermal storage. Such units are generally cored and must be grout-filled to ensure proper performance.

Water

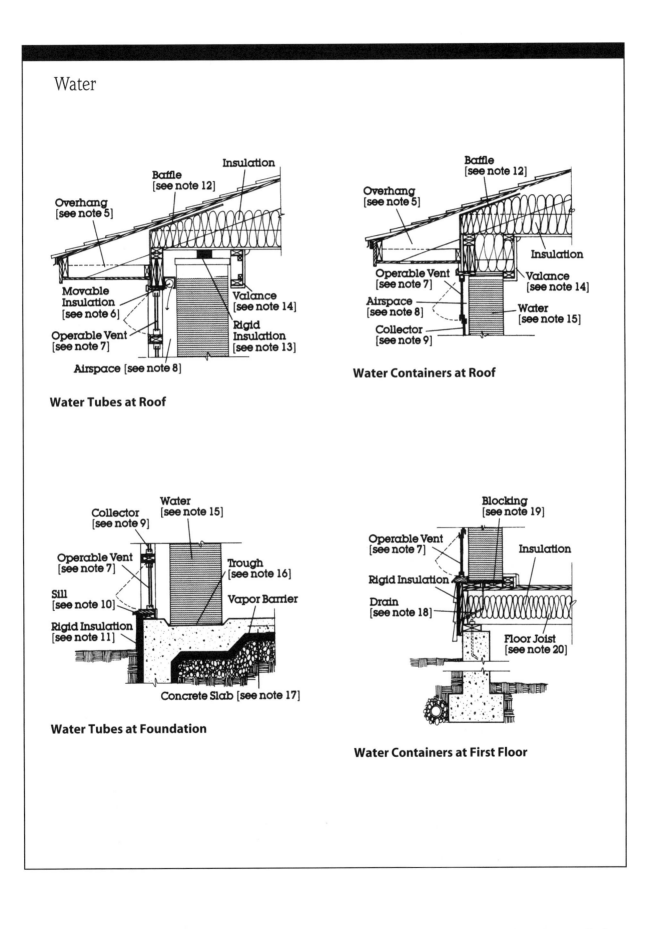

Water Tubes at Roof

Overhang [see note 5]
Baffle [see note 12]
Insulation
Movable Insulation [see note 6]
Valance [see note 14]
Operable Vent [see note 7]
Rigid Insulation [see note 13]
Airspace [see note 8]

Water Containers at Roof

Baffle [see note 12]
Overhang [see note 5]
Insulation
Operable Vent [see note 7]
Valance [see note 14]
Airspace [see note 8]
Water [see note 15]
Collector [see note 9]

Water Tubes at Foundation

Collector [see note 9]
Water [see note 15]
Operable Vent [see note 7]
Trough [see note 16]
Sill [see note 10]
Vapor Barrier
Rigid Insulation [see note 11]
Concrete Slab [see note 17]

Water Containers at First Floor

Blocking [see note 19]
Operable Vent [see note 7]
Insulation
Rigid Insulation
Drain [see note 18]
Floor Joist [see note 20]

THERMAL STORAGE WALL DETAILS

Notes
(Wood Frame with Water Storage)

GENERAL NOTES

1. All footings must bear on undisturbed soil. Adjust footing size, reinforcing, and depth below grade as required by site conditions and/or local code. Where groundwater problems exist, provide sufficient granular fill to prevent water penetration at slab-on-grade.

2. Placement of reinforcing, metal ties, anchor bolts, flashing, and weep holes is to be determined by local building codes and/or accepted practice. Reinforcing in concrete slab is not recommended except where required by local conditions and/or code.

3. Insulation levels at foundation/slab and/or floor, and roof/ceiling must meet or exceed requirements of local building and energy codes. The storage mass should not be insulated. In crawl space or basement construction, it is recommended that the thermal storage wall foundation be insulated on both sides to prevent losses to the outside and to the ground except where the basement or crawl space is heated. In these cases, insulation is not required on the inside.

4. Other roof configurations may be used at the builder's option. Consult local building codes for restrictions and special requirements concerning roof/wall connections, especially in seismic and/or high-wind areas. The roof/attic section should be vented to ensure proper performance of insulation. Vents may be located at sides of roof construction or at soffit and/or ridge vents. Provide gutters and downspouts as required.

DETAIL NOTES

5. Overhang at the collector should be sized to optimize solar gains during heating season and prevent overheating during heating season. (For further information, see "Control Rules of Thumb" in this chapter and "Control Components" in Chapter 7.)

6. Movable insulation can be provided to control nighttime and cloudy-day heat loss and to prevent overheating during the cooling season. Insulation may be installed within the airspace or placed on the exterior of the collector. In the latter case, insulating shutters or panels can be used. Care must be taken to ensure a tight fit between the insulation and the collector to reduce heat loss at the shutter or panel edges. When provided within the airspace, care must be taken to ensure adequate space for proper installation and operation. Where upper and lower portions of the thermal storage wall are separated, movable insulation must be installed in each section. Note that the use of movable insulation can generally be avoided by specifying high-performance glazings and frames for the collector. (For further information, see "Control Components" in Chapter 7.)

7. Portions of the collector should be operable to allow venting of the thermal storage wall during periods of excessive heat gain. Awning-type or other operable windows may be specified and should be equipped with demountable insect screens that can be removed during the heating season.

8. It is generally recommended that the airspace between the glazing and the storage mass be a minimum of ¾" and a maximum of 6" to prevent excessive heat loss.

9. For optimum thermal performance, it is generally recommended that double glazing be provided, preferably a high-performance glazing using one or more of the following: low-e coatings, gas fill, or suspended plastic

films. (See the "Collector Components" section in Chapter 7 for more information on glass or plastic collector materials.) The collector unit should be demountable or externally operable to aid in maintenance and cleaning. The collector frame may be detached from the wall and designed to support the glazing, glazing frame (if preframed), roof, and other related loads, or it may be attached to and supported by the wall system. Framing should be kept to a minimum, since it reduces the effective collector area and may cast shadows, both of which will affect the thermal performance of the wall. All structural framing and connections shall be designed to conform with local building code restrictions and/or accepted practice. Frames should be continuous at edges. 2x framing members bolted to the wall assembly can serve as spacers, ensuring adequate airspace, and should be discontinuous, allowing for free circulation of air behind the collector.

10. Continuous sill sealer is recommended to provide protection against infiltration.

11. It is recommended that the thermal storage wall foundation be insulated on both sides to prevent heat losses to the outside. In heated basements and heated crawl spaces, insulation is not required on the inside. Insulation levels on both sides should be equal and should meet code requirements for foundation insulation. Insulation must be protected where exposed outside above grade. Cement plaster over wire lath or other methods may be employed. Where dampproofing is used, allow for complete curing before applying insulation. Consult insulation manufacturer for recommended installation methods.

12. Provide baffles where necessary to maintain 1″ minimum airspace for venting the attic.

13. The airspace in a thermal storage wall system must be thermally isolated from the adjacent living spaces for optimum performance. Blocking made of rigid insulation serves to provide such isolation and also may provide some lateral bracing for water storage tubes.

14. It is recommended that freestanding water storage containers be braced against lateral movement. Bracing may be in the form of a framed valance.

15. Water, stored in appropriate containers, is an effective material for use in thermal storage wall systems. Suitable containers include fiberglass tubes, polyethylene or steel drums, and metal culverts. Care should be taken to ensure that steel and metal containers are lined with corrosion-resistant materials. In all cases, water should be treated with algae-retardant chemicals. (For further information on the use of water as thermal storage, including descriptions of appropriate containers, see "Storage Components" in Chapter 7.)

16. Troughs should be provided as a precaution against leakage of water from containers or from condensation. Troughs should be formed of corrosion-resistant materials attached or set into the supporting floor system, in order to provide added lateral bracing at the base of the container. Troughs may be designed for a single container or a row of containers. It is generally recommended that each trough be provided with a slight slope of the base to a central drain that is tied to the main plumbing system of the building or other drainage system.

17. Concrete slab should be thickened to take the additional weight of the water containers. Consult local codes for requirements.

18. PVC drains should be provided to eliminate water from drainage trough as required.

19. Blocking is provided beneath the trough to allow space for the drain.

20. Consideration must be given to the additional weight of the water containers. Consult structural design loading tables and local codes to determine suitable grade and spacing of joists, and grade and thickness of the subfloor.

TVA Solar House #2

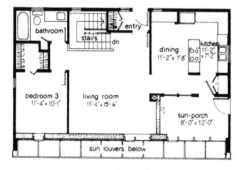

upper level

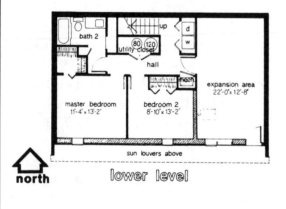

north

lower level

Designed to be built into a south-facing slope, the lower level of this 2,000-sq.-ft. house is nearly hidden from view on three sides. In addition to berming, the home is buffered on the north by a variety of circulation and service functions, including the air-lock front entry, the kitchen, and a bathroom. The house opens up to the south to reveal a two-story thermal storage wall punctured with operable windows for light and view, and an integrated second-floor sun porch, which functions as an attached sunspace.

The thermal storage wall, constructed of grout-filled 12″ concrete blocks, is coated at its exterior with a dark-stained cement plaster to increase solar absorption. A light-colored plaster interior finish retains the thermal integrity of the wall. Operable insulated vents at the top and bottom of the collector frame provide ventilation of the airspace in the summer. Roof and first-floor south wall overhangs are dimensioned to allow the sun to strike the wall in winter and shade it in summer. Wing walls offer added protection against overheating.

The sun porch, with access to the kitchen and dining areas, occupies the southeast corner of the building. The interior concrete wall is directly heated by the winter sun in the morning and early afternoon hours.

Above the sun porch, a thermostatically controlled fan vents heated air through an insulated ceiling duct to remote interior spaces. To cool the sun porch in the summer, an insulated ceiling damper is opened. The attic space, in turn, is ventilated by a thermostatically controlled exhaust fan in the roof.

The home is well insulated, including 2″ of rigid insulation placed at the upper edge of the bermed foundation wall; 1″ minimum R-8 rigid waterproof insulation down to the footings; and R-30 batt insulation in the roof.

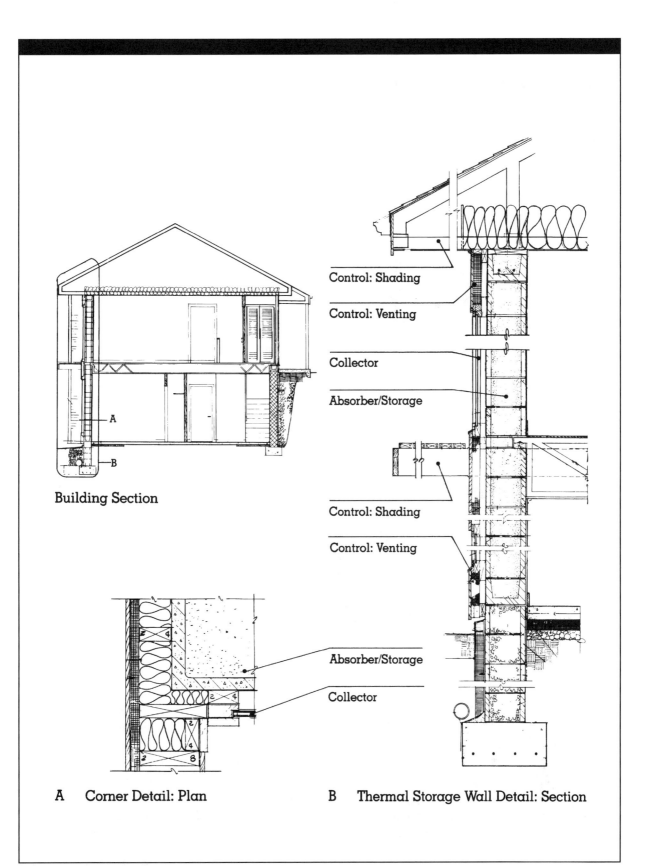

Building Section

Control: Shading

Control: Venting

Collector

Absorber/Storage

Control: Shading

Control: Venting

Absorber/Storage

Collector

A   Corner Detail: Plan

B   Thermal Storage Wall Detail: Section

THERMAL STORAGE WALL CASE STUDY

SSEC Louisville House

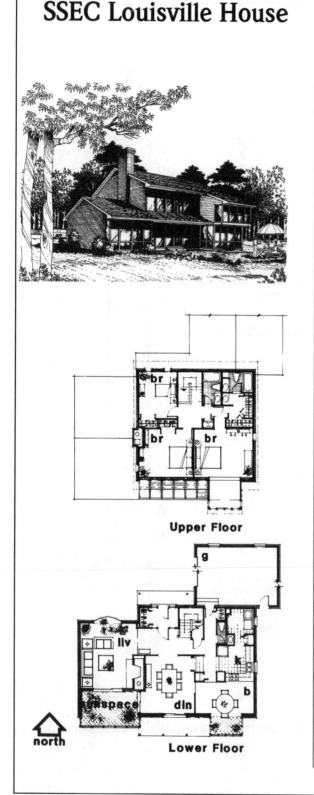

Upper Floor

Lower Floor

north

This 2,300-sq.-ft. two-story home designed for Louisville, Kentucky, is protected on the north by an air-lock entry and garage. The south façade integrates thermal storage wall, attached sunspace, and direct gain systems into a coherent, effective design that substantially reduces energy costs.

The two-story thermal storage wall is composed of 10″ concrete masonry blocks filled solid with grout, with the exterior painted black to increase solar absorption. The double-glazed collectors are wood framed and heavily caulked with a silicone sealant. A plaster interior surface creates an attractive and thermally effective wall finish.

The thermal storage wall is fully vented, providing three modes of operation. During the heating season, the interior vents at the top and bottom of each floor can be opened during the day to circulate heated air through the home, or closed to capture and store the heat in the thermal mass of the wall. In the cooling season, exterior vent panels in the collector serve to remove heat by circulating outside air in the airspace, cooling the wall. For ease of use, a pulley system enables remote operation of these panels from below.

A wooden trellis with angled slats and second-story overhang are both designed as sunscreens to permit the winter sun to strike the wall while preventing direct summer gain.

Flanking the thermal storage wall, two attached sunspaces collect and store heat while providing additional living space. Sliding glass doors allow heat exchange between the single-height solarium and both the living and dining rooms. A brick-veneered west wall and brick paver floor provide heat storage.

A double-height open sunspace creates a dramatic breakfast area and provides additional solar gain. Heat storage is provided by the interior masonry-veneered walls and tile floor. A roof overhang protects this space from overheating.

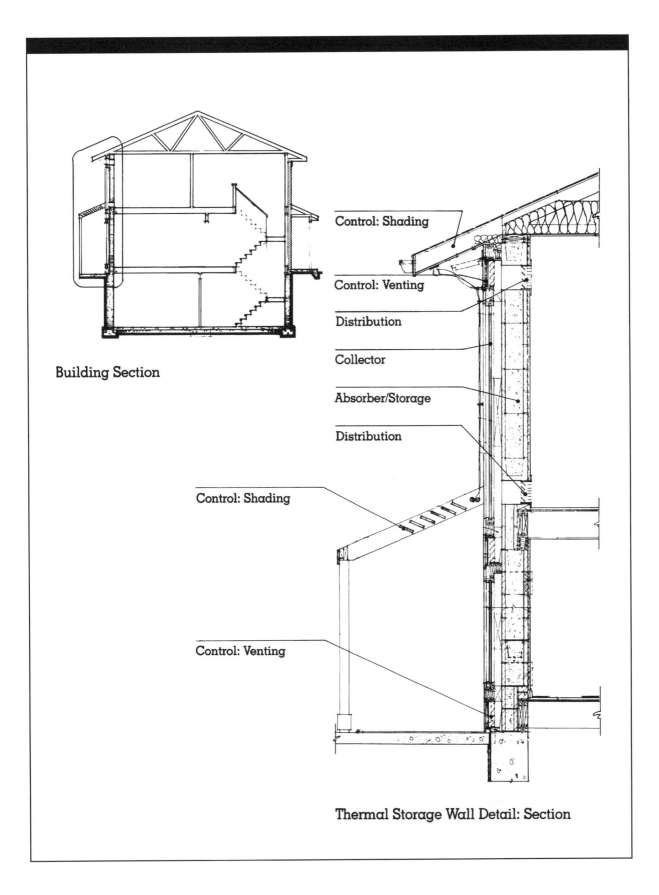

Building Section

Control: Shading

Control: Venting

Distribution

Collector

Absorber/Storage

Distribution

Control: Shading

Control: Venting

Thermal Storage Wall Detail: Section

THERMAL STORAGE WALL CASE STUDY

Pine Hall House

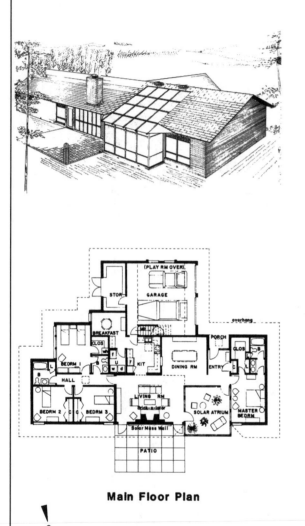

Main Floor Plan

The 2,000-sq.-ft. single-story Winston-Salem, North Carolina, house employs thermal storage wall and attached sunspace systems for passive solar heating. The floor plan is laid out with the garage protruding as a windbreak on the north. The recessed entry and service spaces buffer much of the north façade, allowing the living areas to be located on the south.

The thermal storage wall, which is constructed of three wythes of brick, is located at the center of the living room with glazed doors at each end for daylighting. The wall is vented, with openings at its base to draw cool room air into the airspace and at the top of the wall to deliver warm, solar-heated air into the living areas. Hinged exterior vents in the collector frame are opened in the cooling season to prevent overheating of the space and wall. An overhang protects the thermal storage wall from the direct summer sun.

The thermal storage wall doubles as a fireplace to take advantage of the heat-retaining qualities of the masonry. A brick-veneered interior wall between the kitchen and living room and the brick paver floor provide additional heat storage.

Adjacent to both the living room and main bedroom is a sunspace, or solar atrium. The roof and south wall of the sunspace are glazed, flooding the interior with light and solar heat. Interior walls of the sunspace are also glazed, isolating it from the other living spaces while preserving the openness of the plan. Its interior doors and windows can be opened to release collected heat to the rest of the home. Exterior shades placed over the glazing and two exhaust fans help keep the sunspace cool in the summer.

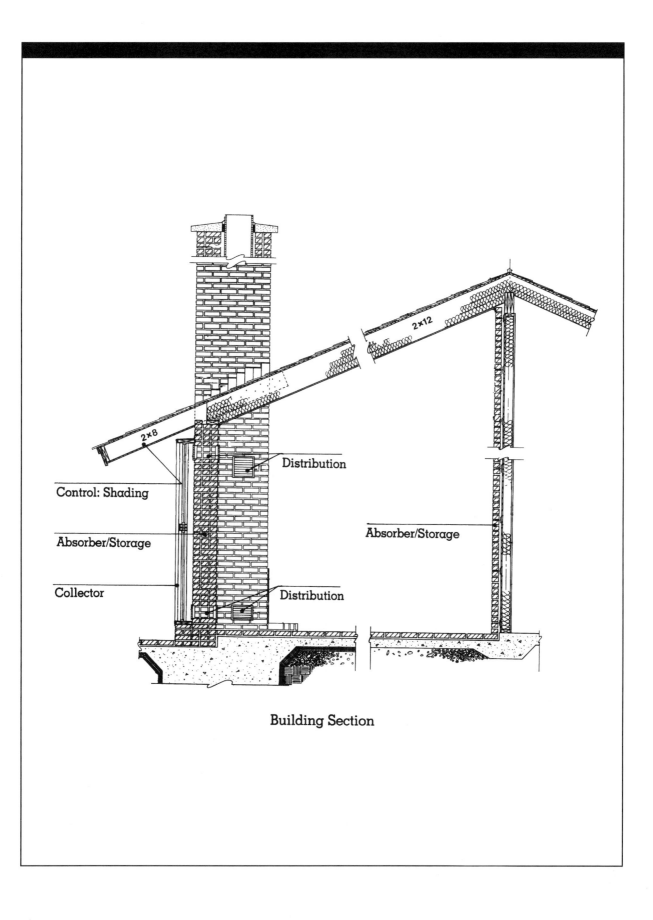

Building Section

THERMAL STORAGE WALL CASE STUDY

PCA Split-Level

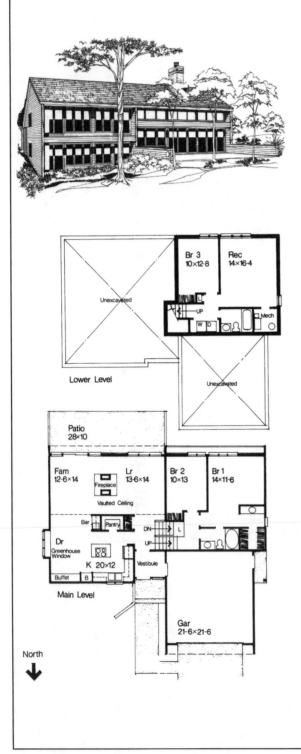

Lower Level

Patio
28×10

Fam
12-6×14

Lr
13-6×14

Fireplace

Vaulted Ceiling

Br 2
10×13

Br 1
14×11-6

Bar   Pantry

Dr
Greenhouse
Window

DN

UP

L

K 20×12

Vestibule

Buffet   B

Main Level

Gar
21-6×21-6

Br 3
10×12-8

Rec
14×16-4

Unexcavated

UP

Mech

W   D

Unexcavated

North

This 2,100-sq.-ft. split-level passive home is designed for a sloping site and benefits from being earth-sheltered on its north and east sides. On the south, concrete masonry unit panels alternate with expanses of operable windows, combining the advantages of the thermal storage wall and direct gain systems.

The partially bermed north entry façade is insulated with R-10 exterior foam board, reducing slab-edge heat losses. The kitchen, a heat-generating space, is ideally placed with the garage, air-lock entry, and other circulation and service areas along the north, buffering the home's major living spaces. Living spaces are concentrated on the southern side of the house with direct access to passive solar gain.

The entry-level concrete slab floor is finished with quarry tile for heat storage. Clerestory windows above the 1½-story living and family rooms permit winter sun to strike most of the floor surface area in these rooms. An energy-conserving fireplace aids in reducing the home's fuel costs.

The south-facing, two-story thermal storage wall is constructed of fully-grouted 8″ concrete blocks with 4″ concrete bricks as the interior finish. For greater absorption, the exterior face of these composite panels is painted black. Generous overhangs and wing walls effectively shade the south wall from summer sun and overheating.

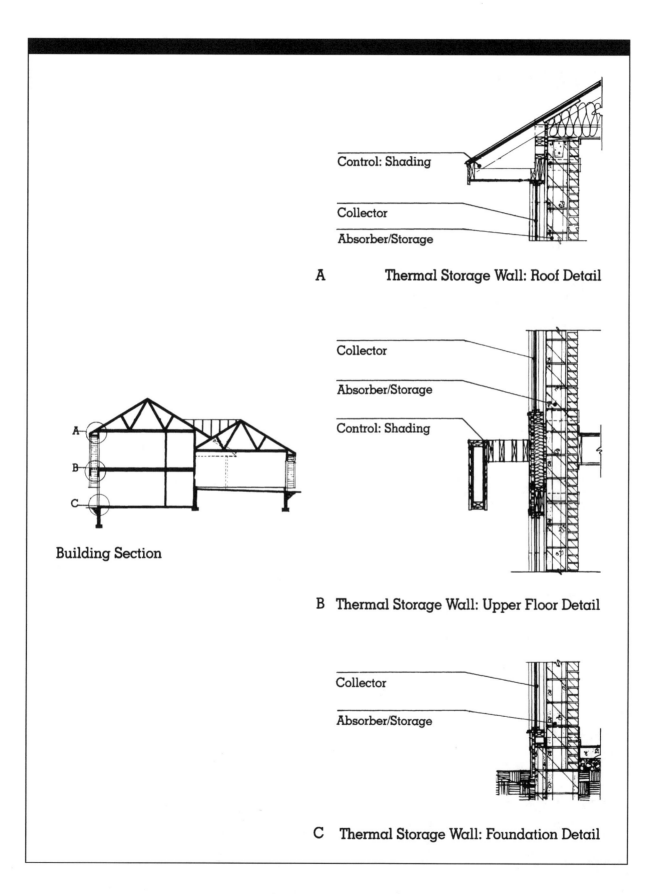

Control: Shading

Collector

Absorber/Storage

A   **Thermal Storage Wall: Roof Detail**

Collector

Absorber/Storage

Control: Shading

B   Thermal Storage Wall: Upper Floor Detail

Collector

Absorber/Storage

C   Thermal Storage Wall: Foundation Detail

Building Section

A

B

C

TVA Solar House #9

A two-story thermal storage wall provides passive solar heating for this 1,200-sq-ft traditional farm-style house. Designed for a flat or slightly sloping site, kitchen and other service and circulation spaces buffer the north. An optional garage can be constructed to the north, further protecting the home.

The south-facing thermal storage wall alternates with operable windows. The wall is designed to be constructed of 12″ heavyweight, grout-filled, hollow-core concrete blocks for effective heat storage.

During the summer, operable exterior insulated vents at the top and bottom of the collector frames allow outside air to enter the airspace, producing potential heat gain to the wall. Roof and intermediate-level overhangs screen the thermal storage wall from heat gain in summer, further reducing the home's cooling requirements. Wing walls offer additional protection from the west.

upper level 549 sf

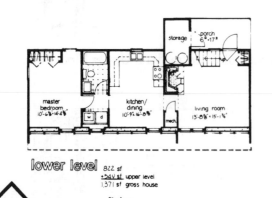

lower level 822 sf
+549 sf upper level
1,371 sf gross house

91 sf pc

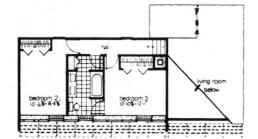

north

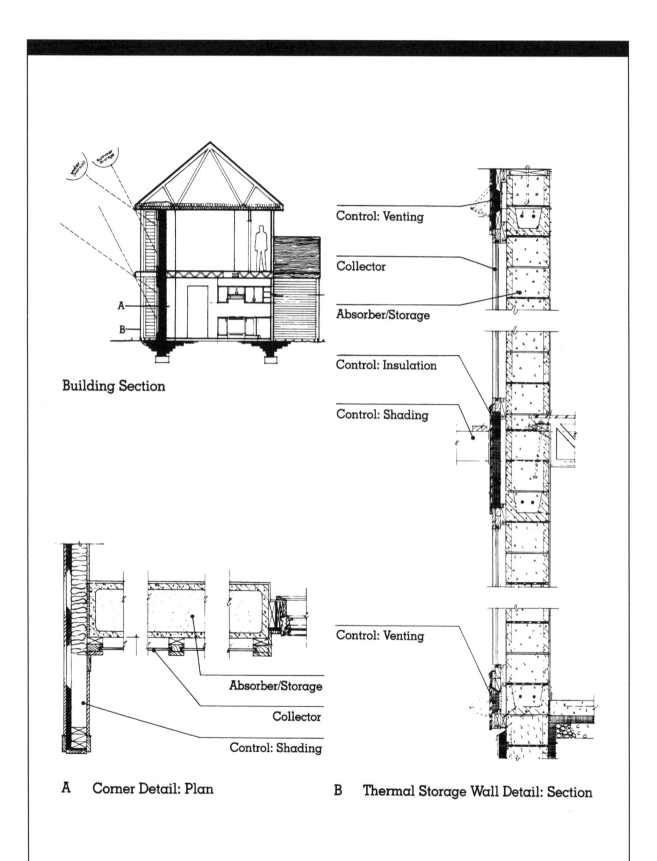

Building Section

Control: Venting

Collector

Absorber/Storage

Control: Insulation

Control: Shading

Control: Venting

Absorber/Storage

Collector

Control: Shading

A   Corner Detail: Plan

B   Thermal Storage Wall Detail: Section

General Shale House

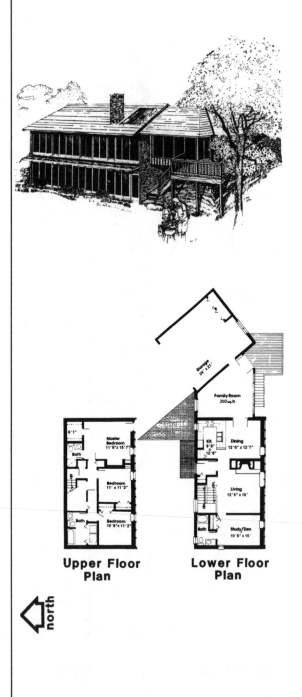

Upper Floor Plan

Lower Floor Plan

north

The 2,350-sq.-ft. house is designed for a site that slopes to the south. Partially earth-sheltered, the home is entered on the upper level from the north, with bedrooms beneath the entry level.

Circulation and service spaces, including an air-lock entry vestibule, provide buffers for the north side of the home. Passive solar heating is provided by thermal storage wall and direct gain systems, covering most of the south façade.

Windows incorporated into the brick and concrete masonry thermal storage wall provide direct gain heating and daylighting. Sunscreens overhang at both floors to protect the south glass from excessive summer heat gain.

An attached sunspace family room that opens onto a second-story deck connects the garage and house proper. The brick pavers laid on a concrete slab floor store solar heat in the winter, tempering the space throughout the day and night. R-5 insulating drapes effectively control nighttime heat losses, and a roof overhang controls summer heat gain.

R-30 ceiling and R-19 wall insulation levels are specified, completing a thermally tight building envelope. Supplementary heating is provided by a wood-burning fireplace.

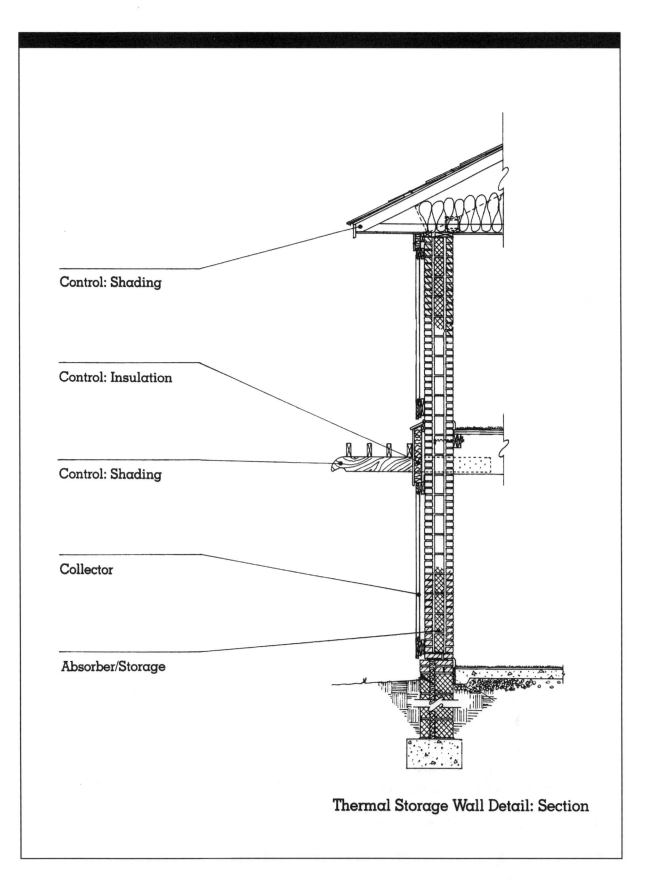

Control: Shading

Control: Insulation

Control: Shading

Collector

Absorber/Storage

Thermal Storage Wall Detail: Section

THERMAL STORAGE WALL CASE STUDY

PEG House #2

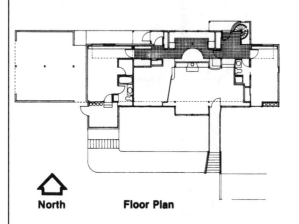

North   **Floor Plan**

The PEG House #2 house combines direct gain with earth-sheltered construction to significantly reduce the energy needed to heat its 2,900 sq. ft. of living space. The living spaces on the north side of the home receive direct sunlight through a band of clerestory windows. A small attached greenhouse provides additional solar gain.

The 260-sq-ft thermal storage wall is constructed using floor-to-ceiling, water-filled fiberglass cylinders behind Teflon-coated translucent glazing panels. Vents at the top and bottom of the wall allow heated air to circulate into the adjacent living spaces. Circulation is controlled by flaps constructed of polyethylene plastic sheets.

Outside, hinged insulated panels with a reflective surface increase incident light on the water wall when they are opened during the day. At night, when closed, their insulation reduces heat loss. The panels can be closed all summer, reducing unwanted heat gain. On the second floor, roll-up canvas shades afford similar protection.

A small greenhouse at the southwest corner of the home contains water storage and serves as a sunroom for the main bedroom. All 224 sq. ft. of the home's direct gain insulative glazing have been fitted with movable R-9 insulating shades to reduce losses. One layer of 6" batt insulation in the walls and two layers in the roof, as well as 2" of rigid polystyrene sheathing at the perimeter foundation wall, help create a thermally tight envelope.

Light entering the clerestory windows on the roof must also pass through the interior horizontal skylights before illuminating the living spaces. Movable reflective insulating shutters between the clerestories and skylights increase the solar gain. Along the hallway beneath the skylights, water-filled steel drums and a masonry floor provide needed thermal storage.

Project
Passive Solar Residence

Designer
Harrison Fraker, Architects
Princeton, New Jersey

Sponsor
Private Individual
Princeton, New Jersey

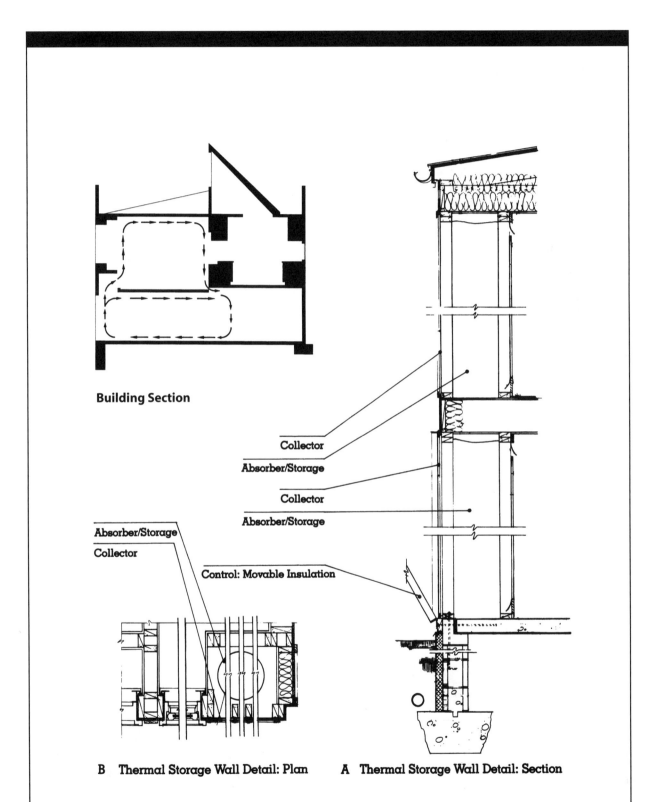

Building Section

Collector

Absorber/Storage

Collector

Absorber/Storage

Absorber/Storage

Collector

Control: Movable Insulation

B   Thermal Storage Wall Detail: Plan   **A   Thermal Storage Wall Detail: Section**

THERMAL STORAGE WALL CASE STUDY

SERI House #7

Second Floor Plan

Main Floor Plan

North

Two thermal storage walls flank an enclosed two-story sunspace with a mass storage wall beyond, providing passive solar heating to this 1,900-sq.-ft. home in Colorado. Coupled with a solar domestic home water system mounted on the roof, this solar design substantially reduces dependence on fossil fuels for heating.

Located at each end of the south wall, the thermal storage panels consist of 12″ heavyweight concrete blocks filled with grout and coated with a heat-resistant black exterior paint and an interior stucco finish. Exterior insulating panels with reflective interiors are raised by hand winches to reduce night heat losses. When lowered, their exposed reflective surfaces serve to increase effective collector gain.

The double-height sunspace, onto which all the living spaces face, is double-glazed, with storage provided in its brick and concrete wall construction and brick paver over 4″ concrete slab floor. Above the sunspace, an operable insulated ceiling turbine vents the sunspace to provide cooling during the summer.

A south-facing clerestory window provides solar gain directly to the north side of the second floor. Its cable-operated insulating shutter panel is coated with an aluminum surface that, when opened, reflects additional sunlight into the space.

Trellis, balcony, and roof overhangs screen the south wall from excessive solar gain in the summer, while insulating shutters, drapes, and shades provide extra thermal protection at night in the winter. Auxiliary heating needs are met by a wood-burning stove and a gas-fired forced-air furnace. Insulation levels of R-30 ceiling, R-19 wall, and R-8 foundation help keep the building envelope heat losses to a minimum.

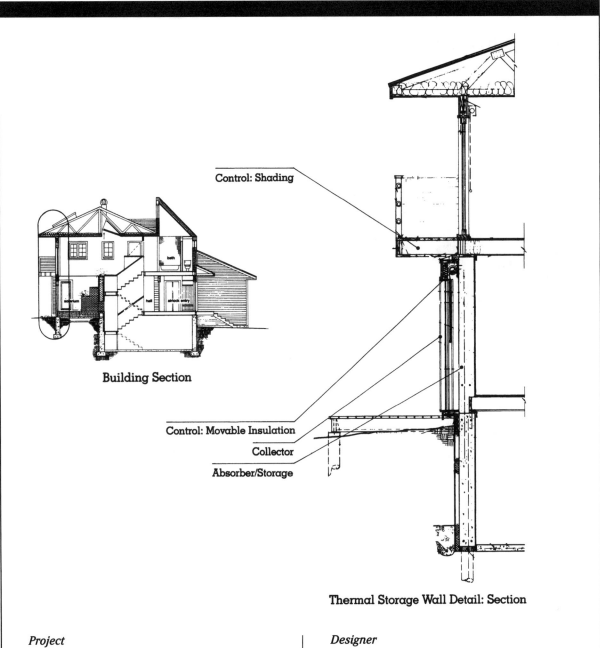

Control: Shading

Building Section

Control: Movable Insulation

Collector

Absorber/Storage

Thermal Storage Wall Detail: Section

Project
SERI House #7

Builder
John Kurowski
Kurowski Development Company
Westminster, Colorado

Designer
David Barrett, AIA
Sunflower Architects/Environmental Designers
Boulder, Colorado

Sponsor
Solar Energy Research Institute
Denver Metro Home Builders Association
Denver, Colorado

THERMAL STORAGE WALL CASE STUDY

Star Tannery House

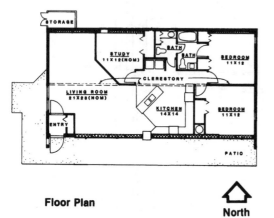

Floor Plan

North

Situated atop a knoll near Winchester, Virginia, the single-story 1,250-sq-ft Star Tannery house employs water thermal storage walls and direct gain for passive solar heating.

An air-lock vestibule at the southwest corner of the house provides entry into the living room through insulated metal doors. Virtually the entire south wall is constructed of the prefabricated water-wall units. A 2′ × 4′ partition wall, finished with gypsum board on the interior,

screens the water wall from view. Above, a row of unobstructed transom windows provides direct gain into the living spaces.

Sunlight strikes the prefabricated water containers, which, in turn, heats the air in the space between the containers and gypsum board. This heat is vented into the living space through vents at the top of the partition wall. Manually operated exterior vents exhaust collected heat to the outdoors during the cooling season.

A light-colored reflective concrete patio slab increases light incident on the water wall. An overhang fitted with movable louvers, landscapings, and wing walls provides shade during the summer.

At mid-roof, a continuous expanse of south-facing clerestory windows brings sunlight into the north side of the home. Another overhang above shades these windows from direct gain in the summer. Light passing through the clerestories strikes the dark-painted 4″ brick placed on the inside of the north wall.

Building envelope heat losses are reduced by R-19 wall and R-30 ceiling insulation levels and 2″ of closed-cell insulation wrapping the foundation wall. A propane-fueled, forced-air furnace supplies backup heating as needed.

Project
Star Tannery House

Builder
Wayne Holt
Holt Brothers Construction
Strasburg, Virginia

Designer
Tim Maloney
One Design, Inc.
Winchester, Virginia

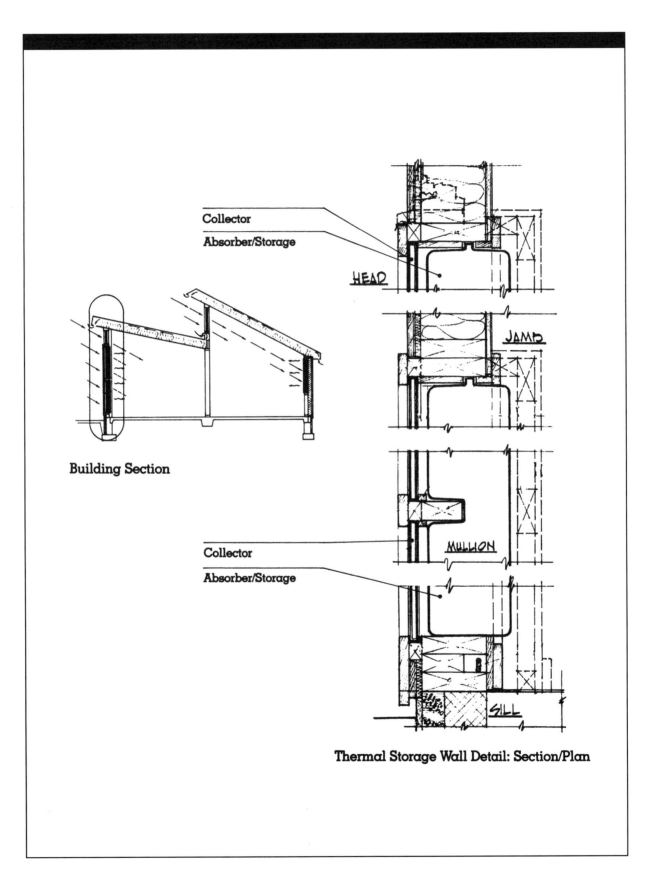

Collector

Absorber/Storage

HEAD

JAMB

MULLION

Collector

Absorber/Storage

SILL

Building Section

Thermal Storage Wall Detail: Section/Plan

5

ATTACHED SUNSPACE

Design Overview

Attached sunspaces are designed to be used primarily for heating and are effective in areas with moderate to severe winter climates. As the name implies, they are spaces designed for passive solar gain that are "attached" to the south side of a building. Such spaces often serve as working greenhouses. In these cases, they are referred to as attached greenhouses or solar greenhouses, to distinguish them from the standard nonsolar varieties that are generally not as well constructed and detailed (see Figure 5.1).

A sunspace can project from the house, or the house can be designed to "wrap around" the sunspace and partially enclose it. The latter configuration has the advantages of: (1) reducing heat losses from the sunspace; (2) transferring heat easily to a greater area of the surrounding house; and (3) allowing for the inclusion of a larger amount of thermal storage material than is possible in a projecting sunspace.

Whether they project from the house or are enclosed by it, attached sunspaces can have two basic floor configurations. In the first and most common, the sunspace floor is level with, or only slightly below or above, the adjacent living area. In the second, the so-called pit sunspace, the floor level is located below the frost line and thus significantly below the floor of the adjacent living spaces. The pit variety has the advantage of increased headroom and of reduced floor and perimeter heat losses due to the relatively constant temperatures of the surrounding earth. A pit sunspace can actually *gain* heat from the ground in winter if, as is often the case, the temperature in the sunspace is allowed to drop below the surrounding subsurface ground temperature. In these instances, the sunspace floor slab need not be insulated (see Figure 5.2).

The solar energy collected and absorbed by an attached sunspace is used to heat both the sunspace itself and the adjacent living areas. The ways in which this energy is stored and distributed form the basis for distinguishing four separate attached sunspace subsystems, which differ significantly from each other in terms of operation and construction: open wall, direct gain, air exchange, and thermal storage wall. Where appropriate in this chapter, each of these subsystems is treated separately, with the construction details organized to reflect this subsystem orientation.

There are two basic modes of operation for any attached sunspace subsystem. In the first, the sunspace serves as an extension of the living

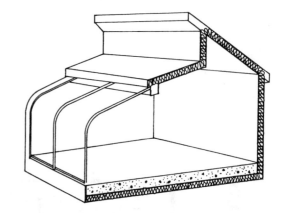

Figure 5.1

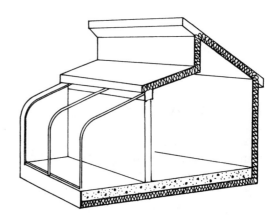

Figure 5.3

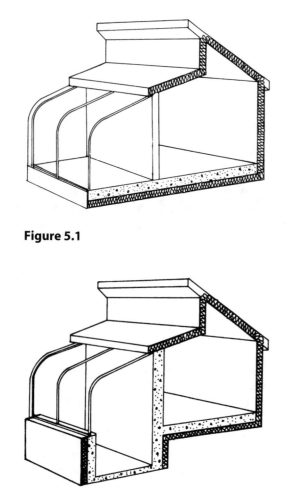

Figure 5.2

Figure 5.4

area. It is *not* thermally isolated from the living space, and its temperature is not allowed to fluctuate outside the comfort range. In most cases, this type of sunspace will require some form of auxiliary energy system to maintain comfortable temperatures (see Figure 5.3).

In the second mode, the sunspace is a separate, distinct area that *is* thermally isolated from the living space. It is not a direct extension of the living space, and its temperature can be allowed to fluctuate outside the comfort range. In this case, an auxiliary energy system is optional and, if present, is used only to heat the sunspace (see Figure 5.4).

Each of the four subsystems, in its pure form, operates in one or the other of these two modes. It should be noted, however, that, very often,

two or more systems are combined to function together. In such hybrid configurations, the actual mode of operation will depend on the particular subsystems involved and the way in which the space is intended to be used. This will, in turn, determine the amount and location of insulation (fixed and/or movable) employed and whether or not an auxiliary energy system is necessary.

Seasonal Operation—Heating

During the heating season, sunlight enters an attached sunspace through the south-facing collector (an expanse of glass or plastic), is absorbed by elements within the sunspace, and is converted to heat. This basic process is the same for all the attached sunspace subsystems. It is only in the next stages of operation (storage, distribution, and control) that these subsystems differ significantly from each other. The following descriptions summarize the operating characteristics for each of the subsystems during the heating season.

OPEN WALL SUBSYSTEM

In this subsystem, the sunspace opens directly to the living spaces and is basically an extension of these areas. Because of this openness, there is a direct, unimpeded transfer of warm air between the two spaces. While the sun is shining, heat is generated in the sunspace, and the resulting warm air moves freely to the adjacent living spaces. Some of this heat is also stored in storage components (e.g., concrete slab floor) located in the sunspace and/or living spaces (see Figure 5.5).

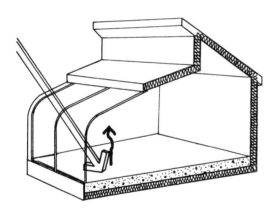

Figure 5.5

This subsystem, unlike the other three that follow, is essentially an extension of the living area, and its temperature is maintained at the same level as that of the other living spaces. The provision of storage material in the open wall sunspace will help dampen temperature fluctuations, but the sunspace in this subsystem will still need to be heated by conventional heating equipment at night and during prolonged periods of cloudy weather. At these times, the direction of heat transfer is reversed, and the sunspace will receive heat from the adjacent living area, as well as from the storage components located in the sunspace itself (see Figure 5.6).

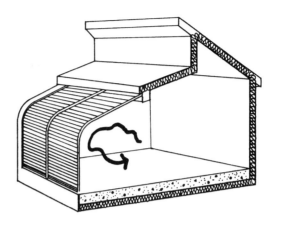

Figure 5.6

In order to prevent excessive loss of this heat, it is recommended that high-performance glazings be used. In mild to moderate climates, double-pane low-e glass would be typical. In colder climates, low-e glass with a gas-filled void (argon or krypton) might be justified. In extreme climates, the use of glazing with suspended films, or the addition of movable insulation, might be warranted. The sunspace floor will also need to be insulated to the same level as the standard living-space floor.

DIRECT GAIN SUBSYSTEM

Although this subsystem is similar to the open wall system in construction, it is generally operated as an isolated space and is typically not provided with backup heating from an auxiliary energy system. The open connection between the sunspace and the living areas is replaced by a glazed, shared wall. Because of the thermal separation that this wall provides, temperatures in the sunspace can be allowed to fluctuate without seriously affecting the amount of heat lost from the living space. However, it is still advisable to double-glaze (at minimum) the shared wall in severe climates (see Figure 5.7).

The use of movable insulation (such as insulating drapes or shades) located at the shared-wall glazing will further reduce heat losses from the living areas. This may not be cost-effective, however, because the sunspace, if properly designed, will act as a buffer between the outside air and the living areas, reducing the rate of heat loss.

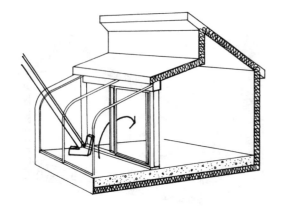

Figure 5.7

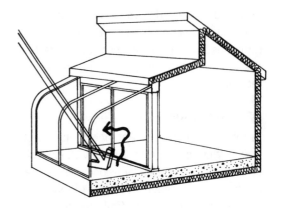

Figure 5.8

Movable insulation will be more effective, however, if placed on the sunspace collector. Such insulation, if correctly operated, will both enhance the sunspace's effectiveness as a heat generator and prolong the period over which comfortable temperatures are maintained in the sunspace. The use of high-performance glazings at both the sunspace collector and the shared wall can eliminate the need for movable insulation in all but the most extreme climates.

Heat generated in the sunspace can be used both to warm the sunspace itself and to supply heat to the adjacent living areas. When providing heat only for itself, the sunspace is acting simply as a climatic buffer for the adjacent living spaces. Some direct gain radiation does reach the living spaces through the glazed shared wall. However, if the glazed shared wall can be opened (e.g., patio doors), the sunspace can provide heated air, in addition to solar radiation, to the living spaces when it is required.

When this heat is no longer desired or when the sunspace is no longer receiving solar radiation, the homeowner can simply close the glazed wall (see Figure 5.8).

AIR EXCHANGE SUBSYSTEM

In this subsystem, the living areas and the sunspace are separated by an opaque frame wall containing operable vents. These vents allow for the transfer of heated air from the sunspace directly to the living areas during periods of heat gain. The vents, which are either manually or auto-

matically operated, can be closed off when heat is no longer wanted or when the sunspace temperature drops below that of the living space (see Figure 5.9).

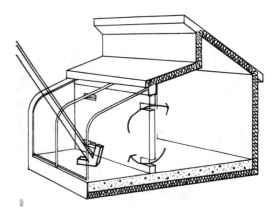

Figure 5.9

Closing the vents effectively turns the sunspace into a buffer zone, reducing the overall heat loss from the living spaces (see Figure 5.10).

Because the temperature difference is reduced, it may not be necessary to insulate this opaque shared wall. One advantage such insulation might have, however, is to reduce heat gain through the wall during the cooling season, especially if the wall receives direct solar radiation during this period.

THERMAL STORAGE WALL SUBSYSTEM

In this subsystem, the shared wall between the living areas and the sunspace is a mass wall that

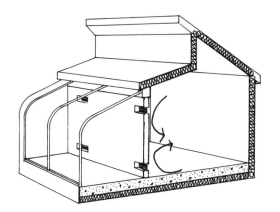

Figure 5.10

functions much like a standard thermal storage wall. In fact, it may be easiest to visualize this subsystem as simply a thermal storage wall with an enlarged airspace between the collector and storage components.

The wall absorbs incoming solar radiation and stores it. The resulting heat then slowly migrates through the wall to the adjacent living area. The wall reradiates the heat it has stored both to the living space and back into the sunspace itself. In doing so, it not only heats the living area but also helps to maintain a relatively constant temperature in the sunspace (see Figure 5.11).

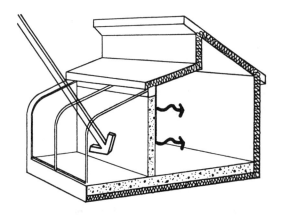

Figure 5.11

Because this sunspace temperature is higher than the surrounding outside air, the sunspace acts as a thermal buffer zone, reducing the amount of heat lost from the living space at night and during prolonged overcast periods. The use

of high-performance glazing or, in extreme climates, movable insulation placed at the collector will significantly improve the overall efficiency of the system. By reducing the amount of stored heat that escapes, higher temperatures will be maintained in the sunspace during the heating season. Due to these higher temperatures, the shared mass wall will have less of a tendency to transfer its heat into the sunspace and will thus provide a greater portion of its heat to the adjacent living areas (see Figure 5.12).

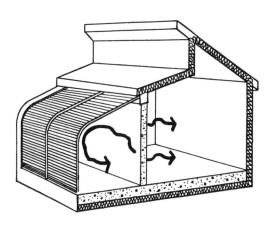

Figure 5.12

The storage wall can also function as a vented thermal storage wall. In this instance, the sunspace is actually a hybrid combination of the thermal storage wall and the air exchange subsystems (see Figure 5.13).

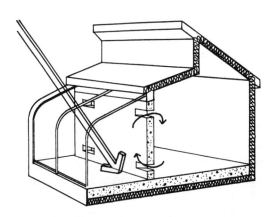

Figure 5.13

Seasonal Operation—Cooling

During the cooling season, the sunspace can easily overheat, adding to the cooling load on the auxiliary system. Therefore, the collector in any of the four subsystems should be well shaded to prevent unwanted heat gain. Deciduous trees and other types of vegetation can be used, as can building elements such as overhangs, louvers, and shades. If movable insulation has already been provided, it can serve a dual purpose and also act as a shading device.

The sunspace should also be properly vented. If possible, low vents, to admit cool air, should be located in the shade on the windward side of the sunspace, and high vents, to exhaust hot air, on the leeward side. These vents can either be operable glazing elements or form part of the frame. Gable vents on the east and west end walls are also possible. In order to reduce infiltration losses at the edges of these vents, it is preferable to have a few large vents serve the space rather than a series of smaller ones with a larger aggregate edge area (see Figure 5.14).

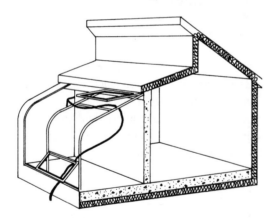

Figure 5.14

If properly managed, the storage mass within the sunspace can also help cool it. Placing vents to allow cool night air to pass over the storage mass will cause the mass to become cooler. If properly shaded from the sun, this cooler mass will absorb heat generated in the sunspace during the day, effectively cooling it and, depending on the subsystem involved, the adjacent living areas as well (see

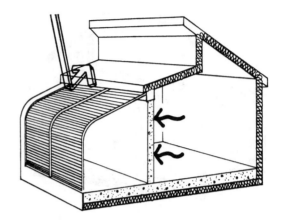

Figure 5.15

Figure 5.15). The mass will then dissipate this collected heat to the night air, completing the diurnal cycle. Openings placed between the sunspace and the adjacent living spaces will enhance the cooling effect of the storage mass by inducing cooled air to circulate through the rest of the home.

The majority of sunspace configurations built consist of hybrid combinations of the subsystems described above. It is not uncommon for a thermal storage wall to include operable vents to allow for direct transfer of heated air, nor for the opaque shared wall in a remote storage subsystem to include windows that allow for some direct gain heating in the living areas. As noted earlier, the thermal performance of such hybrids is, in general, very difficult to quantify. It should be assumed, however, that combining subsystems will not result in significant decreases in overall thermal performance if the general rules of thumb for attached sunspaces are followed.

Advantages

- The sunspace can be used for growing houseplants and/or food.
- The sunspace acts as a buffer zone to reduce heat loss from the adjacent living spaces.
- The sunspace can serve more than one function, including being an extension of the living space.
- The sunspace can become an aesthetic asset to a house.

Disadvantages

- Thermal performance can vary significantly from one design to another, and predicting performance accurately is difficult.

- Construction of the sunspace with high-performance glazings, or with movable insulation, can be expensive.

- If used as a working greenhouse, certain characteristics, such as excess humidity, odors, control of insects, provision for running water, and drainage must be accommodated in the design.

Collectors

As in all passive solar applications, the purpose of the attached sunspace collector is to admit and trap solar energy. Although often perceived as a net energy loser, the large expanse of south-facing glazing in a well-designed sunspace collector actually gains much more heat than it loses, particularly when high-performance glazings are used. The collector component functions in the same way in each of the attached sunspace subsystems, and the design and materials information presented below applies to all four subsystems.

There is a wide variety of possible collector configurations. A large number of sunspaces are site-fabricated to meet specific, and often idiosyncratic, design specifications. The collectors for the majority of these site-built installations are framed in wood, whereas prefabricated, off-the-shelf collector units are usually framed in metal. Both systems have advantages and disadvantages.

Prefabricated systems are generally simple to erect, are relatively impermeable to the effects of weather, and require little maintenance. They can be expensive, and their dimensional modularity may inhibit design and system sizing flexibility. They may also be difficult to insulate in precisely the manner necessary to ensure maximum thermal performance. The metal frame collector system should be equipped with thermal breaks in the frame to reduce heat loss.

Site-built systems can be adapted to any particular design situation and can be insulated and

shaded to meet specific conditions. Unless carefully detailed, however, such systems are notorious for failing to maintain a tight seal against the weather. Special attention must be paid to caulking and sealing the glazing material, and periodic inspections should be made to ensure that the seals are still holding. Rough-sawn or green wood should be avoided in such applications in favor of kiln-dried lumber. Wood should also be treated to resist moisture damage. Copper naphthenate should be used in greenhouse applications, rather than creosote or pentachlorophenol, which give off fumes that are potentially harmful to vegetation. Regardless of the material, the collector frame should be painted a light color in order to reflect more light into the sunspace.

The most common sunspace collector material is glass; it is recommended that high-performance double glazing be used in applications where glass alone, not in combination with any other collector material, is used. For many prefabricated greenhouse manufacturers, double-pane low-e glazing is currently standard.

Materials other than glass, including various forms of fiberglass, acrylics, and polycarbonates, can be used. Each of these has its own advantages and disadvantages. Note, however, that most plastics can discolor, cloud, and degrade over time.

Each collector material can also be used in combination with any of the other materials to maximize the best qualities of each. For example, the roof of the sunspace might be constructed of corrugated fiberglass because of its ease of handling during construction, while the vertical portion might be glass to provide a view to the outside. Combinations and variations such as this should be considered for each individual application. The advantages of using a light-diffusing collector material to promote a balanced distribution of incoming solar energy should also be considered if storage mass is evenly distributed throughout the sunspace.

In general, the most thermally effective sunspace is one in which little or no glazing is placed on the roof. Sunspaces with completely opaque and insulated roofs, however, limit the penetration of sun into the sunspace (often inhibiting plant growth) and are difficult to find in prefabricated models. A sunspace with a partially glazed roof is an excellent compromise between utility and thermal effectiveness.

Usually, collector material on the east and west walls is thermally less efficient than glazing on the south. It is recommended that such walls be opaque and well insulated where possible, or that the house itself "wrap around" the sunspace on the east and west.

COLLECTOR RULES OF THUMB

Orientation

Extend the sunspace along the south wall of the building for the most efficient performance. Orientation can be up to 20° east or west of true south without significant loss in performance. East is generally preferred to allow morning sun to "wake up" the sunspace.

- *Sloped glazing:*   The angle of tilt for any sloped surface of the sunspace collector should be 45° to 60°. The tilt should be slightly flatter (nearer to 45°) in overcast or foggy areas, and slightly steeper (nearer to 60°) in mostly clear and sunny areas.

- *End walls:*   East and west walls of the sunspace should be opaque and well insulated.

"Wrapping" the main building around the sunspace is a good approach.

Sizing

Table 5.1 can be used to determine the collector size.

For example, for Madison, Wisconsin, at 43° NL with an average January temperature of 21.8°F (data available from local and/or national weather bureau), select the closest "Average Winter Outdoor Temperature" (20°F). Reading across the table, it is recommended that 0.9 to 1.5 sq. ft. of glazing be used per square foot of floor area. Because Madison is at a relatively high latitude, the upper end of this range should be employed, and a figure of 1.3 will be adequate. Thus, to heat a living space of 200 sq. ft., 260 sq. ft. of south-facing glazing will be required.

Storage

The four attached sunspace subsystems embody unique approaches to the problem of thermal storage, and each is treated separately below.

OPEN WALL SUBSYSTEM

In this subsystem, solar radiation is absorbed by and stored in the sunspace floor, in water containers placed within the sunspace, and, where applic-

Table 5.1

Average Winter Outdoor Temperature (Clear Day)*	Square Feet of Sunspace Glazing Needed for Each Square Foot of Floor Area**
COLD CLIMATES	
20°F	0.90–1.50
25°F	0.78–1.30
30°F	0.65–1.17
TEMPERATE CLIMATES	
35°F	0.53–0.90
40°F	0.42–0.69
45°F	0.33–0.53

* Temperatures listed are for December and January, usually the coldest months.

** Within each range choose a ratio according to your latitude. For southern latitudes (i.e., 35° NL) use the lower glazing to floor area ratios; for northern latitudes (i.e., 48° NL), use the higher ratios. For a poorly insulated sunspace or building, always use slightly more glazing.

able, in the opaque end walls if they are constructed of suitable materials (see Figure 5.16).

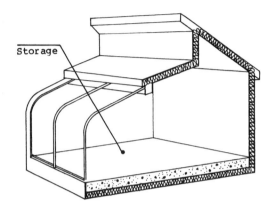

Figure 5.16

Storage elements can also be provided in the living areas and will prove very effective if sunlight can penetrate deeply enough into the living spaces to strike them directly. The majority of the heat reaching the living areas, however, will be in the form of warm air generated in the sunspace during the day.

The storage components in the sunspace and the adjacent living spaces can be made from any of a variety of high thermal storage capacity materials and should be as dark a color as possible to increase absorption of solar radiation.

DIRECT GAIN SUBSYSTEM

In this subsystem, the storage components are the same as in the open wall subsystem and function in a similar manner (see Figure 5.17).

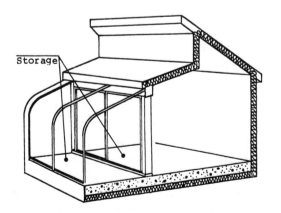

Figure 5.17

The chief difference is that the living area storage components, while still receiving direct solar radiation through the glazed shared wall, do not normally receive convected warm air from the sunspace. The heat collected and stored in the sunspace is available to the living areas only when the shared-wall glazing is opened.

At other times, when the glazing is closed, this heat is used to maintain warm temperatures in the otherwise unheated sunspace. In this mode of operation, the sunspace serves as a buffer zone, reducing heat losses from the adjacent living areas, thereby reducing overall fuel consumption.

In this subsystem, as in the open wall subsystem, the storage elements can be of the same materials and construction as those found in a direct gain system.

AIR EXCHANGE SUBSYSTEM

In this subsystem, the living areas are separated from the sunspace by an opaque shared wall and receive no direct solar radiation. Vents in this wall allow warm air generated in the sunspace to be convected into the living areas (see Figure 5.18).

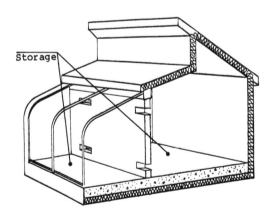

Figure 5.18

As in the other subsystems, storage mass located in the sunspace will absorb and store heat. When heat is required in the living spaces, the wall vents are opened and warm air is allowed to flow from the sunspace into the living areas. When the vents are closed, the stored heat is used to heat the sunspace itself, helping it to act as a thermal buffer, reducing heat losses from the adjacent living areas. Once again, the materials and construction techniques used in direct gain applications are appropriate for the air exchange sunspace storage components.

THERMAL STORAGE WALL SUBSYSTEM

This subsystem acts very much like a thermal storage wall with a much larger airspace between the storage wall and the collector. The mass wall separating the living areas from the sunspace is used to absorb and store solar radiation, which is, in turn, used to heat both the living areas and the sunspace itself. The wall can be built of any of the thermal storage wall materials discussed in Chapter 4, and will be constructed in much the same fashion (see Figure 5.19).

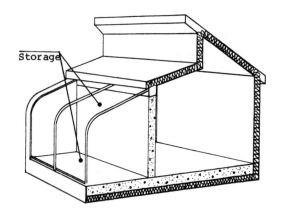

Storage

Figure 5.19

Whatever material is chosen, the sunspace side of the wall should be painted a dark color to increase absorption of incoming solar energy (see Table 7.4 in Chapter 7 for the absorptivities of various materials and colors). The interior surface can be painted or left unfinished. Finishes other than paint, however, will decrease the efficiency of the wall by restricting its ability to reradiate heat. Plaster and wallpaper will have little impact on thermal performance. Gypsum board can also be acceptable over masonry walls if it is attached directly to the wall (not on furring strips), and if care is taken during installation to apply a very thick coat of construction adhesive in order to

increase the thermal connection between the wall and the gypsum board. Finishes that are attached to the wall with furring strips will create an insulating airspace, significantly reducing the performance of the system.

The heat radiating from the storage wall back into the sunspace, along with heat stored in elements within the sunspace itself, will help maintain higher-than-ambient temperatures in this space. As in the other subsystems, these higher temperatures will help reduce heat losses from the adjacent living spaces.

STORAGE RULES OF THUMB

Floors (All Subsystems)

- *Thickness:* Standard slab thicknesses are usually appropriate. Consult "Storage Rules of Thumb" in Chapter 3.

Walls (Thermal Storage Wall Subsystem)

- *Thickness:* The recommended attached sunspace storage wall thickness is 8 to 18".

Vents (Air Exchange Subsystem)

- *Size:* Interior vents should be a minimum of 3 percent of the area of the shared wall between the sunspace and the adjacent living spaces. To achieve a more balanced airflow, upper vents should *not* be located directly over lower vents, but should be moved to one side if possible. Backdraft dampers or operable louvers should be provided for upper vents to prevent reverse thermocirculation.

Control

SHADING

In each of the attached sunspace subsystems, it is recommended that some method for shading the collector be provided to help avoid unwanted summer heat gain. Most devices used in direct gain are applicable for at least the vertical or near-vertical wall section of the collector, including vegetation (trees), trellises, vertical and/or horizontal louvers, and attached awnings.

The glazed portion of the collector roof, however, represents a slightly different shading condition. The most efficient way to shade this area is to use operable wood, aluminum, or plastic roller shades attached directly to the collector, preferably on the outside. Prefabricated collectors are often equipped with these shades integrated into the framing system. In site-built installations, provision should be made for the inclusion of such elements as part of the site-built frame.

Wherever possible, it is recommended that the roof portion of the collector be opaque at its connection to the home. This opaque roof will serve as an overhang for shading the sunspace. In working greenhouse applications, care should be taken to balance the amount of shading with the daylight requirements of the plants (see Figure 5.20).

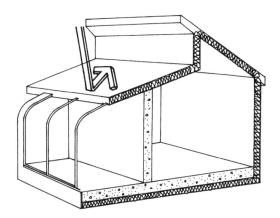

Figure 5.20

REFLECTING

Reflecting panels can be used in any of the attached sunspace subsystems to enhance the amount of solar energy reaching the collector. They should be located to reflect sunlight onto the mass within the space without directing excessive radiation directly onto the plants.

INSULATING—FIXED EXTERIOR INSULATION

In general, all exposed opaque surfaces in the sunspace, including roof and end walls, should be well insulated to reduce heat flow to the exterior. Standard insulating techniques are appropriate, except in the case where a particular construction is intended to function as a storage component. For example, if an end wall in the sunspace is to function as a direct gain storage component, the construction procedures and insulation techniques should follow the discussions and details in Chapter 3.

Foundation insulation will, of course, reduce heat losses. These reductions can be increased if the floor slab is also insulated at its perimeter. However, such perimeter insulation may or may not be advisable, depending on the particular mode in which the sunspace is operated.

If the sunspace is thermally isolated from the living area and its temperatures are allowed to fluctuate freely, under-slab insulation will not be necessary if perimeter insulation is already provided. If the sunspace is not thermally isolated from the living space and/or if an auxiliary energy system is used to maintain temperatures in the sunspace within the comfort range, perimeter insulation and under-slab insulation should be considered. In general, the floor in such sunspaces should be insulated to the same extent as a direct gain floor would be in the same location (see "Insulating—Fixed Exterior Insulation" in Chapter 3).

In general, it is not necessary to provide fixed insulation for the shared wall between the sunspace and the adjacent living spaces in any of the four subsystems. In the open wall and direct gain subsystems, such considerations do not apply. In the air exchange and thermal storage wall, the shared wall need not be insulated if high-performance glazings or movable insulation are provided at the collector. In the thermal storage wall subsystem, insulating the shared storage wall will effectively nullify any passive benefits that the wall might provide.

INSULATING—MOVABLE INSULATION

Movable insulation at the sunspace collector can increase the performance of all four subsystems. Such insulation will reduce heat losses during prolonged overcast periods and at night, as well as prevent unwanted heat gain during the cooling season. In most climates, the use of movable insulation can be avoided by specifying high-performance glazings and thermally broken frames.

If using movable insulation, it is advisable to select or design an insulating system that, when closed, provides a tight air seal between the collector and the sunspace. Sunspace insulating materials are typically suspended from guide wires or run in a track that may be attached to or integrated with the collector frame.

These insulating materials may be bulky and difficult to store if not designed into the collector framing system. Manual operation of movable insulation is often very simple but requires an active commitment on the part of the homeowners. Local codes should also be consulted to assess the eligibility of certain materials for use in exposed situations.

CONTROL RULES OF THUMB

Shading

- *Overhangs:*   An overhang sized to provide a specified level of shading has the advantage of further reducing both the home's cooling energy requirements and potential glare in the cooling season.

The projection of the overhang that will be adequate (that will provide 100 percent shading at noon on June 21) at particular latitudes can be quickly calculated by using the following formula:

Projection (L)

$$= \frac{\text{window opening, i.e. collector (H)}}{F \text{ (see Table 5.2)}}$$

A slightly longer overhang may be desirable at latitudes where this formula does not provide enough shade during the later part of the cooling season (see Figure 3.15). For example, for Madison, Wisconsin, at 43° NL, select an F factor between 2.0 and 2.7 (values for 44° NL). Assuming shade is desired on August 1, choose the lower value of 2.0. If the window opening (H) is 8′, the projection (L) of the overhang placed at the top of the collector will be: 8⁄2 = 4′.

Table 5.2

North Latitude	F Factor*
28°	5.6–11.1
32°	4.0–6.3
36°	3.0–4.5
40°	2.5–3.4
44°	2.0–2.7
48°	1.7–2.2
52°	1.5–1.8
56°	1.3–1.5

* Select a factor according to your latitude. The higher values will provide 100% shading at noon on June 21, the lower values on August 1.

If a collector is located in the sloped roof area, directly above vertical glass, a movable screen that extends across the roof collector and down the vertical glass may be used to shade the sunspace, providing shade for the entire collector area with the same material.

Reflecting

- *Sizing:*   If used, a reflector panel should be the same length as the collector area served and roughly as wide as the collector area is high.
- *Slope:*   A downward slope (away from the collector) of roughly 5° is recommended.

Insulating

- *R-values (fixed insulation):*   Fixed exterior insulation R-values should meet or exceed the levels that would be maintained by the same element in a nonsolar building, which should, in turn, meet or exceed local building code requirements.
- *R-values (movable insulation):*   Rigid movable insulation will typically have an R-value between R-4 and R-9. Insulating drapes and shades, for interior use, will typically have lower R-values.

• *Seals:*   Insulation should provide a tight seal to avoid problems with heat loss at its edges.

Vents (Exterior)

• *Area:*   The exterior vent area should be one-sixth of the area of the wall shared between the living space and the sunspace. The top vents should be one-third larger than the bottom vents. The vertical distance between vents should be as great as possible.

ATTACHED SUNSPACE DETAILS

The drawings on the following pages illustrate common construction detailing for attached sunspace systems. The details are divided into four sections corresponding to the subsystem types discussed above: open wall, direct gain, air exchange, and thermal storage wall.

The four sections suggest one design and material option for each subsystem. Components and materials shown for one subsystem can gen-

erally be substituted for another, provided the basic functional characteristics of the system are unchanged. For example, the various collector components illustrated can be used with any of the subsystem types.

Construction notes follow the details. The notes, referenced from the details, provide guidelines, troubleshooting tips, and other information useful in constructing an attached sunspace.

Open Wall Subsystem

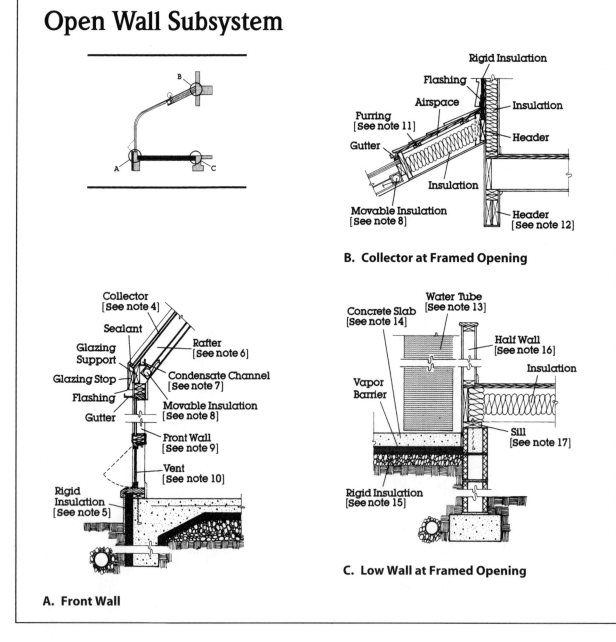

A. Front Wall

B. Collector at Framed Opening

C. Low Wall at Framed Opening

Direct Gain Subsystem

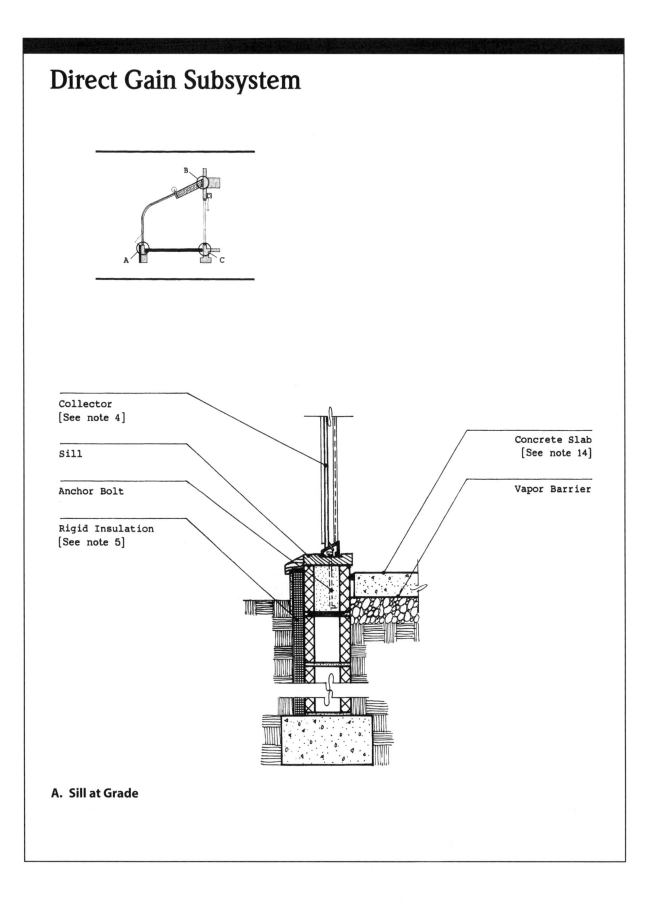

Collector
[See note 4]

Sill

Anchor Bolt

Rigid Insulation
[See note 5]

Concrete Slab
[See note 14]

Vapor Barrier

A. Sill at Grade

ATTACHED SUNSPACE DETAILS

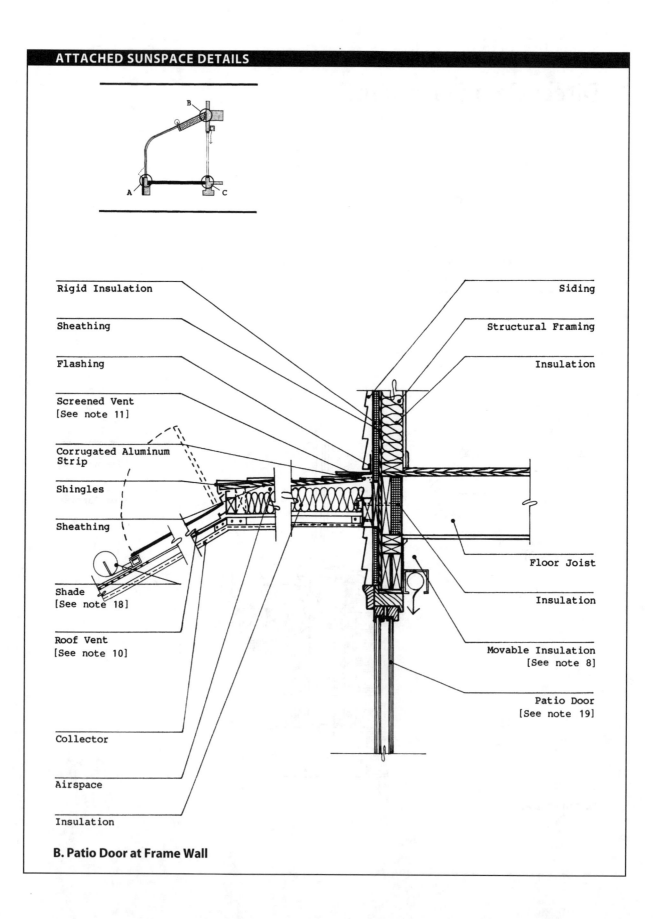

Rigid Insulation

Sheathing

Flashing

Screened Vent
[See note 11]

Corrugated Aluminum
Strip

Shingles

Sheathing

Shade
[See note 18]

Roof Vent
[See note 10]

Collector

Airspace

Insulation

Siding

Structural Framing

Insulation

Floor Joist

Insulation

Movable Insulation
[See note 8]

Patio Door
[See note 19]

B. Patio Door at Frame Wall

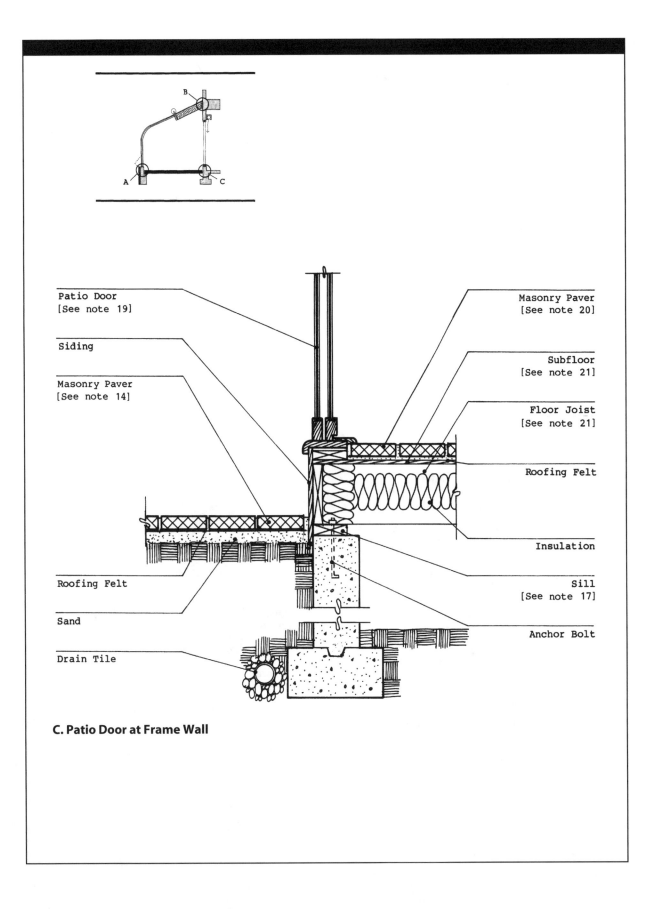

Patio Door
[See note 19]

Siding

Masonry Paver
[See note 14]

Roofing Felt

Sand

Drain Tile

Masonry Paver
[See note 20]

Subfloor
[See note 21]

Floor Joist
[See note 21]

Roofing Felt

Insulation

Sill
[See note 17]

Anchor Bolt

C. Patio Door at Frame Wall

ATTACHED SUNSPACE DETAILS

Air Exchange Subsystem

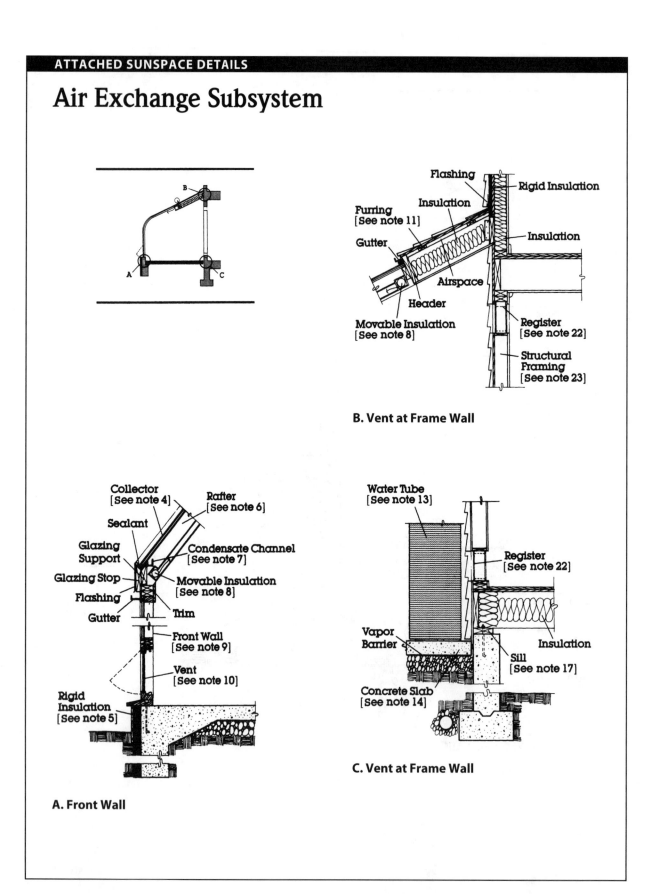

B. Vent at Frame Wall

A. Front Wall

C. Vent at Frame Wall

Thermal Storage Wall Subsystem

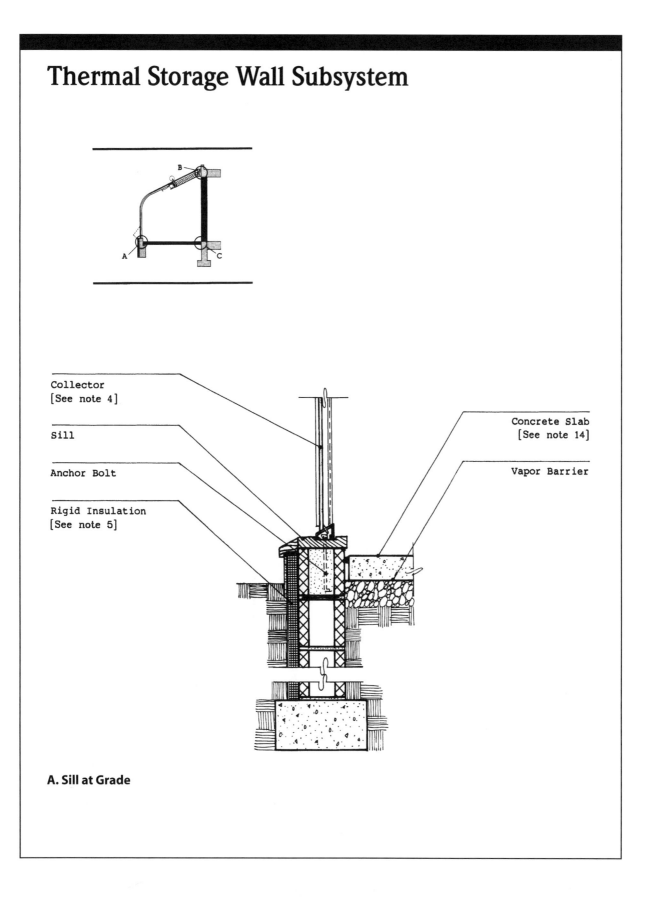

Collector
[See note 4]

Sill

Anchor Bolt

Rigid Insulation
[See note 5]

Concrete Slab
[See note 14]

Vapor Barrier

A. Sill at Grade

ATTACHED SUNSPACE DETAILS

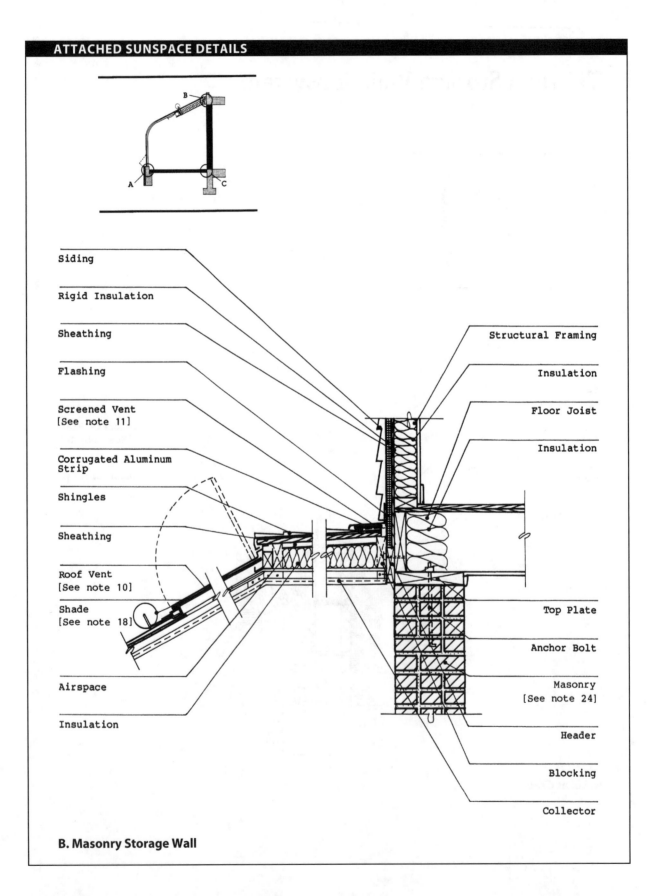

Siding

Rigid Insulation

Sheathing

Flashing

Screened Vent
[See note 11]

Corrugated Aluminum
Strip

Shingles

Sheathing

Roof Vent
[See note 10]

Shade
[See note 18]

Airspace

Insulation

Structural Framing

Insulation

Floor Joist

Insulation

Top Plate

Anchor Bolt

Masonry
[See note 24]

Header

Blocking

Collector

B. Masonry Storage Wall

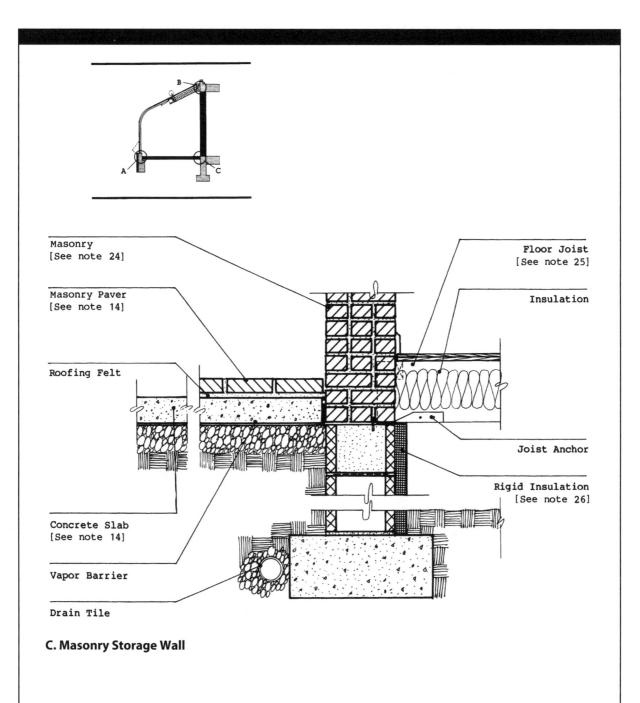

Masonry
[See note 24]

Masonry Paver
[See note 14]

Roofing Felt

Concrete Slab
[See note 14]

Vapor Barrier

Drain Tile

Floor Joist
[See note 25]

Insulation

Joist Anchor

Rigid Insulation
[See note 26]

C. Masonry Storage Wall

ATTACHED SUNSPACE DETAILS

Remote Storage Subsystem

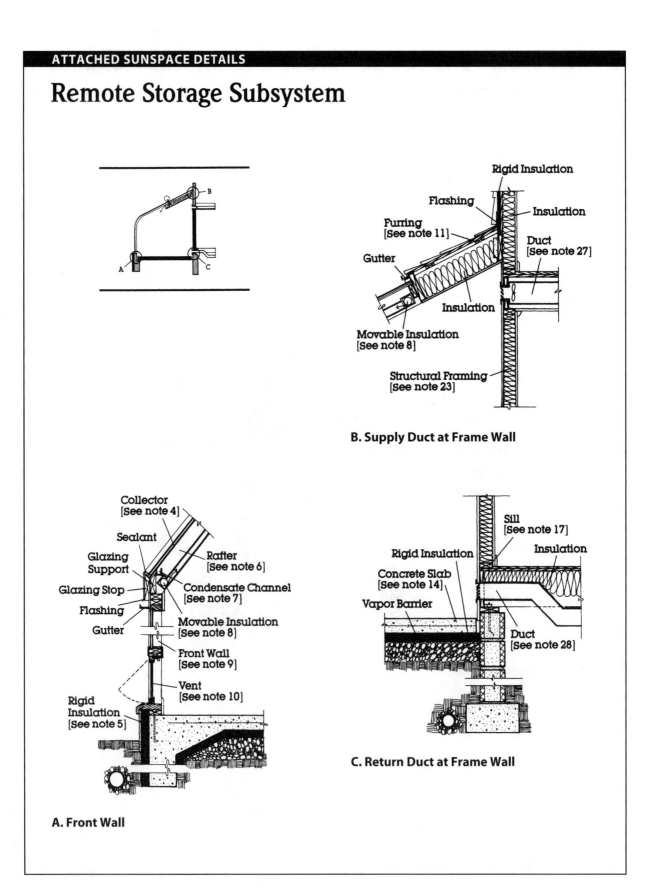

B. Supply Duct at Frame Wall

A. Front Wall

C. Return Duct at Frame Wall

Notes

GENERAL NOTES

1. All footings must bear on undisturbed soil. Adjust footing size, reinforcing, and depth below grade as required by site conditions and/or local code.

2. Provide adequate drainage in the attached sunspace floor, particularly where extensive planting is planned.

3. Insulation levels at foundation/floor, opaque walls, and opaque roof section should meet or exceed requirements of local building and energy codes for roof components.

DETAIL NOTES

4. For optimum thermal performance, it is generally recommended that double glazing be provided, preferably a high performance glazing using one or more of the following: low-e coating(s), gas fill, or suspended plastic film(s). (See the "Collector Components" section in Chapter 7 for more information on glass or plastic collector materials.) Where corrugated plastic glazing is specified, provide continuous blocking cut to conform to the corrugations. The collector frame can be site-built or prefabricated. Site-built systems are generally framed in wood, which should be treated to resist the effects of moisture. Special attention should be paid in these systems to proper sealing and caulking of the glazing material. Prefabricated systems (e.g., standard greenhouses) are generally framed in metal. The frame specified in any such system should be equipped with thermal breaks, and sill connections should conform with manufacturers' specifications and local building codes and/or accepted practice.

5. Foundation and/or front walls may be insulated, but must be protected above grade. Cement plaster or synthetic stucco finish applied on lath may be used, or other finishes may be specified at the builder's option. Consult the insulation manufacturer for recommended installation procedures. Insulation should have an R-value that meets or exceeds the requirements of local building and energy codes for foundations.

6. Sizing of framing members is to be determined by weight of glazing material, loading requirements, and desired clear spans. All structural elements must be designed to meet applicable local building codes and/or accepted practice. High humidity levels in attached sunspaces used as working greenhouses may necessitate treating wood framing members with preservative. Avoid preservatives harmful to plants.

7. Condensate channel is formed by turning up metal flashing.

8. Movable insulation can be provided to reduce nighttime heat loss during the heating season and daytime heat gain during the cooling season. Because of the limited availability of movable insulation specifically designed for attached sunspaces, it may be necessary to site-design and site-fabricate an insulation system for a particular application—for example, an insulating curtain suspended from cables. In most climates, the use of movable insulation can be avoided by specifying high-performance glazings and thermally broken frames.

9. The structure and height of the attached sunspace front wall may vary, depending on design and use. The wall may be glazed, with insulated masonry. Reinforcing, thick-

ness, provisions for weep holes, longitudinal drains, and waterproofing are to be determined by site conditions, local building codes, and/or accepted practice.

10. Operable glazing units should be provided to vent the sunspace to the outside during the cooling season. Intake vents should be as low in the sunspace wall as possible, while exhaust vents should be high, either near the ridge or high in the gable ends (see "Seasonal Operation—Cooling" in this chapter). Some greenhouse manufacturers provide roof vents. Side vents are also available and suitable.

11. Opaque roof section must be vented to ensure proper performance of insulation. Vents may be located at the roof/wall connection or at sides of roof construction. Furring is provided as required to allow air to circulate.

12. Sunspace and adjacent living areas open directly to each other for natural air exchange between the two spaces. Headers over opening are to be designed for loading and clear span per local building codes and/or accepted practice. (For further information, see "Open Wall Subsystem" in this chapter.)

13. Water, stored in appropriate containers, is an effective material for thermal storage. Suitable containers are fiberglass tubes, polyethylene and/or steel drums, and metal culverts. Care should be taken to ensure that steel and metal containers are lined with corrosion-resistant materials. In all cases, water should be treated with algae-retardant chemicals. (For further information on the use of water as thermal storage, including descriptions of appropriate containers, see "Storage Components" in Chapter 7.)

14. Concrete slab-on-grade and any of the wide variety of standard and interlocking concrete masonry unit pavers or standard brick pavers on slab-on-grade are suitable for ther-

mal storage. (For further information, including finishes and construction techniques, see "Interior Floor Types" in Chapter 3.)

15. In cooler climates, it is generally recommended that rigid insulation be placed under masonry floors that are acting as storage components in attached sunspaces, particularly when the sunspace is open to the living spaces. The use of rigid insulation is recommended in all cases to reduce perimeter heat loss.

16. A low wall will not restrict free circulation of air between the sunspace and adjacent living areas. Consult local codes for structural requirements. (For further information, see "Open Wall Subsystem" in this chapter.)

17. Continuous sill sealer is recommended to provide protection against infiltration.

18. Exterior movable shades can be provided for protection against solar heat gain during the cooling season. Such shades are typically aluminum, wood, or fabric (see "Control Components" in Chapter 7).

19. It is recommended that the patio door adjacent to the living space be double glazed, preferably with high-performance glazing. Installation is according to manufacturers' specifications. (For further information, see "Direct Gain Subsystem" in this chapter.)

20. For information on masonry pavers used for direct gain storage, including recommended installation procedures, see "Interior Floor Types" in Chapter 3.

21. Consideration must be given to the additional weight of pavers. Consult structural design loading tables and local codes to determine suitable grade and spacing of joists, and grade and thickness of subfloor. Expansion joints should be provided, as required, at the connection between masonry floors and stud or masonry walls to prevent cracking.

22. Vents from the top of the attached sunspace distribute heat into the adjacent living area, and vents at the bottom return cooler air from the living space to the sunspace.

23. Insulation is not required in the structural frame wall separating the attached sunspace and living spaces. (For further information, see "Air Exchange Subsystem" in this chapter.)

24. Alternate storage wall materials can be specified at the builder's option. (For further information on thermal storage wall materials and configurations, see "Wall Types" in Chapter 4.)

25. Floor joists must bear on solid masonry not less than 4″ thick. Fire-cut joists as required.

26. It is recommended that walls at the crawl space/unheated basement foundation be insulated to prevent heat losses through the wall. Insulation levels should meet or exceed building and energy code requirements for foundation insulation.

27. Air handling ducts can be connected to vents at the top of the attached sunspace to move heated air to other areas of the house. A small, low-velocity fan can be incorporated into the duct system to ensure proper airflow. (For further information on fans, see "Distribution Components" in Chapter 7.)

28. To facilitate proper airflow, a cold-air return must be provided. A return-air duct can be connected to a vent at the bottom of the attached sunspace, with the cold air supplied from a floor register at the rear of the house.

ATTACHED SUNSPACE CASE STUDY

TVA Solar House #5

Upper Plan 656 sf

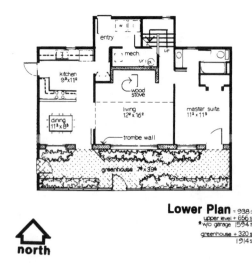

Lower Plan = 938 sf
upper level + 656 sf
* w/o garage 1594 sf
greenhouse + 320 sf
1914 sf

north

An attached sunspace spans the entire south side of this 1,870-sq-ft two-story house designed for a flat or slightly sloping site. The sunspace combines thermal storage wall and direct gain subsystems to create a space that is well matched to the major living spaces of the home. Circulation and service spaces, including the kitchen, entry, utility room, and bathroom, buffer the colder north wall.

The wall and roof of the attached sunspace are constructed of double-glazed operable window units that can be insulated in the evening by a movable curtain. Solid masonry floor pavers are laid mortarless over a 6" sand bed to retain heat. Heated air is circulated between the sunspace and the living space by opening adjoining windows and doors.

The 12" heavyweight concrete masonry unit thermal mass wall is filled solid with grout and finished with a dark plaster on the greenhouse side to increase solar absorption. An optional wood-burning stove next to an interior masonry wall provides auxiliary heat. An opaque section of the sunspace roof serves as a sunscreen for the thermal storage wall during the cooling season.

During the summer, heat generated within the living space can be vented to an attic and then exhausted to the exterior through louvered vents. The greenhouse/sunspace is vented by a wall-mounted fan and operable glazing panels in the collector assembly.

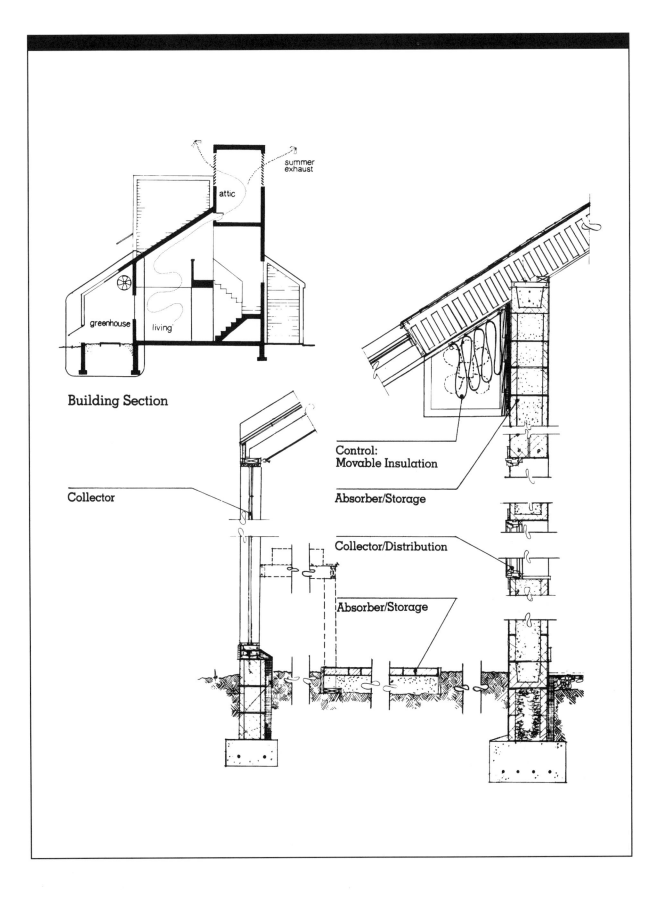

summer
exhaust

attic

greenhouse

living

Building Section

Collector

Control:
Movable Insulation

Absorber/Storage

Collector/Distribution

Absorber/Storage

ATTACHED SUNSPACE CASE STUDY

PCA Two-Story House

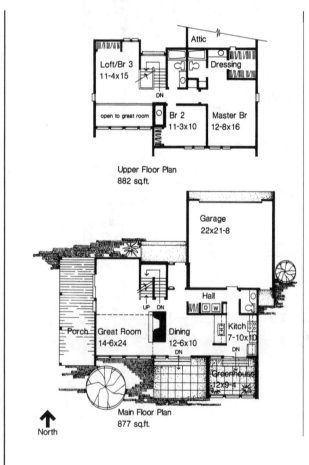

Upper Floor Plan
882 sq.ft.

Loft/Br 3
11-4x15

Attic

Dressing

open to great room

Br 2
11-3x10

Master Br
12-8x16

DN

Garage
22x21-8

Hall

UP   DN

Porch

Great Room
14-6x24

Dining
12-6x10

Kitch
7-10x10

DN

DN

Greenhouse
12x9-4

Main Floor Plan
877 sq.ft.

North

Attached sunspace, patio, and covered porch areas enhance the openness of this 1,800-sq.-ft. two-story passive house. The garage, air lock, and entry vestibule below and closets, bath, and stair above created an effective north-wall thermal buffer zone.

Adjacent to the kitchen, the south-glazed sunspace easily lends itself for use as a breakfast room or working greenhouse. Its concrete slab-on-grade floor provides solar storage. The sliding glass doors are used to control heat flow between the sunspace and the major living spaces. The great room receives direct gain heat, which is stored in the quarry tile floor. The tile rests on 1½″ of concrete to provide the necessary depth of masonry.

During the summer, wing walls and overhangs to the south protect interior spaces by controlling glare and unwanted heat gain.

A double-height space in the great room facilitates heated-air circulation to the upper floors. Supplementary direct gain heating is provided by a row of clerestory windows, which also enhance the open feeling of this design. The R-13 exterior wall and R-38 external ceiling and floor insulation help control heat flow through the building envelope throughout the year.

Designer
John D. Bloodgood, P.C.
Des Moines, Iowa

Sponsor
Portland Cement Association
Skokie, Illinois

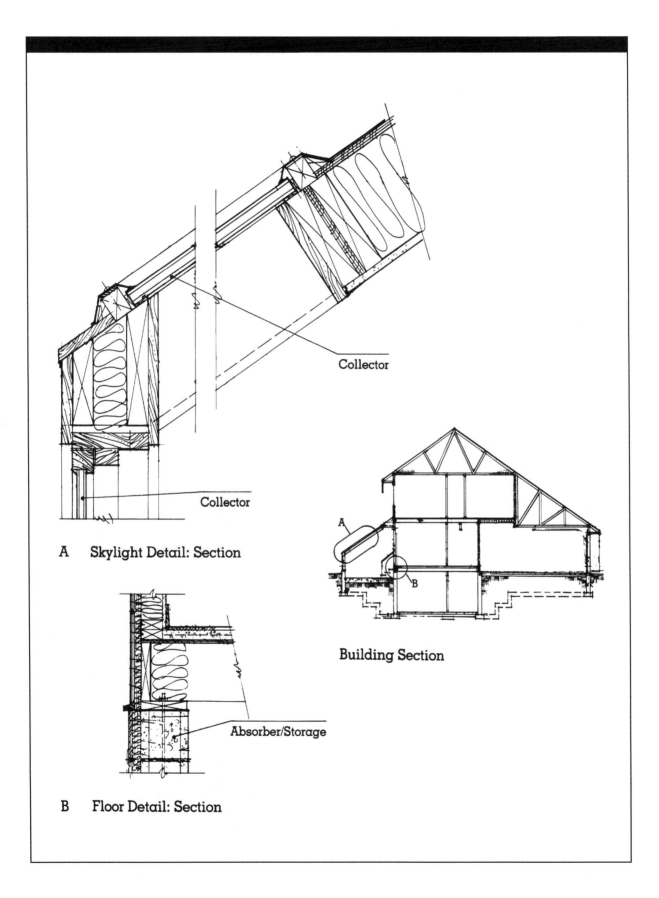

A   Skylight Detail: Section

Collector

Collector

Building Section

B   Floor Detail: Section

Absorber/Storage

La Vereda House

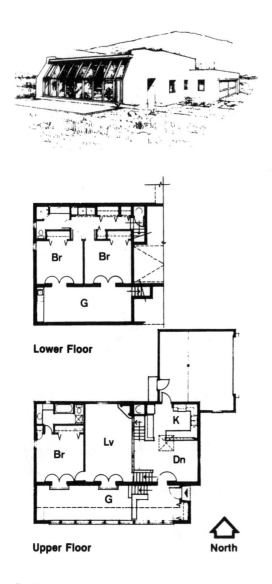

Lower Floor

Upper Floor   **North**

Project
La Vereda House #4

Builder/Designer
Susan Nichols
Communico, Inc.
Santa Fe, New Mexico

A double-height expanse of greenhouse stretches along the south wall of this split-level home in Santa Fe. Designed for a slightly sloping site, this wood-framed home is partially bermed on the east, west, and north, with trees to the north offering winter wind protection. Heat, which collects in the sunspace, is stored in an adobe wall and rock bed located underneath the first floor of the home.

A solid roof and projecting overhang shade the adobe wall from the summer sun. The attached sunspace is constructed using both tilted and vertical south glazing. In addition to the adobe wall and rock bed, a concrete slab topped with flagstone provides sufficient thermal mass storage.

Doors cut through the adobe wall between the greenhouse and the living spaces can be opened to allow heated air, generated in the sunspace, to flow throughout the home. During the summer, sunspace heat is exhausted by wind turbines located in the greenhouse ceiling.

The rock bed contains 810 cu. ft. of storage beneath the kitchen and dining room. On top of the 1½″ to 2″-diameter rocks, a layer of polyethylene film and a 1″ setting bed of sand provide a base for the 4″ concrete slab, which is finished with tile. A thermostatically controlled fan at the top of the sunspace draws heated air through ducts to a plenum along the north side of the rock bed. Heat is transferred to the rocks and radiates through the slab. Return air is ducted through a plenum back to the greenhouse, completing the loop. The rock bed is insulated, improving its thermal performance.

The 8″ concrete masonry foundation wall is sheathed in 2″ of rigid R-9 polystyrene with a plaster coating. Ceiling insulation varies between R-30 and, where a combination of rigid polystyrene and fiberglass batt insulation is applied, R-52. Walls are insulated to a level of R-33.

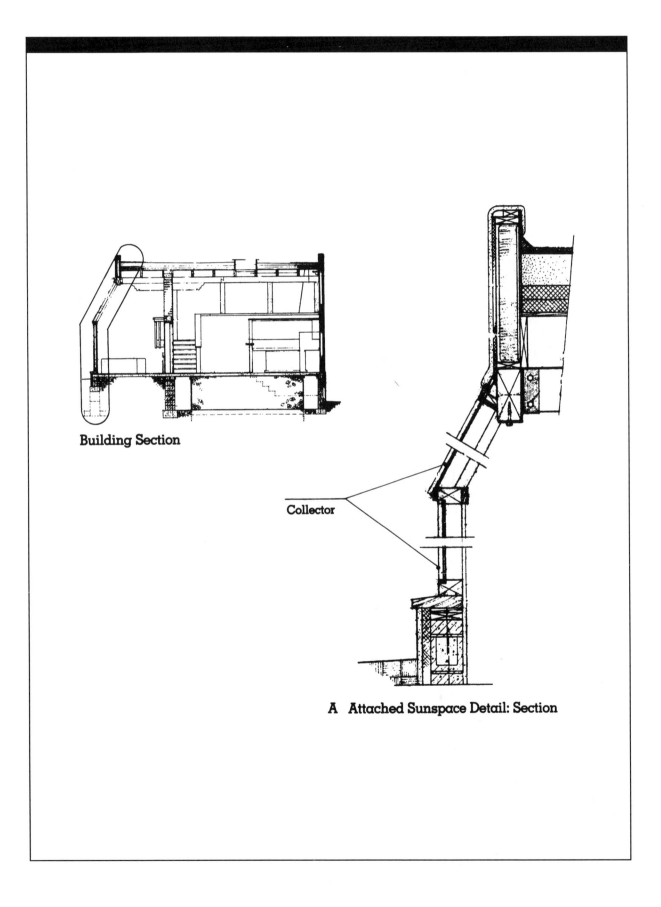

Building Section

Collector

A Attached Sunspace Detail: Section

SSEC Atlanta House

2nd floor

1st floor

north

A two-story attached sunspace incorporates a water wall and phase-change materials for thermal storage in this 2,300-sq.-ft. home in Atlanta. Living spaces on the upper floor are buffered from heat losses to the north by service and circulation spaces and, on the ground floor, by an air-lock entry vestibule and garage.

The foundation wall is constructed of 8″ concrete blocks with exterior rigid insulation, protected above grade with an applied plaster coating. R-38 roof and R-20 wall insulation aid in reducing heat losses.

Sliding glass doors provide both direct access and air distribution from the sunspace to the dining room. Above the dining room, the main bedroom overlooks the sunspace through windows inserted between three panels containing additional thermal mass storage in the form of thermal storage rods filled with phase-change materials.

Two thermostatically controlled fans at ceiling level are mounted at either end of the solar porch. One of the fans is opened to the exterior to cool the space in the summer. The other fan operates in the winter, distributing heated air through ducts in the ceiling into the great room.

The triple-height expanse of southern glazing is capped by wooden trellis work at the first two floors, and with a roof overhang above. Both devices serve as sunscreens to prevent direct solar gain in the cooling season.

The attached sunspace contains a water wall of nine 55-gallon black drums stacked three by three, providing a significant amount of thermal mass. The sunspace heat is supplemented by heat generated in a partial basement below. Air heated in both spaces is allowed to rise naturally into the living spaces above.

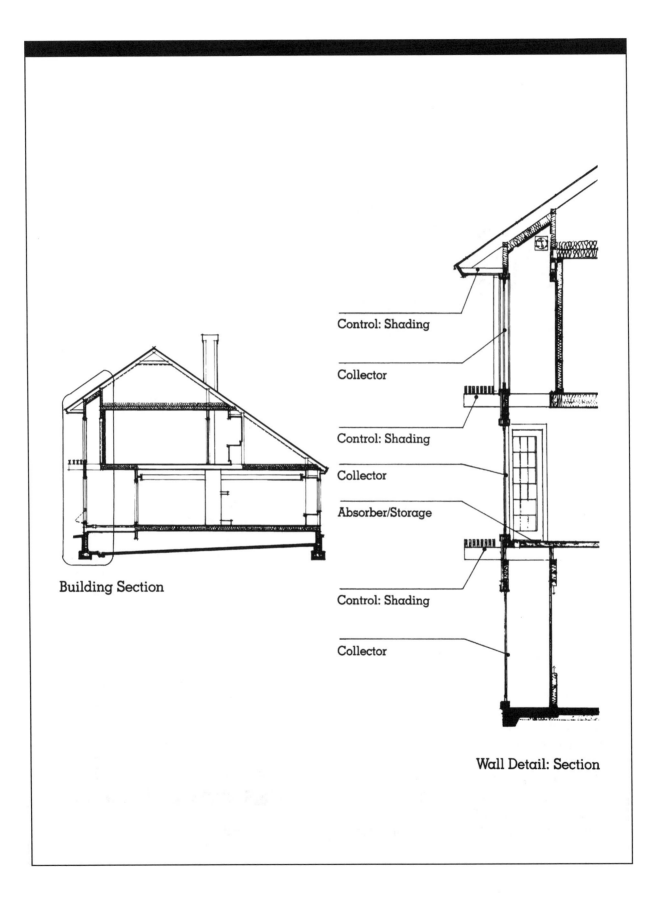

Building Section

Control: Shading

Collector

Control: Shading

Collector

Absorber/Storage

Control: Shading

Collector

Wall Detail: Section

ATTACHED SUNSPACE CASE STUDY

PEG House #1

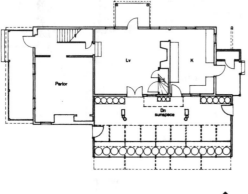

Floor Plan

North

The 500-sq.-ft. lean-to greenhouse/dining room addition to the 1,900-sq.-ft. Hamill house of Princeton, New Jersey, serves the dual function of increasing living space and reducing the home's heating requirements. Thermal storage is afforded by water-filled cylinders, masonry wall construction, and the slate floor, all contained within the sunspace.

First- and second-floor doors and windows in the masonry wall at the back of the attached sunspace can be opened to allow heat flow into the adjacent living spaces. The full-time use of the sunspace as an added living space requires that the space be well insulated with movable insulation at the glazing.

One hundred square feet of double-glazed vertical collector and 500 sq. ft. of tilted collector glass over Plexiglas® comprise the south wall of the sunspace. The insulating curtain with an interior reflective coating operates on a track and cable system to reduce nighttime heat loss. Two wood-burning stoves provide auxiliary heat.

The solid roof and end walls of the addition offer protection against overheating. Upper glazing panels can be opened with a rod-and-arm mechanism to ventilate the sunspace, forming a 36' continuous vent. A shading screen is hung in front of the glazing to reduce the seasonal cooling requirements.

Seventeen water-filled 55-gallon storage drums are placed adjacent to the vertical glazing. On the exterior, hinged shutters reflect more light onto the drums when opened during the day. When closed at night, they insulate the lower glazing against heat losses. Additional water storage is provided by ten 18"-diameter and three 12"-diameter fiberglass cylinders, which line the north wall of the sunspace.

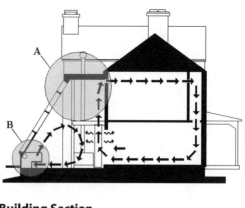

Building Section

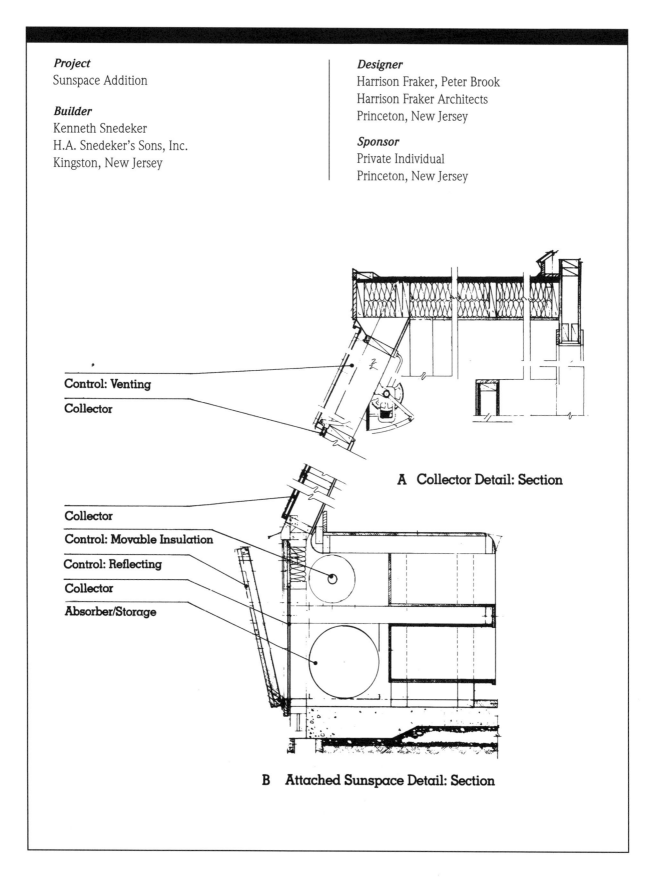

Project
Sunspace Addition

Builder
Kenneth Snedeker
H.A. Snedeker's Sons, Inc.
Kingston, New Jersey

Designer
Harrison Fraker, Peter Brook
Harrison Fraker Architects
Princeton, New Jersey

Sponsor
Private Individual
Princeton, New Jersey

Control: Venting

Collector

A Collector Detail: Section

Collector

Control: Movable Insulation

Control: Reflecting

Collector

Absorber/Storage

B   Attached Sunspace Detail: Section

CONVECTIVE LOOP

Design Overview

Convective loop systems are designed to be used exclusively for heating. They are effective in any location with substantial heating requirements, although they are most appropriate in moderate and severe climates. One major advantage of a convective loop system is that it is thermally isolated, and often physically separated, from the living spaces of the home.

As discussed in the previous chapters, direct gain, thermal storage wall, and attached sunspace systems are potential sources of heat loss during overcast periods and during the night. Control components are typically required in such systems to reduce these losses. Because they are thermally isolated from living spaces, however, convective loop systems are not subject to such heat losses, reducing—and, in some cases, eliminating—the need for control components.

Isolating solar gains, however, requires that the distribution component and storage component (not required in some convective loop configurations) be carefully designed, detailed, and constructed.

The major element in a convective loop design is the solar collection panel. These panels, fre-quently referred to as thermosiphon air panels (TAPs), are similar in appearance and operation to active solar panel collectors. Unlike active solar panels, which are generally roof mounted, however, the TAP is typically mounted on the exterior wall in a vertical position (see Figure 6.1) or below the floor line at a steep angle (see Figure 6.2).

Convective loop systems operate on the basic principle that hot air rises. As in all passive systems, the collector in a convective loop admits sunlight, which strikes an absorber surface and is converted to heat. In the convective loop, however, this absorbed heat is transferred to the air surrounding the absorber instead of being directly stored by thermal mass. The heated air rises inside the TAP until it passes through a vent located at the top and is distributed directly into the home. As this air passes out through the upper vent, it is replaced by cooler air entering through a vent located near the bottom of the panel (see Figure 6.3).

All the air movement in such a system is, in principle, by natural convection, although there may be certain designs in which a small fan is required.

Previously, systems of this type included options for remote storage, usually in the form of

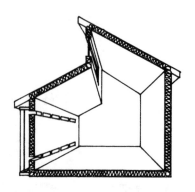

Figure 6.1

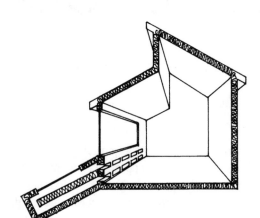

Figure 6.2

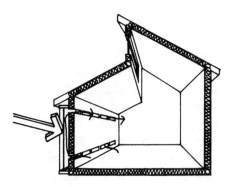

Figure 6.3

under-floor rock beds (see Figure 6.4). Although these systems can operate effectively, they have generally not proven to be practical. Reasons for this include:

• High cost of storage system and distribution

• Difficulty in accessing, cleaning, and maintaining rock storage

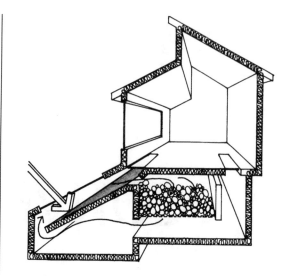

Figure 6.4

• Associated indoor air quality issues

• Typically, only useful with large collector areas

Because of the difficulties with rock storage, this element of convective loop systems will not be reviewed in detail. Two examples of convective loop systems with rock storage are included in the case studies, however, so that the system can be understood in principle.

Transpired Solar Collectors

A new type of convective loop design, recently developed by Conserval (a private solar heating and energy conservation company) and the U.S. Department of Energy's National Renewable Energy Lab, is known as the transpired solar collector. Using a significantly different approach than the other systems described in this chapter, the transpired solar collector is designed to be a ventilation air preheating system for use in conjunction with building HVAC equipment.

In the transpired solar collector, the use of glazings of any type has been eliminated. The collector consists of a corrugated aluminum sheet, painted a dark color and perforated with hundreds of tiny holes. The collector is installed on a south-facing building wall, mounted a few inches off of the surface to create a vertical air plenum. This plenum is connected to the outside

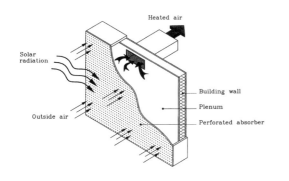

Heated air

Solar radiation

Outside air

Building wall

Plenum

Perforated absorber

Figure 6.5

air intake of the building's HVAC system (see Figure 6.5). The elimination of any glazing, plus the simplicity of the installation, make the transpired collector an economical, low-maintenance convective loop alternative.

The operation of the transpired collector is straightforward. Radiation from the sun is absorbed by the dark panels and heats the air in the plenum. Using fans from the HVAC system, or additional fans added to the collector, fresh air is continuously drawn through the holes in the panels, preheated through solar radiation, and directed to the air intake of the HVAC system as needed. The air plenum is also effective at recapturing heat escaping from the building wall, and using this to assist in the preheating process.

On sunny days, the transpired solar collector is capable of absorbing up to 80 percent of the solar radiation that strikes it, and can raise the temperature of the incoming air by 30° to 50°F. Under cloudy conditions, the system is still able to absorb diffuse light and provide some air preheating, albeit at lower levels. These increases in the air temperature, although not nearly as high as those in the glazed convective loop systems, have proven to be significant, with heating cost reductions demonstrated at $1 to $3 per square foot (depending on the cost and type of fuel used).

Because transpired solar collectors are designed to preheat air for HVAC systems, their primary use is for buildings with large ventilation requirements, notably commercial or institutional buildings. Some newer residences, however, which are built for energy efficiency, have very low air infiltration/exfiltration rates, and

thus do employ mechanical ventilation. In these instances, the transpired solar collector may be an appropriate system to consider. It should also be noted that transpired collectors are most cost-effective in cold, sunny climates.

As a new technology, the full uses and potential of this system are still being determined. In particular, the use of transpired collectors as an actual building finish is one that is actively being explored.

Seasonal Operation—Heating

During the heating season, sunlight is transmitted through the collector (usually glass or plastic) of the convective loop TAP and strikes the absorber surface. The absorber, which is typically a black-colored metallic surface, converts the sunlight to heat. Since metal or other materials used as absorbers are good conductors of heat, the air surrounding the absorber will quickly be heated and rise in the panel and through the outlet vent. Cooler makeup air will be drawn from the room into the panel inlet, starting a flow of heat that continues throughout the daylight hours. The heat generated in the convective loop panel is distributed directly into the living spaces.

This basic process is the same for all convective loop system configurations. However, it is in the design, operation, and construction of the components that two basic subsystems can be distinguished. In the discussions that follow, these subsystem types, referred to as vertical and U-tube panel subsystems, are treated separately.

VERTICAL PANEL SUBSYSTEM

In this subsystem, the TAP is mounted directly on the south-facing wall, outside the insulation, thermally isolating the panel from the living spaces. Vertical panel systems are usually constructed without storage, delivering heat directly to the living spaces through vents at the top of the panel. Cooler makeup air is drawn into the panel through vents at the bottom of the panel (see Figure 6.3).

Due to the high cost and complexity of construction, remote storage should be considered for the vertical panel configuration only when the system is designed to provide a substantial percentage of the home's total heating requirements.

To prevent warm room air from being drawn back into the panel during cloudy periods or at night, simple backdraft dampers are typically provided at the vents. This system configuration, without storage, is inexpensive to construct, requires little maintenance, and is one of the most effective passive solar designs. In principle, it functions similarly to a Trombe wall, except that thermal mass is not used.

U-TUBE PANEL SUBSYSTEM

As its name implies, the TAP in the U-tube subsystem is constructed in the form of a "U" with the cool inlet air drawn down one side of the panel and warm outlet air rising up the opposite side (see Figure 6.6).

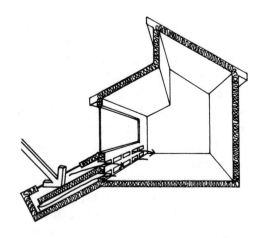

Figure 6.6

This panel configuration has some inherent advantages. If carefully designed and constructed, the panel is self-damping, eliminating the need for control features such as dampers. In the evening or during cloudy periods, the air in the panel cools. This cool air is trapped in the panel and cannot rise up into the living space. Therefore, unlike the TAP design in the vertical panel subsystem, a damper is not required, further simplifying this passive system.

The close proximity of the inlet and outlet vents provides a second advantage for the U-tube. If the vents are located near the floor, distribution to the subfloor storage is direct and,

consequently, less expensive and simpler to construct than distribution in a vertical panel system. In addition, in the below-floor-level location, less of the south side of the home is covered by the TAP.

The U-tube subsystem can be used without storage. As in the vertical panel subsystem, storage is required only when the panel is to deliver sufficient heat to satisfy a substantial portion of the total home heating needs. The system is "activated" when sun shining on the panel heats the absorber, in turn heating the surrounding air and causing it to rise into the living spaces. Cooler room air is drawn into the inlet vent, completing the loop.

The U-tube subsystem without storage is inexpensive to construct (although generally more expensive than the vertical panel subsystem), requires little maintenance, and has a high efficiency relative to the other passive system types.

Seasonal Operation—Cooling

Since convective loop systems are designed for heating only, they are inactive during the cooling season. In the vertical panel subsystem, the TAP should be completely isolated from the living space and the storage component by closing the dampers so that any residual heat can be prevented from reaching the home. In addition, it is recommended that the TAP be well shaded or simply covered with an opaque material to prevent unwanted heat buildup in the panel (see Figures 6.7 and 6.8).

An unshaded TAP that is not vented, sometimes referred to as "stagnating," can reach fairly

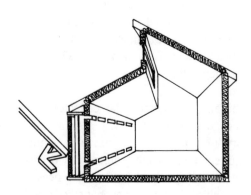

Figure 6.7

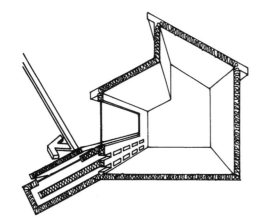

Figure 6.8

high temperatures. At such temperatures, panel seals are stressed, materials often warp, and the absorber surface can be damaged.

Advantages (not including Transpired Solar Collectors)

- The convective loop is the most thermally efficient of all the passive system types.

- If designed without storage, the convective loop is relatively inexpensive and simple to construct.

- The convective loop system is isolated from the living space, allowing the homeowner to completely control heat gains and losses to and from the system.

- The TAP can be physically separated from the home, allowing greater freedom in the design of the home itself.

Disadvantages

- Unless careful attention is paid to its design, the TAP can be an aesthetic liability.

- Unlike the direct gain and attached sunspace, which can provide other amenities such as light and additional living space, the convective loop has only one function—providing heat.

- If mounted on the south-facing wall, the vertical panel subsystem can obstruct light and view. Conversely, the U-tube subsystem, if mounted below the floor line, may impose

specific constraints on site grading, landscaping, and use of outdoor areas.

- Care must be taken to clean and maintain the system to ensure good indoor air quality.

Collector

The collector component of the convective loop system, as in the other passive system types, admits solar radiation onto the absorber and traps the heat generated. The collector in a convective loop is usually part of a thermosiphon air panel, whose operation is discussed earlier in this chapter. The TAP is simply an insulated box, glazed on one side, with an absorber plate inside. Air inlets and outlets are provided to remove the heat generated at the absorber.

The collector glazing material can be glass or plastic. Since the temperatures within the TAP can be expected to reach 300°F, however, materials that will deteriorate at high temperatures should be avoided.

The glazing materials should be specified in large sheets to minimize the mullion area in the frame. Single glazing is recommended for all except severe climates, where tempered double glazing should be specified.

Each glazing layer should be set into the frame with sufficient tolerance to allow for ¾″ expansion in both directions, again, due to the high operating temperatures. A generous amount of silicone caulking is advisable to accommodate this expansion while keeping the unit airtight and weather-tight. The seals should be periodically checked, since some separation may occur in the first few months of operation.

The frame can be constructed of wood or metal, although wood is recommended for site-built TAPs. In the U-tube configuration, the TAP is often completely exposed, and care should be taken to provide insulation on all sides. In the vertical subsystem TAP, the frame wall of the home forms the backing for the unit, and standard batt insulation thickness is commonly specified. In both cases, exposed wood should be treated to prevent rot. If the frame is metal, it should be separated from the absorber to prevent conductive heat losses to the outside. If the frame is wood, rough-sawn and green wood should be avoided in favor of kiln-dried lumber. Any paint used on the frame should be resistant to high temperatures.

COLLECTOR RULES OF THUMB

- *Orientation:*   Orient the convective loop collector panel to face south. Orientations up to 20° east or west of true south will not significantly affect performance.

- *Design:*   The TAP system can be wall-mounted, as in the vertical subsystem configuration, or below the floor line for U-tube construction. Floor-line systems should be tilted to an angle of not less than 45°. The optimum tilt is an angle equal to the location latitude plus 10° (see Figure 6.9). For example, a tilted panel in Madison, Wisconsin, at 43° NL should be constructed and mounted at a 53° angle (43° + 10°) to the ground.

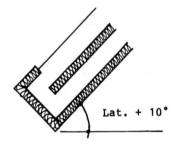

Figure 6.9

- *Area:*   The collector area should equal from 20 percent to 40 percent of the area to be heated. The height of the collector is typically from 6' to 18' but should not be less than 4'. For example, if a 300 sq. ft. living room is to be heated, the collector area should be from 60 to 120 sq. ft. If 8' high, the unit would be from 8' to 16' wide.

- *Number of glazings:*   Single glazing is generally recommended except in severe climates, where high-performance glazing should be specified.

Absorber

Unlike the other passive systems, the absorber in a convective loop system is a distinct element whose only function is to absorb solar radiation and convert it into heat. This heat is, in turn, transferred to the airstream, which passes either over or through the absorber material. In effect, the absorber works very much like the heating element in a standard convection heater.

The absorber material is typically metal, painted black to effectively absorb solar radiation. The metal surface heats up quickly when exposed to the sun and rapidly transfers this heat to the surrounding air. Paint applied to the metal absorber plate must be able to withstand operating temperatures above 300°F without deterioration. Black enamel paint over a suitable primer or an appropriate selective surface material can be specified (see "Absorber Components" in Chapter 7).

The absorber plate is typically corrugated metal decking or expanded metal lath, the latter being used where the airstream flows through, rather than over, the absorber material. The actual design, configuration, and material selection of the absorber component will differ for the U-tube and vertical panel subsystem types; therefore, each is discussed separately below.

VERTICAL PANEL SUBSYSTEM

There are three configurations for the absorber plate in the vertical panel subsystem. In the first, described as a back pass absorber, air flows between the absorber plate and the inside wall (see Figure 6.10).

The major advantage of the back pass design is that the airflow is separated from the cold collector component by a dead airspace. Since an airspace is a good insulator, heat losses between the moving airstream and the outdoors will be minimized. In addition, dust and dirt that enter the channel from the home cannot settle on the glazing, which would otherwise eventually reduce the amount of transmitted solar radiation. For these reasons, this configuration is favored in many TAP installations.

In the front pass design, the airstream passes in front of the absorber plate (see Figure 6.11). The absorber can be fastened directly to the stud wall, simplifying construction and reducing costs. Of the three configurations, however, the front pass is the least efficient, since the moving airstream, which is heated by the absorber, is at the same time losing some of its heat to the cold glazing.

The third, and most efficient, absorber design is the dual pass. As its name implies, a dual pass absorber is constructed to allow the airstream to move both in front of and behind the absorber plate (see Figure 6.12).

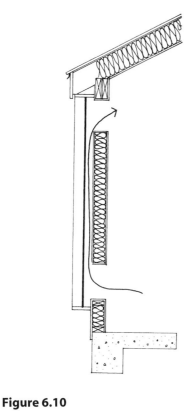

Figure 6.10

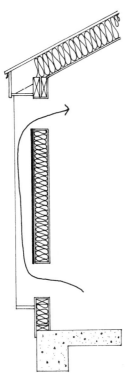

Figure 6.11

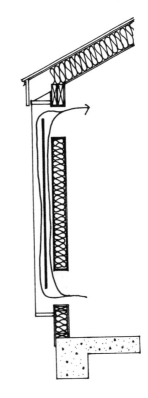

Figure 6.12

The effectiveness of this configuration lies in the fact that air is a poor conductor of heat. Therefore, it is advantageous to expose as much of the moving airstream to the absorber plate surface as possible. A dual pass, by allowing air to pass on both sides of the absorber, exposes twice as much surface area to passing air as does either the back or front pass. Of the three configurations, however, the dual pass is the most difficult and expensive to construct.

One practical and effective option for the front and dual pass absorber configurations is to use five or six layers of slit-and-expanded metal lath

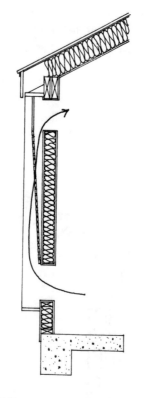

Figure 6.13

(typically used for plaster work) as the absorber (see Figure 6.13). The lath is placed on the diagonal, increasing the heat-transfer surface between absorber and air. The surface behind the absorber is covered with a light-colored or polished surface to reflect any sunlight that penetrates the lath back onto the absorber surface.

At night in the heating season, the absorber and adjacent airstream will cool below the temperature of the living space. If unimpeded, this cool air will drop, entering the living space through the lower vent. This flow of cool air, called reverse thermocirculation, will rob heat from the living space unless dampers are provided. Dampers can be automatically or manually operated and should be placed on the upper and lower vents. It is designed to open in the direction of warm-air flow and close at other times, preventing reverse thermocirculation.

U-TUBE SUBSYSTEM

The TAP in the U-tube subsystem is constructed with a central partition around which the air-

stream flows, collecting heat from the absorber plate. The absorber is usually found in one of two locations, depending on the direction of airflow. In the most common configuration, the air flows from behind to in front of the central divider, then directly into the living space. The absorber is placed on the central divider, much like the front pass configuration in a vertical TAP (see Figures 6.11 and 6.14). This design can be modi-

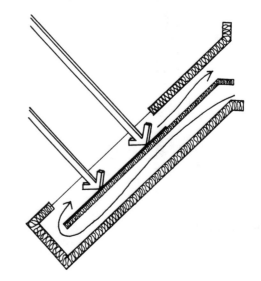

Figure 6.14

fied to the diagonal pass-through design discussed earlier in this chapter, in which case the absorber is constructed of slit-and-expanded metal lath (see Figure 6.15).

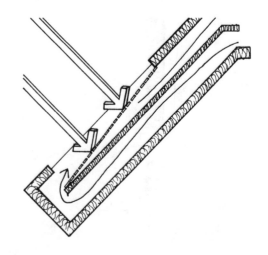

Figure 6.15

In the second configuration, known as the reverse flow tube, air enters through the top vent of the TAP and flows around the center divider and out the lower vent. The center divider is glazed in this design, with the absorber placed behind it (see Figure 6.16). This design has lower

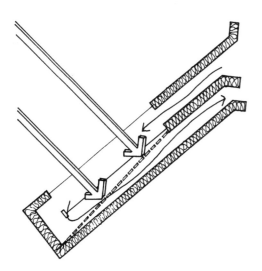

Figure 6.16

heat losses to the outside than the front pass, since the air is heated by the absorber *after* it passes the cold glazing. This reverse flow configuration is primarily used in cases where it is advantageous for the lower vent to be the air outlet (see the discussion of slab floor storage in "Storage," later in this chapter).

The U-tube TAP, if carefully designed, can be self-damping. When detailing the TAP, the top of the exterior glazing should be below the lowest point of the outlet vent (see Figure 6.17). If the glazing is above this level, dampers similar to those described earlier in this chapter for the vertical panel subsystem will need to be specified.

ABSORBER RULES OF THUMB

- *Area:* The area of the absorber should be slightly larger than, and directly behind, the collector glazing.

- *Flow channel:* The depth of the flow channel (D) should be 1/20 the length (L) of the glazing for diagonal absorbers and 1/15 (L) for flat plate, vertical absorbers (see Figure 6.18).

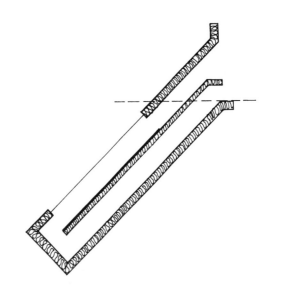

Figure 6.17

For example, if the glazing is 8′ long, the flow channel should be 5″. The channel in a U-tube TAP should be the same depth on both sides of the central divider.

- *Airspace (back pass vertical panel):* The airspace between the absorber and glazing in a back pass vertical TAP should be from 5⁄8″ to 1¾″.

Storage

Convective loop systems are generally designed without a storage component, providing heat only during the daytime when the sun is shining.

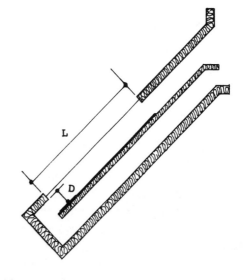

Figure 6.18

If large collector areas are specified, however, the amount of heat generated in the TAP can, at times, exceed the heating requirements of the home. If storage, such as a radiant slab, is provided, this excess heat produced by the TAP can be stored for use at night and during overcast periods.

Since the TAP produces hot air that is distributed to storage, the storage component can be located virtually anywhere in the home. However, two design guidelines should be considered when selecting the storage location: (1) the storage material in most cases will be heavy and will impose structural considerations if placed above the foundation; and (2) the system will operate more effectively if the storage is placed *above* the TAP.

These design guidelines have led to the development of the slab-on-grade, or radiant slab, design. In slab-on-grade storage, hot air from the TAP is circulated under the floor slab of the home and out through vents at the back of the slab (see Figure 6.19). As the warm air is passed under the

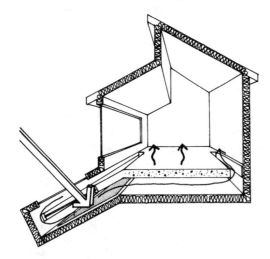

Figure 6.19

slab, heat is absorbed into the masonry. As in a direct gain floor, this heat is slowly released throughout the day and night. Therefore, the floor should not be covered with a carpet or other material with insulating properties. Insulation should, conversely, be placed under the air channel to reduce heat losses to the ground.

The TAP outlet for under-slab distribution is generally the lower vent; therefore, a reverse flow panel design should be specified (see "Ab-

sorber" earlier in this chapter). The slab-on-grade storage system is generally easy to construct and to operate. It should be noted, however, that since air is vented directly to the living space, the underslab plenum must be kept clean and dry to avoid indoor air quality problems. Periodic inspection of the underslab area should be part of ongoing maintenance.

Distribution

In convective loop systems, the distribution component moves air between TAP, living space, and (if used) storage. For systems designed without storage, distribution is required only when the TAP is not located adjacent to the living spaces. This is rarely the case, and most convective loop systems without storage are designed to allow the TAP to deliver heated air directly into the living space through vents.

If remote storage is provided, hot air coming out of the TAP should be delivered with as little loss of heat through the distribution system as possible.

Generally, the distribution system consists of insulated ducts connecting TAP, storage, and living space. Air movement is by natural convection, although, in some instances, the use of a small fan, placed in the opening of the duct, is advisable. A fan is particularly recommended in designs where the TAP outlet vent is located above the storage component.

In a vertical panel subsystem design with radiant slab storage, heated air is taken off the top of the TAP and distributed initially through insulated ducts that run between the upper floor joists or roof trusses. Vertical runs, connecting the ducts to the plenum underneath the floor slab, can be enclosed in an interior partition wall. The heated air travels from the vertical ducts to the underslab plenum, where it is used to charge the underside of the floor slab. Heat flow into the living space is by radiation through the floor slab, by convection through floor registers, or by both methods. After the air passes through the underslab plenum, it is collected in a return plenum and distributed back to the TAP through vertical return ducts. In this type of distribution system, fans will be a necessity for adequate air movement.

In the U-tube subsystem, as noted above, the TAP is frequently adjacent to the storage. Distribution between the TAP and the radiant slab is through a reverse flow panel design. Heat rising from the absorber panel is distributed through the lower panel vent into an adjacent underslab plenum. The heated air charges the underside of the floor slab, and is also, in some cases, fed directly into the living space through floor registers at the north side of the room (see Figure 6.19). Return air is provided to the TAP through floor registers directly above the upper TAP inlet vents, at the south side of the living space.

DISTRIBUTION RULES OF THUMB

- *Design:* In all cases, the distribution system should be designed to be free of any obstructions that would impede airflow. Duct runs should be designed to be direct and to contain as few turns as possible.

- *Vent openings:* Vent openings between the TAP and living space should be the same width as the flow channels. Continuous linear diffusers (available from most mechanical equipment distributors) are recommended for vents used for direct distribution.

Control

SHADING

To avoid excessive heat buildup in the TAP during the cooling season, it is recommended that a covering be placed over the collector glazing. A sheet of opaque material, such as plywood or rigid insulation, which is roughly the size of the TAP, secured at the edges, will prevent solar heat from reaching the absorber. Considerations should be made for the appearance of the panels, particularly in the vertical panel subsystem design.

If a vertical TAP is used, the façade of the home should be designed to allow the collector to be completely covered without obstructing the view out of the windows. Simple overhangs and other conventional shading devices are *not* recommended, since they will not sufficiently reduce the potential heat buildup to prevent deterioration of the TAP materials.

INSULATING—FIXED INSULATION

Fixed insulation is generally specified for three parts of a convective loop system: the thermosiphon air panel, the distribution component, and the underside of the supply plenum below the radiant floor slab. In the TAP construction of the vertical panel subsystem, insulation is placed between the studs on the inside of the TAP to the same levels as those specified for the rest of the home. The insulation and studs should be covered with a smooth material, such as gypsum board, which allows the air to flow unimpeded through the TAP.

In a U-tube subsystem, the TAP is frequently exposed on all sides and will require a complete insulation "wrap" to reduce heat losses from the sides and back. In addition, the central divider should be constructed of an insulating material to reduce heat flow between the air channels. In both cases, a rigid insulation, such as rigid fiberglass boards or certain types of polyisocyanurate (which can withstand operating temperatures of up to 300°F), is recommended. Polystyrene is emphatically *not* recommended in TAP construction. It is also recommended that, if used, rigid fiberglass board be covered to prevent direct exposure of the fibers to the moving air stream.

In a radiant slab design, insulation should be placed underneath the horizontal plenum that feeds the exposed concrete slab above it. This insulation is necessary to reduce heat losses to the ground during the heating season.

If ducts are used to distribute warm air from the TAP, they should be insulated to reduce heat losses. Insulation is particularly important if the ducts run in an unheated space, such as a basement or crawl space.

CONTROL RULES OF THUMB

Insulating

- *Fixed insulation:* R-8 insulation is recommended in the construction of the TAP in a U-tube subsystem design. The central divider should be insulated with R-5 to R-8 insulation. Ducts used for warm-air distribution should be wrapped with R-4 insulation.

CONVECTIVE LOOP DETAILS

The drawings on the following pages illustrate common construction detailing for convective loop systems. The details are divided into two detail pages and are intended to simply suggest a few options among the many convective loop system configurations possible.

The two detail pages illustrate typical construction features for the vertical panel and U-tube panel subsystems, respectively. The vertical panel subsystem is shown in both back and dual pass configurations. Panel constructions can be used both with and without thermal storage.

The details are followed by a set of construction notes, referenced from the details. The notes contain guidelines, troubleshooting tips, and other information useful in constructing a convective loop system.

Wall Collector

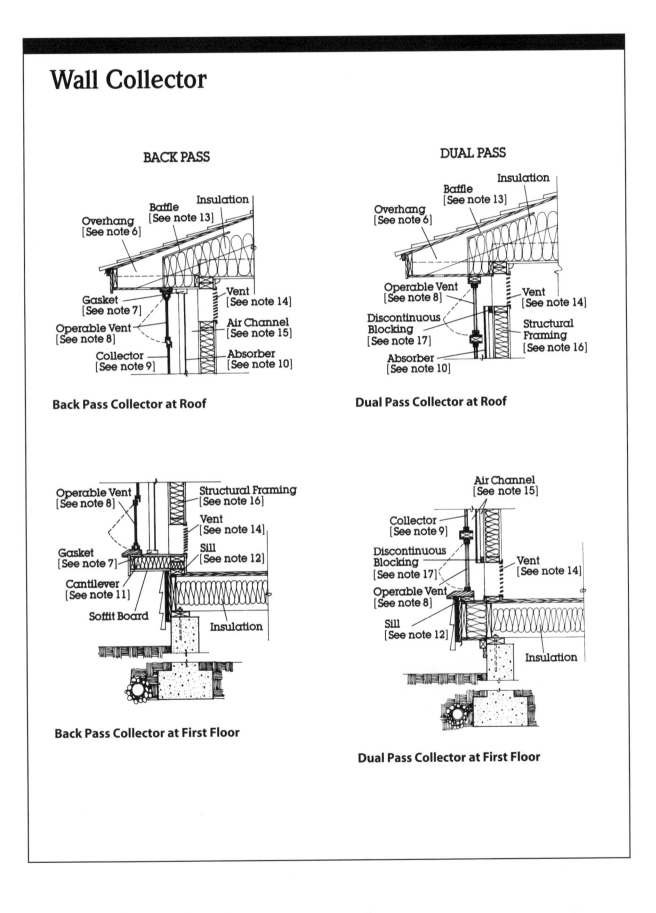

BACK PASS

Overhang [See note 6]
Baffle [See note 13]
Insulation
Gasket [See note 7]
Vent [See note 14]
Operable Vent [See note 8]
Air Channel [See note 15]
Collector [See note 9]
Absorber [See note 10]

Back Pass Collector at Roof

DUAL PASS

Overhang [See note 6]
Baffle [See note 13]
Insulation
Operable Vent [See note 8]
Vent [See note 14]
Discontinuous Blocking [See note 17]
Structural Framing [See note 16]
Absorber [See note 10]

Dual Pass Collector at Roof

Operable Vent [See note 8]
Structural Framing [See note 16]
Vent [See note 14]
Gasket [See note 7]
Sill [See note 12]
Cantilever [See note 11]
Soffit Board
Insulation

Back Pass Collector at First Floor

Air Channel [See note 15]
Collector [See note 9]
Discontinuous Blocking [See note 17]
Vent [See note 14]
Operable Vent [See note 8]
Sill [See note 12]
Insulation

Dual Pass Collector at First Floor

CONVECTIVE LOOP DETAILS

Below-the-Floor Collector

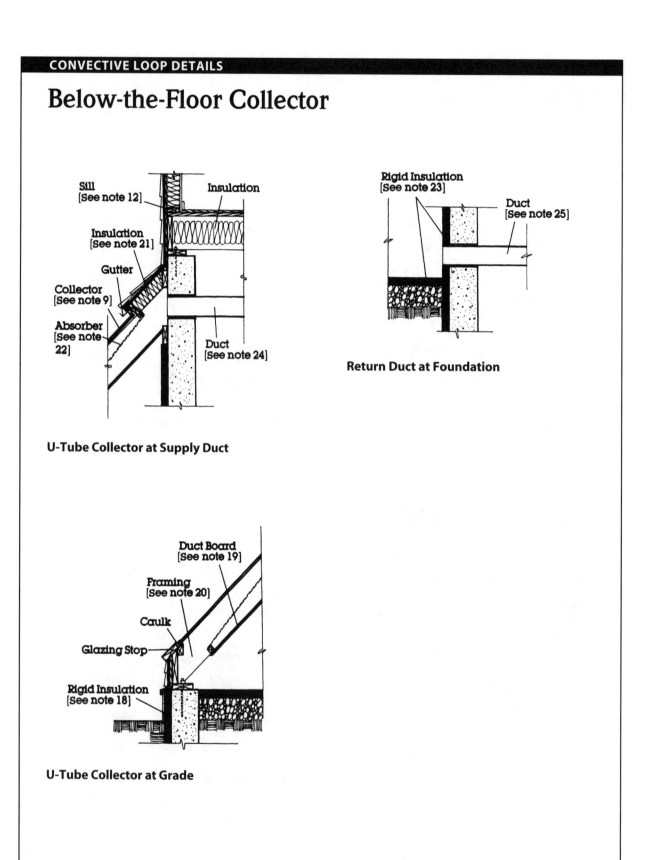

U-Tube Collector at Supply Duct

Return Duct at Foundation

U-Tube Collector at Grade

Collector Notes

GENERAL NOTES

1. All footings must bear on undisturbed soil. Adjust footing size, reinforcing, and depth below grade as required by site conditions and/or local code. Where groundwater problems exist, provide sufficient granular fill to prevent water penetration at slab-on-grade. Reinforcing in concrete slab-on-grade construction is not recommended except where required by local conditions and/or code. Expansion joints should be provided, as required, at the connection between concrete or masonry floors and stud or masonry walls to prevent cracking.

2. Sizing of headers is to be determined by local building codes and/or accepted practice.

3. Insulation levels at foundation, floors, walls, and ceiling must meet or exceed the requirements of the local building and energy codes.

4. Other roof configurations may be used at the builder's option. Consult local building codes for restrictions and special requirements concerning roof/wall connections, especially in seismic and/or high-wind areas. The opaque roof must be vented to ensure proper performance of the insulation. Vents are typically located at the overhang soffits and at the ridge, depending on the roof construction. An airspace is provided to allow for circulation.

5. Provide gutters and downspouts as required.

DETAIL NOTES

6. Overhang at collector should be sized to optimize solar gains during heating season and prevent overheating during cooling season.

7. A strip gasket, such as ethlylene propylene diene monomer (EPDM), at the top and bottom of the corrugated metal absorber plate will provide an airtight seal at the edges. Care must be taken to ensure that the gasket material is able to withstand the high temperatures generated in the space.

8. Portions of the collector should be operable to allow venting of the TAP during periods of excessive heat gain. For indoor air quality considerations, the operable units are also critical to allow periodic cleaning and maintenance of the TAP, particularly when the air is directly vented into the building. Awning-type or other operable windows may be specified and should be equipped with demountable insect screens that can be removed during the heating season.

9. For optimum thermal performance, it is generally recommended that double glazing be provided, preferably a high performance glazing using one or more of the following: low-e coating(s), gas fill, or suspended plastic film(s). (See the "Collector Components" section in Chapter 7 for more information on glass or plastic collector materials.) The collector unit should be demountable or externally operable to aid in maintenance and cleaning. The collector frame may be detached from the frame wall and designed to support the glazing, glazing frame (if preframed), roof, and other related loads, or it may be attached to and supported by the frame wall. Framing should be kept to a minimum, since it reduces the effective collector area and may cast shadows, both of which will affect the thermal performance of the wall. All structural framing and connections shall be designed to conform with local

CONVECTIVE LOOP DETAILS

building code restrictions and/or accepted practice. Frames should be continuous at edges.

10. The absorber should be a lightweight material, such as corrugated roof metal, providing maximum heat transfer and maximum surface area. (For further information, see "Absorber Components" in Chapter 7.)

11. The collector assembly is supported on a cantilever. Care must be taken to ensure that insulation levels meet or exceed requirements of local building and energy codes. Sizing of members is to be determined by loads and local building codes and/or accepted practice.

12. Continuous sill sealer is recommended to provide protection against infiltration.

13. Provide baffles where necessary to maintain 1″ minimum airspace for venting the attic.

14. Operable vents at top of the adjacent wall area are provided to allow heated air to enter living spaces, while low vents draw cooler room air into the collector assembly, completing the "loop." Heated air may also be ducted from vents at the top to remote storage for later use. (For further information, see "Storage" and "Distribution," earlier in this chapter.)

15. It is generally recommended that the air channel depth should be $\frac{1}{15}$ the length of the glazing for flat plate absorbers and $\frac{1}{20}$ the length of the glazing for diagonal mesh absorbers. (For further information, see "Absorber Rules of Thumb" in this chapter.)

16. Stud framing should be as required to support the roof and other loads. Insulation levels should meet or exceed requirements of local building and energy codes. The air channel side of the stud wall should be finished with a smooth-surfaced sheathing to augment airflow.

17. Discontinuous blocking is provided to allow free airflow on both sides of the absorber plate.

18. Cement or synthetic stucco (applied on lath) over exterior insulation may be used. Other finishes may be specified at the builder's option, but rigid insulation must be protected where exposed above grade.

19. The air channel is created by nailing a rigid sheathing material to the underside of the framing members. It is recommended that an insulative material, such as duct board, be specified. (See notes on fixed insulation earlier in this chapter.)

20. Framing must be sized to support the glazing system.

21. Opaque, insulated framing should be provided to reduce heat loss at the top of the collector assembly. The length of the opaque portion should be sufficient to extend below the bottom of distribution ducts from the collector assembly.

22. Three to five layers of expanded wire mesh are recommended for the absorber. Other materials may be specified at the builder's option. (For further information, see "Absorber Components" in Chapter 7.)

23. Rigid insulation is recommended to control heat loss and to reduce the introduction of ground vapor and odors into the airflow. In areas with drier soils and low water table, a 6-mil polyethylene sheet may suffice.

24. A blockout in the foundation must be provided to allow for distribution of heated air to living spaces and/or remote storage. Lintels should be designed and reinforced as required by local codes and/or accepted practice. Ductwork should be insulated to

prevent heat loss. (For further information, see "Distribution" in this chapter.)

25. A blockout in the foundation must be provided for the return air ducts bringing cooler air from living spaces and/or remote stor-

age, completing the "loop." Lintels should be designed and reinforced as required by local codes and/or accepted practice. (For further information, see "Distribution" in this chapter.)

SERI #1—Lobato House

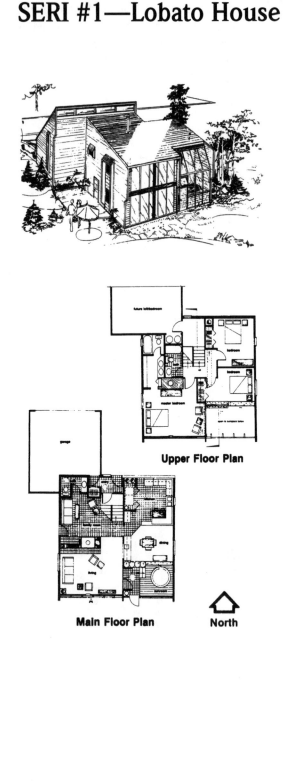

Upper Floor Plan

Main Floor Plan   **North**

This 2,300-sq.-ft. home in Boulder, Colorado, was designed under a program sponsored by the Solar Energy Research Institute (SERI) and employs a convective loop system for passive solar heating. Heated air from a two-story thermosiphon air panel and an attached sunspace is stored in a rock bed and the thermal mass within the living space. The distribution of heated air within the system is augmented by small fans.

Partial earth berming, air-lock entry vestibules, and the garage act as thermal buffers on the minimally glazed north side of the home. To the south, a double-height attached sunspace is well integrated into the plan and serves as a focal point for recreational activities.

The 216 sq. ft. of south-facing thermosiphon air panels in the living and bedroom areas are glazed with patio door replacement glass. Sunlight transmitted through these collectors is absorbed by a black aluminum screen in the airspace between the glazing and the stud wall. This absorbed heat is transferred to the air passing up through the airspace. Induction fans circulate the heated air through insulated ducts into a rock storage bed, which stores the heat for eventual radiant release through the floor slab.

Located at the southeast corner of the house, the double-height sunspace provides additional passive heating. Vertical and sloped south-wall glazing allows sunlight to strike water storage containers on the north wall. The water storage is comprised of four water-filled fiberglass tubes, each holding 450 gallons. Additional thermal mass is afforded by 12″ of exposed aggregate concrete wall. Beneath the tubes, brick pavers on a concrete slab further supplement the storage mass. Heated air from the sunspace is transferred to adjacent spaces through operable doors and windows.

Project
Lobato House (SERI #1)

Builder
Tom Fowler
Heritage Construction
Boulder, Colorado

Designer
Rudy Lobato
Rudolph Lobato & Associates
Longmont, Colorado

Sponsor
Solar Energy Research Institute
Denver Metro Home Builders Association
Denver, Colorado

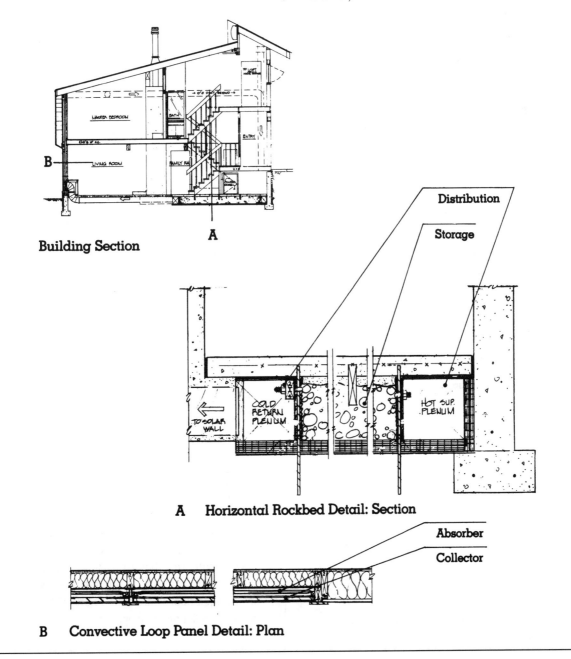

Building Section

A   Horizontal Rockbed Detail: Section

B   Convective Loop Panel Detail: Plan

CONVECTIVE LOOP CASE STUDY

Ashelman House

Upper Floor

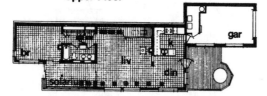

Lower Floor

North

A convective loop system provides passive solar heating to the 2,155-sq.-ft. Ashelman house in Martinsburg, West Virginia. Built into a south-facing slope, the home is buffered on the north by a service area and an air-lock entry. The house is fully exposed on the south, where thermosiphon air panels below the first floor collect solar heat. Although this type of system is not generally suggested, this case study of rock-bed storage is included to explain the general principles of the system.

An attached sunspace (solarium) and an open-air sun deck flank the south-facing living spaces on the lower level. Above, bedrooms are connected by a bridge from the main entry overlooking the double-height direct gain living room. Masonry construction throughout, including precast 4' concrete panels supporting the sod roof, tile over the slab floors, and five 55-gallon water-filled storage drums placed in the sunspace, contribute to the thermal mass of the home.

The 12' × 32' tilted array of air panels is constructed using one layer of tempered glass over five layers of expanded metal lath painted flat black to increase solar absorption. The assembly lies within an 8" airspace and is backed by 2" of urethane insulation. Four inches of rigid Styrofoam insulate the cold-air return channel behind the panels.

A rock bed containing 4"- to 8"-diameter rocks provides backup storage for the solar heat collected in the panels. Panel-heated air rises into the rock-bed storage area beneath the home. Manually controlled vents in the living-space floor are opened to allow warm air to rise directly into the living quarters, if required. Cooler return air is ducted into the rock-bed storage through floor vents on the north side of the home, completing the loop.

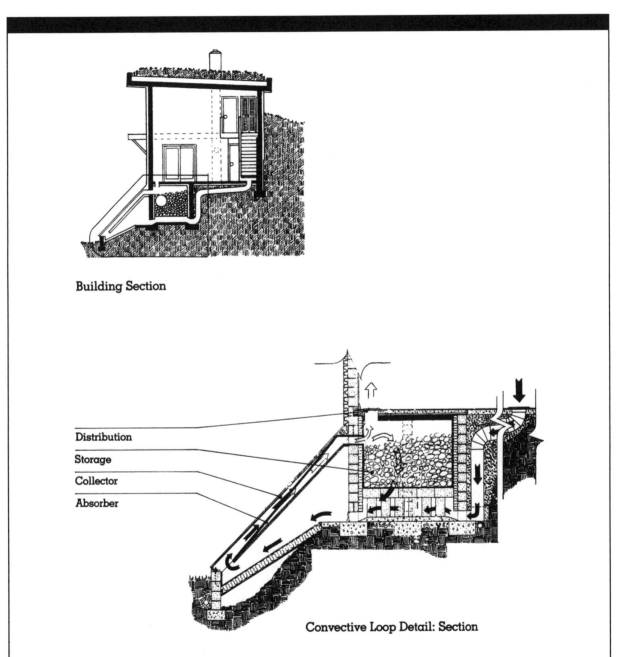

Building Section

Distribution
Storage
Collector
Absorber

Convective Loop Detail: Section

Roof overhangs and intermediate trellises shade the south wall during the cooling season.

Removable insulation over the panels has been added since construction to significantly reduce temperatures in the panels during the summer.

Project
Ashelman House

Builder/Designer
Randall Ashelman
Randall Ashelman–Natural Sun Homes
Berkeley Springs, West Virginia

Sponsor
U.S. Department of Housing and Urban
  Development
U.S. Department of Energy
Washington, D.C.

CONVECTIVE LOOP CASE STUDY

TEA House

The TEA House in Massachusetts utilizes thermosiphoning air panels along its south wall, creating a convective loop system for passive solar heating. This design illustrates the simplicity with which a standard design can be modified to supplement heating requirements with a passive solar system. It is particularly appropriate for application to existing structures because the air panels can be installed on almost any south wall, regardless of the configuration of the floor plan.

The panels consist of clear glass covering corrugated aluminum absorber plates, which are painted black. In the back pass design, as it is called, top and bottom vents in the insulated wall allow air to move between absorber plates and the gypsum-board finish. Sunlight passing through the collector glazing strikes the aluminum plates, where it is absorbed as heat. The heat is transferred through the plate to warm the air in the airspace. This heated air rises through the channel and passes into the house through the upper vent. At the same time, denser, cool air from the home enters the channel through the lower vents to replace the displaced heated air.

This thermosiphoning effect naturally circulates heat through the house in a convective loop during the day. A 4-mil polyethylene backdraft damper over the bottom grill restricts nighttime heat loss from reverse thermosiphoning. Additionally, insulated vent covers on hinges can be latched closed at night to further reduce heat loss, as well as during the cooling season to prevent heat gain. This system design does not require storage and, as a result, provides heat only during the daytime. The panels can be covered with an opaque panel during the summer to reduce the possibility of rapid deterioration.

Project
TEA House

Designer
TEA Foundation, Inc.
1 West St.
Keene, NH 03431

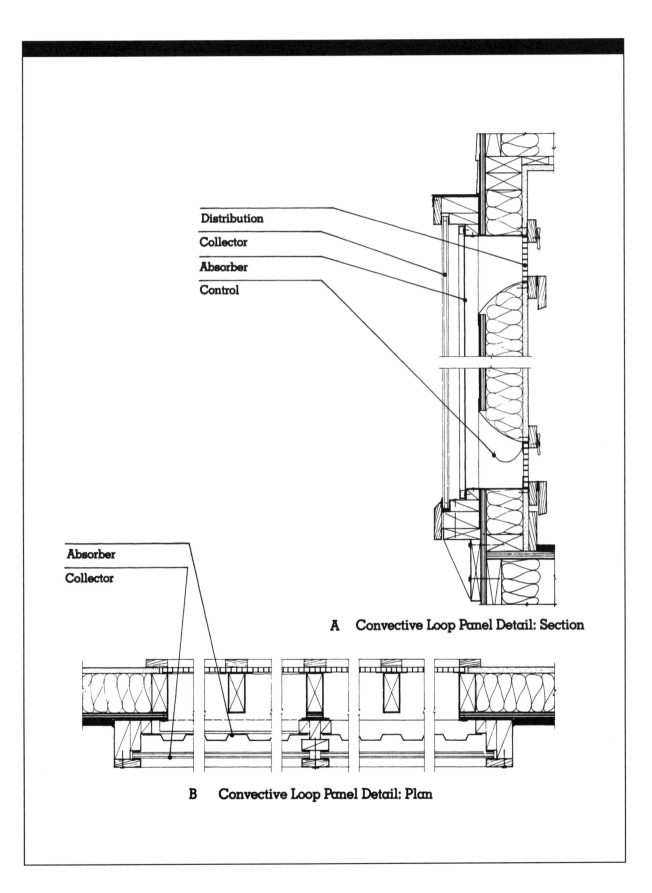

Distribution

Collector

Absorber

Control

A   Convective Loop Panel Detail: Section

Absorber

Collector

B   Convective Loop Panel Detail: Plan

Introduction

This chapter presents construction and thermal performance information that will aid in specifying the materials illustrated in the construction details in Chapters 3 through 6. For the most part, the materials designated in these details are intended to represent typical, rather than specific, products.

Once a particular detail has been selected and material dimensions determined using the rules of thumb, specific materials or products can be specified using the information in this chapter. In most cases, the materials illustrated are available from a number of manufacturers. In instances where unique or specific products are discussed, individual manufacturers are identified and their products listed.

To simplify this material selection and specification process, the chapter is divided into subsections by component type, including (1) collector components, (2) absorber components, (3) storage components, (4) control components, and (5) distribution components. Each component section is further subdivided with discussions focusing on issues relevant to that subject area.

The collector components section includes (1) a review of the basic characteristics of passive

solar collectors; (2) a discussion of the fenestration options for passive solar installations, including types of glazing materials and frame types; and (3) a brief discussion of caulking and sealants appropriate for passive solar applications.

The section on absorbers covers a general discussion of the function of the absorber, the types of products available to use as absorbers, and their performance characteristics. Two tables accompany the discussions. The first lists specific manufacturers of selective-surface products and general absorber materials. The second provides absorptivities of various common building materials.

The storage components section is divided into four subsections covering the various storage materials presented in the construction details (chapters 3 through 6): (1) concrete masonry, (2) concrete, (3) brick, and (4) water. Each of these subsections includes, where relevant, a general description of the basic composition and typical dimensions of the materials; a discussion of relevant construction issues, including finishes (exterior and interior), color, and texture; and a definition and discussion of the specific physical properties that affect the thermal performance of each material. Tables are presented that provide data, of a general nature, with regard to that material type and, where appropriate, specific products.

The discussion of the distribution components provides a brief review of the applicability of distribution to the basic system types and general guidelines useful in component design.

The control components section is subdivided into three sections covering shading, reflecting, and insulating components.

Each section outlines the function of these components and the techniques for their proper operation in the basic passive systems.

Collector Components

Introduction

The collector is the portion of a passive solar system that admits solar energy and traps the heat it generates. This heat is absorbed by other elements in the system and is then stored for later use or distributed directly to the living spaces. The collector thus forms an integral part of every passive heating system.

The collector can be as simple as a standard window unit or as elaborate as a large, site-built sunspace with both vertical and tilted glazing. In all cases, the collector is composed of three basic elements:

- *Glazing*—Composed of some form of glass or plastic that allows radiant energy to strike the absorber or storage component while restricting the outflow of the heat energy.

- *Collector frame*—Supports the glazing material.

- *Caulking and sealants*—Ensure that the entire installation is airtight and weather-tight and able to operate at peak efficiency.

These elements can be combined in a large variety of configurations whose performance in passive solar installations is dependent on the orientation and tilt of the collector; the thermal properties of the specific glazing material employed (see the following section); the *net* area of the material being used for collection (exclusive of frame); the size and type of frame being used; the effectiveness of the caulking and/or sealants being used; and the overall con-

figuration of the collector (glazing material and frame).

Collector Types

The number of possible designs for passive collectors is virtually limitless—from simple, off-the-shelf window units to solid walls of glass or plastic that can cover the entire south side of a house. Some of the more common configurations and their possible applications are shown in Figure 7.1. The choice of glazing materials in these configurations has increased widely over the past 10 years. Options include high-performance glazings (see following section) and plastics such as acrylics and polycarbonates. Table 7.1 compares the advantages and disadvantages of some of these materials.

High-performance collector elements (including glass, spacers between glass panes, and frames) for residential applications have become more commonplace over the past decade. These elements help windows lose less heat in cold weather and gain less heat in hot weather. Many also reduce glare and maintain a relatively high level of daylight penetration into the space. The configurations of window units vary, but the basic elements include low-emittance (low-e) coatings on glazings and interpane films; coatings with low shading coefficient and high daylight transmittance; glazings with low shading coefficient with the appearance of clear glass; multiple air layers using suspended plastic films between panes; inert gases instead of air in the interpane space(s); insulating "warm edge" spacers on the glass units; and improved frame designs, including thermally broken metal frames and low-conducting composite materials. Windows that incorporate these features are now available nationally from leading manufacturers, such as Marvin Windows, Weather Shield, Hurd, Andersen Windows, Pella, Semco, and others.

LOW-E GLAZINGS

Low-e glass is the most important development in glazing technology of the past decade, and has had a significant impact on passive solar heating and cooling. In fact, low-e glass now makes such passive solar techniques as adjustable shading

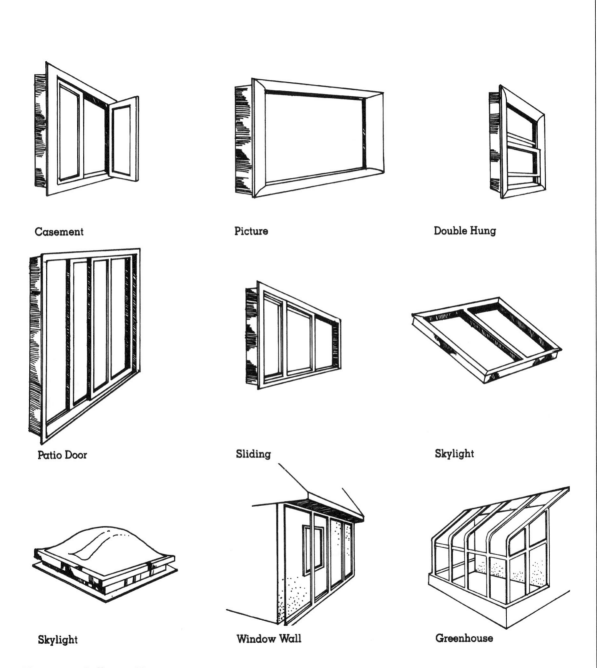

Casement   Picture   Double Hung

Patio Door   Sliding   Skylight

Skylight   Window Wall   Greenhouse

Figure 7.1 Collector Types

Table 7.1   *Glazings: Advantages and Disadvantages*

	ADVANTAGES	DISADVANTAGES
GLASS	• high optical clarity • excellent selective transmission properties • excellent weatherability • heat, air pollution and UV resistant • readily available in multipane units, with tints, coatings and/or gas fills to improve thermal and optical properties • low thermal expansion • long lifespan	• breaks easily • heavy • often difficult to install in large sheets
ACRYLIC	• high optical clarity • lightweight and easy to handle • some impact resistance • insulation and transmission values of base material (single pane, untinted and uncoated) similar to glass • some blockage of UV transmission • frosted acrylic available with light-diffusing properties (often used in skylights) • available with tints • fabricated in curved shapes	• scratches easily, although abrasion-resistant coatings are available • buckles and cracks if not properly installed • significant expansion and contraction characteristics • not normally available with selective coatings, or in sealed, gas-filled units • will sag at high temperatures • flammable, can release toxic fumes when burning • medium lifespan
POLYCARBONATE	• high optical clarity • very high impact strength • insulation values of base material (single pane, untinted and uncoated) slightly better than glass or acrylic, similar solar transmission to acrylics • available in insulating, extruded multicell sheets • available with tints • fabricated in curved shapes	• scratches easily, although abrasion-resistant coatings are available • becomes brittle and can yellow after prolonged exposure to the sun, unless protective treatments are added • not normally available with selective coatings, or in sealed, gas-filled units • flammable, can release toxic fumes when burning

Table 7.1 *(Continued)*

	ADVANTAGES	DISADVANTAGES
FIBERGLASS REINFORCED POLYESTER	• lightweight, easy to handle • high strength and durability with coatings such as Tedlar® • low UV transmission • flat and corrugated sheets available • highly insulating, transluscent panel assemblies available, combining double layers with a fiberglass fill	• solar transmittance reduced when UV coatings are added • will yellow and "blossom" without coatings • not normally available with selective coatings, or in sealed, gas-filled units • flammable, can release toxic fumes when burning • medium lifespan

and movable insulation—common a decade ago—less economical when compared to low-e performance. Low-e glass admits less solar heat than uncoated clear glass, is more insulating, and requires no adjustment by the resident. Low-e glass is fabricated by coating a pane with layers of metal or metal oxide a few atoms thick. The coating emits very little radiation in the long-wave (infrared) spectrum. This means that if the interior low-e glass pane gets warm in the winter, it will radiate little heat to the exterior, cold pane of the window. The net effect is to diminish heat loss from the building interior in cold weather, and to reduce heat gain in hot weather.

The location of the low-e coating in the window assembly affects its performance. On a double-pane window, the four glass surfaces are numbered consecutively, starting with the surface exposed to the outside (Figure 7.2). A low-e coating on surface 3 of the glazing reduces the ability of the inner pane to radiate outside, and is most effective in buildings requiring long periods of heating. A low-e coating on surface 2 of the glazing reduces the ability of the outer pane to radiate toward the conditioned space, and is therefore recommended for cooling applications. Some manufacturers also offer low-e coatings on both surface 2 and surface 3. These glazings have a higher R-value (by about 5 percent to 10 percent), and a lower shading coefficient (less solar heat admitted) than single-coating glazings.

Heat Mirror™ glazings vary from a common low-e coated plastic layer in the space between two panes of glass. The space can be air-filled or gas-filled. In effect, this creates a "triple-pane" window in only a 1"-thick glass assembly. Low-e coatings can be applied to either the glass or film. Heat Mirror™ reports a center-of-glass U-value of 0.26, compared to 0.33 for most low-e applications. With gas-fill, this U-value can go as low as 0.17. Hurd Windows, for instance, offers Heat Mirror™ units that achieve R-values in the range of R-3 to R-4.

Visonwall produces another high-end window, suitable for very cold climates. The U-values of Visionwall windows range from 0.51 to 0.14,

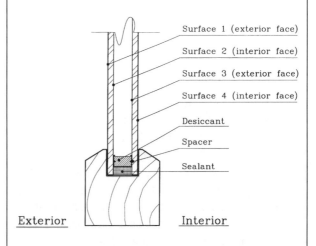

Figure 7.2 Window Section with Insulating Glass

yielding R-values of R-2 to R-7. The distinctive characteristic of the Visionwall window is its exceptional thermal-break system system in the frame, which renders the whole-window U-value almost equal to the center-of-glass U-value.

When windows have R-values in the 4 to 6 range, they do not feel cold during winter. As a result, the occupants feel more comfortable in the house at lower temperatures. (As a rule of thumb, if a person is seated by a window, for every 1°F increase in the window surface temperature, the air temperature in the house can be lowered by 1.4°F without affecting comfort.)

Another important characteristic of a window's thermal performance is the decrease in shading coefficient of low-e glass versus uncoated glass. Glazings with lower shading coefficients admit less solar heat. Low-e glass can maintain a clear appearance while reducing solar gain by 20 percent to almost 50 percent. Consequently, a building can have low-e glass with different solar characteristics on the west and north sides, for instance, yet the glass will be practically identical in appearance.

Low-e coatings are referred to as either "soft" or "hard." Soft coatings are sputtered onto the glass surface and they can be more easily scratched or marred. For this reason, the coating is always applied to the inner face of glass or film in multipane applications. Hard coatings are applied using a pyrolitic process, can be used on any glass surface, and have overcome the sometimes objectionable blue-green tints of earlier glazings. The emittance of soft coatings is very low, and, as a result, these coatings also achieve the highest R-values, 10 percent to 20 percent higher than those of hard coatings.

Insulating Spacers

Spacers are used to keep the layers of glass in an insulating unit separated at a uniform distance. In addition, spacers must provide a moisture seal for the glazing unit, accomodate stress from thermal expansion and contraction, and provide a gas-tight seal for units using inert gas fills (see section below). Standard spacers are typically made of aluminum with an organic sealant. Bescause of the high conductivity of aluminum, these spacers can degrade the overall R-value of the glazing unit.

Better spacers, designed for use in high-R-value glazings, utilize lower-conducting metals, such as stainless steel, plastics ranging from silicone to hardened polyurethane, or wood. Research shows that an entire fenestration unit with insulating spacers can achieve R-value improvements ranging from 5 percent to more than 15 percent. The high percentage improvements are obtained for glazings with very low U-values. In addition, "warm edge" spacers, as they are sometimes known, can decrease the potential for moisture condensation at the edge of the glass units. This can be an important attribute in colder climates.

INERT GASES

The interpane spaces of fenestration units can be filled with nontoxic inert gases that are less conductive than air, such as argon (combined with sulfur hexafluoride) or krypton. Argon gas windows have R-values that are 5 percent to 30 percent better than those of air-filled windows. Krypton gas can raise the R-value by up to 50 percent. There has been some concern about the long-term efficiency of the fenestration, in the event that the gas escapes. However, research indicates that only 10 percent to 20 percent of the gas may be lost over a 20-year period.

Frame Material

As the R-values of glazings have improved in recent years, more attention is being paid to the fenestration frame materials, which can have a significant impact on the overall thermal performance of a fenestration unit. Because frames typically represent 10 percent to 30 percent of the overall area of a window, highly conductive frame materials can result in lower unit R-values, counteracting the benefits obtained from high-performance glazings (see "Collector Selection" section below).

The range of frame materials available includes aluminum, aluminum with thermal breaks, wood, vinyl, fiberglass, engineered thermoplastics, and composite materials. Aluminum frames are generally available as manufactured window and door units, as well as custom enclosures such as sunspaces and "storefront" glazed walls (suitable as the collector in a thermal storage wall). Wood frames are available as manufactured window and door units, or can be custom built by the user for many of the passive solar collector types. The plastic and composite materials are typically available in manufactured window and door units only.

In general, aluminum frames have the worst thermal characteristics, due to the high conductivity of the material. A typical aluminum frame has an R-value in the range of R-0.45 to R-0.5. Adding a thermal break to the aluminum frame increases its R-value to about R-1. Wood and vinyl frames typically have R-values in the range of R-2 to R-3, while insulated vinyl and fiberglass frames can have R-values as high as R-5. It should be noted that the highly conductive materials (particularly aluminum without a thermal break) not only can lose heat, but can also cause condensation and frost buildup on the frames in very cold weather.

In addition to their thermal properties, frame materials have other important attributes, including durability, maintenance requirements, appearance, and environmental impact. Aluminum frames are generally very durable and require little maintenance, provided a good-quality finish is specified. Wood, while susceptible to rot, is still considered durable if properly maintained. Refinishing of wood frames will be required periodically. Vinyl and fiberglass, like aluminum, are considered durable, low-maintenance products, although their suitability in some of the passive solar components (such as a thermal storage wall) may not be advisable due to the extreme temperatures that can occur. Similarly, the newer composite materials, while promising as frame materials in standard windows and doors, are as yet untested in the extreme conditions that occur in the thermal storage wall and convective loop systems. Environmentally sensitive frame options include recycled aluminum frames, composite frames using recycled content materials, and wood from sustainable species for custom frames.

Commercially available frame and glazing assemblies have the advantage of being readily available off-the-shelf and are usually of consistent quality. In passive installations that require some degree of nonstandard construction, however, commercially available units may not offer the flexibility of a site-built system designed for a specific installation.

For example, the collectors on thermal storage walls require exterior operation for periodic cleaning and seasonal ventilation. Few commercially available collectors can be operated in this fashion, because their hardware is designed for interior operation. If such units are not adapted for special use, they will need to be mounted with their interior face (and finish) to the exterior, exposed to the weather, in order to be operated from outside. Sliding patio doors with key locks can be used successfully in these conditions, but for most other off-the-shelf collectors, it will be necessary to make some arrangement with the manufacturer to install the necessary hardware on the outside of the stock product. In the case of site-built collector assemblies, such maintenance and operation problems should be considered before designing and building the framing system.

Collector Selection

There are a number of considerations in selecting windows for passive solar performance. As a general rule in any passive application, using large individual units to cover a given collector area (such as one large picture window, as opposed to several smaller units) will decrease the overall amount of framing and will thus increase the net collector area exposed to the sun. From the standpoint of energy conservation, this arrangement will also reduce the amount of perimeter framing exposed to the environment and, consequently, will reduce the amount of heat loss due to infiltration through the framing. Similarly, using a unit with less crack length, as in a single-hung versus a double-hung window, will also reduce infiltration. Considerations such as these must be weighed against other criteria, such as cost, ease of maintenance, aesthetic preference, and availability, to arrive at the best collector design for a given application.

When assessing a material's suitability for a specific situation, special attention should be paid to a product's "weatherability" and its maximum operating temperature. Thermal storage walls and convective loop panels, in particular, can generate extremely high working temperatures (150°F to 300°F) and can put a severe strain on certain collector materials.

When comparing the cost effectiveness of several glazing types during the design phase, it is important to consider the possibility of reducing the size, and therefore the cost, of the HVAC system. Always compare and use R-values of entire fenestration units rather than R-values of center-of-glass areas. The former can be more than 30 percent lower than the latter in the case of metal frames without thermal breaks. Rating information on window units is now available from the National Fenestration Rating Council (1300 Spring St., Suite 120, Silver Spring, MD 20910; 301-589-NFRC). NFRC ratings reflect not only glazing performance, but also that of frame materials incorporating thermal breaks. Such ratings now make comparisons between units within a manufacturer's line, and with windows by other manufacturers, far easier. Table 7.2 presents a sample listing of window types and comparisons.

During construction, if glass types vary by orientation, clearly mark the fenestration units and check the installation. Also check that the glass is mounted in the frame as specified. For example, tinted panes must be located on the exterior. Low-e coatings should be applied to either surface 2 or 3 if the units are to deliver good passive solar performance.

Sealants and Caulking

All collector installations need to be carefully caulked and sealed. In the case of nonvented thermal storage walls, where temperatures can be in excess of 150°F, or convective loop panels, which experience temperatures up to 300°F, recaulking may be necessary after the first several months of operation to ensure efficient future performance. The seal should be airtight but able to be broken in case the panel must be removed.

Absorber Components

Introduction

Generally located on the surface of the storage material, the absorber converts solar radiation into heat. When sunlight strikes a material, it is, in part, reflected, effectively reducing the amount of solar radiation that can be absorbed. Conse-quently, absorber materials are usually dark, minimizing heat losses due to reflection. In the process of converting sunlight to heat, the temperature of the absorber rises. If the absorber forms the surface of the storage component, as in a thermal storage wall, the heat moves into and is stored in the thermal mass. In this case, the surface of the wall itself is considered the absorber.

Typically, the surface is painted a dark color to enhance its ability to absorb solar radiation and convert it to heat. This is the case in direct gain, thermal storage walls, and attached sunspace systems, where the storage and absorber are the same material, and the absorber is simply the south-facing surface of the storage material. In such cases, a coat of dark paint will aid in the absorption function. Certain storage materials, such as colored concrete, brick, or textured concrete masonry units, are naturally dark and do not require a coat of paint.

Materials used to enhance the absorber performance, such as paint applied to masonry in a thermal storage wall or a direct gain application, may be exposed to temperatures of 200°F or higher. Care must be taken to ensure that paints or other material applied to the absorber can withstand these extreme temperatures without degradation. If the storage is remote from the absorber, or if storage is not provided, the absorber transfers its heat to the surrounding air. In this case, the absorber is often a metal plate, a material well suited to quickly transferring heat to a moving airstream. The entire plate is the absorber, and provides no other system function. This type of absorber is used in convective loop systems. Again, care must be taken to coat the metal surface with paints that can withstand the high temperatures (up to 300°F in convective loop panels) without degrading.

For these applications, corrugated metal roofing is a suitable absorber material. Depending on the type of absorber plate required (see Chapter 6), expanded metal lath can also be used. Usually, three to five layers of lath are specified to allow the air stream to circulate *through* the absorber, thereby coming in contact with the largest possible area of absorber and enhancing heat transfer.

Table 7.2 *Window Comparison Chart*

Characteristic	1	2	3	4	5	6	7	8	9	10	11	12
General glazing description	Single-glazed clear	Single-glazed bronze	Double-glazed clear	Double-glazed bronze	Double-glazed clear	Double-glazed bronze	Double-glazed low-e	Double-glazed low-e	Double-glazed spectrally selective	Double-glazed spectrally selective	Triple-glazed low-e super-window	Triple-glazed clear
Layers of glazing and spaces (outside to inside)	1/8" clear	1/8" bronze / 1/8" clear	1/8" clear / 1/2" air / 1/8" clear	1/8" bronze / 1/2" air / 1/8" clear	1/8" clear / 1/2" air / 1/8" clear	1/8" bronze / 1/2" air / 1/8" clear	1/8" clear / 1/2" argon / 1/8" low-e (0.20)	1/8" low-e (0.08) / 1/2" argon / 1/8" clear	1/8" low-e (0.04) / 1/2" argon / 1/8" clear	1/8" low-e (0.10) / 1/2" argon / 1/8" clear	1/8" low-e (0.08) / 1/2" krypton / 1/8" clear / 1/2" krypton / 1/8" low-e (0.08)	1/8" low-e / 1/2" air / 1/8" clear / 1/2" air / 1/8" clear
Center-of-glass												
U-factor	1.11	1.11	0.49	0.49	0.49	0.49	0.30	0.26	0.24	0.27	0.11	0.31
SHGC	0.86	0.73	0.76	0.62	0.76	0.62	0.74	0.58	0.41	0.32	0.49	0.69
SC	1.00	0.84	0.89	0.72	0.89	0.72	0.86	0.68	0.47	0.38	0.57	0.81
VT	0.90	0.68	0.81	0.61	0.81	0.61	0.74	0.78	0.72	0.44	0.68	0.75
Frame												
Type	Aluminum no th. break	Aluminum no th. break	Aluminum no th. break	Aluminum no th. break	Wood or vinyl	Wood or vinyl	Wood or vinyl	Wood or vinyl	Wood or vinyl	Wood or vinyl	Insulated vinyl	Wood or vinyl
U-factor	1.90	1.90	1.00	1.00	0.40	0.40	0.30	0.30	0.30	0.30	0.20	0.30
Spacer	—	—	Aluminum	Aluminum	Aluminum	Aluminum	Stainless	Stainless	Stainless	Stainless	Insulated	Stainless
Total window												
U-factor	1.30	1.30	0.64	0.64	0.49	0.49	0.33	0.30	0.29	0.31	0.15	0.34
SHGC	0.79	0.69	0.65	0.55	0.58	0.48	0.55	0.44	0.31	0.26	0.37	0.52
VT	0.69	0.52	0.62	0.47	0.57	0.43	0.52	0.56	0.51	0.31	0.48	0.53

Note: All values for total window are based on a 2-foot by 4-foot casement window
* Key: U-factor—The rate of heat loss (non-solar) through a material or assembly. Expressed in Btu/hr-ft²-°F. The lower the U-value, the better the material's insulating value.
SHGC—Solar Heat Gain Coefficient
SC—Shading Coefficient
VT—Visible Transmittance

Thermal Properties

The performance of the absorber component depends partially on two properties of the material used for the surface finish of the absorber: absorptivity and emissivity. Absorptivity is a measure of the material's ability to absorb solar radiation while minimizing losses due to reflection. As a result, white and light colors are poor absorber-finish colors.

Emissivity is a measure of the material's ability to emit the collected solar energy and is associated with a loss of solar heat otherwise usable by the passive system. Therefore, the surface of the absorber facing the sun should have a high absorptivity and a low emissivity.

Most materials typically specified as finish material have both high absorptivities and high emissivities. However, there are a few products currently available that exhibit high absorptivity and low emissivity characteristics. These products, referred to as selective-surface materials, are typically available in sheets designed to be adhered to the face of the storage component.

Table 7.3 illustrates these properties of four commonly used absorber materials. The absorptivity of concrete, if left unfinished, is 0.65, indicating that 65 percent of the solar radiation striking the surface of, for example, a thermal storage wall, is absorbed. Simply painting the concrete with a flat black paint can increase the absorptivity to 0.96. However, the emissivity is also fairly high, at 0.87.

Material #3 on the table is a currently available selective-surface material. As can be seen from the table, the absorptivity of this material is approximately the same as the black paint, but the emissivities are much lower, which is an indication of its superior performance as an absorber finish material.

In general, where standard materials, such as black paint, are used as finish materials, a high absorptivity is usually associated with a high emissivity. Table 7.4 lists absorptivities for standard materials. If selective-surface materials are not specified, this table can be used as a guide to the comparative performances of readily available finishes as absorbers.

It is also worth giving consideration to the environmental impact of the material selected. It is better to use materials with recycled content, and paints with low volatile organic compounds (VOCs), to reduce off-gassing and to maintain good indoor air quality.

Storage Components

Introduction

Once the collectors of the system have been properly selected, designed, located, and constructed, a great deal of heat in the form of solar energy will enter the passive solar system. The

Table 7.3   *Characteristics of Absorber Materials*

Material	Product Name and Manufacturer	Absorptivity	Emissivity
1. Exposed and unfinished concrete	—	0.65	0.87
2. Flat black latex paint (nonselective)	Various	0.96	0.87
3. Black chrome-coated copper foil, 24″ wide strips, w/pressure-sensitive adhesive backing	Solar—L—Foil MTI Solar Inc. 220 Churchill Avenue Somerset, NJ 08873 (201) 246-1000	0.95	0.11
4. Aluminum (polished and unfinished)	—	0.12	0.09

Table 7.4 *Solar Absorptivity of Various Materials**

Material	Value
Optical flat black paint	.98
Flat black paint	.95
Black lacquer	.92
Dark gray paint	.91
Black concrete	.91
Dark blue lacquer	.91
Black oil paint	.90
Stafford blue bricks	.89
Dark olive drab paint	.89
Dark brown paint	.88
Dark blue-gray paint	.88
Azure blue or dark green lacquer	.88
Brown concrete	.85
Medium brown paint	.84
Medium light brown paint	.80
Brown or Green lacquer	.79
Medium rust paint	.78
Light gray oil paint	.75
Red oil paint	.74
Red bricks	.70
Uncolored concrete	.65
Moderately light buff bricks	.60
Medium dull green paint	.59
Medium orange paint	.58
Medium yellow paint	.57
Medium blue paint	.51
Medium Kelly green paint	.51
Light green paint	.47
White semi-gloss paint	.30
White gloss paint	.25
Silver paint	.25
White lacquer	.21
Polished aluminum reflector sheet	.12
Aluminized Mylar film	.10
Laboratory vapor deposited coatings	.02

This table is meant to serve as a guide only. Variations in texture, tone, overcoats, pigments, binders, etc. can vary these values.

* Data obtained from: *Passive Solar Design Handbook, Volume Two: Passive Solar Design Analysis* by J.D. Balcomb et al. (see Bibliography).

amount of heat that can be utilized and the measure of comfort afforded in the living space are largely functions of the storage characteristics of the system. In the winter, for example, the sun shines for only a few hours during the day, while the majority of home heating needs are at night. A well-designed, well-constructed storage system will make the sun's energy available in the living space, protecting against overheating during the day and providing needed heat in the evening.

The discussions that follow present basic information on materials that can be used as passive solar storage components. A storage component can generally be constructed of any of a variety of materials that exhibit a high capacity to store heat. The most commonly used residential construction materials that fit this criterion are those in the masonry family. Water, in suitable containers, represents an alternative method of thermal storage.

The possibility of using masonry materials as structural components of the building provides the potential of combining the cost of structure and storage materials. This has resulted in establishing masonry as the most popular storage material in passive solar homes. Water, although inexpensive, requires a container for effective use, which can be costly and difficult to integrate into the design.

Table 7.5 presents a comparison of the major storage component materials. It is meant only as a quick reference guide for use in selecting a material in the early design stages. Each of these material types, appropriate for use in a passive design, is discussed below in detail.

In each discussion, the following information is presented: a definition of the material and a discussion of typically available shapes and sizes; a review of construction issues specifically related to the materials used in passive solar applications; and an analysis of the thermal performance characteristics of the material.

Concrete Masonry

Concrete masonry units (concrete block, concrete brick, and concrete block paving units), referred to as CMUs, are composed primarily of

Table 7.5 *Characteristics of Primary Thermal Mass Storage Materials*

Material	Typical Thickness (in.)	Volume to Store 100 Btus (ft³)	Weight to Store 100 Btus (lbs.)	Comments
Concrete Masonry Unit	12–18	43.3	4,545	Can be structural
Concrete	12–18	33	4,762	Can be structural
Brick	16–18	40.65	5,000	Can be structural
Water	6–12	16 (133 gal)	1,000	Inexpensive, locally available, container required
Stone (loose fill)	N/A	72	5,000	Inexpensive, locally available, container required

Portland cement, graded aggregates, and water. They are fabricated into specific shapes from machine-molded, very dry, no-slump concrete. The resulting elements are then exposed to an accelerated curing procedure and subsequently dried to reduce the moisture content to specified levels. Concrete masonry has traditionally been used both as a structural material in above- and below-grade walls and as an exposed finish material on walls and floors.

Concrete masonry construction is based on a modular dimensional system whose base module has been established as 4″ vertically and 4″ horizontally (nominal measurements). Standard dimensions for CMUs are equal to the nominal size minus the thickness of one ⅜″ mortar joint. Thus, the common 8″-high by 16″-long concrete block is actually 7⅝″ × 15⅝″ (see Figure 7.3).

Regardless of their dimensions, CMUs are manufactured as either hollow or solid units. Due to their reduced weight and ease of handling, hollow units are used more frequently than solid ones. In most passive solar construction, however, it is recommended that concrete masonry units used for storage be solid, or hollow with grout-filled cores, to increase the overall efficiency of the passive system (a specification for the grout to be used in CMU cores is included later in this chapter).

A sampling of the large variety of sizes and shapes of concrete masonry units available in the market today is presented in Figures 7.4 through 7.13.

CONSTRUCTION

In most passive solar installations, construction with concrete masonry will follow standard practice. The only major departures from typical construction are (1) placing insulation on the *outside* of a CMU being used for direct gain storage (e.g., an exterior CMU wall); (2) the use of solid or grout-filled, as opposed to hollow, units to store heat; and (3) the use of heavyweight rather than lightweight block. These changes require only

(Text continues on p. 247.)

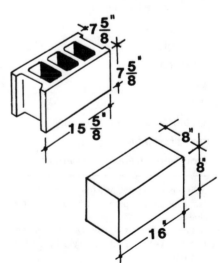

Figure 7.3

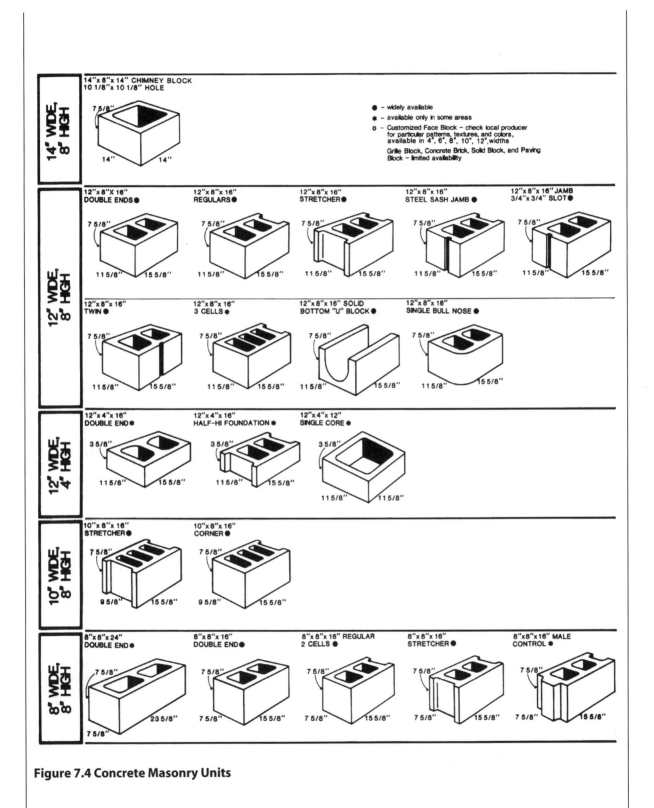

Figure 7.4 Concrete Masonry Units

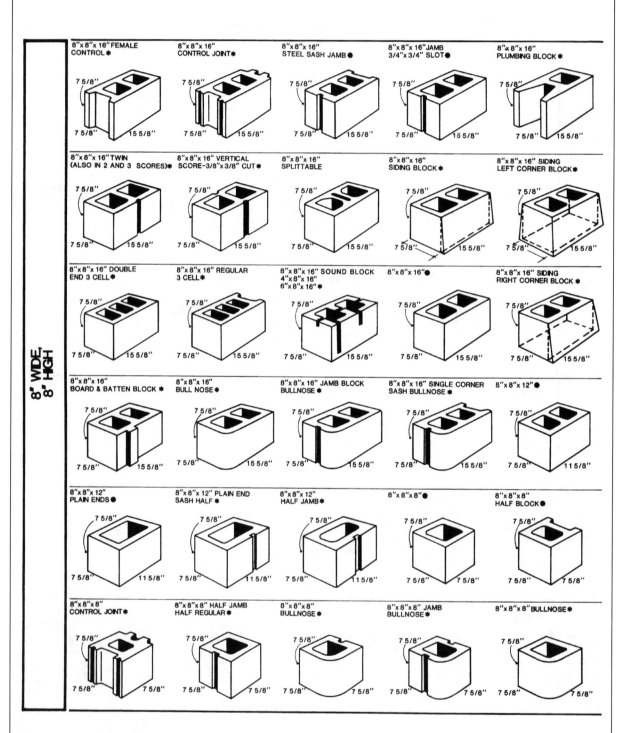

Figure 7.5 Concrete Masonry Units

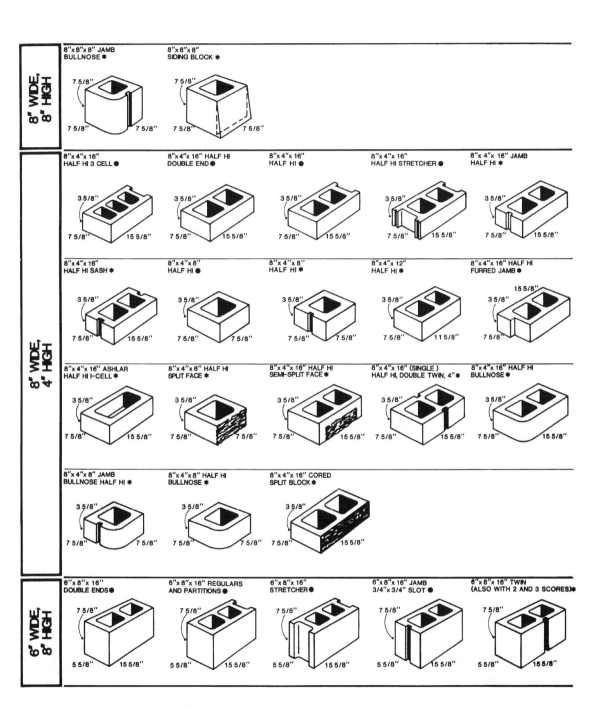

Figure 7.6 Concrete Masonry Units

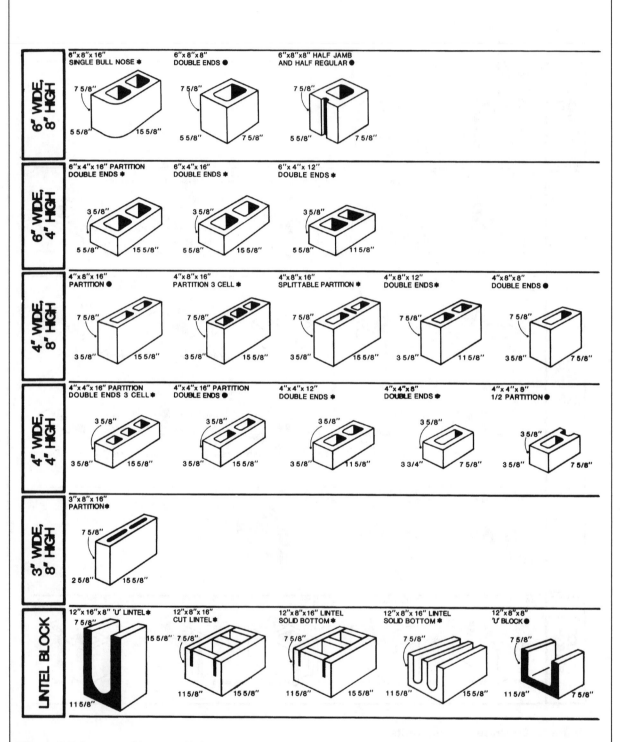

Figure 7.7 Concrete Masonry Units

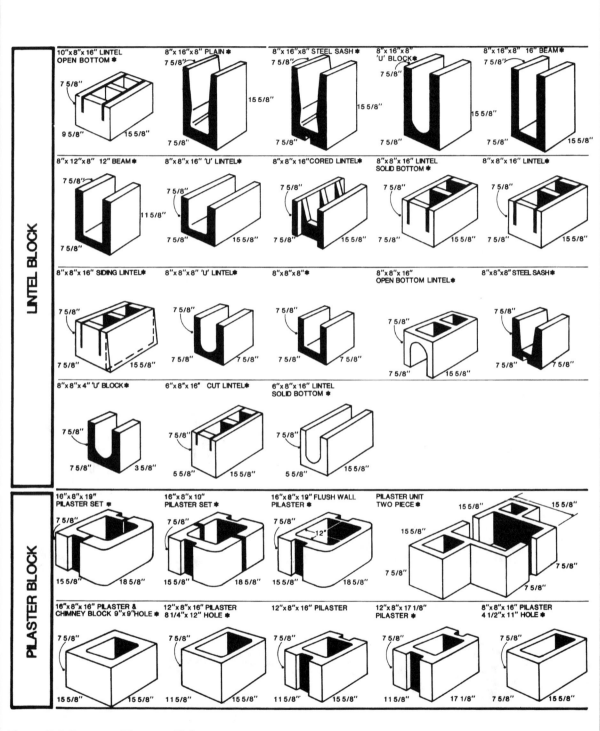

Figure 7.8 Concrete Masonry Units

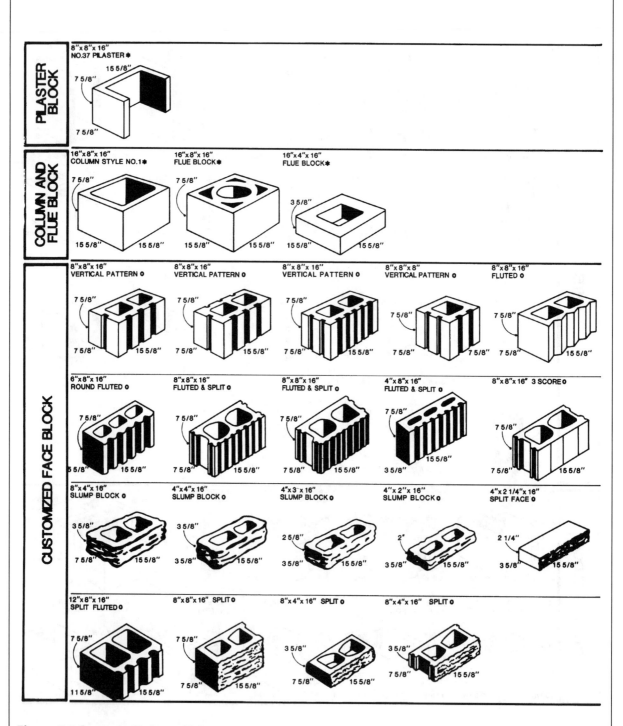

Figure 7.9 Concrete Masonry Units

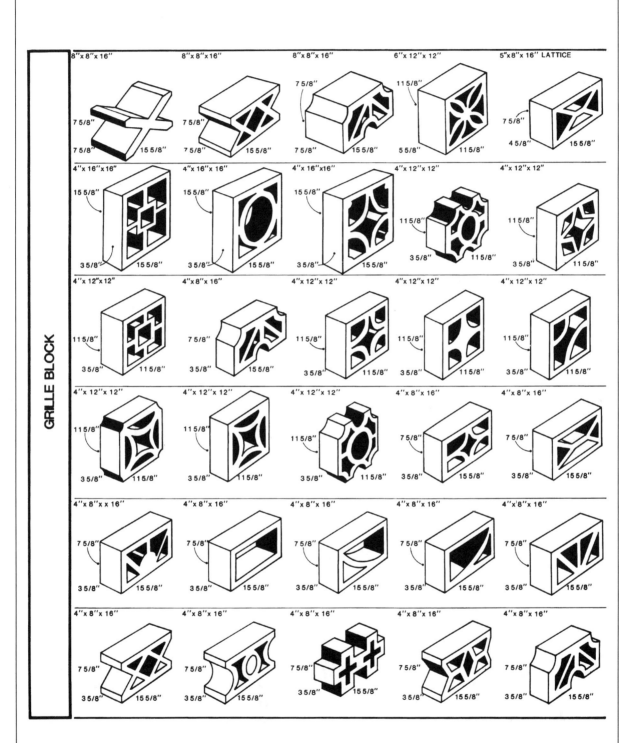

Figure 7.10 Concrete Masonry Units

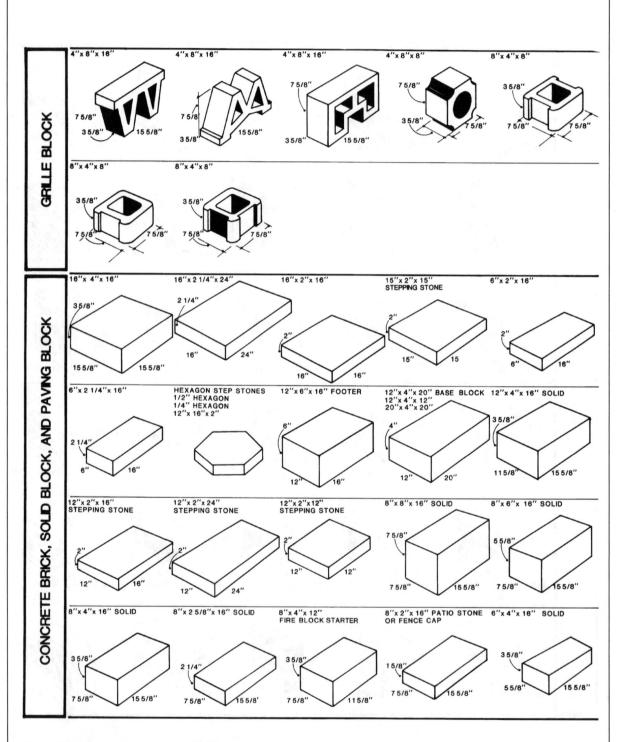

Figure 7.11 Concrete Masonry Units

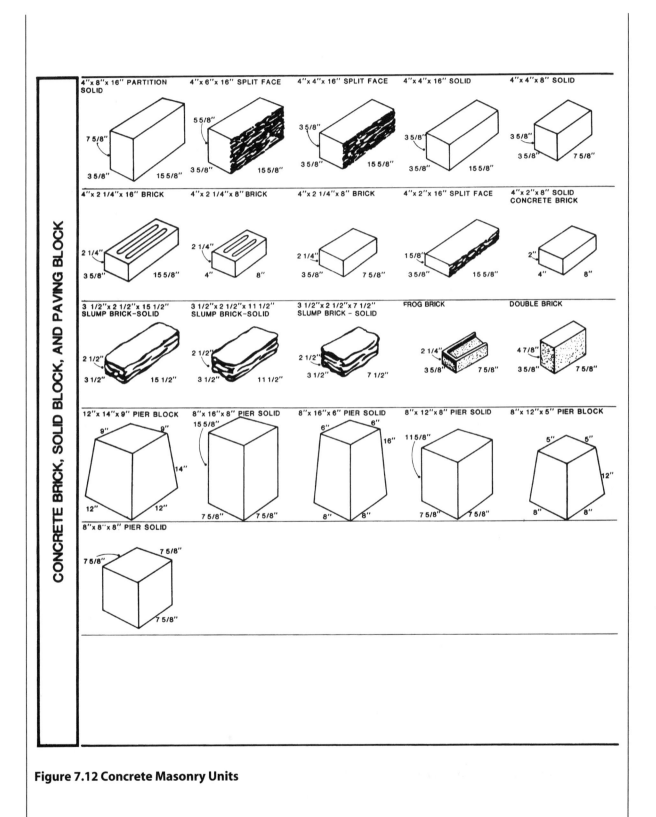

Figure 7.12 Concrete Masonry Units

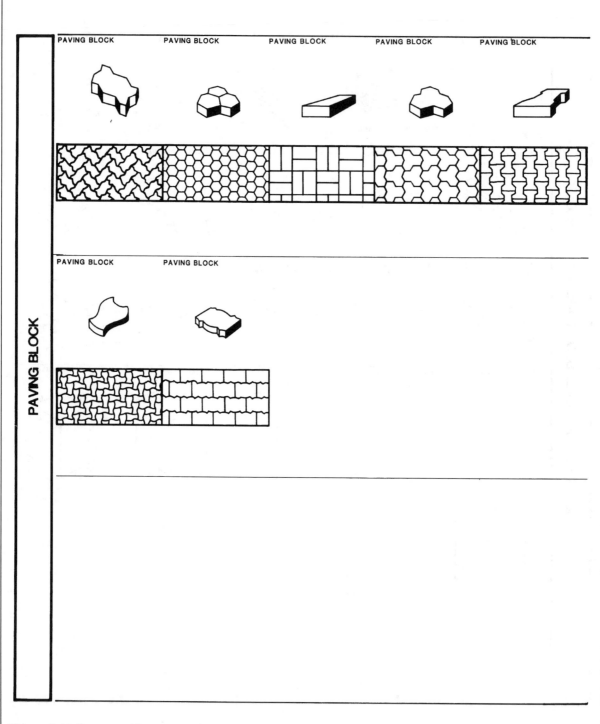

Figure 7.13 Concrete Masonry Units

minor modifications to the building process, which are described in the details in chapters 3 through 6.

FINISHES

In thermal storage wall and attached sunspace construction, the exterior face of a CMU wall is used to absorb and store heat and is protected from the environment by the collector glazing. Unfinished concrete masonry of a dark color performs best in these conditions. In direct gain systems with exterior wall storage, however, the outside face of a solid CMU wall is not protected by the collector glazing. In this situation it is typical, if not required, to use some form of insulation and finish to prevent stored heat from traveling through the wall and being lost to the outside, severely reducing the thermal performance of the overall system.

There are a variety of methods for finishing the exterior of a concrete masonry wall being used for direct gain storage. Because it is recommended that insulation be placed on the *outside* of exterior walls being used for direct gain storage, such finishes will need to be applied *over* this insulation. In a standard masonry bearing wall configuration, stucco or siding can be applied over insulation that has been adhered and fastened to the CMU wall. In typical exterior CMU veneer wall construction, the configuration of the materials can be inverted, moving the masonry to the inside for heat storage and the insulated bearing frame wall to the outside. Siding is then applied in the conventional manner.

Such external finishes will affect the thermal performance of a direct gain storage component only insofar as they increase the effective insulation value of the wall. If a wall that is absorbing heat at its interior face is well insulated on its exterior, it will retain more of the heat energy imparted to it and will thus serve as a more effective solar energy storage medium.

It is recommended that interior finishes be kept to a minimum to preserve the inherent thermal performance capabilities of the CMU. For example, if a finish, such as wood paneling or gypsum board, is applied to the interior face of a wall intended to absorb and store solar energy, it

will reduce both the amount of heat that reaches the wall and the amount that is reradiated from it to the space. This is especially true when covering a CMU paver floor or CMU radiant floor system with carpet, which is emphatically *not* recommended. A good rule of thumb is to assume that, relative to other finish materials, the higher the insulating value of a given finish, the more it will inhibit the passive thermal performance of the component to which it is applied. Several acceptable finish materials, such as tile products, can be effectively combined with concrete masonry construction (for further information, see the discussion of finishes for concrete storage components later in this chapter).

It should also be noted that a variety of concrete masonry products, such as architectural block, have been designed specifically as finish materials and are suitable for residential construction.

Carrying this concept one step further, it is obvious that putting insulation on the interior surface of the CMU used for energy storage is extremely counterproductive and will essentially nullify any passive benefits that might have been derived from the component. It is for this reason that it is recommended that no passive storage component (wall, floor, or roof/ceiling) be insulated on its interior face.

COLOR

Where concrete masonry is used both to absorb and to store solar energy, the surface exposed to solar radiation should be as dark a color as possible to increase absorption of light and heat. Other surfaces in a space that are not being used for storage, such as standard wood frame walls, should be light in color in order to reflect more light to the darker storage material (for a listing of the solar absorptivity characteristics of various colors/materials, see Table 7.4).

In the case of concrete masonry, natural color can vary from light to dark grey and also to tints of buff, red, or brown, depending on the color of aggregate, cement, and other mix ingredients. Again, it is recommended that the darker tones be specified when the CMUs are being used unfinished for heat storage. In customized units, specific dark colors can be requested from the manufacturer.

Concrete masonry can also be painted or stained. Care must be taken to specify paints or stains that do not degrade when subjected to high temperatures in applications where such temperatures are expected (e.g., thermal storage walls).

Another possible finish is the so-called selective surface, a foil that has a very high absorptivity of incoming solar radiation but a very low emissivity of heat. Such foils can be very effective at increasing the thermal efficiency of passive solar storage components, and manufacturers' data should be referenced for specific performance characteristics (for further information, see "Absorber Components" earlier in this chapter).

TEXTURE

One final note should be added concerning customized CMUs that have architecturally finished faces. Such units present a greater amount of exposed surface area for heat exchange to the surrounding air than do standard flat-surfaced CMUs. It might be assumed that such increased exposure might influence the performance of installations using these materials, but this has not, as yet, been proven to be true. Until more accurate data are compiled in this regard, it is recommended that customized CMUs be used interchangeably with standard units in passive solar storage applications.

THERMAL PROPERTIES

From the point of view of thermal performance in a passive solar application, the most important material characteristics of any particular concrete masonry unit are its conductivity, density, specific heat, and thickness.

A material's conductivity (k) is a measure of how readily the material will transfer or "conduct" heat: the higher the conductivity, the faster the heat will travel through a material. In general, thermal performance increases as conductivity increases.

The remaining three basic material characteristics (density, specific heat, and thickness) can also be used as indicators of anticipated thermal performance. When multiplied together, they yield the so-called thermal storage capacity of a specific unit of material. Essentially, this characteristic is a measure of the ability of a given unit of material to store heat. The higher the thermal storage capacity, the greater the amount of heat the unit can absorb and store.

In the case of concrete masonry, the specific heat for the majority of available units remains basically constant. Thus, the major variables that will determine the thermal storage capacity of a CMU are its density (measured in pounds per cubic foot) and its thickness.

In general, concrete masonry units can be divided into two broad categories of material density:

- *Dense or normal weight*—Employing sand, gravel, crushed stone, or air-cooled blast-furnace slag as aggregate.

- *Lightweight*—Using expanded shale, clay, and slate, expanded blast-furnace slag, sintered fly ash, coal cinders (fly ash), or natural lightweight materials such as pumice or scoria.

By weight, concrete masonry is considered lightweight if its density is 105 lb/ft^3 or less, medium weight if 105 to 125 lb/ft^3, and normal weight if more than 125 lb/ft^3. It is recommended that the heavier-weight CMUs be used in passive solar storage applications.

The weight of any specific concrete masonry unit will be a function of the density of the concrete used and the volume of this concrete in the particular unit. In the case of hollow units, the volume of concrete is equal to the overall volume of the unit minus the volume of the cores. The concept of "equivalent solid thickness," used for rating a unit's fire-resistance capability, comes to mind in this regard as a method for visualizing the "real" shape of a hollow-core block (see Figure 7.14).

In terms of thermal performance, however, such a model is misleading. In passive solar applications where concrete masonry is being used as a storage medium, an 8″ hollow block with a 50 percent core area does not perform like a 4″ solid unit. Heat transfer through the webs and across the airspaces formed by the cores is not uniform,

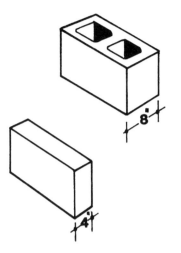

Figure 7.14

and the amount of heat reaching the far side of the block is considerably less in an 8″ hollow unit than it is in a 4″ solid one.

It is for this reason that filling all hollow concrete masonry cores when they are used as passive solar storage media is recommended (grout, small-size normal-weight aggregate, or other materials are suitable). For the purpose of analysis, when the grout or other material in the cores is of different density from that of the CMU itself, a weighted average of the densities involved should be used. The density of the joint mortar employed should be considered to be the same as that of the CMU itself.

Table 7.6 presents thermal performance data for a variety of CMUs with different thicknesses, densities, and grout types. The table can be used for general performance comparisons between the various material combinations presented. It should be noted that the conductivity (k) values presented are for the CMU material only.

In general, the higher the thermal storage capacity of a given unit, the better its performance from a passive solar point of view. This should be kept in mind when selecting a specific CMU for a specific installation. For example, if a nominal 8″ CMU wall is desired for a particular passive installation, the combination of unit density and grout type that results in the highest possible thermal storage capacity should generally be specified (subject to local cost considerations).

For grout types and block densities not covered in the tables, a good rule of thumb is to assume that, for a given unit thickness, the higher the density of the unit and/or of the grout, the greater the overall thermal storage capacity. It can also be assumed that the thermal storage capacities for thicknesses greater than 12″ will roughly equal the sum of the capacities of smaller units which, when added together, will equal the total overall thickness desired. For example, the thermal storage capacity per square foot for a 20″-thick wall of 80-lb-density block and 100-lb grout will roughly equal the sum of the capacities of one 8″ and one 12″ block wall (12.4 + 19.2 = 31.6) or of two 10″ walls (15.8 + 15.8 = 31.6).

It should be noted that some concrete masonry manufacturers in the United States produce CMUs with higher densities than those listed in Table 7.6. Should higher densities be required, local manufacturers of concrete masonry units should be consulted in advance. CMU that is made with fly ash, a waste material, has less environmental impact.

Concrete

Concrete is essentially a mixture of two elements: aggregate and paste. The paste is made of Portland cement and water, and it binds the aggregate (sand plus gravel or crushed stone) into a solid mass as it hardens, due to a chemical reaction between the cement and water. The paste is usually from 25 percent to 40 percent of the total volume of the concrete, with aggregates comprising the remainder.

Concrete can be separated into the following four general categories based on density:

- Insulating lightweight concrete (30 to 90 lb/ft^3)—Using pumice, scona, perlite, vermiculite, or diatomite as aggregate.

- Structural lightweight concrete (85 to 115 lb/ft^3).

- Normal weight concrete (135 to 160 lb/ft^3)—Using sand, gravel, crushed stone, or blast-furnace slag (fly ash) as aggregate.

- Heavyweight concrete (160 to 400 lb/ft^3)—Using barlite, limonite, magnetite, ilmenite, hematite, iron, or steel slugs as aggregate.

Table 7.6 *Concrete Masonry Unit Physical Properties*

Unit Thickness*	Unit Density[a]	Specific Heat 0[b]	Thermal Storage Capacity[c]			R-Value[d]			Conductivity[e]
3″	80	.22	3.5			0.95			2.5
	95	.22	4.1			0.72			3.3
	105	.22	4.5			0.66			3.6
	125	.21	5.2			0.39			6.1
	135	.21	5.6			0.29			8.1
			A	B	C	A	B	C	
4″	80	.22	3.5	5.9	6.6	n/a	n/a	n/a	2.5
	95	.22	4.0	6.5	7.2	n/a	n/a	n/a	3.3
	105	.22	4.5	6.9	7.6	n/a	n/a	n/a	3.6
	125	.21	5.0	7.3	8.1	n/a	n/a	n/a	6.1
	135	.21	5.5	7.8	8.5	n/a	n/a	n/a	8.1
6″	80	.22	5.3	9.1	10.2	1.79	1.84	1.37	2.5
	95	.22	6.3	10.0	11.2	1.58	1.61	1.17	3.3
	105	.22	6.9	10.7	11.8	1.45	1.48	1.06	3.6
	125	.21	7.9	11.5	12.5	1.21	1.24	.85	6.1
	135	.21	8.5	12.1	13.1	1.08	1.11	.76	8.1
8″	80	.22	6.3	12.4	14.1	2.07	2.48	1.83	2.5
	95	.22	7.6	13.7	15.4	1.79	2.18	1.56	3.3
	105	.22	8.4	14.4	16.1	1.64	2.01	1.42	3.6
	125	.21	9.5	15.3	17.0	1.35	1.68	1.15	6.1
	135	.21	10.2	16.0	17.7	1.21	1.49	1.02	8.1
10″	80	.22	7.2	15.8	18.4	2.22	3.10	2.22	2.5
	95	.22	8.5	17.1	19.7	1.92	2.75	1.92	3.3
	105	.22	9.5	18.1	20.7	1.76	2.55	1.76	3.6
	125	.21	10.8	19.0	21.5	1.45	2.15	1.45	6.1
	135	.21	11.7	19.9	22.3	1.30	1.92	1.30	8.1
12″	80	.22	8.4	19.2	22.5	2.39	3.73	2.64	2.5
	95	.22	9.9	20.7	24.1	2.06	3.32	2.29	3.3
	105	.22	10.9	21.7	25.1	1.88	3.08	2.10	3.6
	125	.21	12.5	22.9	26.1	1.54	2.59	1.75	6.1
	135	.21	13.5	23.9	27.1	1.38	2.31	1.57	8.1

* 3″ units solid CMU pavers.
A Cores hollow.
B Cores filled with 100 lb/ft² grout.
C Cores filled with 130 lb/ft² grout.
n/a data not available
[a]—Units of lb/ft³
[b]—Units of btu/lb·°F
[c]—Units of btu/ft²·°F
[d]—Units of hr·°F/ft²·btu
[e]—Units of btu·in/hr·ft²·°F

MINIMUM REQUIREMENTS FOR NON-STRUCTURAL GROUT*

Where concrete masonry walls are grouted for the purpose of increasing thermal storage capacity, i.e., non-structural purposes, the grout may consist of a mixture of Portland cement, aggregate and water.

Portland cement shall conform to the requirements of ASTM C-150, Standard Specification for Portland Cement, or ASTM C-595, Specification for Blended Hydraulic Cements.

Aggregate shall conform to the requirements for fine aggregate of ASTM C-33, Standard Specification for Concrete Aggregates (except that the grading requirements need not apply), or ASTM C-404, Standard Specification for Aggregates for Masonry Grout.

Grout shall consist of a mixture of Portland cement and aggregate proportioned such that the aggregate to cement ratio does not exceed 12:1; and sufficient water to permit the mixture to flow readily, without segregation, into the cores of the masonry.

*Courtesy of the National Concrete Masonry Association
2302 Horse Pen Road
P.O. Box 781
Herndon, Va. 22070

The most commonly used concrete is normal weight, and this general type is recommended for most passive solar applications. Structural lightweight is appropriate for use as floor fill over structural wood floors.

Concrete can be used in a wide variety of wall, floor, and roof/ceiling applications that make use of either cast-in-place or precast elements. In the single-family, detached residential sector, the use of precast concrete elements is quite uncommon. Cast-in-place concrete, on the other hand, is commonly used for footings, foundation/basement walls, and slabs-on-grade. Although the possible thicknesses of cast-in-place elements in such applications are basically infinite, dimensions are generally as follows:

- Walls—6″, 8″, 10″, or 12″
- Structural floors—4″ to 8″
- Slabs-on-grade—3″ to 6″
- Floor Fill—1½″ to 2½″
- Roofs/ceilings—Not applicable.

Precast elements also come in a wide variety of possible dimensions. The most common thicknesses are listed below.

- Solid slabs and tees—2″, 3″, 4″, 5″, 6″, and 8″ (tee thickness is for slab portion only, exclusive of stem).
- Hollow-core slabs—6″, 8″, 10″, and 12″.

Lengths can vary, as can widths, for solid slabs. Widths for tees and hollow-core slabs are generally 2′, 4′, or 8′.

CONSTRUCTION

In most passive installations, construction with concrete will follow standard practice. The only major departure from typical construction is placing insulation on the outside of concrete used for direct gain storage (e.g., in a solid concrete exterior wall). This change requires only minor modifications to the building process and is fully covered in the construction details in chapters 3 through 6.

FINISHES

In thermal storage wall and attached sunspace construction, the exterior face of a concrete wall is used to absorb and store heat and is protected from the environment by the collector glazing. Unfinished concrete of a dark color performs best in these conditions. In direct gain systems, however, the exterior face of a solid concrete wall is not protected by the collector glazing. If the concrete is exposed directly to the environment and is not protected by some form of insulation and finish, stored heat will travel through the wall and be lost to the outside, severely reducing the thermal performance of the overall system.

There are a variety of methods for finishing the exterior of a concrete wall, including paint, stain, stucco, and siding. Placing insulation on the *outside* of exterior walls being used for passive solar energy storage requires that such finishes be applied *over* this insulation. Methods of applying these finishes are discussed in Chapter 3.

Exterior finishes will affect the thermal performance of a direct gain storage component only insofar as they increase the effective insulation of that component. If a wall that is absorbing heat at its interior face is well insulated on its exterior, it will retain more of the heat energy imparted to it and will thus serve as a more efficient solar energy storage medium.

It is recommended that interior finishes be kept to a minimum in order to preserve the inherent thermal performance capabilities of the concrete itself. For example, covering the interior face of a concrete storage component, such as a direct gain wall, with gypsum board or wood paneling will reduce both the amount of solar energy that reaches the wall and the amount that is reradiated from it to the space. This is especially true of covering a concrete-slab floor with wall-to-wall carpet, which is not recommended.

An acceptable range of choices for concrete wall and floor finishes can be found in various ceramic tile materials. Details for the installation of tile over concrete and masonry walls and floors may be obtained from the Tile Council of America, Inc., P.O. Box 326, Princeton, NJ 08542.

A general rule of thumb in assessing the effects that coverings have on thermal performance is that the higher the insulating value of a given finish, the more it will inhibit the passive thermal performance of the component to which it is applied. Relative to the finish materials suggested in the accompanying discussions, gypsum board and paneling have high insulative properties.

Carrying this concept one step further, it is obvious that putting insulation on the interior surface of a concrete component (e.g., a direct gain wall) used for energy storage is extremely counterproductive and will essentially nullify any passive benefits that might have been derived from the installation. It is for this reason that it is recommended that no passive solar storage component (wall, floor, or roof/ceiling) be insulated on its interior face.

Special mention must be made concerning finishes for slab-on-grade floors that are used for thermal storage. As previously mentioned, such floors should never be covered with carpet. One alternative to carpet is to stamp the slab, while wet, with any one of a variety of surface textures. If done with proper care, this technique will result in a very handsome floor surface that can be waxed or polished and that will retain its inherent thermal performance capability. Imaginative layouts of the control joints can also help make standard wood-float or steel-trowel finished slabs more attractive. Alternate finished surfaces, such as exposed aggregate, brick or CMU pavers, and tile, mentioned earlier, can also be used effectively.

COLOR

Where concrete is used both to absorb and to store solar energy, the surface exposed to solar radiation should be as dark a color as possible to increase absorption of light and heat. Other surfaces in a space, such as wood frame walls, which are not being used for storage, should be light in color in order to reflect more light to the darker storage material (for a list of the solar absorptivity characteristics of various colors/materials, see Table 7.4).

Colored concrete can be produced by utilizing colored aggregate, by adding color pigments, or both. The concrete can also be stained or painted. It is recommended that paints or stains that do not degrade when subjected to high temperatures be specified in applications where such temperatures are expected (e.g., thermal storage walls).

Another possible finish is the so-called selective surface, a foil that has a very high absorptivity of incoming solar radiation but a very low emissivity of heat. Such foils can be very effective at increasing the thermal efficiency of passive solar storage components, and manufacturers' data should be referenced for specific performance characteristics (for further information, see "Absorber Components" earlier in this chapter).

TEXTURE

Exposed concrete can also be textured in a number of different fashions. Patterns can be created by the particular mold employed, or the aggregate can be exposed by a number of different methods, including washing, brushing, using retarders, scrubbing, abrasive blasting, tooling, or grinding. The net result of such techniques is to expose more surface area for heat exchange with surrounding air.

It might be assumed that such increased exposure would influence the heat storage performance of components using these textured concretes, but this has not, as yet, been proven to be true. It is therefore recommended that textured and unfinished concrete be used on the basis of aesthetic preference in passive solar storage applications.

THERMAL PROPERTIES

From the point of view of thermal performance in a passive solar application, the most important material characteristics of a particular concrete mixture are its conductivity, density, specific heat, and thickness.

A material's conductivity (k) is a measure of how readily the material will transfer or "conduct" heat: the higher the conductivity, the faster the heat will travel through a material. In general, thermal performance increases as the conductivity increases.

The remaining three basic material characteristics (density, specific heat, and thickness) can also be used as indicators of anticipated thermal performance. When multiplied together, they yield the so-called thermal storage capacity of a specific unit of material. Essentially, this characteristic is a measure of the ability of a given unit of material to store heat. The higher the thermal storage capacity, the greater the amount of heat the unit can absorb and store.

In the case of concrete, the specific heat for the majority of mixtures and densities commonly used in residential construction varies only slightly. Thus, the major variables that will determine the thermal storage capacity of a concrete component are its density (measured in pounds per cubic foot) and its thickness.

As discussed above, concrete can be divided into four broad density classifications:

- Insulating lightweight—30 to 90 lb/ft^3.
- Structural lightweight—85 to 115 lb. ft^3.
- Normal weight—135 to 160 lb/ft^3.
- Heavyweight—160 to 400 lb/ft^3.

Table 7.7 presents thermal performance data, including thermal storage capacity, for a variety of concrete densities and thicknesses. The table can be used for general performance comparisons between various thickness/density combinations.

The higher densities for heavyweight concrete are not shown, since this is not a very common building material and is principally used for radiation shielding. Its heavier density will improve its thermal performance in a passive solar application, but the exact extent of this improvement is not known. If use of heavyweight concrete is anticipated, manufacturers' specifications should be referenced, where possible, for specific thermal performance data.

In general, the higher the thermal storage capacity of a given component, the better its performance from a passive solar point of view. This should be kept in mind when selecting a concrete mixture for a specific installation. For example, if an 8″ concrete wall is desired for a particular passive installation, the density that results in the highest possible thermal storage capacity should generally be specified (subject to cost considerations).

It can also be assumed that the thermal storage capacities for thicknesses greater than 12″ will roughly equal the sum of capacities of smaller thicknesses, which, when added together, will equal the total overall dimension desired. For example, the thermal storage capacity per square foot of a 20″-thick wall will roughly equal the sum of the capacities of one 8″ and one 12″ wall (14.7 + 22.0 = 36.7) or of two 10″ walls (18.3 + 18.3 = 36.6).

To reduce environmental impact, consider using concrete that contains recycled aggregate and/or fly ash, an industrial waste product.

Table 7.7 *Concrete: Physical Properties*

Unit Thickness	Unit Density[a]	Specific Heat[b]	Thermal Storage Capacity[c]	R-Value[d]	Conductivity[e]
2″	20	0.24	0.9	2.86	0.70
	50	0.23	1.9	1.34	1.50
	70	0.22	2.6	0.90	2.20
	90	0.22	3.3	0.60	3.30
	100	0.22	3.6	0.48	4.20
	110	0.21	3.9	0.38	5.30
	130	0.21	4.6	0.22	9.10
	145	0.21	5.0	0.15	13.30
3″	20	0.24	1.2	4.29	0.70
	50	0.23	2.9	2.01	1.50
	70	0.22	3.9	1.35	2.20
	90	0.22	4.9	0.90	3.30
	100	0.22	5.5	0.72	4.20
	110	0.21	5.8	0.57	5.30
	130	0.21	6.8	0.33	9.10
	145	0.21	7.6	0.23	13.30
4″	20	0.24	1.6	5.72	0.70
	50	0.23	3.9	2.68	1.50
	70	0.22	5.2	1.80	2.20
	90	0.22	6.6	1.20	3.30
	100	0.22	7.3	0.96	4.20
	110	0.21	7.6	0.76	5.30
	130	0.21	9.1	0.44	9.10
	145	0.21	10.2	0.30	13.30
5″	20	0.24	2.0	7.15	0.70
	50	0.23	4.8	3.35	1.50
	70	0.22	6.5	2.25	2.20
	90	0.22	8.2	1.50	3.30
	100	0.22	9.2	1.20	4.20
	110	0.21	9.7	0.95	5.30
	130	0.21	11.4	0.55	9.10
	145	0.21	12.7	0.38	13.30

Table 7.7   *(Continued)*

Unit Thickness	Unit Density[a]	Specific Heat[b]	Thermal Storage Capacity[c]	R-Value[d]	Conductivity[e]
6″	20	0.24	2.5	8.58	0.70
	50	0.23	5.8	4.02	1.50
	70	0.22	7.6	2.70	2.20
	90	0.22	9.9	1.80	3.30
	100	0.22	10.9	1.44	4.20
	110	0.21	11.5	1.14	5.30
	130	0.21	13.7	0.66	9.10
	145	0.21	15.3	0.45	13.30
8″	20	0.24	3.2	11.44	0.70
	50	0.23	7.6	5.36	1.50
	70	0.22	10.2	3.60	2.20
	90	0.22	13.3	2.40	3.30
	100	0.22	14.7	1.92	4.20
	110	0.21	15.4	1.52	5.30
	130	0.21	18.1	0.88	9.10
	145	0.21	20.3	0.60	13.30
10″	20	0.24	4.0	14.30	0.70
	50	0.23	9.7	6.70	1.50
	70	0.22	13.4	4.50	2.20
	90	0.22	16.6	3.00	3.30
	100	0.22	18.3	2.40	4.20
	110	0.21	19.8	1.90	5.30
	130	0.21	22.8	1.10	9.10
	145	0.21	25.3	0.75	13.30
12″	20	0.24	4.8	17.16	0.70
	50	0.23	11.5	8.04	1.50
	70	0.22	15.4	5.40	2.20
	90	0.22	19.9	3.60	3.30
	100	0.22	22.0	2.88	4.20
	110	0.21	23.0	2.28	5.30
	130	0.21	27.4	1.32	9.10
	145	0.21	30.4	0.90	13.30

[a]—Units of lb/ft^3
[b]—Units of $btu/lb \cdot °F$
[c]—Units of $btu/ft^2 \cdot °F$
[d]—Units of $hr \cdot °F/ft^2 \cdot btu$
[e]—Units of $btu \cdot in/hr \cdot ft^2 \cdot °F$

Brick

A brick is generally defined as a small building unit, solid or cored, formed from clay or shale into a rectangle, and hardened by heat. A brick is referred to as "solid" when the net cross-sectional area is 75 percent or more of its gross cross-sectional area. Most "cored" units are in this category. A brick is referred to as "hollow" when the net cross-sectional area is less than 75 percent but more than 40 percent of its gross cross-sectional area. It is recommended that all hollow bricks used for passive solar storage be fully grouted in addition to regular mortaring.

These general categorizations comprise a number of specific brick types that differ from each other in terms of texture, color, degree of water absorption, strength, and durability. These differences, however, do not significantly affect the thermal performance characteristics of the majority of brick types.

Brick should be specified by the appropriate American Society for Testing and Materials (ASTM) standards:

- ASTM C-216—Standard specification for facing brick (solid masonry units made from clay or shale)

- ASTM C-62—Standard specification for building brick (solid masonry units made from clay or shale)

- ASTM C-652—Standard specification for hollow brick (hollow masonry units made from clay or shale)

- ASTM C-902—Standard specification for pedestrian and light traffic paving brick

- ASTM C-126—Standard specification for ceramic glazed structural clay facing tile, facing brick, and solid masonry units

Brick construction is based on a modular system of dimensions for all standard products. Table 7.8 lists some of the typical industry sizes. The dimensions of the units listed in the table are "nominal." Actual dimensions are equal to the nominal dimension minus the thickness of the mortar joint with which the unit is designed to be laid. In general, such mortar joints are either ⅜″ or ½″ thick. Thus, a brick that is nominally 4″ × 2⅔″ × 8″ can be 3½″ × 2¼″ × 7½″ or 3⅝″ × 2¼″ × 7⅝″, depending on the specifications for a particular application. Note that the vertical dimension does not always change, and the difference in mortar joint size is made up in the coursing of the brick as it is constructed.

Although some solid brick units are manufactured without cores, most bricks are cored to some degree to reduce unit weight and to improve firing, resulting in a denser and more durable product.

The cores in solid brick units will not significantly affect the thermal performance of brick masonry used in passive solar storage applications. The process of laying brick usually results in the cores being filled with mortar, and thus the thermal storage is not significantly different from comparable solid units. When using hollow brick units as the thermal storage material, however, large cores should be grouted.

Illustrated in Figures 7.15 and 7.16 are some of the representative sizes and shapes of bricks currently available.

CONSTRUCTION

In most passive installations, construction with brick will follow standard practice. The only major departure from typical construction is placing insulation on the *outside* of a brick being used for direct gain storage (e.g., in a solid brick exterior wall). This and other changes require only minor modifications to the building process and are fully covered in the details illustrated in chapters 3 through 5.

FINISHES

In thermal storage wall and attached sunspace construction, the exterior face of a brick wall is used to absorb and store heat and is protected from the environment by the collector glazing. Unfinished brick of a dark color performs best in these conditions. In direct gain systems, however, the exterior face of a solid brick wall is not protected by the collector glazing. If this exterior face is exposed directly to the environment and is not protected by some form of insulation and finish, stored heat will travel through it and be

Table 7.8 *Brick: Typical Sizes*

Nominal Dimensions			Joint Thickness	Manufactured Dimensions			Modular Coursing*
t	h	l		t	h	l	
4″	2²/₃″	8″	3/8″	3⁵/₈″	2¹/₄″	7⁵/₈″	3C = 8″
4″	4″	12″	3/8″	3⁵/₈″	3⁵/₈″	11⁵/₈″	1C = 4″
4″	4″	12″	1/2″	3¹/₂″	3¹/₂″	11¹/₂″	1C = 4″
6″	4″	12″	3/8″	5⁵/₈″	3⁵/₈″	11⁵/₈″	1C = 4″
6″	4″	12″	1/2″	5¹/₂″	3¹/₂″	11¹/₂″	1C = 4″
8″	4″	12″	3/8″	7⁵/₈″	3⁵/₈″	11⁵/₈″	1C = 4″
8″	4″	12″	1/2″	7¹/₂″	3¹/₂″	11¹/₂″	1C = 4″
12″	4″	12″	3/8″	11⁵/₈″	3⁵/₈″	11⁵/₈″	1C = 4″
12″	4″	12″	1/2″	11¹/₂″	3¹/₂″	11¹/₂″	1C = 4″
6″	5¹/₃″	12″	3/8″	5⁵/₈″	4⁷/₈″	11⁵/₈″	3C = 16″
6″	5¹/₃″	12″	1/2″	5¹/₂″	4³/₄″	11¹/₂″	3C = 16″
8″	5¹/₃″	12″	3/8″	7⁵/₈″	4⁷/₈″	11⁵/₈″	3C = 16″
8″	5¹/₃″	12″	1/2″	7¹/₂″	4³/₄″	11¹/₂″	3C = 16″
4″	8″	8″	3/8″	3⁵/₈″	7⁷/₈″	7⁷/₈″	1C = 8″
4″	8″	8″	1/2″	3¹/₂″	7¹/₂″	7¹/₂″	1C = 8″

t = thickness
h = height
l = length
* Dimensions are for the number of courses indicted (e.g. 1C = 1 course).

lost to the outside, severely reducing the thermal performance of the overall system.

There are a variety of methods for finishing the exterior of a brick wall being used for direct gain storage. Because it is recommended that insulation be placed on the *outside* of exterior walls used for direct gain storage, such finishes will need to be applied *over* this insulation. In a standard masonry bearing wall configuration, stucco or siding can be applied over insulation that has been adhered and fastened to the brick wall. In typical brick veneer wall construction, the configuration of the materials can be inverted, moving the masonry to the inside for heat storage and the insulated bearing frame wall to the outside. Siding can then be applied in the conventional manner.

Neither of these configurations, however, provides a brick appearance on the outside of the house. In order to obtain this appearance while maintaining the passive solar performance characteristics of interior brick masonry, a cavity wall can be specified. If well insulated, such a wall will provide both the aesthetic appeal of brick on the exterior (exterior wythe) and the heat storage capacity of brick on the interior (interior wythe). The cavity insulation will ensure that stored heat will not be lost, while still providing a brick appearance on the exterior.

It is recommended that interior finishes be avoided in order to preserve the inherent thermal performance capabilities of the brick itself. For example, if a finish such as wood paneling or gypsum board is applied to the interior face of a brick wall intended to absorb and store solar energy, it will not only hide the brick, but will also reduce both the amount of heat reaching the wall and the amount reradiated from the wall back to the space. This is especially true of covering a brick paver floor with wall-to-wall carpet,

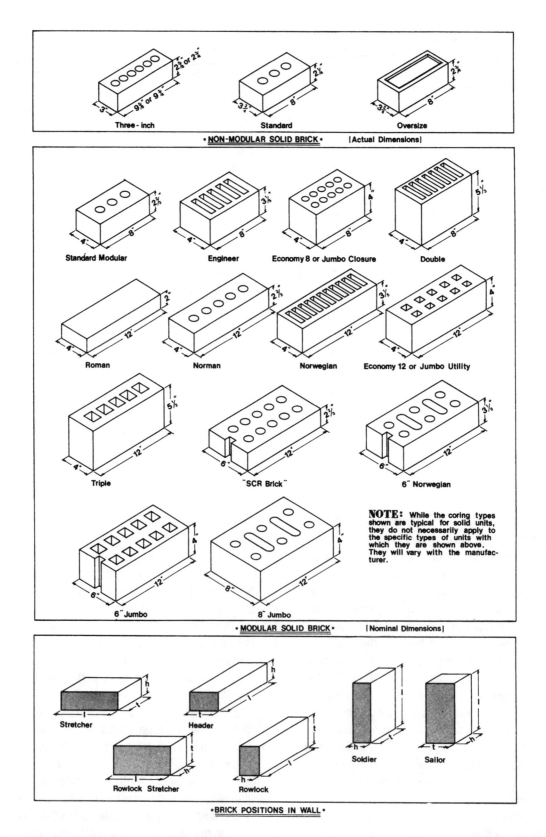

NOTE: While the coring types shown are typical for solid units, they do not necessarily apply to the specific types of units with which they are shown above. They will vary with the manufacturer.

Figure 7.15 Brick: Typical Shapes

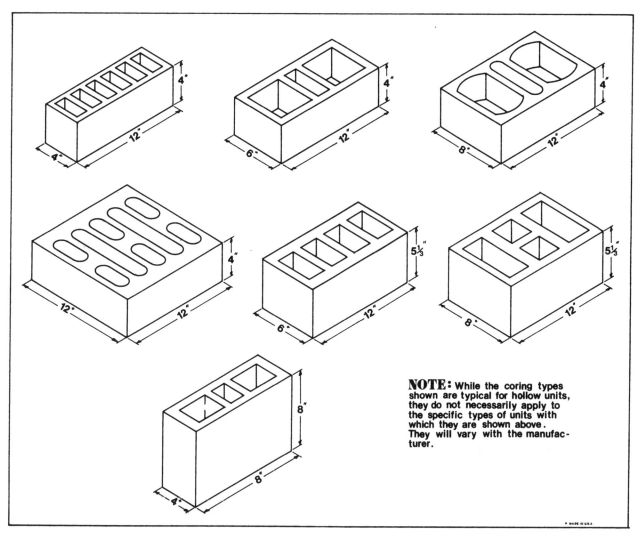

NOTE: While the coring types shown are typical for hollow units, they do not necessarily apply to the specific types of units with which they are shown above. They will vary with the manufacturer.

★ MODULAR HOLLOW BRICK ★   [Nominal Dimensions]

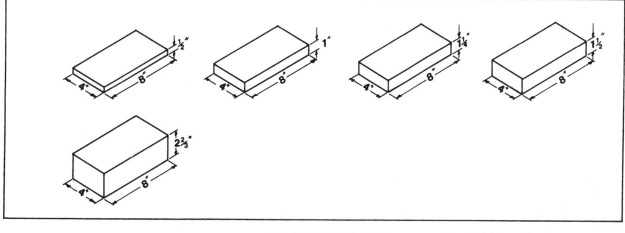

★ MODULAR PAVING BRICK ★   [Nominal Dimensions]

Figure 7.16 Brick: Typical Shapes

which is not recommended. Although the exact negative effects of such coverings have not been quantified, a good rule of thumb is to assume that, relative to other finish materials, the higher the insulating value of a given finish, the more it will inhibit the passive thermal performance of the material to which it is applied.

Carrying this concept one step further, it is obvious that putting insulation on the interior surface of a brick component (e.g., direct gain wall) used for energy storage is extremely counterproductive and essentially nullifies any passive benefits that might have been derived from the component. It is for this reason that it is recommended that no passive solar storage component (wall, floor, or roof/ceiling) be insulated on its interior face.

COLOR

Where brick is used both to absorb and to store solar energy, the surface exposed to solar radiation should be as dark a color as possible to increase absorption of light and heat. Other surfaces, such as standard frame walls, that are not being used for storage should be light in color in order to reflect as much sunlight as possible onto the darker storage material.

Although black is the most desirable storage material color from a thermal performance point of view, certain of the darker natural brick colors (browns, blues, and reds) will perform almost as effectively. Using the exposed natural brick will avoid maintenance problems that might result from the use of paint (for a listing of the solar absorptivity characteristics of various colors/ materials, see Table 7.4).

Brick with a glazed ceramic coating should be avoided, since the finish will reflect some of the solar radiation striking it. Many brick manufacturers, however, can supply brick with dull black ceramic glazed faces that perform as well as the dull finishes on natural colored brick.

Another possible finish is the so-called selective surface, a foil that has a very high absorptivity of incoming solar radiation but a very low emissivity of heat. Such foils can be very effective at increasing the thermal efficiency of passive solar storage components, and manufacturers' data should be referenced for specific performance characteristics (for further information, see "Absorber Components" earlier in this chapter).

TEXTURE

Although it would seem at first glance that rough-textured brick, by providing more surface area for the collection of energy, would be more effective than smooth brick for energy storage, this is not the case. It appears that brick texture does not have a major impact on the performance of passive solar installations, and any desired texture can be used without significant loss or gain in effectiveness.

THERMAL PROPERTIES

In terms of thermal performance, the most important material characteristics of a brick unit are its conductivity, density, specific heat, and thickness.

A material's conductivity (k) is a measure of how readily the material will transfer or "conduct" heat. The higher the conductivity, the faster the heat will travel through a material. In general, thermal performance increases as the conductivity increases.

The remaining three basic material characteristics (density, specific heat, and thickness) can also be used as indicators of anticipated thermal performance. When multiplied together, they yield the so-called thermal storage capacity of a specific unit of material. Essentially, this characteristic is a measure of the ability of a given unit of material to store heat. The higher the thermal storage capacity, the greater the amount of heat the unit can absorb and store.

In the case of brick, the specific heat for the majority of units commonly used in residential construction remains basically constant. Thus, the major variables that will determine the thermal storage capacity of a brick unit are its density (measured in pounds per cubic foot), which varies only slightly, and its thickness.

Table 7.9 presents thermal performance data, including thermal storage capacities, for a variety of bricks with different thicknesses and two different densities. The table can be used for general performance comparisons between the various brick types presented.

Table 7.9 *Brick: Physical Properties*

Brick Type[1]	Unit Thickness	Unit Density[a]	Specific Heat[2b]	Thermal Storage Capacity[3c]	R-Value[d]	Conductivity[e]
Paver	1⅝″	120	0.24	3.90	0.36	5.00
Paver		130	0.24	4.23	0.20	9.00
Paver	2¼″	120	0.24	5.40	0.50	5.00
Paver		130	0.24	5.85	0.27	9.00
Common	4″	120	0.24	8.70	0.80	5.00
Facing		130	0.24	9.43	0.44	9.00
Common	6″	120	0.24	13.50	1.20	5.00
Facing		130	0.24	14.63	0.66	9.00
Common	8″	120	0.24	18.30	1.60	5.00
Facing		130	0.24	19.83	0.88	9.00
Common	10″	120	0.24	23.10	2.00	5.00
Facing		130	0.24	25.03	1.10	9.00
Common	12″	120	0.24	27.90	2.40	5.00
Facing		130	0.24	30.23	1.32	9.00
Common	16″	120	0.24	37.50	3.20	5.00
Facing		130	0.24	40.63	1.76	9.00

[1] When using hollow units grouted, use values for common brick. When using paving units, use values for facing brick.
[2] Specific heat may vary from 0.20 to 0.26; 0.24 is typical.
[3] Thermal storage capacities are for actual dimensions of units listed.
[a]—Units of lb/ft³
[b]—Units of btu/lb·°F
[c]—Units of btu/ft²·°F
[d]—Units of hr·°F/ft²·btu
[e]—Units of btu·in/hr·ft²·°F

In general, the higher the thermal storage capacity of a given unit, the better its performance in a passive solar application. This should be kept in mind when selecting a specific brick for use as a storage component. It is evident from Table 7.9 that thicker bricks will have higher thermal storage capacities and, within the rule of thumb guidelines set out in chapters 3 through 6, will generally perform better than thinner units.

It can also be assumed that the thermal storage capacities for thicknesses greater than 16″ will roughly equal the sum of the capacities of smaller units which, when added together, will equal the overall thickness desired. For example, the thermal capacity per square foot of a 20″-thick wall of facing brick will roughly equal the sum of the capacities of one 8″ and one 12″ wall (18.3 + 27.9 = 46.2) or of two 10″ walls (23.1 + 23.1 = 46.2).

Mention should be made of the potential use of magnesia brick as a passive storage medium. Magnesia brick exhibits much higher thermal conductivities than clay and shale brick. It is not, however, markedly superior in its capacity to store heat. Rather, it is capable of delivering more heat to the interior of a space and insulating against losses from the space. Such a capability can be useful in situations where relatively rapid heat transfer is desired, but it can also have the drawback of causing a space to overheat during sunny days. Because magnesia brick is also significantly more expensive than common brick, its advantages and disadvantages should be carefully weighed before it is substituted for common brick in passive solar applications.

Little documentation is available regarding the thermal performance of the various types of mortar that can be used in brick construction. Therefore, when conducting a thermal performance analysis, it is recommended that a brick installation be considered solid brick without any mortar joints at all. This is equivalent to assuming that the mortar will exhibit the same thermal performance characteristics as the brick itself.

An environmentally sensitive choice is brick that contains manganese, a waste product from battery manufacture. Manganese brick is a rich brown color with a somewhat metallic finish.

Water

Within the same volume, water can store more than twice as much heat as masonry. Thus, to store a given amount of heat, less than one-half the volume and approximately one-fifth the weight of water will be required compared to a storage system utilizing masonry materials.

When evaluating water as a storage material for a passive solar system, however, two aspects of its use must be considered and evaluated. First, the use of water requires that it must be contained, and the cost of the container, although generally low, will need to be considered. Second, unlike masonry materials, which can also provide structural support, water storage containers are not designed as structural elements of the home and frequently require framing for bracing.

Although water containers, due to their high storage capacity, can be narrower than masonry, the specification, design, and placement of the containers must be carefully planned and constructed. Site assembly, however, is almost always faster and easier than for masonry, since the containers are prefabricated and are quickly filled on site.

CONSTRUCTION

As with all storage materials, water storage for passive solar systems should be located in direct sunlight. To function efficiently, the water storage container should present a large amount of surface area both to the sun, for absorption of heat, and to the living space, for release of the heat. In addition, a few basic characteristics, discussed below, will need to be considered before a water thermal storage system is specified.

CONTAINERS

Containers can be designed to be left exposed, with their surface providing the interior finish, or may be enclosed in walls or incorporated into features such as planters or window seats. The less expensive the container, the more likely it is to be of the concealed type. Care must be taken, when containers are concealed, that they not be inadvertently punctured (for example, by nails in hanging artwork).

Unfortunately, covering water containers will degrade the overall system performance. One of the most common applications in which the containers are concealed is in a thermal storage wall. Where a frame wall is constructed to cover the containers, the wall sheathing, typically gypsum board, will need to contain vents at both the bottom and the top of the wall to allow heat to flow into the adjacent living space.

Regardless of the type of container chosen for water storage, the water itself will need to be chemically treated to prohibit the growth of algae or other organisms within the container. In addition, all metal containers should be coated either by the manufacturer or at the site to prevent rust or corrosion.

The most widely used containers are tubes, culverts, and drums, which can be used alone or in combination (see Figure 7.17). All have inherent advantages and disadvantages. The following provides a brief description of each of the major container types.

- *Tubes*—Plastic tubes made of fiberglass, high-density polyethylene, and other materials can be used for water thermal storage. They are often left exposed and freestanding for functional and aesthetic reasons. Before filling, the tubes are lightweight and easy to install but must be handled carefully to prevent cracking or puncturing. Most plastic tubes have the

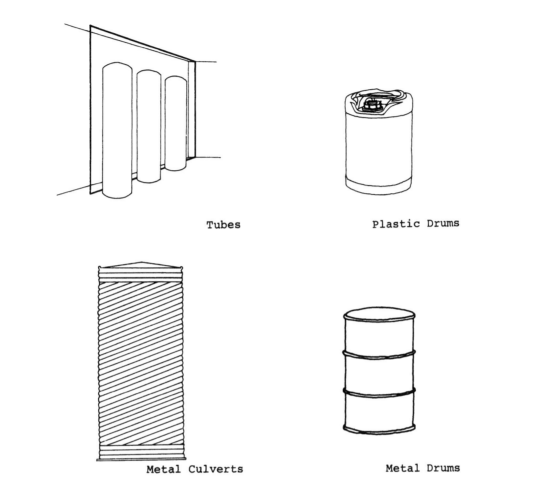

Tubes

Plastic Drums

Metal Culverts

Metal Drums

Figure 7.17

advantage of being noncorrosive and are available in sizes ranging from 14″ to 23″ in diameter, and 2′ to 3′ or more in height.

- *Metal culverts*—Culvert pipe, available from pipe supply houses, can be used for water storage. Culverts can be cut to any height, providing more design flexibility than is possible with plastic tubes. Further, culverts are generally sturdier than plastic and less subject to damage, although their heavier weight will need to be considered in sizing the supporting foundation.

  Culverts can be painted, but should first be treated with two coats of zinc chromate primer. Typically, a plate is welded to the bottom and a covering cap is fabricated from sheet steel. Culverts must be treated to resist corrosion, and it is generally recommended that a plastic liner bag be installed to further protect against leaks. Culverts are generally available in diameters of 12″ and larger.

- *Metal drums*—Thirty- and 50-gallon metal drums can be used as water storage containers. However, their use is recommended in applications where their industrial appearance is not objectionable. Drums are generally low in cost, but they are difficult to clean and may need to be treated to prevent corrosion.

  If drums are to be specified, be sure to check on the former contents to ensure against toxic reactions. Drums are available from chemical supply companies and/or drum manufacturers.

COLOR

When water is used both to absorb and to store solar energy, the surface exposed to solar radiation should be as dark a color as possible to increase absorption of light and heat. Other surfaces in the space, such as wood frame walls, that are not being used for storage should be light in color in order to reflect more light to the darker storage material (for a listing of the solar absorptivity characteristics of various colors and materials, see Table 7.4).

Color can be applied to water storage systems in two ways. In the first, and most common, the container surface can be painted, or the container can be ordered in a dark color. Plastic containers can be ordered in dark colors, while metal is often painted in the field with a suitable primer applied first. An effective alternative involves specifying a translucent or transparent container material and treating the water with a dark dye.

Water containers can also be finished with a selective surface, a foil that has a very high absorptivity of incoming solar radiation but a very low emissivity of heat. Such foils can be very effective at increasing the thermal efficiency of passive solar storage components, and manufacturers' data should be referenced for specific performance characteristics (for further information, see "Absorber Components" earlier in this chapter). In the case of water storage systems, such a foil should be placed on the side of the container that faces the sun.

TEXTURE

The texture of the water storage container can vary, depending on the material specified. Most metal or plastic containers are smooth. In general, however, the surface texture will not have a significant impact on performance.

THERMAL PROPERTIES

From the point of view of thermal performance in a passive solar application, the most important material characteristics of a particular water storage system are its conductivity, density, specific heat, and thickness.

A material's conductivity (k) is a measure of how readily the material will transfer or "conduct" heat. The higher the conductivity, the faster the heat will travel through a material. In general, thermal performance increases as the conductivity increases.

The remaining three basic material characteristics (density, specific heat, and thickness) can also be used as an indication of anticipated thermal performance. When multiplied together, they yield the so-called thermal storage capacity of a specific unit of material. Essentially, this characteristic is a measure of the ability of a given volume of water to store heat. The higher the thermal storage capacity, the greater the amount of heat that can be absorbed and stored.

In the case of water, the specific heat and the density are constant. Therefore, the only variable that will influence thermal storage capacity is the thickness. The performance of a water storage system will increase and temperature fluctuations within the living space will decrease as thickness increases.

Table 7.10 presents thermal performance data for a variety of water container thicknesses. The thicknesses listed are for rectangular containers, and the values will need to be adjusted for cylindrical containers.

Comparing the thermal storage capacity values in Table 7.10 with corresponding values for masonry materials will confirm the use of water as a suitable storage material. As stated earlier, the storage capacity per unit of thickness far exceeds that of masonry materials, a factor that should be seriously considered in designing the storage component.

Environmentally sensitive options include recycled water storage containers of plastic or metal.

Distribution Components

The distribution components move heat or "coolth" throughout the passive system, including into the living space where it is finally utilized. In most system designs, the distribution component receives little consideration. In these instances, such as direct gain design, the distribution of heat is by natural means (e.g., movement of air from space to space), and particular products or materials do not need to be specified.

In thermal storage wall design, the only instance in which distribution is considered is in the design of a vented wall. The vents in this case are considered the distribution component.

Table 7.10 *Water: Physical Properties*

Unit Thickness	Unit Density[1]	Specific Heat[2]	Thermal Storage Capacity[3]
4″	62.32	1.0	20.8
5″	62.32	1.0	26.0
6″	62.32	1.0	31.2
7″	62.32	1.0	36.4
8″	62.32	1.0	41.6
9″	62.32	1.0	46.8
10″	62.32	1.0	52.0
11″	62.32	1.0	57.2
12″	62.32	1.0	62.4
13″	62.32	1.0	67.6
14″	62.32	1.0	72.8
15″	62.32	1.0	78.0
16″	62.32	1.0	83.2
17″	62.32	1.0	88.4
18″	62.32	1.0	93.6

[1] Units of lb/ft^3
[2] Units of btu/lb·°F
[3] Units of btu/ft^2·°F

These are normally standard vents used in conventional heating design.

The use of distribution with attached sunspaces will vary, depending on the subsystem selected. The open wall and direct gain subsystems generally distribute heated air by natural means, although fans can be used in some cases to increase system performance. In the air exchange subsystem, air movement is through vents, and, as for thermal storage walls, the vent alone typically constitutes the distribution component.

Methods of heat distribution in the attached sunspace radiant slab represent the most significant example of distribution components. In this design, where heat is to be delivered to the slab (often not adjacent to the collector and absorber) a system of ducts will need to be provided. These ducts should be tightly taped and otherwise sealed and insulated to reduce system heat losses. In most cases, a low-velocity fan should be installed in the ducts to assist in the movement of air.

The operation of the fan is generally thermostatically controlled. The thermostat senses the temperatures in the living space and at the collector/absorber to determine whether the heat should be diverted into storage.

Selection, operation, and control of the fan(s) will vary, depending on the design of the system and the products specified. Manufacturers' literature should be consulted in this regard. Information on specific products is currently available from mechanical equipment manufacturers and suppliers.

Control Components

Introduction

Due to the development of high-performance glazings, the use of many control components has become less essential and, in some cases, unnecessary. Previous problems associated with single-pane or double-pane collectors, including substantial heat loss at night and the increased cooling loads in the summer, have been minimized by the lower U-values and low shading coefficients possible with many glazing assemblies. Control components still have their place, however, particularly in extreme and harsh climates.

The three basic types of control components are shading, reflecting, and insulating. Shading is a cooling-season measure that reduces the amount of solar heat that reaches the living spaces. Reflecting, conversely, is a heating-season control device whose purpose is to increase the amount of collected solar heat. Insulating devices slow the movement of heat into, and out of, the living spaces.

Insulating components are divided into two categories: fixed and movable. Fixed insulation generally remains in place throughout the year. Movable insulation, as its name indicates, is moved into position, typically on a daily basis.

Many of the products used in one type of control application can also be used in another, such as a reflector, which, if shut in the evening, provides insulating value. Products that can serve a dual role often provide the highest dollar return in energy savings for dollar invested.

Each of the three control components—shading, reflecting, and insulating—is covered in a separate discussion below. The relative importance of the components will vary depending on home design and geographical location.

Shading

In most passive systems, some form of shading is required to prevent overheating during the cooling season. Shading devices can be placed on either the inside or the outside of the collector glazing.

If placed on the exterior, the shade will intercept direct solar radiation before it strikes the collector. Shades can be fixed or movable. Fixed exterior shading is not as effective as movable exterior shading, since it will block some of the sunlight from reaching the collector during the heating season. However, fixed shading is generally less expensive and less prone to maintenance problems than movable shading. Examples of common shading devices on the exterior include simple overhangs, awnings (fixed or adjustable), trellises, and shutters.

Shading devices placed inside the collector are not as thermally efficient as those placed on the exterior because they allow sunlight to penetrate into the space, where it can cause some heat gain. However, this heat buildup is usually restricted to the window surface and can be vented. To reduce the amount of heat reaching the living space, the interior shade should have edges sealed at the top, bottom, and both sides.

Interior shades are typically light in color to reflect sunlight back out the window before it can be converted to heat. The major advantage of interior shades is that they are typically easier to operate and maintain than most operable exterior elements.

Interior fixed shades are rarely specified. Some examples of interior shading components include roller shades, drapes, and movable panels. The components are especially effective if they can also be designed to provide insulation during the day in the cooling periods and at night in the heating periods (see "Insulating" later in this chapter).

TYPES OF SHADING DEVICES

A vast variety of shading products and configurations can be effective in passive solar applications. Selection will depend largely on ease of construction and operation, aesthetics, and cost. It is important to remember that, regardless of the system selected, the shading device will not be effective if it is not operated appropriately. Therefore, convenience and ease of operation are of foremost importance in the selection process of this control component.

The following are brief descriptions of the most commonly specified shading devices. Examples are shown in Figure 7.18.

- *Trellises and overhangs*—Simple trellises and overhangs are popular and inexpensive exterior shading options. Since they are fixed, they must be sized to reduce the amount of sun reaching the collector in the cooling season,

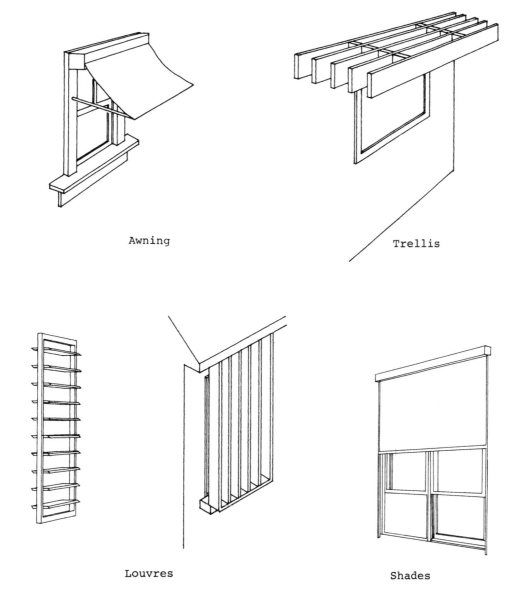

Awning

Trellis

Louvres

Shades

Figure 7.18

while allowing as much sunlight as possible to strike the collector in the heating season.

Trellises and overhangs are usually simple extensions of the roofline and typically do not require any maintenance. By encouraging air movement across the collector glazing, trellises are slightly more effective than overhangs in reducing the cooling requirements.

- *Roll shades*—Roll shades can be installed on the exterior or interior. They can be solid or translucent, allowing some light into the living spaces. All fabrics used should be resistant to ultraviolet degradation, and exterior applications must be weather-resistant.

Interior applications may be designed with insulative materials to combine shading and insulating benefits. In addition, interior shades should be provided with seals at the edges to further restrict the flow of heat into the living space.

- *Awnings*—Awnings may be fixed or movable. As mentioned earlier, fixed awnings should be sized to reduce heat gain during the cooling season yet allow for solar gain during the heating season. In order to reduce possible maintenance problems, movable awnings should be removed and stored during the heating months. Movable awnings provide the flexibility required to provide shade only when needed, adjusting to the angle of the sun. Operation of movable awnings can be either manual or motorized.

- *Louvers*—Louvers can be installed on the exterior or interior. In either location, movable, adjustable louvers can reduce solar gain and glare and also provide insulating and/or reflecting qualities.

  Louvers or slats can be horizontal or vertical. The latter configuration is particularly effective for southeast and southwest exposures. Both horizontal-mounted and vertical-mounted louvers are available. Operation may be manual or motorized.

Reflecting

Unlike a shading device, whose function is to limit the amount of solar heat in the passive system, a reflector is designed to enhance the collection of solar energy.

Reflectors increase the effective collector area by increasing the amount of solar heat passing through the glazing. The reflective surface acts like a mirror, reflecting much of the sunlight that strikes it. If properly oriented, the sunlight can be reflected onto the glazing, increasing the amount of solar heat available to the passive system. This increase in collected solar heat can, in effect, be considered to be the equivalent of adding the additional glazing area that would have been required to provide the same amount of heat.

Some significant performance increases can result from reflectors used in areas where local site obstructions, such as large trees or other homes, shade the collector at certain times of the day or year. A well-designed reflector can increase solar heat collection as much as 30 percent to 40 percent in certain situations.

Reflectors can be movable or fixed. A movable reflector in a passive solar system is most com-

monly constructed or purchased as a rigid panel with a highly reflective surface, such as aluminum or foil, on one side. A typical installation might include either vertical or horizontal hinges to permit the panel to close over the collector during periods of heat loss. The reflector is nearly always designed to double as movable nighttime insulation and, for ease of use, can be motorized to operate automatically.

Even if such panels are not feasible or not desired for certain applications, the performance of a passive solar system can be improved (although not as significantly as with a movable reflective surface) through the use of fixed reflectors. Concrete patios or white gravel planting beds adjacent to the collector, light colors on exterior walls, and decks or balconies with light-colored finishes are all examples of how reflective benefits can be obtained from standard fixed building components designed as reflectors.

CONSTRUCTION

Movable reflectors are typically fabricated specifically for the job. This "one-off" approach is generally necessary, since the requirements for different applications tend to vary.

Panels can be readily fabricated, incorporating insulation characteristics as well, by finishing the face of a rigid insulation board with a reflective material. All panels exposed to the outside should be weather-resistant, and operation should be made as simple as possible.

Table 7.11 contains the reflectivities of various materials. These values should be used for comparative purposes. The actual amount of sunlight reflected onto and through the collector will vary with time of year, location, angle of reflector, weather conditions, collector design, and material selection.

Insulating

Passive solar insulating components can be separated into two basic categories: fixed insulation that is permanently installed to reduce heat loss from a system's storage components, and movable insulation that is usually located at the collector and that is operated periodically to reduce nighttime and cloudy-day heat loss (during the

Table 7.11 *Reflectivity Values of Various Surfaces*

Surface	Reflectivity (%)
Aluminum Foil, bright	92–97
Aluminum Sheet	80–95
Aluminum-Coated Paper (polished)	75–84
Steel, galvanized, bright	70–80
Aluminum Paint	30–70
Brick	30–48
Paint (white)	75
Marble (white)	45
Concrete	40
Cement	27
Gravel	13
Grass	6

heating season) and daytime heat gain (during the cooling season).

FIXED INSULATION

In order to be effective, fixed insulation must be placed on the exterior surface of storage components that would otherwise be directly exposed to the outside. This type of installation will prevent the heat absorbed and stored at the interior surface of, for example, a direct gain floor or wall from being lost to the outside environment. If standard practice is followed and insulation is placed on the *inside* face of a storage component, the passive system is rendered ineffective.

Any of the materials commonly used for residential insulation can be employed as fixed exterior insulation for passive solar storage elements. The methods for attaching this insulation to the storage elements may differ slightly from standard practice, but those differences require only minor modifications to standard construction practices (see chapters 3 through 6).

Today's range of insulation products offers a number of environmentally sensitive materials. Cellulose (from recycled newsprint), recycled expanded polystyrene (EPS), extruded poly-styrene (XPS) insulation containing no chlorofluorocarbons (CFCs), fiberglass with recycled content, and recycled cotton insulation are some of the choices commercially available.

MOVABLE INSULATION

Movable insulation comes in a variety of forms, including rigid panels, insulating shutters, and insulating drapes and shades. Depending on their physical characteristics, these devices can be used on the exterior or the interior of the collector. Interior applications are generally easier to operate and maintain, and they avoid degradation due to weathering. Exterior applications have the advantage, during the cooling season, of also acting as exterior shades.

If interior movable insulation is used, the side facing the glass should be light-colored to reflect sunlight and thereby avoid heat buildup in the airspace between the insulation and glass. This buildup can occur even on sunny winter days if the insulation is left in place. Therefore, all interior movable insulation should be light-colored on the side facing the glass, whether it is used to prevent summer heat gain or not.

The most distinctive characteristic of movable insulation is that it is operable and, in general, must be managed on a day-to-day basis. Although some varieties can be thermostatically controlled, the majority require some operation, either manual or automatic switch-controlled. The choice of product will depend, of course, on cost and ease of operation, as well as on thermal effectiveness.

A variety of movable insulation product types can be installed on either the interior or the exterior of the windows. All will function well if properly installed and operated, and a mix of types will probably be appropriate for the typical home. Each product type is briefly discussed below. Some typical products of these types are shown in Figures 7.19 and 7.20.

INTERIOR MOVABLE INSULATION PRODUCTS

- *Drapes*—Insulating drapes commonly employ quilted fabrics, reflective liners, or multiple layers of materials to help reduce heat flow.

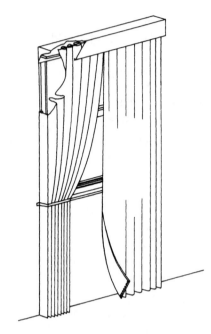

Drapes

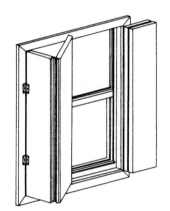

Shutters

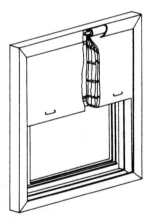
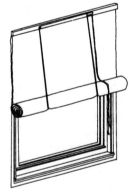
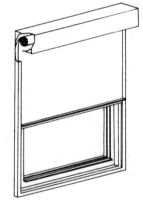

Shades

Figure 7.19

Manufacturers' specifications should be consulted for rated R-values, but performance in the R-1 to R-4 range can be expected.

Attention must be paid to sealing the edges, tops, and bottoms of drapes, particularly if the R-value of the drapes is R-4 or higher. Velcro™ or magnetic strips can be used at the edges, and weights in the bottom hem are appropriate if the drapes reach the floor or rest on the windowsill. If they fall past the sill but do not reach the floor, special detailing will be required to ensure a continuous seal at the bottom.

Standard drapes, not specifically designed to have a significant R-value, can nonetheless pro-

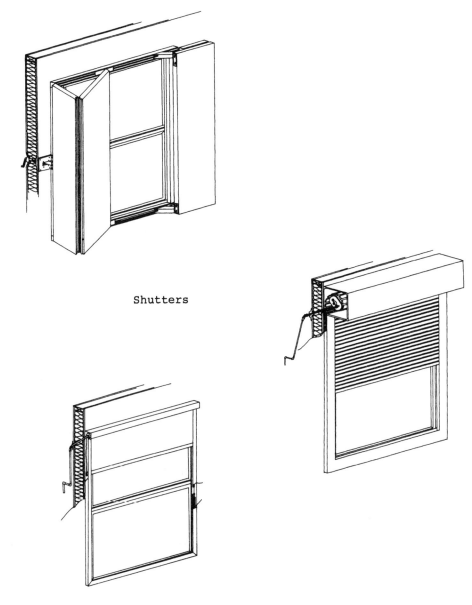

Shutters

Rolldown Shutters

Figure 7.20

vide some insulating benefit if they are properly sealed at the edges and bottom. The R-value for sealed, standard drapes is approximately R-1.

• *Shades*—Insulating shades can be regular, quilted, or multilayered and can incorporate fiberfill, insulating airspaces, or heat-reflective materials. R-values range roughly from R-3 to R-12, and, again, manufacturers' specifications should be consulted for precise values.

As in the case of insulating curtains, edge and bottom seals are critical to the effective performance of insulating shades. Velcro or magnetic strips can be used (sides and bottom) to seal shades to the window frame, or side tracks can be mounted on the frame with the bottom of the shade fitting into an additional track or simply resting on the sill. In the latter case, a small piece of foam plastic material attached to the bottom of the shade may be desirable to ensure a tight seal.

Insulating shades may be bulky relative to more standard varieties and may require larger valances.

Standard shades, not specifically designed to have an insulating capability, can provide some insulating benefit if properly sealed at edges and bottom. Again, an estimated R-value of R-1 should be assumed for well-sealed shades.

- *Shutters*—Insulating shutters are typically fabricated from rigid insulating boards (polystyrene, polyurethane, or polyisocyanurate) sandwiched between some form of finish material. Performance will generally range from R-4 to R-8 per inch of insulation, depending on the material used.

  Typical shutter configurations are hinged, bifold, or track mounted. In any configuration, there should be a tight fit between the shutters and frame, and all edges should be well sealed. Manufacturers' recommendations should be followed for sealing, or common weatherstripping details can be applied.

- *Panels*—Removable insulating panels are similar to insulating shutters in configuration, except that they are not mechanically attached to the window frame but are removed and stored after each use. Such panels should be detailed so that edges are continuously sealed with materials such as Velcro, magnetic strips,

or tight-fitting buttons that hold the panel firmly against the frame.

EXTERIOR MOVABLE INSULATION PRODUCTS

- *Shutters and panels*—Insulating exterior shutters and panels are constructed and perform similarly to those placed on the interior, except that they require operation from the outside or special detailing to allow operation from the inside of the home. As in the case of interior insulation, all edges should be well sealed.

- *Roll-down shutters*—Exterior shutters are typically made from interlocking wood, aluminum, or PVC slats. A range of product R-values is available. Side tracks on rolldown shutters should be detailed to provide a tight seal, as should the bottom of the shutter where it meets the sill.

CONSTRUCTION

In many passive systems, the installation and operation of movable insulation may be difficult. For this reason, it is strongly recommended that, where used, consideration be given to movable insulation components at the earliest stages of design. This will ensure that the passive system, as a whole, operates at optimum performance levels. It is also advisable to consult manufacturers' recommendations when specifying movable insulation components to ensure that proper allowances and clearances are provided.

GLOSSARY

ABSORBER—A solid surface, usually dark-colored, which is exposed to, and struck by, sunlight, and which transforms radiant solar energy to heat energy.

ABSORPTANCE—The ratio of the radiation absorbed by a surface to the total energy falling on that surface, measured as a percentage.

ABSORPTIVITY—See Absorptance.

ACTIVE SOLAR SYSTEM—A system that uses mechanical devices and an external energy source, in addition to solar energy, to collect, store, and distribute thermal energy (heat).

AIR CHANGE—The replacement of a quantity of air in a volume within a given period of time. This is expressed in number of changes per hour. If a house has 1 air change per hour, all the air in the house will be replaced in a 1-hour period.

AIR-LOCK ENTRY—A vestibule enclosed with two airtight doors for permitting entrance while limiting air or heat exchange.

AMBIENT TEMPERATURE—The prevailing temperature outside a building.

ANGLE OF INCIDENCE—The angle that the sun's rays make with a line perpendicular to a surface.

ANNUAL FUEL REQUIREMENT—Annual heating load divided by the product of the mechanical plant efficiency (MPE) (usually obtainable from the equipment manufacturer) and the fuel conversion factor.

APERTURE—The part of the south-facing glazing that contributes to solar heating; literally, an opening.

ASHRAE—The American Society of Heating, Refrigerating and Air Conditioning Engineers.

AUXILIARY ENERGY SYSTEM—Equipment utilizing energy other than solar, both to supplement the output provided by the solar energy system (as required by the design conditions) and to provide full energy backup requirements during periods when the solar heating or domestic hot water systems are inoperable.

AUXILIARY HEATING FRACTION (AHF)—The part of the total building heating requirements supplied by the auxiliary heating system.

AZIMUTH—The angular distance between true south and the point on the horizon directly below the sun.

BACKUP SYSTEM—See Auxiliary Energy System.

BERM—A manmade mound or small hill of earth.

BLACK BODY—A theoretically perfect absorber.

273

BTU (BRITISH THERMAL UNIT)—Basic heat measurement, equivalent to the amount of heat needed to raise 1 lb. of water 1°F.

BTU/DD/FT² (HEATED AREA)—A unit commonly used to express the inherent ability of the building shell to resist heat loss.

BUILDING ENVELOPE—The elements of a building that enclose conditioned spaces through which thermal energy may be transferred to or from the exterior.

BUILDING LOAD COEFFICIENT (BLC)—A rough measure of the insulating quality of the home, exclusive of the south facade, used in estimating the solar savings fraction (SSF), which is the percentage of heating needs supplied by the passive solar system.

BUILDING SKIN CONDUCTANCE—The weighted average conductance of all the components of the building skin.

CALORIE (CAL)—The quantity of heat needed to raise the temperature of 1 gram of water 1°C. One calorie is approximately 0.004 Btu.

CLERESTORY—A vertical window placed high in a wall near the eaves or between a lower roof and a higher roof, used for light, heat gain, and ventilation.

COLLECTOR—An area of transparent or translucent glazing commonly located on the south-facing side of the home.

COLLECTOR EFFICIENCY—The amount of energy gathered by a collector compared to the amount striking it.

COMFORT RANGE—The range of climatic conditions within which people feel comfortable.

COMPONENT—An individually distinguishable product that forms part of a more complex product (i.e., subsystem of a system).

CONDUCTANCE (C)—The quantity of heat (Btus) that will flow through 1 sq. ft. of material in 1 hour, when there is a 1°F temperature difference between both surfaces. Conductance values are given for a specific thickness of materials, not per inch of thickness.

CONDUCTIVITY (K)—The quantity of heat (Btus) that will flow through 1 sq. ft. of material 1″ thick, in 1 hour, when there is a temperature difference of 1°F between both surfaces.

CONTROL—A device or devices that regulates heat flow between the building and the exterior.

CONVECTION—The transfer of heat by movement of a fluid (liquid or gas).

CONVECTION, FORCED—Heat transfer through a medium, such as air or water, by currents caused by a device powered by an external energy source.

CONVECTION, NATURAL—Heat transfer of a fluid, such as air or water, that results from the natural rising of the lighter, warm fluid and the sinking of the heavier, cool fluid.

CONVECTIVE LOOP—A passive system in which a fluid, typically air, is circulated in a closed path induced by rising hot air and falling cold air.

COOLING SEASON—The period(s) during the year when the outside temperature and humidity conditions require that the living spaces must be naturally or mechanically cooled to be comfortable.

COOLTH—A term used to describe the quality of a material at a lower than ambient temperature. Coolth is to cooling as warmth is to heating.

DECLINATION—A deviation, as from a specific direction or standard. Used primarily in relation to magnetic declination (magnetic variation), which is the angle between true north and magnetic north. The declination varies with different geographical areas.

DEGREE-DAY (DD), COOLING—See Degree-Day, Heating, except that cooling degree days are measured as the variation of degrees above, not below, the standard temperature (usually 65°F).

DEGREE-DAY (DD), HEATING—A unit of heat measurement equal to 1°F variation below a standard temperature (usually 65°F) in the average temperature of one day. If the standard is 65°F and the average outside temperature for one day is 50°F, then the number of degree-days recorded for that day would be 15.

DELTA T (Δ T)—A difference in temperature.

DENSITY—The mass of a substance, which is expressed in pounds per cubic foot.

DESIGN LIFE—The period of time during which a heating, cooling, or domestic hot water system is expected to perform its intended function without requiring maintenance or replacement.

DESIGN TEMPERATURE—A designated temperature close to the most severe winter or summer temperature extremes of an area, used in estimating heating and/or cooling demand.

DIFFUSE RADIATION—Sunlight that is scattered by air molecules, dust, water vapor, and translucent materials.

DIRECT GAIN (DG)—A passive system in which solar radiation is admitted directly into the conditioned (or living) space, where it is converted to heat and stored.

DIRECT RADIATION—Light that has traveled a straight path from the sun, as opposed to diffuse radiation.

DISTRIBUTION—The method by which heat is delivered to the living areas.

DRY BULB TEMPERATURE—A measure of the sensible temperature of the air.

ECONOMIC EFFICIENCY—Maximizing net benefits or minimizing costs for a given level of benefits.

EFFICIENCY—In solar applications, the amount of useful solar energy collected, divided by the amount of solar energy available to the collector.

EMISSIVITY—The ability to radiate heat in the form of long-wave radiation.

EMITTANCE—The ratio of the amount of heat radiated by a surface to the amount that would be radiated by a black body at the same temperature. Emittance values range from 0.05 for brightly polished metals to 0.96 for flat black paint.

ENERGY—The capacity for doing work. It takes a number of forms, which may be transformed from one into another, such as thermal (heat), mechanical (work), electrical, and chemical; customarily measured in kilowatt-hours (kWh) or British thermal units (Btu).

ENERGY TRANSPORT SYSTEM—The portion of heating and domestic hot water systems that contains heat transfer fluids and transports energy throughout the system.

EQUINOX—Either of the two times during the year when the sun crosses the celestial equator and when the length of day and night are approximately equal. These are the autumnal equinox, on or about September 22, and the vernal equinox, on or about March 22.

FIRST COST—A measure of the initial cost of a component or system.

FLAT PLATE COLLECTOR—A panel of metal or other suitable material that converts sunlight into heat. The solar radiative absorbing surface is essentially flat, and the aperture and absorber are similar in area and geometry.

GLAZING—A covering of transparent or translucent material (glass or plastic) used for admitting light. Glazing reduces heat losses from reradiation and convection. Examples: windows, skylights, greenhouses, and clerestories.

GREENHOUSE EFFECT—The ability of a glazing material to both transmit short-wave solar radiation into a space and trap long-wave heat generated by the conversion of the short-wave radiation into heat.

GROSS FLOOR AREA—The sum of the areas of all floors of a building, including basements, cellars, mezzanine, and intermediate floored tiers, and penthouses of headroom height, measured from the exterior faces of exterior walls or from the centerline of the walls separating buildings.

GROSS WALL AREA—The gross area of exterior walls consists of all opaque wall areas (including foundation walls, areas between floor spandrels, peripheral edges of floors, window areas including sash, and door areas) where such surfaces are exposed to outdoor air and enclose a heated or mechanically cooled space, including areas between two such spaces.

HEAT—The form of energy that is transferred by virtue of a temperature difference.

HEAT CAPACITY—The property of a material defined as the quantity of heat needed to raise 1 cu ft of the material 1°F; numerically, the density multiplied by the specific heat.

HEAT EXCHANGER—A device specifically designed to transfer heat between two physically separated fluids.

HEAT GAIN—An increase in the amount of heat contained in a space, resulting from solar radiation and the flow of heat through the building envelope, plus internal heat gain.

HEAT LOSS—A decrease in the amount of heat contained in a space, resulting from heat flow through walls, windows, roof, and other building envelope components.

HEAT LOSS COEFFICIENT (UA)—The rate of energy transfer through the walls, roof, and floor of a house, calculated in Btus per hour per degree F (Btu/hr/°F).

HEAT SINK—A substance that is capable of accepting and storing heat, and therefore may also act as a heat source.

HEAT TRANSFER MEDIUM—A medium—liquid, air, or solid—that is used to transport thermal energy.

HEATED SPACE—Space within a building that is provided with a positive heat supply to maintain the air temperature at 50°F or higher.

HERS—Home Energy Rating System; a system used to determine efficiency of home energy consumption.

HVAC SYSTEM—A system that provides, either collectively or individually, the processes of comfort control, including heating, ventilating, and/or air-conditioning within or associated with a building.

HYBRID SYSTEM—A solar heating system that combines active and passive techniques.

INCIDENT ANGLE—The angle between the incident ray from the sun and a line drawn perpendicular to the solar collector surface.

INDIRECT GAIN PASSIVE SYSTEM—A solar heating system in which sunlight first strikes a thermal mass located between the sun and a space. The sunlight absorbed by the mass is converted to heat and then transferred into the living space.

INFILTRATION—The uncontrolled inward air leakage through cracks and interstices in any building element and around windows and doors of a building, caused by the pressure effects of wind and/or the effect of differences in the indoor and outdoor air density.

INSOLATION—The total amount of solar radiation incident on an exposed surface measured in Btus per hour per square foot (Btu/hr/ft²) or in Langleys.

INSULATION—A material having a relatively high resistance to heat flow and used principally to reduce heat flow.

INTERNAL HEAT GAIN—Heat generated by equipment, appliances, lights, and people.

ISOLATED GAIN PASSIVE SYSTEM—A system in which solar collection and heat storage are isolated from the living spaces.

LIFE-CYCLE COST—A measure of total system cost, including initial, maintenance, and operating costs over the system's life span. The accumulation generally includes a discounting of future costs to reflect the relative value of money over time.

LOAD COLLECTOR RATIO (LCR)—The building load coefficient (BLC) divided by the total passive solar collector area. The LCR is used to determine the solar savings fraction.

LOW-E GLASS—Low-e glass is coated with layers of metal or metal oxide a few atoms thick. The coating emits very little radiation in the long-wave (infrared) spectrum. The net effect is to diminish heat loss from the building interior in cold weather, and to reduce heat gain in hot weather.

MAGNETIC SOUTH—South as indicated by a compass; it changes markedly with latitude.

MECHANICAL PLANT EFFICIENCY—The efficiency of the mechanical system, usually obtainable from the equipment manufacturer.

MICROCLIMATE—The climate of a defined local area, such as a house or building site, formed by a unique combination of factors such as wind, topography, solar exposure, soil, and vegetation.

MMBTU—Million (10⁶) Btus. The predominant unit of measure for energy in the United States.

MOVABLE INSULATION—Insulation placed over windows, clerestories, skylights, and other glazing when needed to prevent heat loss or gain, and removed for light, view, venting, or heat.

NATURAL VENTILATION—See Ventilation, Natural.

NIGHT INSULATION (NI)—See Movable Insulation.

NOCTURNAL COOLING—Cooling by night-time radiation, convection, and evaporation.

OPAQUE—Impenetrable by light.

OUTSIDE AIR—Air taken from the outdoors and, therefore, not previously circulated through the system.

PASSIVE SOLAR SYSTEM—An assembly of natural and architectural components, including collectors, thermal storage device(s), and transfer fluid, which converts solar energy into thermal energy in a controlled manner and in which no fans or pumps are used to accomplish the transfer of thermal energy.

PAYBACK—A traditional measure of economic viability of investment projects. A payback period is defined in several ways, one of which is the number of years required to accumulate fuel savings that exactly equals the initial capital cost of the system.

PEAK LOAD—The design heating and cooling load used in mechanical system sizing. Usually set to meet human comfort requirements 93 percent to 97 percent of the time.

PERCENT SOLAR—A crude measure of the amount of heating or cooling provided by a solar system, compared to the total demand.

PHASE-CHANGE MATERIAL—A material, such as salt or wax, that stores thermal energy when the material melts, and releases heat when it solidifies.

PLENUM—A chamber used for the even distribution of air entering into and exiting from remote storage systems.

POWER—In connection with machines, power is the time rate of doing work. In connection with the transmission of energy of all types, power refers to the rate at which energy is transmitted. In customary units, it is measured in watts (W) or British thermal units per hour (Btu/hr).

R-VALUE—A unit of thermal resistance used for comparing insulating values of different materials. The reciprocal of the conductivity (U-value). The higher the R-value of a material, the greater its insulating capabilities (see Thermal Transmittance; U-Value).

RADIATION—The direct transport of energy through a space by means of electromagnetic waves.

RADIATION, SOLAR—See Solar Radiation.

RECOVERED ENERGY—Energy utilized that would otherwise be wasted from an energy utilization system.

REFLECTANCE—The ratio of the light reflected by a surface to the light falling on it.

REFLECTED RADIATION—Solar radiation reflected by light-colored or polished surfaces. It can be used to increase solar gain.

REFRACTION—The change in direction of light rays as they enter a transparent medium, such as water, air, or glass.

RESISTANCE (R)—The tendency of a material to reduce the flow of heat (see R-Value).

REVERSE THERMOCIRCULATION—The convective circulation that occurs when a warm fluid is cooled, causing it to drop (see Thermocirculation).

ROCK STORAGE SYSTEM—A solar energy system in which the collected heat is stored in a rock bin for later use. This type of storage can be used in an active, hybrid, or passive system. However, rock storage is primarily used with a system that circulates air as the transfer medium between the collector and storage, and from the storage to the heated space. Because of maintenance problems, and the fact that high-performance glazings perform so well, rock storage is rarely, if ever, used.

SELECTIVE SURFACE—A coating with high solar radiation absorptance and low thermal emittance, used on the surface of an absorber to increase system efficiency.

SENSIBLE HEAT—Heat that results in a temperature change

SHADING COEFFICIENT (SC)—The ratio of the solar heat gain through a specific glazing system under a given set of conditions to the total solar heat gain through a single layer of clear, double-strength glass under the same conditions.

SOLAR ALTITUDE—The angle of the sun above the horizon, measured in a vertical plane.

SOLAR CONSTANT—The amount of radiation or heat energy that reaches the outside of the earth's atmosphere.

SOLAR HEATING FRACTION (SHF)—The percentage of heating needs supplied by the passive solar system.

SOLAR RADIATION—Electromagnetic radiation emitted by the sun.

SOLAR RETROFIT—The application of a solar heating or cooling system to an existing building.

SOLAR SAVING FRACTION (SSF)—The difference in auxiliary heat required with and without the solar collection aperture (solar wall). The "nonsolar" building is simply the same building without a solar wall.

$$SSF = \frac{\text{solar savings}}{\text{reference net thermal load}}$$

or

$$SSF = \frac{1 - \text{auxiliary heat required by solar building}}{\text{auxiliary heat required by nonsolar building}}$$

SOLAR TIME—The hours of the day reckoned by the apparent position of the sun. Solar noon is that instant on any day at which the sun reaches its maximum altitude for that day. Solar time is very rarely the same as local standard time in any locality.

SOLAR WINDOW—An opening that is designed or placed primarily to admit solar energy into a space.

SPECIFIC HEAT—The number of Btus required to raise the temperature of 1 lb. of a material 1°F in temperature.

SPECULAR—Resembling, or produced by, a mirror, polished metal plate, or other reflector device.

STORAGE—The assembly used for storing thermal energy so that it can be used when required.

STRATIFICATION—In the context of solar heating, the formation of layers in a substance in which the top layer is warmer than the bottom.

SUN-TEMPERED—A structure that is designed or oriented to take into account climatic conditions but that does not possess strict passive features, such as thermal mass.

THERMAL BREAK—An element of low heat conductivity placed in such a way as to reduce or prevent the flow of heat.

THERMAL CAPACITY—See Heat Capacity.

THERMAL CONDUCTANCE—See Conductance.

THERMAL ENERGY—Heat possessed by a material resulting from the motion of molecules that can do work.

THERMAL MASS—A thermally absorptive component used to store heat energy. In a passive solar system, the mass absorbs the sun's heat during the day and radiates it at night as the temperatures drop. Thermal mass can also refer to the overall amount of heat storage capacity available in a given system or assembly.

THERMAL STORAGE CAPACITY—The ability of a material, per square foot of exposed surface area, to absorb and store heat; numerically, the density times the specific heat times the thickness.

THERMAL STORAGE ROOF—A passive system in which the storage mass is located on the roof. Mass can be water or masonry, and usually has movable insulation.

THERMAL STORAGE WALL—A passive system in which the storage mass is a wall located between the collector and the living space(s) to be heated. The mass can be a variety of materials, including water or masonry.

THERMAL TRANSMITTANCE (U)—Overall coefficient of heat transmission (air-to-air) expressed in units of Btu per hour per square foot per degree F. It is the time rate of heat flow. The U-value applies to combinations of different materials used in a series along the heat flow path: single materials that comprise a building section, cavity air spaces, and surface air films on both sides of a building element (see U-Value).

THERMOCIRCULATION—The convective circulation of fluid, such as water or air, that occurs when warm fluid rises and is displaced by denser, cooler fluid in the same system.

THERMOSIPHON—See Thermocirculation.

TILT ANGLE—The angle of a collector relative to the ground. A rule-of-thumb collector angle for winter heating is the latitude + 10°, while the rule for year-round heating is the latitude − 10°.

TIME LAG—The period of time between the absorption of solar radiation by a material and its release into a space. Time lag is an important consideration in sizing a thermal storage wall.

TRANSLUCENT—Having the characteristic of transmitting light but causing sufficient diffusion to eliminate perception of distinct images.

TRANSMITTANCE—The ratio of radiant energy transmitted through a transparent or translucent substance to the total radiant energy incident on its surface.

TRANSPARENT—Having the characteristic of transmitting light so that objects or images can be seen as if there were no intervening material.

TROMBE WALL—Another name for a thermal storage wall, named after its inventor, Dr. Felix Trombe.

U-VALUE—The number of Btus that flow through 1 sq. ft. of roof, wall, or floor, in 1 hour, when there is a 1°F difference in temperature between the inside and the outside air, under steady-state conditions. The U-value is the reciprocal of the resistance or R-value (see Thermal Transmittance; R-Value).

VAPOR BARRIER—A layer of material, resistant to the flow of water in the gaseous state, used to prevent condensation of water within insulation or dead-air spaces.

VENTILATION, FORCED—The mechanically assisted movement of fresh air through a building using some sort of fan or blower.

VENTILATION, INDUCED—The thermally assisted movement of fresh air through a building, such as by thermocirculation.

VENTILATION, NATURAL—The unassisted movement of fresh air through a building.

WATER WALL—A passive technique for collecting solar energy. Water walls are usually black, water-filled containers exposed to the sun. These collect and store heat, which is then used to warm a living space.

WET BULB TEMPERATURE—The lowest temperature attainable by evaporating water into the air.

WYTHE—Each continuous vertical section of a wall one masonry unit in thickness and tied to an adjacent vertical section or sections.

ZONE—A space or group of spaces within a building with heating and/or cooling requirements sufficiently similar so that comfort conditions can be maintained throughout by a single controlling device.

BIBLIOGRAPHY

The following is a selected bibliography of publications that will provide additional information on topics covered in the *Handbook*.

AIA Research Corporation. *A Survey of Passive Solar Buildings.* Washington, DC: U.S. Department of Energy, 1980.

———. *A Survey of Passive Solar Homes.* Washington, DC: U.S. Department of Energy, 1980.

———. "Passive Cooling." *Research & Design Quarterly,* Vol. 11, No. 3. Washington, DC, Fall 1979.

———. "Passive Technology." *Research & Design Quarterly,* Vol. 11, No. 1. Washington, DC, January 1979.

———. *Solar Dwelling Design Concepts.* Washington, DC: U.S. Government Printing Office, 1976.

American Institute of Architects. *Environmental Resource Guide: Building Materials.* Washington, DC: American Institute of Architects, 1994.

American Society of Heating, Refrigeration, and Air Conditioning Engineers. *ASHRAE Handbook of Fundamentals.* Atlanta: ASHRAE Publications, 1996.

Ander, Gregg D. *Daylighting: Performance and Design.* New York: Van Nostrand Reinhold, 1995.

Anderson, Bruce, ed. *Solar Building Architecture.* Cambridge, MA: MIT Press, 1990.

Anderson, Bruce, and Michael Riordan. *Solar Home Book.* Andover, MA: Brick House Publishing Co., 1987.

Balcomb, J. Douglas. *DOE: Passive Solar Handbook, Vols. 1, 2, & 3.* New York: Van Nostrand Reinhold, 1984.

———. *Energy Savings Obtainable Through Passive Solar Techniques.* Los Alamos, NM: Los Alamos Scientific Laboratory, 1978.

———. *Passive Solar Buildings.* Cambridge, MA: MIT Press, 1992.

Balcomb, J. Douglas, et al. *Passive Solar Design Handbook, Volume 2: Passive Solar Design Analysis.* Springfield, VA: National Technical Information Service, U.S. Department of Commerce, 1980.

Banham, Rayner. *The Architecture of the Well-Tempered Environment.* Chicago: The University of Chicago Press, 1969.

Beattie, Donald A., ed. *History and Overview of Solar Heating Technologies.* Cambridge, MA: MIT Press, 1997.

Brown, G. Z. *Sun, Wind, and Light: Architectural Design Strategies.* New York: John Wiley & Sons, 1985.

Brown, Robert J. and Rudolph R. Yanuck. *Life Cycle Costing: A Practical Guide for Energy*

Manager. Atlanta: Fairmont Press, Inc., 1980.

Butti, Ken and John Perlin, *A Golden Thread.* New York: Cheshire Books/Van Nostrand Reinhold, 1980.

Carmody, John, Stephen Selkowitz, and Lisa Heschong. *Residential Windows.* New York: W. W. Norton & Co., 1996.

Cook, Jeffrey, ed. *Passive Cooling.* Cambridge, MA: MIT Press, 1990.

Crosbie, Michael J. *Green Architecture: A Guide to Sustainable Design.* Washington, DC: AIA Press, 1994.

Danz, Ernst. *Sun Protection: An International Architectural Survey.* New York: Praeger, 1967.

de Winter, Francis, ed. *Solar Collectors, Energy Storage, and Materials.* Cambridge, MA: MIT Press, 1991.

Evans, Benjamin. *Daylight in Architecture.* New York: McGraw-Hill, 1981.

Givoni, Baruch. *Man, Climate, and Architecture.* London, England: Applied Science Publishers, 1976.

Halacy, Dan. *Home Energy.* Emmaus, PA: Rodale Press, 1984.

Heschong, Lisa. *Thermal Delight in Architecture.* Cambridge, MA: MIT Press, 1979.

Hopkinson, R. G. and J. D. Kay. *The Lighting of Buildings.* London, England: Faber and Faber, 1972.

Hulstrom, Roland L. *Solar Resources.* Cambridge, MA: MIT Press, 1989.

Hunn, Bruce, ed. *Fundamentals of Building Energy Dynamics.* Cambridge, MA: MIT Press, 1996.

Johnson, Timothy E. *Solar Architecture: The Direct Gain Approach.* New York: McGraw-Hill, 1981.

———. *Low-E Glazing Design Guide.* Boston: Butterworth Architecture, 1991.

Jones, Robert W. and Robert D. McFarland. *The Sunspace Primer.* New York: Van Nostrand Reinhold, 1984.

Knowles, Ralph J. *Energy and Form.* Cambridge, MA: MIT Press, 1974.

———. *Sunlighting as Formgiver for Architecture.* New York: Van Nostrand Reinhold, 1986.

Larson, Ronald W., and Ronald W. West, eds. *Implementation of Solar Thermal Technology.* Cambridge, MA: MIT Press, 1995.

Lewis, Dan, Charles Michael and Paul Pietz, Total Environmental Action. *Design of Residential Buildings Utilizing Natural Thermal Storage.* Springfield, VA: National Technical Information Service, U.S. Department of Commerce, 1979.

Mackenzie, Dorothy. *Design for the Environment.* New York: Rizzoli, 1991.

Marshall, Harold E., and Rosalie T. Ruegg. *Energy Conservation in Buildings: An Economics Guide for Investment Decisions,* NBS Handbook 132. Washington, DC: U.S. Government Printing Office, 1980.

———. *Simplified Energy Design Economics.* National Bureau of Standards Publication 544. Washington, DC: National Bureau of Standards, 1980.

Mazria, Ed. *The Passive Solar Energy Book.* Emmaus, PA: Rodale Press, 1979.

McCullagh, James C., ed. *The Solar Greenhouse Book.* Emmaus, PA: Rodale Press, 1978.

Moore, Fuller. *Concepts and Practice of Architectural Daylighting.* New York: Van Nostrand Reinhold, 1985.

Nisson, J. D. Ned and G. Dutt. *The Superinsulation Book.* New York: John Wiley & Sons, 1985.

Olgyay and Olgyay. *Solar Control and Shading Devices.* Princeton, NJ: Princeton University Press, 1976.

———. *Design with Climate.* Princeton, NJ: Princeton University Press, 1973.

Passive Cooling Handbook. Berkeley, CA: Lawrence Berkeley Laboratory, 1980.

Passive Solar Design: An Extensive Bibliography. Springfield, VA: National Technical Information Service, U.S. Department of Commerce, 1978.

Passive Solar Industries Council. *Designing Low-Energy Buildings* (with ENERGY-10 software). Washington, DC: Passive Solar Industries Council, 1996.

Passive Solar Industries Council and the National Renewable Energy Laboratories. *Passive Solar Design Strategies: Guidelines for Home Build-*

ing (with BuilderGuide software). Washington, DC: PSIC and NREL, 1989, revised 1995.

Professional Builder. *Energy and the Builder.* Chicago: Cahners Publishing Company, 1977.

Shurdliff, William A. *Thermal Shutters and Shades.* Andover, MA: Brick House Publishing Company, Inc., 1980.

Selkowitz, Stephen. *Windows for Energy Efficient Buildings,* Vol. 1, Nos. 1–2. Berkeley, CA: Lawrence Berkeley Laboratory, 1980.

Solar Energy Research Institute. *Analysis Methods for Solar Heating and Cooling Applications,* 3rd ed. Golden, CO: U.S. Department of Energy, 1980.

———. *The Design of Energy-Responsive Commercial Buildings.* New York: Wiley-Interscience, 1985.

Southern Solar Energy Center. *Passive Retrofit Handbook.* Atlanta: Southern Solar Energy Center, 1981.

Steven Winter Associates, Inc. *Suntempering in the Northeast: A Selection of Builders' Designs.* Boston: Northeast Solar Energy Center, 1980.

Strong, Steve, with William G. Scheller. *The Solar Electric House.* Still River, MA: Sustainability Press, 1993.

Sustainable Building Technical Manual. Washington, DC: Public Technology, Inc., 1996.

Total Environmental Action, Inc. *Passive Solar Design Handbook, Volume 1: Passive Solar Design Concepts.* Springfield, VA: National Technical Information Service, U.S. Department of Commerce, 1980.

Watson, Donald. *Designing and Building a Solar House.* Charlotte, VT: Garden Way Publishing, 1977.

———. *Designing Passive Solar Buildings to Reduce Temperature Swings.* Los Alamos, NM: Los Alamos Scientific Laboratory, 1975.

Watson, Donald, ed. *Energy Conservation Through Building Design.* New York: McGraw-Hill, 1979.

———. *The Energy Design Handbook.* Washington, DC: American Institute of Architects, 1993.

Watson, Donald, and Kenneth Labs. *Climatic Building Design.* New York: McGraw Hill, 1983, revised 1995.

West, Ronald E., and Frank Kreith, eds. *Economic Analysis of Solar Thermal Energy Systems.* Cambridge, MA: MIT Press, 1988.

Wilson, Alex, *Thermal Storage Wall Design Manual.* Albuquerque, NM: Modern Press, 1979.

Wright, D. *Natural Solar Architecture: A Passive Primer.* New York: Van Nostrand Reinhold Co., 1978.

INDEX

Page numbers shown in italics, followed by a *t*, refer to tables; page numbers shown in italics only refer to illustrations.